CLIMATE AND HUMAN MIGRATION

There is growing concern that the impacts of anthropogenic climate change will generate large-scale population displacements and forced migration in coming decades. Reports in the popular media periodically conjure up worrying images of millions of 'environmental refugees' flooding into developed countries and cities. Are these concerns well grounded? What is the present state of research and knowledge of the linkages between climate and migration? What might the future implications and priorities be for concerned researchers, policy makers, and the general public?

Robert A. McLeman provides a comprehensive review of how physical and human processes interact to shape migration, using simple diagrams and models to guide the reader through the climate-migration process. While climate change will undoubtedly affect future migration patterns and behavior, the potential outcomes are far more complex than the environmental refugee scenario suggests. This book applies standard concepts and theories used in climate and migration scholarship to explain how events such as Hurricane Katrina, the Dust Bowl, African droughts, and floods in Bangladesh and China have triggered migrations that have not always fit the environmental refugee storyline. Lessons from past migrations are used to predict how future migration patterns will unfold in the face of sea level rise, food insecurity, and political instability, and to review options for policy makers.

This book provides the first comprehensive review of climate and human migration. It will prove invaluable for advanced students, researchers, and policy makers in climate change impact and adaptation studies, migration and demography, geography, environmental studies, environmental sociology, political and public policy studies, and environmental governance.

Robert A. McLeman is a geography professor at Wilfrid Laurier University, Waterloo, Canada; a former diplomat; and an award-winning teacher. He specializes in understanding how the natural environment influences the well-being of households and communities. His research investigates historical drought-related migration on the Great Plains; adaptation to climate change in remote and resource-dependent communities; drivers of modern-day settlement abandonment; and the effects of environmental events and conditions in Africa, Asia, and the Caribbean on international migration to Canada. In writing this book, Dr. McLeman drew his inspiration from years of scholarly research and past professional experiences. His scholarly articles on migration as an adaptation to climate are widely cited, and have featured prominently in reports of the Intergovernmental Panel on Climate Change. Government agencies in Canada, Europe, and the United States have frequently sought his advice on policy issues related to climate change, migration, and security. He is a frequent contributor on environmental issues to French-language and English-language public radio in Canada and the United States, and he enjoys teaching introductory classes in environment studies and engaging the wider public in citizen science.

'McLeman eschews the hyperbole and screaming headlines that often surround this topic to unpack the complex and still evolving connections between climate change and migration. His analysis is both broad and deep in its reach and avoids the pitfalls that commonly plague the climate change and migration literature.'

– Geoffrey Dabelko, Ohio University

'This book is excellent. In *Climate and Human Migration*, Dr. McLeman offers accessible explanations of this tremendously complex association – convoluted processes become understandable. In this way, the book will be valuable in the university classroom. Dr. McLeman also offers a thorough summary of varied literature scattered across multiple scientific disciplines. In this way, the book will be valuable to both social and natural scientists. And finally, with his logical and level-headed approach to a topic that is sometimes presented in controversial and exaggerated terms, this book will be useful to practitioners and policy makers. Highly recommended.'

– Lori Mae Hunter, University of Colorado at Boulder;
Editor-in-Chief of *Population and Environment*

'We've needed this book for some time now. While the "flood of climate refugees" idea (scare?) can have a certain appeal, and its "connect the dots" logic a certain policy utility, Robert McLeman's exceptionally well-researched and readable book reveals we are way off the mark in thinking that the migration repercussions of climate change will be simplistic. *Climate and Human Migration* will be very valuable for research and teaching about the human dimensions of climate change. But perhaps those who need to read it most are the policy makers in various countries who are pondering (and in some cases already formulating) perilous and dangerous policies based on the simple, unelaborated view of how migration and climate change interact.'

– Jon Unruh, McGill University

CLIMATE AND HUMAN MIGRATION

Past Experiences, Future Challenges

ROBERT A. MCLEMAN

Wilfrid Laurier University

CAMBRIDGE UNIVERSITY PRESS

CAMBRIDGE
UNIVERSITY PRESS

32 Avenue of the Americas, New York, NY 10013-2473, USA

Cambridge University Press is part of the University of Cambridge.

It furthers the University's mission by disseminating knowledge in the pursuit of
education, learning, and research at the highest international levels of excellence.

www.cambridge.org
Information on this title: www.cambridge.org/9781107606708

First published 2014

Printed in the United States of America

A catalog record for this publication is available from the British Library.

Library of Congress Cataloging in Publication data
McLeman, Robert A.
Climate and human migration : past experiences, future challenges / Robert A. McLeman.
pages   cm
Includes bibliographical references and index.
ISBN 978-1-107-02265-2 (hardback) – ISBN 978-1-107-60670-8 (paperback)
1. Human beings – Effect of climate on.   2. Climatic changes.   3. Human beings –
Migrations.   4. Human geography.   I. Title.
GF71.M35   2013
304.8–dc23   2013029365

ISBN 978-1-107-02265-2 Hardback
ISBN 978-1-107-60670-8 Paperback

For Anna, Coleen, and Sophie

Contents

Figures

Tables

Preface

Over the past decade or so various sources have produced reports and studies warning that climate change and sea level rise will cause hundreds of millions of people to become environmental refugees in coming decades. One prediction issued in 2005 estimated that by the year 2010 climate change would create 50 million environmental refugees worldwide (thankfully, that prediction proved wrong). Just the same, these concerns have prompted scholars, refugee advocates, and international organizations to call for new policies and laws to protect those whom climate change might displace. National intelligence agencies have commissioned studies of the security implications of climate change–induced displacement, and on two occasions the United Nations (UN) Security Council has held discussions on what ought to be done. UN Environment Programme officials have reported that the Darfur conflict was in part caused by climate change, while the popular media has identified groups living on the Alaskan coast, on Micronesian atolls, and in Africa's Lake Chad region as the world's first 'climate change refugees'. In short, it has become widely accepted that climate change–driven migration will have a significant impact on our future well-being, and for some people it may already be doing so.

I agree that the risks posed by anthropogenic climate change do indeed have the potential to cause large-scale population displacements in many countries. Extreme climate events already do so, as we have seen in recent years through examples like Hurricane Katrina and severe droughts in East Africa. However, the environmental refugee scenario (or more precisely, 'climate change refugee' scenario) is only one of the many ways climate affects migration patterns and behavior, most of which do not make the headlines and do not enter into public discussions about climate change. These include a wide range of diverse examples, a sample of which include: drought-induced changes in marriage-related migration in Ethiopia; influxes of temporary labor migrants to Bangladesh's cities during monsoonal floods; changing pastoralist movements in West Africa; and the ongoing flow of financially secure retirees from the northeastern United States to the Sun Belt. None of these are refugee scenarios. To varying degrees, the migrant in each of these examples exercises some degree of discretion and control over the duration and destination of migration and, indeed, over the decision of whether to migrate in the first place.

Climate change and sea level rise will have impacts across the whole spectrum of migration, from voluntary to involuntary. It will place some people in refugee-like situations but will create migration opportunities for others. It will make some places more desirable ones in which to live and make others less desirable. It will affect migration within countries and between them. In most cases, future climate-related migration will not unfold as a simple stimulus-response process, where one unit of climate change (however we might measure it) triggers a corresponding additional unit of migration. Rather, migration will be shaped by the interaction of climatic processes with cultural, economic, political, and social processes. How do we know this? Because this is how it already works. A good amount of scholarly research, generated in a variety of disciplines and fields, shows that people exposed to even the severest of droughts, storms, floods, and other climatic phenomena undertake a wide range of adaptation and adjustment strategies, which may or may not include migration. The adaptations they pursue and, if these do include migration, the duration and destinations they select, are shaped by access to social networks and to financial resources, cultural heritage, the freedom to migrate legally, and a whole host of other factors that may have little or no direct connection with climate.

My motivation for writing this book is straightforward. If we are to better understand how climate change will affect future migration, to produce reliable forecasts of that migration, and to formulate sound plans and policies at national and international levels, it is important that we base our considerations on a well-grounded understanding of how climate influences migration patterns and behavior more broadly. This requires thinking beyond the speculative climate change refugee scenarios and avoiding normative prescriptions for action that are not based on empirical evidence (of which there are already more than enough in circulation). Just as no one would seriously contemplate making international monetary policy on the basis of back-of-the-envelope calculations of worst-case scenarios, national and international migration policies will not and should not be made on the basis of unproven fears and untestable guesstimates of environmental refugees. We need reliable empirical research grounded in a sound understanding of the physical processes of climate and the human processes that influence migration. Generating this will require natural scientists to become more engaged with social science research on migration; social scientists will need to become better versed in the basic physical science of climate; and policy makers and policy influencers must become more familiar with both.

As a contribution to this end, this book provides a state-of-the-science introduction to the subject of climate and migration; at least, as good as I can muster. It starts with the basic premise that climate-related migration is neither a simple stimulus-response process nor an unknowable set of chance outcomes. Instead, it treats migration as an outcome of a larger set of processes by which individuals and households adapt not only to climate itself, but to the interaction of climatic events and conditions with cultural, economic, political, and social processes. I use as a shorthand for this the 'MESA' function, suggesting that migration (M) under conditions of climatic variability or change is a function of the particular climatic conditions to which a given population is exposed (E), its relative sensitivity (S) to such conditions, and the available adaptation (A) options other than migration. I am very conscious of scale here, recognizing that both climatic and human processes play out in different ways over different spatial and temporal scales. Instead of broad-brush assertions about how the MESA function plays out on the ground, I supplement it with a simple process diagram of how migration emerges within an adaptive human-environment system, with household access to capital helping the system generate particular migration outcomes (don't worry, it will make sense by the time you reach it in Chapter 3 at Figure 3.9). The connections and flows shown in the diagram are reinforced by applying it to known examples of climate-related migration, thereby teeing up the final chapters in which future challenges are discussed using the same language and concepts. Although the nonacademic reader may at times find the large number of citations distracting, the book is deliberately and thoroughly referenced so that it might serve as a one-stop shop for readers who desire no more than a single resource, while simultaneously pointing out promising next directions to those who want to plunge into the subject in much greater depth.

The book has three general sections. Chapters 1 through 3 provide the theoretical, conceptual, and methodological backdrop for a contemporary study of climate and migration. Chapter 1 gives a general overview of how the subject has been approached in the past and the directions in which research is currently moving. Chapter 2 reviews the broad scholarly field of traditional migration research and introduces the key concepts and theories used in it. Chapter 3 reviews the theories and concepts used in climate impacts and adaptation research. It combines them with those introduced in the preceding chapter to provide a systems-based approach to understanding how migration patterns emerge and are modified as vulnerable populations adapt to climatic events, variability, and change.

The second section of the book – the 'past experiences' referred to in the subtitle – applies the theories, concepts, and approaches from the first section to specific examples of climate-related migration. These are organized according to the three types of climatic events most commonly associated with migration: extreme weather events (Chapter 4), floods (Chapter 5), and droughts (Chapter 6). Each of these chapters follows a similar progression. It begins with an overview of the physical processes that give rise to the event in question, keeping in mind that the reader may not have a strong grounding in the natural sciences. It next identifies the cultural, economic, political, and social processes that put people in positions where they are exposed to such events and describes the range of adaptations that may be undertaken by those exposed. Some of these may be initiated at the community, household, or individual scale; others require action by higher-level organizations and institutions. Each chapter then focuses on the various shapes and forms migration can take as people adapt to the climatic event in question, using examples drawn from across the globe. Each chapter in the second section concludes by exploring in detail well-known examples like flooding in Bangladesh, the Great Plains Dust Bowl, and Hurricanes Mitch and Katrina and drawing generic lessons from them.

The final section of the book takes the lessons learned from earlier chapters and applies them to future challenges. Chapter 7 considers the potential impacts of mean sea level rise on migration and examines the strengths and weaknesses of existing and proposed national and international regulatory frameworks for managing future climate-related migration. Particular attention is paid to issues of statelessness that could conceivably emerge from this dynamic. Chapter 8 considers the security dimensions of climate-related migration in terms of international political stability and in terms of food security, and in doing so identifies much-needed areas for future research. The chapter and the book itself conclude with a discussion of how even though we may not know precisely how climate change will play out in the future, and even though climatic events will undoubtedly occur that catch us by surprise, we know enough from present-day experience to anticipate how migration behavior and patterns may respond.

I began writing this book in 2011 and finished in early 2013, but the thinking that went into it began twenty years ago, when I was living and working in Hong Kong. At that time I was working for the Canadian foreign service at my country's diplomatic mission there, while simultaneously taking my Master of Science degree at the University of Hong Kong. My master's dissertation, which attempted to combine the environmental science I was learning in school with what I was learning about migration during my day job, was entitled 'A management strategy for potential human population movements as a result of climate change'. When I flip through it now, its crudeness and quaintness make me smile. Still, I wish I had attempted to publish it then, for it would be more than a decade before I published my first scholarly article on the subject (McLeman and Smit 2006a). In the meantime, I continued taking diplomatic postings, specializing in many different aspects of international migration, including interviewing refugees in Kosovo; helping skilled workers travel to Canada under the North American Free Trade Agreement; training airline staff to spot migrant smuggling; and, generally interacting with migrants and people who work with migrants on a daily basis. By the time I gave up foreign service to do my PhD, I had asked close to ten thousand people their motivations for wanting to go to Canada to visit, study, work, or live permanently.

I never met anyone who said they wanted to move to Canada because of climate change (granted, I never specifically asked that question). Most people were motivated by the sorts of things you might imagine: a desire to be with friends and relatives, to work, to pursue economic opportunities or a higher education, or because they did not feel safe or secure in the place where they presently lived. I did, however, regularly meet people who said they were seeking the clean air and natural environment in Canada; usually these were people who lived in congested or polluted urban areas (I wonder if those migrants who have since been stuck in a Toronto traffic jam feel the same way now). One example sticks out in my mind. Back in the early 1990s, I was interviewing a young Taiwanese couple with a son about ten years old. When I asked them why they wanted to leave Taiwan, they answered 'the environment'. Now, that particular week China was rattling its sabers at Taiwan and threatening to invade it. This happened regularly back then, and occasionally still does when China thinks its tiny cousin is getting too big for its britches. In any event, given the headlines and the context of our preceding conversation, I thought they meant the political environment. When I rephrased the question to ask why they wanted to move to Canada, I got the same answer: the environment. As I started to clue in, the couple explained that their son was asthmatic and that the air pollution was awful in Taipei (as I had experienced on a recent visit there). They had been to Vancouver for a family vacation, and found their son could breathe more easily there, and that had motivated them to migrate to Canada. In other words, they were environmental migrants, but not environmental refugees.

My point in concluding this preface with this story is that environmental factors (and climatic events would be one subset of these) can, and sometimes do, influence migration, but the influence may be subtle and not obvious to the outsider. The causality behind any migration decision is complex, and so even though in this book I speak in terms of general behaviors, interactions, patterns, and trends, migration is for the most part a decision made by individuals and households for reasons particular to their personal circumstances.

Acknowledgments

While my name appears on the cover, many others made this book possible. First and foremost, without the support and encouragement of my wife, daughters, and extended family, I could not have written a word. Through my empirical research I have had many great friends, supporters, and collaborators. My knowledge of and continued fascination with the Dust Bowl migration is the direct result of help received from Doris Weddell, Earl Shelton, and Ray Rush of Kern County, California, and from the Rider family, Earl Strebeck, and the late Dick Mayo of Sequoyah County, Oklahoma. Had I not already promised my daughters the dedication, this book would have been dedicated to Mr. Mayo. The people of Herbert, Saskatchewan, Geoff Cunfer, and Simon Evans, have also taught me much about migration on the Great Plains. The good people of Addington Highlands and North Frontenac are thanked collectively; too many of them have supported my research over the years to be named individually.

My research program, which led directly to this book, has been financially supported by the Canadian taxpayer in various ways, particularly through grants received from the Social Science and Humanities Research Council and Natural Resources Canada – thank you. I began this book in the comfortable and supportive work environment provided by the Department of Geography and Faculty of Arts at the University of Ottawa. I will thank here by name Dean Antoni Lewkowicz on behalf of all my former colleagues there, several of whom I continue to collaborate with. I presently enjoy a similarly comfortable and supportive environment in the Department of Geography and Environmental Studies at Wilfrid Laurier University in Waterloo, Ontario, Canada, and would like to thank the WLU Research Office for providing a book preparation grant to help me get this manuscript to the publisher less late than it would have been. Speaking of the publisher, my sincere appreciation goes to Matt Lloyd for providing me the chance to write this book, and the Cambridge University Press staff for making it look presentable. Cambridge University Press also secured five anonymous reviewers whose comments made this book a better one. The best of the chapters that follow are the ones for which Kate Shipley Coddington and Elizabeth

Fussell provided detailed comments on earlier drafts. Peter Todd did the original cartography for maps found in this book, and they look sharp.

Some truly remarkable professional and academic colleagues need to be acknowledged. On behalf of all the many good people I worked with at Citizenship and Immigration Canada, I would like to thank Brian Davis, Jim Versteegh, Audrey Tomick, and Greg Chubak, who were the most instrumental in my transition from foreign service to academia. Professor Barry Smit of the University of Guelph took a chance on me when I arrived from Vienna looking to pursue my PhD, and is still a great supporter of my research. John Smithers, Craig Johnson, Alice Hovorka, and Harald Bauder of Guelph are also thanked, as is my former PhD lab partner and continued collaborator, James Ford. Several years of being an associate of the Strategic Natural Resources Management Group of the International Institute for Sustainable Development enabled me to collaborate with excellent people, and to publish with Oli Brown and Anne Hammill on climate, migration, and security issues. Thank you to Hank Venema for making it happen. Franz Laczko and the International Organization for Migration also helped me publish on that topic. My numerous past coauthors (whose numbers include excellent former graduate students) are thanked. Mike Brklacich deserves a special shout-out for his long-standing support. My past collaborator Lori Hunter receives my admiration for her many achievements in our field. She also receives my thanks for her personal support and for introducing me to a group of world-class demographers whose names appear in many of the works cited in this book. If we chatted in sight of the Flatirons, I'm talking about you.

The UK Government Office for Science, Neil Adger, and Richard Black are thanked for including me in the Foresight study of global environmental migration, a remarkable achievement from which I learned much. The European Science Foundation, Thomas Faist, and Jeanette Schade are thanked for including me in two remarkably forward-looking conferences on climate change and migration that galvanized me to look more closely at how migration affects the adaptive capacity of those left behind. Visits to Cornell University got me thinking about the linkages between climate, migration, and food security, and Chris Barrett was the catalyst for these (thanks also go to Lindy Williams of Cornell). The U.S. National Academies of Science are also thanked.

Not being sure where in this list to put him, so James William Buffett is thanked here.

The final and most important acknowledgment goes to you, the reader. I hope what you find in the following pages is worth the time you spend looking at it, even if you end up not agreeing with how I've represented the subject. If you are a student reading this book, whether by choice or because some professor forced you to do so, I hope it inspires you to pursue your own research in this area.

1

An Introduction to the Study of Climate and Migration

1.1 Introduction

Climate influences human migration. Sometimes the influence is direct and obvious, such as when people flee their ruined homes in the wake of a hurricane or tornado and do not return. Sometimes its influence is more subtle, such as when a string of dry years prompts an aging farmer to decide it is time to sell the land to a younger family and move to town. Sometimes climate's influence is nested so deeply in interwoven chains of past events that we no longer notice how it has shaped where, how, and why we live in the places we do. It is not some random act of chance nor deliberate human plans that led southern England, southeastern Australia, and northern New Zealand to become the most densely populated regions of their respective countries, home to urban centers that continue to draw migrants from around the world. Climate played a role.

It is estimated that there are approximately 215 million international migrants worldwide (UN DESA 2011). Relatively few of them migrated for reasons directly and obviously tied to climate. If asked why they moved, most would likely answer that it was because of family reasons, or to search for work or new opportunities. Some might say they had to, because their household had grown too big to be able to support them. An unfortunate number, perhaps 20 per cent of the total, would answer that they had no choice, that they were forced to move because of violence, persecution, or natural disasters (some of which might be climatic in origin). Because climate is in proportional terms so rare a proximate cause of migration, scholars who specialize in migration research have largely tended to consider it in passing, if they consider it at all. Check any textbook used to teach undergraduate courses in migration over the past few decades, and you will find few mentions of climate.

Since the 1980s, natural scientists have accumulated convincing evidence that human activity is causing unprecedented changes to the atmosphere, and that we have entered an era of rapid, human-induced climate change. Warnings that this will create hundreds of millions of environmental refugees in coming decades have led a small but growing number of scholars to reconsider the relationship between climate and migration. Their research is showing that climatic events and conditions will likely have a greater influence on migration in the future. However, that influence will most often be felt as part of a complex interplay with cultural, economic, political, and social factors that shape human migration behavior and patterns. Further, migration in the context of changing climatic events and conditions is not a discrete, stimulus-response phenomenon, but is typically one of a range of possible outcomes that may result as people adapt to changes occurring around them. The evidence that leads to this conclusion comes from careful examinations of past and present migration events, using a variety of theoretical, conceptual, and methodological approaches to tease out the contribution of climate and the nature of its interaction with other factors. These theories and concepts have been drawn from the natural and social sciences and employ a range of quantitative, qualitative, and geospatial imaging methods. This book provides a summary of relevant scholarship on the relationship between climate and migration, and is intended to serve as a starting point for scholars wishing to pursue further research in this emerging field.

In addition to the basic premise that climate can and does influence migration, several other basic premises underpin this book, which have been drawn from the current literature on the subject:

- The influence of climate on migration occurs in concert with cultural, economic, political, and social factors that are human in origin.
- Migration can be understood as an outcome of processes by which human populations adapt to climatic variability and change.
- Past examples can be used as evidence and learning devices for understanding future linkages between climate and migration.
- When the theories, concepts, and methods used in the often unconnected fields of migration and climate change research are brought together, they provide a powerful toolkit for the scholar.

Before launching this chapter with a review of the longer history of the study of climate and migration, it is worth noting that this book avoids as much as possible making value-laden judgements of whether migration events are good or bad, desirable or undesirable. There is no shortage of others willing to do so. The perspective taken here is that *migration happens*. Governments and institutions may wish to control and organize migration to suit their own purposes, as is discussed in Chapter 2, but the reality is that even in regimes where people's mobility is officially restricted, people will migrate when it is in their interest to do so. Any migration has its costs and benefits for the migrant, for members of the migrant's extended family and social network, and for the larger populations of sending and receiving areas alike. Raising barriers to migration raises the costs of migration, and may therefore restrict the numbers of people able to migrate, but even odious, repressive regimes like in North Korea or the former 'democratic'[1] Republic of East Germany have found it impossible to fully control and prevent migration and mobility. Migration is therefore analyzed here simply as a phenomenon that may or may not occur depending on circumstances, with the emphasis on identifying the circumstances accurately.

1.2 A Long View of the Influence of Climate on Human Migration

Climate has always been an important influence on human settlement and migration patterns. For the two hundred thousand or so years that *Homo sapiens* has been on the planet, climate and its interactions with other environmental processes have helped shape human population numbers, distribution, densities, longevity, and well-being. Until fairly recently in that long history – that is, until ten thousand to fifteen thousand years ago – climate and other environmental forces were likely among the foremost direct and indirect influences on human migration (Lamb 1982, Fagan 2004). The role of migration in the course of human development, from our earliest origins in East Africa to our settlement and colonization of all the continents (save Antarctica) and major islands of the Earth, from being primarily hunter-gatherers to mostly city dwellers, may be read in a variety of ways. One of these is to look at migration as part of a continual and ongoing process of adaptation. Within this context of adaptation it is possible to better understand the role that climate has played, and continues to play today, in influencing migration.

Adaptation is a process that takes on a variety of forms, including biological changes, behavioral changes, and technological changes (Smit and Wandel 2006). Adaptation implies a stimulus for change – that is, the adaptation of something to something. Evolutionary theory tells us that organisms, including humans, are continually adapting to environmental stimuli so as to enhance the chances that they and their offspring will survive to reproduce. In some regions, such as the northernmost Arctic, the Antarctic, and the great deserts, climatic conditions are so harsh that, after two hundred thousand years, they remain largely beyond the range to which humans have biologically adapted. Humans cannot safely live in such environments for any extended amount of time without implementing a significant amount of technology to overcome our biological limits. This is the first and most obvious way that climate has influenced human population movements, by delineating the human habitat – the regions of the world to which it is biologically safe to migrate and settle.

The distribution and density of human settlements within our climatologically defined habitat is neither uniform nor random. Climate as it is experienced on the ground varies spatially according to latitude, longitude, elevation, proximity to large bodies of water, and other physical factors. Interactions between climate and other elements of the natural environment shape the availability and distribution of resources

---

[1] It seems to be common that countries that use the word *democratic* in their official name are not democratic at all.

Figure 1.1. Remains of an early settler's farm near the abandoned settlement of Rose Hill, Ontario. The farm was established in the late nineteenth century by a migrant from southern Ontario. The short growing season and poor soils of the region put it on the margins of suitability for agricultural crops; the elevated, north-facing location made this a very poor location for a farm. Nearby villages situated on south-facing locations remain inhabited today. Photo by author.

and ecosystem services critical for human survival and well-being. Even over very short distances climatic conditions exhibit considerable variability. In northern temperate regions, for example, the south side of a hill may experience very different temperature regimes and therefore support different vegetation, animal species, soil conditions, and water availability than the north side of the same hill (Figure 1.1). These regional and local variations in climatic conditions interact with other ecological processes to render certain locations more desirable than others for human settlements.

The Earth's climate is continually changing over long periods of time because of natural processes, from ice age to warm period and back again to ice age. Climate is also inherently variable over short periods of time, from season to season and from one year to the next, obliging human populations to adapt to variations and extremes in temperature and precipitation.

Throughout the longer course of history, there have been many times and places where climatic conditions have changed beyond the capacity of people to adjust to them through in situ adaptation (i.e. behavioral or technological adaptations that do not require migration), leading populations in whole or in part to respond by migrating elsewhere. Some have been short-duration events that led to migration at local and regional scales, and many modern examples are included in the chapters that follow. Other periods in human history have seen long-duration, global-scale climatic events that led to pronounced changes in population and settlement patterns across wide regions. Captivating and well-researched accounts of such events have been published by scholars including Mike Davis (2001), Jared Diamond (2005), Brian Fagan (2004, 2008, 2009), Michael Glantz (2001), and Hubert Lamb (1982), meaning there is no need to replicate them in this book. It is, however, worth mentioning briefly a few examples from centuries past that today's scholars frequently invoke in discussions of the relationship between climate and migration.

1.3 Notable Examples from the Long Past

One example that scholars have drawn on is that of the medieval warm period (MWP), which lasted from approximately the tenth century to the early fourteenth century, with its peak occurring in the twelfth century (Mann et al. 2008).[2] During that period, average temperatures across much of Europe, Central Asia, Africa, and the Americas rose to levels similar to or even warmer than those experienced today, making them among the highest global average temperatures since the last ice age.[3] The impacts of these warm centuries were particularly favorable in Europe, where climate in the previous millennium had been highly variable, characterized by long periods of harsh winters, droughts, extreme storm events, and sea level change along the coasts (Lamb 1982, Grove 2002). Medieval warming created a benign climate that led to increased European agricultural productivity and expansion northward of warm weather crop production, including the establishment of vineyards in southern England (Grove 2002). It was during this period that Scandinavian Norse began migrating to and colonizing North Atlantic islands. Fully functioning, permanent Norse settlements were established on the Faroes, Iceland, and Greenland, with smaller, ephemeral hunting and fishing settlements built on the island of Newfoundland (Dugmore, Keller, and McGovern 2007).

In contrast with the beneficial climate experienced in Europe, the onset of the MWP in the tenth century brought a series of prolonged, severe droughts to Central America that coincided with the collapse and depopulation of the great cities of the Mayan empire in Central America (Haug et al. 2003, Wahl et al. 2007). A variety of human factors have been cited as having interacted with climate to precipitate that collapse, including intercity warfare, deforestation that led to soil erosion and loss of ground

---

[2] This period is also sometimes referred to as the Medieval Climate Anomaly.
[3] In East Asia, the tenth through the twelfth centuries were relatively cool, that region having experienced a much warmer period of average temperatures during the seventh to ninth centuries (Lamb 1982).

water, and an increasingly hierarchical and rigid political system that was insufficiently flexible to adapt to changing environmental conditions (Shaw 2003, Orlove 2005). In the American southwest, large pueblos and the famous Anasazi cliff settlements of Chaco Canyon and Mesa Verde arose in the first centuries of the MWP, only to be abandoned over a relatively short period in the twelfth century in the face of severe droughts (Lekson and Cameron 1995). In Asia, climatic conditions were highly variable during the MWP; Fagan (2004) suggests the expansion of the Mongol empire of Genghis Khan and his successors from the Central Asian steppes into China and Europe may have been necessitated by persistent dry conditions on the steppes in the early twelfth century.

The MWP was followed by a general decline in temperatures in the northern hemisphere that culminated between the sixteenth and nineteenth centuries in what has been described as a 'Little Ice Age' (Grove 1988). During this period, European winters became longer and colder, ice skating was widely enjoyed in the Netherlands, and England's River Thames froze over on several occasions (Robinson 2005, Huntley 2012). Agricultural settlements in marginal areas were abandoned in Britain and continental Europe. Norse settlements were abandoned on Greenland, and the population of Iceland fell by a third by the year 1700 (Lamb 1982). Tremendous storms struck the northern European coast on several occasions, causing erosion and the abandonment of numerous coastal settlements (Clarke et al. 2002). In West Africa, the great empire of Mali collapsed in the late sixteenth century during a period of repeated catastrophic flooding in the Niger valley followed by severe droughts upstream at Timbuktu (Makaske et al. 2007). In India, the recently built capital city of Fatehpur Sikri had to be abandoned for lack of water (Hillel 1991).

In addition to these longer-term shifts in climate has been the influence of the El Niño Southern Oscillation (ENSO) on human well-being. A phenomenon that takes its name from a Peruvian observation that it is often experienced during the Christmas period, ENSO describes a period when prevailing trade winds in the south-central Pacific Ocean weaken, allowing warm surface waters from Australia and Indonesia to migrate eastward to the normally cold-water coast of the Americas (Glantz 2001). ENSO events occur irregularly, anywhere from three to seven years apart, and can last for a matter of months or as long as two years. When they occur, ENSO events trigger significant changes in prevailing weather patterns across much of the globe. Traditionally dry areas can experience heavy precipitation, while typically wet areas can experience drought, and this can have implications for the success of human settlements (Caviedes 2001). For example, Davis (2001) observed that famines that occurred in India during the period of British colonial rule often coincided with ENSO events. The 1998 Yangtze River floods that displaced tens of thousands of Chinese families (discussed in greater detail in Chapter 5) occurred during an ENSO event (Ye and Glantz 2005).

These examples are just a few of many in which large-scale population displacements and migrations have occurred during climatic events of the past (see McLeman 2011a for further examples). However, the simultaneous occurrence of a major climate event and a significant event in human history does not prove that the former caused the latter. With migration events of long ago our access to details about human systems and local- and regional-scale climate conditions is limited, so it is necessary to be cautious about assuming that climate caused migration, and to consider whether other concurrent events of a political, social, or economic nature may have been more proximate causes, or if it was some combination of all of these. By way of analogy, consider modern-day famine events that have led to distress migration in parts of Africa and Asia. Droughts can serve as catalysts for famine events by causing sudden declines in local food availability and in the incomes of food producers, but typically there is a range of other contributing causes, such as political instability, economic crises, or conflicts that make the population vulnerable to famine in the first place (Watts and Bohle 1993, Maxwell and Fitzpatrick 2012). Sen (1981) demonstrated how even in the absence of a significant downturn in food production people can go hungry because of structural inequities within the political-economic system. So when we see streams of starving refugees pouring across international borders, as is occurring in Somalia as this chapter is being written, to what extent is climate truly the proximate causal factor? After all, droughts are a recurrent and widespread phenomenon in Africa, and other parts of that continent are also experiencing precipitation shortfalls at this moment; why is it that Somalis are fleeing starvation while others are not? Evidently, climatic conditions alone are not determining their fate.

It is worth noting that these historical examples are well-known and dramatic events of a scale that cannot help but capture the attention of researchers. It would be surprising if ruined Viking settlements on the Greenland coast, Mayan temples surrounded by jungle, or the abandoned cliff dwellings of Mesa Verde did not arouse scholars' curiosity. But the reality is that most past events of climate-related migration have undoubtedly gone unnoticed and undocumented, even instances when entire settlements have been abandoned (McLeman 2011a). This is still the case today. Events like Hurricane Katrina grab not just headlines but the attention of scholars interested in environmental migration, even though less spectacular environmental events elsewhere in the United States cumulatively exert a greater force on migration (Gutmann and Field 2010). A solid understanding of how climate and migration processes interact requires an ability to account not only for the spectacular, infrequent event, but also for the more subtle and mundane ones.

1.4 Avoiding Climatic Determinism

In the first part of the twentieth century, a school of thought emerged among geographers that has since been called 'environmental determinism'[4] (Peet 1985). The

---

[4] Gemenne (2011a) provides a more detailed account of the influence of environmental determinism on present-day research, which is highly recommended.

scholars associated with this line of thinking identified broad trends in human development, conditions, and behavior, and sought to link these with environmental conditions, including climate, in a stimulus-response fashion (Holt-Jensen 1980). Ellsworth Huntington (1907), for example, was one of the first English-language scholars to consider the role of climate in shaping settlement patterns in China. However, in pursuing their ideas, environmental determinist scholars like Huntington, Ellen Churchill Semple (1911), and others developed unsupportable explanations for the linkage between societies and environment. For example, Huntington (1924) created maps comparing national industrial output to global temperature regimes, which showed (probably to no one's surprise) that industrial output was highest in northern hemisphere nations, which also happened to have relatively cool and temperate climates. Through this simple association, conclusions were made that cooler climates made for harder-working people, while warmer climates produced less industrious cultures and lifestyles, ignoring or downplaying social, economic, and political history and events like colonialism and slavery. Later scholars retreated from this sort of logic, and for much of the second half of the twentieth century, research on the role of climate as an influence on human behavior generally, and on migration in particular, became quite rare.

Not until the 1980s, when a new term, *environmental refugees*, was coined in a time of famine-related migration in Africa (El-Hinnawi 1985, Jacobson 1988) did scholars once again turn their attention to the effects of climate on migration. It is not coincidental that this same period was one of tremendous expansion in scientific research on the causes and impacts of anthropogenic climate change. Papers began to appear warning that sea level rise, more extreme storm events, and widespread floods and droughts would displace millions of people worldwide in coming decades (Milliman, Broadus, and Gable 1989; Lewis 1990; McGregor 1992; Myers 1993). The first report issued by Working Group II of the Intergovernmental Panel on Climate Change (IPCC) made similar warnings (Tegardt, Sheldon, and Griffiths 1990). Political scientists working on international security issues picked up on the topic as well, most notably Homer-Dixon (1991), whose work influenced an *Atlantic Monthly* article entitled 'The Coming Anarchy' (Kaplan 1994), which became required reading among senior staff in the Clinton administration (Dabelko 1999; see Chapter 8 for more detailed analysis of the securitization of climate and migration research). Little of this newfound interest in climate and migration came from scholars that had been traditionally engaged in migration research, but instead emanated from other fields like natural hazards, global change, biology, ecology, climate science, political science, and law. To a significant extent this has remained the case until quite recently. A result is that much of what scholars currently know about the relationship between climate and migration has been developed in relative isolation from the theoretical, conceptual, and methodological practices of the broader scholarly field of migration research. To avoid lapsing into a new paradigm of 'climatic determinism' that focuses on the role of climate to the exclusion of other influences on migration, it is important to knit the theoretically grounded knowledge of migration behavior that has been developed over long periods of time by its specialists with the empirical evidence of climate-related migration that has been generated in recent decades through research in other fields.

1.5 Who Are Climate Migrants Today?

There is presently no mechanism for recording the global number of climate-related migrants and the circumstances behind their movement, and it is unlikely one will be developed any time soon. If it were somehow possible to conduct a census of the global numbers right now, what types of people might be included? The range of possibilities is actually quite broad, and the distinction is fuzzy between someone who might logically be called a climate-related migrant and someone who might not. Obvious people to include in this category would be those forced to relocate following droughts, floods, and extreme weather events of recent years, such as Somalis who fled their homes during the 2011 drought, Pakistanis displaced by severe floods in 2010 and 2012, and residents who left New Orleans and resettled elsewhere in the wake of Hurricane Katrina. Also to be included would be the thousands of wealthy retirees from Canada and the northern United States who retire to the sunny climes of Florida and Arizona each year. True, there are many cultural and economic factors that contribute to that migration, but it is the Sun Belt they seek out, not the Corn Belt or the Rust Belt. These all seem like fairly uncontroversial groups to include in this imaginary climate-migrant census, and they represent extremes from largely voluntary to largely involuntary migrants.

As this impromptu census continues, the enumeration decisions would become more difficult. Take this case for an example. In July 2011, thousands of people were evacuated from Anishnabe First Nation communities in northwestern Ontario, Canada, because of forest fires, and were flown to more southern cities until the fires were extinguished a few weeks later. Let's say the evacuation occurred around the time of our census – should they be included? Since the evacuation was only temporary, probably not; migration, as is seen in the next chapter, implies an evacuation of more-than-temporary duration. But there might be some evacuees whose homes were destroyed and who decided not to return; they should probably be counted. And what about an Anishnabe teenager who, having never been to a southern Ontario city before, falls in love with the bright lights and decides not to go back even once it is safe to do so? Should she be counted? After all, the proximate cause of her having to leave home in the first place was forest fire. What if it turns out that the forest fires were caused by arson and not by the natural, climate-related event of a lightning strike – does that mean all the evacuees should automatically be disqualified from our census? As we start parsing who is a climate-related migrant and who is not, recurring problems of causality and reductionism emerge.

For the purposes of this book, it is important to be aware that such fine distinctions exist, and that the decision to label someone a climate migrant may have legal and practical implications (see Chapter 7), but it is not necessary to get bogged down in the fine details. In each of the examples just cited – sun-seeking snowbirds, flooded-out farmers, those fleeing drought, and forest fire evacuees – there exists a range of other causal factors for migration with which climatic conditions interact and serve as a catalyst. A simple working description that will be used for the remainder of this book is this:

Climate-related migration occurs when climatic conditions, weather events, changes in those events and conditions, and/or their physical impacts are among the easily recognizable influences on migration, but they need not be the sole cause of the migration event.

The phrase 'easily recognizable' is used deliberately, knowing there is room for debate over what that exactly means. It is included because many human events, migration or otherwise, when analyzed down to the most minute, tiniest constituents, could reveal some connection to climate. The purchase of a particular house could have been influenced by the breeze felt by the house hunter when she visited it for the first time, or the decision to move to Florida to take a job there may have been influenced by memories of a winter vacation taken there years earlier.

The four clear examples listed earlier share a number of characteristics that are common features of climate-related migration. One is that in each event, there are people who migrated from the place of origin and others who remained behind. Not everyone has fled rural Somalia, not all flooded-out Pakistani farmers abandoned their land, not all wealthy New Yorkers retire to the sun, and most Anishnabe evacuees did go back to their northwestern Ontario homes. In other words, a single climatic event or set of conditions can stimulate a variety of responses among those exposed, some people migrating, others not. As seen in subsequent chapters, even in the case of climate-related migrations involving tens or even hundreds of thousands of people, such as the Great Plains drought migrations of the 1930s and hurricane-related migrations in the Caribbean basin of the past two decades, many more people did not migrate as compared with those that did. This is another reminder to look at migration in the context of adaptation and in the context of what we know about migration behavior more generally, and not in simple cause-effect terms.

Furthermore, a single climatic event can lead to a variety of different types of migration response in terms of duration of the migration, destination, and number of household members participating. In Somalia, some fled to locations within the country, either to other parts of the countryside or to Mogadishu; others fled to Kenya or Ethiopia. In rural Pakistan, some of those displaced by flooding have settled in other rural locations and some have moved to the city. In some cases the whole family has migrated; in others, only certain members have moved to the city in hopes of sending back remittances. Some people displaced by Hurricane Katrina returned to New

Orleans, others resettled elsewhere in Louisiana, while still others migrated to urban centers in neighboring states. Chapter 3 of this book takes these and other parameters of climate-related migration and combines them with basic theories of migration and climate adaptation behavior to create a simple conceptual framework to help make sense of the wide range of examples and case studies of climate-related migration described in Chapters 4, 5, and 6.

1.6 Fears for the Future

There is a growing concern among scholars and policy makers that in coming decades the impacts of anthropogenic climate change will make some regions less suitable for human habitation and stimulate population movements on scales not seen in living memory. This concern is valid. The long view of human history shows that even relatively modest shifts in global climate regimes have significant impacts on population patterns; the difference in average temperatures between the Medieval Warm Period and the Little Ice Age was no more than a degree or two Celsius, depending on the location (Diaz et al. 2011). It would be naïve to think that future changes in average temperature of similar or greater scale would have no effect on migration patterns around the world. How great the migration response to climate change will be in coming decades is an open question. A small number of forecasts made in recent years have generated a healthy discussion and debate. Perhaps the best-known such forecast was offered by ecologist Norman Myers (2002), who suggested that by the mid to late twenty-first century, the world might see 200 million environmental refugees[5] from the combined effects of global warming, sea level rise, land degradation, and other global environment changes. This estimate has since been cited in other reports, most notably the Stern Report (Stern 2007), which attempted to put a dollar value on the impacts of climate change. At time of writing, Myers's is the only global estimate of future environmental migration that has appeared in a peer-reviewed scholarly journal, so it is understandable that it is often cited, even if the figure is based on best guesses (Brown 2008). The non-peer-reviewed literature has generated other estimates, with a noteworthy one having come from the nongovernmental organization (NGO) Christian Aid, a respected organization with a long-standing commitment to bettering the lives of the poor. It suggested future displacements could be much higher than those suggested by Myers, perhaps reaching as many as a billion people displaced by mid century in absolute worst-case scenarios (Christian Aid 2007).

How reliable are such forecasts? Frankly, it is difficult to know, for embedded within them are assumptions about the behavior of Earth systems as they adjust to the forcing effects of additional greenhouse gases, the extent of future levels of greenhouse gas emissions, and the capacity of people to adapt to the impacts – all things

---

[5] A discussion of the term *environmental refugee* and its implications is found in Chapter 7 of this book.

that cannot be predicted with any certainty. There are risks to making such predictions should they turn out wrong. For example, in 2005, the Environment and Human Security program at the United Nations University (UNU) in Bonn reported that by the year 2010 rising sea levels, desertification, and water scarcity would generate up to 50 million environmental refugees.[6] The release of the report, which made use of thematic maps also found in *Le Monde Diplomatique's Atlas de l'environnement* to identify regions particularly at risk, was timed to coincide with a UN promotion of an international disaster reduction day (Adam 2005). When 2011 arrived without any evidence of said refugees, a fair amount of jest was made of the prediction in the media and on the Internet (Bojanowski 2011). Hindsight is always perfect but, even so, the basic principles on which such a prediction was made were flawed. It was obviously assumed that the rate of onset of the expected changes in the Earth's climate regimes would be much faster than what the physical science suggests. In particular, it was a puzzling decision to link a large upswing in population displacement over five years to sea level rise, which is occurring at an average rate of about 3 mm/year (IPCC 2007). The prediction may have been based on a very loose definition of *refugee* that would include people temporarily displaced from their homes as well as those forced to relocate indefinitely. It also seems clear the prediction was based purely on identification of populations exposed to climate risks and did not account for adaptation, something that is discussed in Chapter 3.

This does not mean to say there were no climate-related or other environmental events that caused great suffering and displacement between 2005 and 2010; in fact, there were. For example, the Centre for Research on the Epidemiology of Disasters EM-DAT database recorded 2,152 climate-related disaster events having occurred worldwide during this period, linked to almost two hundred seventy thousand deaths (CRED 2013).[7] No count is made of how many people may have been temporarily or permanently displaced by these, but it is reasonable to assume that many were. The UNU prediction encompassed a much broader range of phenomena in addition to disaster events but, even so, it seems most unlikely migrant numbers would have approached anywhere near 50 million.

The point is simply this: if they are to be reliable, any predictions of future population movements for climate-related reasons must be grounded in a sound understanding of the basic physical science behind climatic phenomena, must reflect the recognition that migration is but one way people respond and adapt to the impacts of climatic phenomena, must consider the roles played by governments and institutions, and must be consistent with established evidence of migration behavior. The

---

[6] Access to the original report has since been removed from UN websites, although references to the press releases that accompanied the launch of the report still widely abound on the Internet.

[7] The EM-DAT database contains entries for geotechnical disaster events (e.g. earthquakes, volcanoes), epidemics (which can be influenced by climate, depending on the method of transmission), industrial accidents, and other disasters that do not have any direct link with climate. These categories are not included in the estimates given in the paragraph earlier.

prediction of 50 million by 2010 was made to capture public attention, which it did – far more than any scholarly research on climate-related migration published in the years since. Having so easily been found to be incorrect, it contributes to public skepticism of climate science generally, and particularly casts doubts on forecasts of 200 million or more to be displaced by climate change by mid century – even though such predictions are within the realm of possibility, if not probability.

1.7 Forecasting the Future by Understanding the Past

At no point in human history have greenhouse gases been pushed to such high levels. Global temperatures and mean sea levels are already changing at rates much faster than at any period in thousands of years (IPCC 2007). It is consequently difficult to know for certain what the impacts of anthropogenic climate change will be on any aspect of the human condition, migration included. However, this does not mean scholars interested in climate-related migration are without tools for predicting the future. There is a range of modelling techniques available, including macroeconomic models, spatial vulnerability models, hazard analysis models, and agent-based models, among others (McLeman 2012). Often, the key challenge in creating such models is not finding the climate data to make them work, but acquiring the necessary population data. Even the most basic of census data are not available at a global level, although there is an ongoing effort led by the UN Department of Economic and Social Affairs to have these collected by mid decade. At regional and national levels, there can be sufficient data about population and environmental conditions to undertake insightful studies, with several good examples cited in the pages that follow (e.g. Henry et al. 2004; Gutmann et al. 2005; Barbieri et al. 2010; Feng, Krueger, and Oppenheimer 2010; Massey, Axinn, and Ghimire 2010; McLeman et al. 2010; Kniveton, Smith and Wood 2011; Gray and Mueller 2012a, b; Nawrotzki, Riosmena, and Hunter 2012). Only a few of these studies have attempted to project climate-related migration numbers into the future, but it is only a matter of time before more do.

The present book takes a different approach in considering the future, one that has been described elsewhere as forecasting by analogy (Glantz 1988). The basic premise is that it is possible to gather information about the processes, interactions, and characteristics of future events or phenomena by identifying and studying analogous examples from the past or present. The use of historical analogs as learning devices is common in the social sciences generally (Hannon 1997). Analog-based methods have been applied in a number of studies that have sought to understand future impacts of climate change and human responses to them, such as those that have looked at adaptive responses to groundwater depletion and droughts (Glantz and Ausubel 1988; Easterling et al. 1992, McLeman et al. 2008; see Ford et al. (2010) for a detailed review of the use of analogs in climate change research). The success of the technique depends on the significance of similarities between a future event and its analog, not merely the number of similarities (Jamieson 1988). Researchers must be careful to identify clearly the significant characteristics shared between an event and its analog, not to overstretch comparisons, and to recognize that human knowledge systems and technologies change with the passage of time (Jamieson 1988). Another implicit assumption is that, while the decisions of individuals can be highly variable from one to the next even when placed in similar circumstances, the collective behavior of people in similar circumstances may exhibit characteristic patterns and processes, about which some degree of generalization may be made. Of course, this assumption is implicit in virtually all social science research; after all, if human behavior were purely random and therefore by definition unknowable, there would be no need for social scientists.

With these caveats well in mind, this book undertakes an extensive review of the migration and climate change adaptation scholarship to generate some basic conceptual tools for looking systematically at the interaction between climatic and human processes that give rise to migration. It applies these tools to the three most important categories of climate-related phenomena that are known from past experience to be linked to migration – extreme weather events, floods, and droughts – which in turn sets the stage for a review of the emergent challenges of mean sea level rise, political instability caused by climate-related migration, food insecurity, and migration responses to unexpected climatic events and worst-case scenarios. The chapters on emergent challenges include discussion not only of hazard-type events but also of the more subtle influences of climate. They also introduce important questions of governance and policy. Throughout the book, a wide range of specific examples from living memory are canvassed to look at how climate and nonclimatic processes interact to create the potential for migration; how migration decisions are made under such circumstances; what factors influence decisions to migrate and, if so, to where; what forms of migration are most likely to emerge in terms of temporal and spatial scale; and some of the implications of migration beyond the migrant herself or himself. In doing so, this book hopes to offer a glimpse into the future through better understanding of the past and present.

1.8 Chapter Summary

Several key points underpin this book. The first is that climate has always had an influence on human settlement and migration patterns. Climate-related migration occurs when climate conditions, weather events and/or their physical impacts are among the easily recognizable influences on migration, but they need not be the sole cause of the migration event. Climatic changes can operate over a range of time scales and spatial scales, from sudden onset events that cause localized pulses of distress migration to long-term shifts in climatic regimes that unfold over the course of decades or centuries to change the habitability of regions. Migrants may be attracted to particular destinations because of favorable climatic conditions that create opportunity; they may also be influenced to leave particular locations because of unfavorable or adverse climate events or conditions. A single climate event or condition may generate multiple types of migration responses. Climate influences migration through spectacular, infrequent events as well as in more subtle, less noticeable ways, with the latter likely being more important influences on migration in aggregate terms. Migration is only one of many possible ways people adapt to take advantage of new opportunities or reduce their exposure to adverse climatic conditions and events.

Scholarly research on climate-related migration is a relatively recent pursuit, and has developed separately from the main body of migration scholarship. By bringing together the theories, concepts, and methods used in mainstream migration research and in climate impacts and adaptation research, researchers have a powerful set of tools at their disposal. These tools are needed. There is good reason to be concerned that anthropogenic climate change will increase the influence of climate on migration in coming years. Making predictions of future climate-related migration at global scales remains challenging, but with reliable population data existing models can be applied to studies done at local or regional scales. Past examples of climate-related migration can be used as evidence and learning devices for understanding future linkages between climate and migration. There is plenty of room for more research on climate and migration, and you, the reader, are strongly encouraged to jump in!

2

Why People Migrate

2.1 Introduction

Scholars in many disciplines pursue migration research from a variety of perspectives, each discipline bringing with it a range of favorite theoretical and methodological tools (Brettell and Hollifeld 2007). No grand unifying theory exists that explains human migration behavior in all its aspects, and there are no signs that one is soon to be developed. There is, however, great complementarity in the various ways scholars have sought to explain migration, each such method making its own useful contribution to a broader understanding. In exploring migration in the context of human adaptation to climate, it is useful to first review important explanatory concepts from across disciplines and describe how these can help clarify human migration behavior more generally.

The migration process can occur across a range of spatial and temporal scales, and involve many potential actors, institutions, and systems. From the perspective of an individual migrant, the process spans the period from when he or she first contemplates the possibility of moving, through the decision-making process, the act of moving, and on into the period of adjustment at the destination. For some migrants, the process may eventually include a return to the place of origin, or lead to becoming a member of a translocal or transnational community that maintains connections and perpetuates migration between the sending and the receiving area. For migrants who travel short distances and remain within their same cultural community, the migration process may be relatively uncomplicated. For migrants travelling long distances to settle in new and unfamiliar places, migration may be a long and arduous process, with integration into the destination population never completed within the migrant's own lifetime, but continued by subsequent generations.

The migration process as experienced by the individual does not exist in a vacuum; it is nested within larger sets of dynamic and interconnected cultural, economic, environmental, political, and social processes that shape human behavior more generally. A decision to migrate today may be the product of any number of antecedent

16

conditions and events. And, once acted upon, the decision to migrate generates new sets of risks and opportunities not only for the migrant, but for his or her social network, and for the sending and receiving communities as well. Migration is more than simply a movement across physical space; it is a change in the trajectory of an individual and those connected to that individual through social space.

The aim of this chapter is to provide the nonspecialist a clear overview of current scholarly understanding of the migration process and to introduce a set of basic theories, concepts, and terms that:

- Have been used in a wide variety of settings to explain and interpret how migration decisions are made and the factors that shape migration behavior generally;
- Can be used to describe and analyze in a systematic fashion known examples of migration related to droughts, floods, extreme weather events, and other climate-related phenomena; and
- Will be combined in Chapter 3 with scholarship that considers human vulnerability and adaptation to climatic variability and change in order to create a conceptual framework that shows the interactions between climate and migration within the context of an adaptive human-environment system.

2.2 Basic Assumptions of Modern Migration Research and Their Origins

Present-day English-language migration scholarship traces much of its theoretical, conceptual, and methodological origins to the work of German-born English scholar E. G. Ravenstein (1852–1913). In 1885 and again in 1889, Ravenstein published articles entitled 'The Laws of Migration', in which he outlined a series of generalized statements about migration behavior. The 'laws' he describes vary somewhat between the two publications and draw upon earlier publications in which Ravenstein offered his thoughts on why people undertake migration. Box 1 provides a summary of Ravenstein's laws based on Grigg (1977), with the language updated to make the terms consistent with present usage.

Box 1. Summary of Ravenstein's Laws, based on Ravenstein 1889, Grigg 1977

Ravenstein's 'Laws of Migration' include findings that:

- the majority of migrants travel only short distances
- migration proceeds in a step-by-step fashion, in that people move from remote parts of the rural area to less remote places, from village to town, and from town to city
- the farther the distance travelled, the more likely the migrant is destined to an urban center
- migration in one direction generates migration in the opposite direction
- people who live in urban centers are less likely to undertake migration than people living in rural areas

- females are more likely than males to migrate within their country of birth, but males are more likely to undertake international migration
- most migrants are individual adults; entire households rarely undertake more than local moves
- the population of urban centers grows more from migration than it does from natural increase
- the rate of migration increases in concert with commercial and industrial expansion and with improvements in transportation
- most migration flows from rural areas to urban centers
- the major causes of migration are economic

All but the last of the laws listed in Box 1 can be tested directly using common statistical data about populations. As researchers often still do today, Ravenstein used census data to develop his theories. By the late nineteenth century, the United Kingdom, along with many other European countries, Canada, and the United States, had established periodic censuses that recorded data including residents' place of birth, enabling Ravenstein to make a coarse identification of migrants and nonmigrants.[1] In describing the spatial scale of migration, Ravenstein used jurisdictional boundaries as his guide: local movements took place within one's county of birth, short-distance migration occurred when one moved to an adjacent county, and long-distance migration occurred when one moved farther afield (Grigg 1977). Given the transportation technologies of the day, such categorizations were reasonable, but to understand present-day migration patterns a different set of spatial categorizations is more helpful, and is introduced later in this chapter.

Ravenstein's laws remain widely cited today, and several have proven through subsequent research to still be reliable. Around the world, most migration today does indeed flow from rural areas to urban centers (Weeks 2008). The periods in which the transition to urbanization commenced vary by continent. In Western Europe, large-scale rural-to-urban migration was already occurring in the nineteenth century, as witnessed by Ravenstein; by the early twentieth century it had spread to the Americas, and in the last half-century to the Asian and African continents (Weeks 2008). It is widely reported that over half the global human population today lives in urban areas, although population statistics contain definitions of *urban* that vary from one jurisdiction to another, some including settlements of only a few thousand or less (Cohen 2003). Considerable variation is also seen in urbanization rates by continent and region, with more than 80 per cent of South Americans, Europeans, and Australians

---

[1] It is worth noting that many countries today still do not take a census at regular intervals, one factor that makes it difficult to obtain precise calculations of global migrant numbers. The United Nations Department of Economic and Social Affairs Statistical Division is coordinating an ongoing effort to have every country carry out some form of national census by 2014 so as to generate a general global census (McLeman 2012).

living in urban areas, while in many countries in South Asia and Africa the majority of the population still resides in rural areas (Cohen 2003).

Ravenstein's statement that migration occurs more often as the movement of individuals than of entire households also holds generally true although, as is shown later in this chapter, the role of the household in shaping the migration decisions of individuals should not be overlooked. Later research has shown that young adults are the most likely migrants of all, a refinement that Ravenstein's data did not allow him to make (Grigg 1977). Ravenstein also demonstrated foresight in identifying gender as an important factor in migration. The patterns in female migration he observed in nineteenth-century England are not universal today; many long-distance migrants today are females, often disproportionately so in the case of countries like the Philippines, Indonesia, and Sri Lanka (United Nations 2009, Gaetano and Yeoh 2010). Nonetheless, Ravenstein's insight was a forerunner to the growing body of research on gender dimensions of migration, which has become increasingly influential on migration scholarship generally (Silvey 2004).

The assertion that most migration takes place over relatively short distances generally holds true to this day (Samers 2010). Twentieth-century scholars suggested the existence of a 'distance-decay' effect in that the longer the distance between two places, the fewer human interactions, including migration, that are likely to occur between them (Hägerstrand 1967, Lewis 1982). However, exceptions to the distance-decay effect exist, and did in Ravenstein's day. For example, in moving from the English countryside to London or Manchester, a migrant then or now might bypass any number of possible alternative destinations along the way.[2] Scholars in recent decades have proposed a variety of explanations for why migration does not always follow the shortest or most direct pathways, including such things as gravity models, immigrant gateway cities, and a super-order of global cities, all variations on a theme that larger centers exert a disproportionate attraction for migrants across wider spatial areas as compared with smaller centers (Borjas 1994, Sassen 2001, Lewer and Van den Berg 2008). While these concepts refine matters somewhat, rules of thumb about distance effects and migration are not foolproof, and can at times be very misleading, particularly in the context of present-day international migration. For example, none of these concepts usefully explains why the three leading source countries of international migration to Canada in 2009 were China, the Philippines, and India, while Canada's only contiguous neighbor, the United States, provided less than a third as many permanent migrants as any of the large Asian source countries (Figure 2.1).

---

[2] This also casts doubt on Ravenstein's assertion that migration proceeds in a step-by-step fashion from less densely populated regions to progressively more densely populated centers, an assertion for which subsequent scholars have found no strong evidence (Grigg 1977). In a study of migration patterns in the United States, Plane, Henrie, and Perry (2005) found that the attractiveness of larger centers as migration destinations varies considerably by age group.

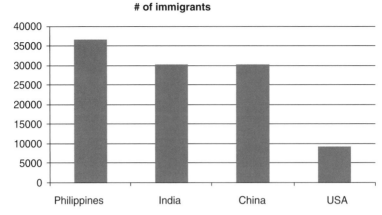

Figure 2.1. Selected source countries of permanent residents immigrating to Canada in 2010.
Data source: Citizenship & Immigration Canada (2010) http://www.cic.gc.ca/english/resources/statistics/facts2010/permanent/10.asp

Ravenstein was also accurate in recognizing that migration cannot be seen simply as discrete, unidirectional flows from point A to point B, but that migration patterns are embedded within other social, economic, and cultural networks and exchanges. Not only does the potential exist for a counter-flow of migration from destination to source region (including return migration), new in-flows of people to the migrant source region from other places may also take place, thereby generating new migration networks (see Massey et al. 1993, Faist 1998, Greiner 2011). In discussing the formation of such networks, Ravenstein introduced the concept of *push and pull*, which implies that migration is shaped by the combined effects of forces operating at a migrant's place of origin and at potential destinations. Push forces predispose or incent an individual or household to consider migration, while pull forces shape the comparative attractiveness of alternative settlement locations. Push-pull terminology continues to appear regularly in present-day discussions of migration. Its simplicity makes it a useful shorthand for acknowledging that migration decisions are influenced by a combination of factors, but it is essential to recognize that the push-pull concept greatly simplifies a complex process.

2.3 Spatial and Temporal Dimensions of Present-Day Migration

In Ravenstein's studies, a migrant was someone who no longer lived in the place where he or she was born, and this continues to be at the heart of how migration is defined. In an oft-cited article on theories of migration, Everett Lee defined migration as 'a permanent or semi-permanent change of residence' (1966: 49). This definition, which is broadly consistent with those used by many migration scholars today, adds to Ravenstein's working definition by suggesting that in addition to requiring a change of residence, migration has a temporal component. Going to work in the morning and coming back in the evening does not make one a migrant; no change of residence has occurred. Similarly, travelling for a vacation or a business trip does not qualify one as a migrant. Evacuating a city in advance of a tropical storm would also not constitute migration. However, Lee's definition does allow for the possibility of a dual intention on the part of the migrant: a first order intention to assume a new place of residence for a period of time, with the possibility of resuming residence at the previous location.

Lee also noted that his definition encompasses someone who moves across town just as it does someone who moves internationally, even though the processes and mechanisms influencing the latter are typically far more complex than those influencing the former. At the same time, by centering the temporal dimension of migration on the concept of residence, Lee's definition does not account for the migration movements of groups such as homeless transients, migrant workers, nomadic pastoralists, and other residence-less people. Migration scholars and demographers have often tended to deal with this definitional inconsistency by simply ignoring residence-less groups on the basis that they constitute a small proportion of the actual global population (Weeks 2008: 265). The present book does not exclude or ignore such groups. Although in absolute global terms they are small in numbers, in many countries and regions such people constitute notable sectors of society, and the nature of their livelihoods and their mobility may place them at a high level of exposure to climatic variability and change. Furthermore, continuously migrating populations, local mobility, and long-distance international migrants can be all accommodated within a framework of existing theories and concepts with little difficulty.

A first step in investigating the influence of climate on migration processes is to settle on clear terminology for describing the range of temporal and spatial possibilities of migration. A contemporary of Lee's, Nancie Gonzalez (1961), suggested a clear typology that captures the temporal possibilities of migration, and is used in this book:

- seasonal
- temporary nonseasonal
- recurrent
- continuous
- indefinite

One small adjustment has been made to Gonzalez's typology, substituting the term *indefinite* for *permanent*, simply to allow for the possibility that migrants may leave their place of origin with no fixed intention to return, but at a later stage in life decide to go back.

The terminology Ravenstein used to describe the spatial scales across which migration occurs were useful for his purposes, but this book employs a more geographically precise set of terms that are more consistent with today's scholarship and with the structure of governing bodies and institutions engaged in migration policy and planning:

- intra-urban migration = movements within urban centers;
- internal migration = migration within state political boundaries, which can be further described as rural-to-rural, rural-to-urban, or urban-to-rural migration depending on the direction of flow;
- international migration = movement across state boundaries, which can be further modified as intraregional (i.e. migration between nearby states); interregional (between more distant states, such as from Bangladesh to the Persian Gulf States), and/or intercontinental.

2.4 General Theories of Why People Migrate

Describing the possible spatial and temporal dimensions of migration is relatively straightforward; understanding the underlying causal reasons for migration is less so. Why do people migrate? Ravenstein suggested that most migration is economic in nature. This is an example of a normative statement that he could not have tested empirically using the census data available to him, and which still today is not easily tested using census data alone. Without direct questioning of migrants to ascertain their motivations, causality can at best be only inferred from secondary data. As with any question of human social behavior, migration theories must be continually developed, empirically tested, and refined to explain why people do the things they do. Yes, economic factors do influence the migration behavior of some groups and individuals some of the time, but scholars have developed a raft of other theories about how and why migration may be initiated, sustained, and transformed. A great many books, edited volumes, and scholarly journal articles have been dedicated to describing and critiquing these various theories of migration, an exercise that will not be repeated here. Instead, a brief summary now follows of the theoretical explanations most commonly referred to by scholars, with the reader seeking a more detailed treatment referred to works such as those by Brettell and Hollifield (2008), Castles and Miller (2009), de Haas (2010), Samers (2010), and Weeks (2008).

Some theories relate to the front end of the migration process (i.e. the decision to leave one place for another) while others consider the tail end (i.e. how migrants become incorporated into their destinations). It is worth seeing these theories not as competing options, but as a kit of useful explanatory tools with which scholars and policy makers can equip themselves. It is also worth noting that, in terms of sheer volume, the greatest amount of English-language scholarship on migration tends to be weighted toward international migration, even though international migrants make up a smaller part of the global migrant population (King and Skeldon 2010). Because many aspects of these theories have been developed to explain international population movements, they may not always work well at other spatial scales.

2.4.1 Economic Theories of Migration

A first set of theories draws upon basic principles of neoclassical economics, in which individuals are assumed to make rational choices about where they will live and work (Faist 1997). The migration options available to any given individual are based on his or her human capital – that is, marketable skills, training and aptitudes, and knowledge of labor market opportunities (Sjaastad 1962, Todaro 1969, Borjas 1989). It is assumed individuals will seek to maximize their income, and will therefore move to where they expect to get the highest wages given their human capital. It would therefore logically follow that migration would typically flow from low-income to high-income locations, or from areas of high unemployment to low unemployment. Such patterns have been observed empirically within the United States, but less so within Europe, for reasons probably not explainable solely by economics (Greenwood 1997). Migration flows driven by wage or employment differentials emerge more freely within countries than between them, since other factors such as government regulation of labor markets and borders constrain international population movements. Indeed, governments and international trade organizations often deliberately favor and facilitate the movement of higher-paid/higher-skilled workers across borders while restricting migration opportunities of lower-paid/lower-skilled workers (Lalonde and Topel 1997). The result is a segmented labor market within which only certain people enjoy the full opportunity of maximizing their incomes through migration (Piore 1979). This can in turn generate concerns about 'brain drains' where poorer areas and regions lose their brightest and most talented residents to wealthier places, a phenomenon that may adversely affect the economic development of the places left behind (Beine, Docquiera, and Rapoport 2001).[3] Because borders are less open to them, lower-skilled workers seeking to move to higher-paying areas often get pushed into more clandestine or higher-risk forms of migration, raising their potential for becoming victims of exploitation. The resulting emergence of organizations that profit from facilitating illegal migration or trafficking is consistent with standard economic models of migration and not a departure from them (Salt 1997).

A variation of income maximization models is something Massey and colleagues (1993) have called 'new economic theory', which holds that migration can be driven by household-level strategies that seek to diversify income sources and reduce exposure to hardship and risk (Stark 1991; see de Haas 2010 for a more detailed review). In other words, the desire to avoid losses can be as powerful a motivation for migration as is the desire to acquire wealth. So it is, for example, that in various cultures young adults will leave their parents' home for another city or region in search of job opportunities in order to remit money back (Connell and Conway 2000, Adger et al. 2002). Massey and colleagues (1993) suggest this type of migration strategy

---

[3] The belief that 'brain drain' is a bad thing for the sending area is a contended one, as shown later in this chapter.

is more likely to be prevalent in areas where other options for reducing risk, such as insurance, lending institutions, and financial and commodity markets are unavailable. Rain (1999) describes in wonderful detail how seasonal migration of young adults is a key livelihood strategy of households living in dryland West Africa, a phenomenon discussed further in Chapter 6.

2.4.2 Structural Theories

Other theories place greater emphasis on broader-scale influences on migration, recognizing that in many cases migrants or people contemplating migration do not have complete liberty or agency with respect to their decision or potential destinations. Faist (1997), Castles and Miller (2009), and Black et al (2011) suggest classifying these broader influences as macro-, meso-, and micro-level structures. Theories of migration that focus on the combined influences of macro-level structures, such as demographics, culture, politics, economics, and globalization, can be generally described as world systems approaches (Portes 2010). Increased worldwide connectivity through improved transportation and communication systems has been cited as a key factor in facilitating international migration, by making longer-distance movements easier (Samers 2010). At the same time, globalized economic forces can constrain migration or actively channel population flows in particular directions. For example, dependency theorists suggest that Western-style globalized capitalism has undermined development in the world's poorer countries, with neoliberal government trade policies and international organizations like the International Monetary Fund and World Bank helping to reinforce this dynamic (Watts 2000). This in turn creates conditions that dispossess the poor, especially rural poor, and drive them to migrate to cities or to other countries in search of low-wage employment (for an example from Peru, see Massey and Capoferro 2006). Scholars drawing upon the systems theories of Wallerstein (1979) go farther and suggest the world is increasingly moving to a single economic system, of which a fundamental attribute is the creation of have-not regions hosting large pools of low-wage, exploitable laborers to be drawn upon as needed (Cohen 1987). Guest worker programs, by which countries agree to regulate the movement of labor migrants from the economically weaker to the stronger, can be interpreted as macro-level efforts to institutionalize the creation of migrant labor pools, as can China's system of internal migration control through the household registration or *hukou* system (see later in this chapter).

Once migration movements become established between one place and another, micro-level structures in the form of social, cultural, and economic networks may emerge that, once they reach a critical mass, facilitate additional migration and assist in the integration and settlement of newcomers (Castles and Miller 2009).[4] Massey

---

[4] Faist (1997) actually labels these social networks as meso-structures and casts the micro-level of influence as values, resources, and capital belonging to the individual. There is no consensus within the scholarship as to the exact boundaries between the micro, meso, and macro.

and Espinosa (1997) have shown, for example, how migrant social networks are key drivers of migration between Mexico and the United States. Not only do networks facilitate migration, but they can lead to the development of permanent transregional or transnational social spaces within which flow ideas, goods, services, and money, thereby linking sending and receiving areas ever more tightly (Faist 1998). Migrant networks can also develop within countries (Lawson 2000), a well-known example being the large-scale migration out of the southern Great Plains 'Dust Bowl' to California during the 1930s, which was greatly facilitated by extended family networks (Gregory 1989, McLeman 2006; see case study Chapter 6).

Between these micro- and macro-level structures are meso-level structures that help mediate migration flows (Castles and Miller 2009). These include such things as employment and recruitment agencies, lawyers, consultants, smuggling organizations, traffickers, and those who provide loans for people to undertake migration. Marriage agents exist in many parts of the world, facilitating the acquisition and movement of spouses, typically women, often across long distances (Wang and Chang 2002). Some of these meso-structures operate legitimately in the light of day; others are blatantly illegal and exploitative in nature. In one sense they are nothing new; meso-level organizations as different from one another as railway companies and slave traders had a role in shaping historical population patterns in the United States (White 2008, Klein 2010).

2.4.3 Theories of Settlement and Integration

The settlement and integration portion of the migration process is complex, and has generated its own body of scholarship looking at issues like the development and transformation of ethnic minorities and enclaves, and the ability of newcomers to become accepted members of their new communities (Castles and Miller 2009). The experience of newcomers has a significant impact on the social, economic, and cultural attributes of destination and sending areas. Most obviously, when migrants can rapidly integrate and succeed in their new communities, it may serve as an incentive to others to migrate as well. However, the inverse in not always true; that is, the lack of an open and welcoming reception at the destination is not necessarily a disincentive or deterrent to further migration. Laws that prohibit French schoolgirls from wearing headscarves or that allow Arizona police officers to detain people who look suspiciously like undocumented migrants are unlikely to stop Muslim migration to France or Mexican migration to the U.S. southwest (Ho 2010, Tissot 2011). Some states choose to actively facilitate integration and offer the possibility of naturalization – that is, offer full citizenship to newcomers. Others offer citizenship only on an ethnic basis, meaning that newcomers can never fully participate in the receiving society. Why some states do so and others do not is a question beyond the scope of this book.[5] What is particularly important for the study of climate-related migration

---

[5] Readers interested in exploring such questions might start with Shachar and Hirschl (2007).

is simply to recognize that the outcomes of settlement and integration processes have effects on both sending and receiving areas.

2.5 Common Concepts in Migration Theory

Several key concepts are common across theoretical explanations of migration and merit a little extra attention. The first is *path dependency*, a broad social science concept that recognizes that decisions made in the present, including migration, do not emerge out of thin air, but are shaped by past events (Hansen 2002). Future migration movements are more likely to follow routes where previous events have created favorable conditions. One obvious example is the legacy of past European colonization of other parts of the world. For example, it is not coincidental that intercontinental migrants from the West African nations of Cape Verde, Ghana, and Cote D'Ivoire often make their destinations Portugal, the United Kingdom, and France, respectively (Cardoso 2010, Michalowski 2010, Somerville and Cooper 2010). Shared language and cultural familiarity between former colonial power and former colony create conditions that favor the social and economic success of these migrants. Residents of former colonies also often enjoy entry and residency privileges nationals from other countries lack, reducing one of the common barriers to international migration. For example, when volcanic activity required the abandonment of much of the Caribbean island nation of Montserrat, residents did not resettle just anywhere; most went to either the United Kingdom (the overseeing colonial power) or to Antigua, a nearby island that was also once a British colony (Skinner 2002).

A concept associated with path dependency is that of *cumulative causation* (Massey 1990), which suggests that once a migration movement becomes established between two places, even should the conditions that initiated the movement wane, new driving forces can emerge that reinvigorate or perpetuate the movement. For example, Massey and Espinosa (1997) found in studies of migration from Mexico to the United States that, while economic factors were initially at the core of this movement, social networks and the obligations and resources that are transmitted along them (also described as *social capital*) became a new stimulus for migration. As another example, during the 1920s, falling commodity prices and rising interest rates led thousands of rural residents to migrate from the southern Great Plains to the expanding economy of California (McLeman 2006). The next decade, a new and even greater wave of migrants followed when the combined effects of drought, the Great Depression, and agricultural restructuring hit the Great Plains. Fussell and Massey (2004) have observed that cumulative causation tends to operate much more strongly in reinforcing migration out of rural areas than out of (or between) urban areas, a result of rural social networks tending to be stronger than more anonymous and opportunistic urban ones.

A third important concept is that migration is related to the *human life course*. Certain types of migration behavior or events are more likely to occur among certain age cohorts, reflecting how the social and economic advantages and disadvantages of migration vary over the course of one's lifetime (Plane, Henrie, and Perry 2005). Young adults are generally more mobile than other age cohorts. Their migration decisions and patterns are often strongly influenced by labor market opportunities, making them active participants in rural-to-urban migration. Labor market forces can also combine with social and cultural factors to generate migration patterns particular to young people (Gibson and Argent 2008). For example, members of what is often referred to as the 'creative class' (i.e. artists, entertainers, scholars, and so forth) tend to migrate immediately upon completion of their postsecondary training to places with high densities of other members of this class (Hansen and Niedomisyl 2009). As people age and settle into more established patterns of employment and community, it is generally believed that labor markets have a decreasing effect on migration decisions. Noneconomic factors become even more influential as one approaches retirement, with quality of life issues and concerns like health services, proximity to loved ones or caregivers, and environmental amenities becoming more important. In North America, the most visible manifestation of this is in the hundreds of thousands of 'snowbirds', wealthy retirees who participate in an annual seasonal movement between cooler and sunnier climes (McHugh, Hogan, and Happel 1995). Bures (1997) has identified a particular group of people called the 'near-elderly', who are approaching retirement but still participating in the labor force, and who have their own migration tendencies that distinguish them from middle-aged people and from retirees.

A final key concept that is critical to analyzing migration behavior is that of *structure and agency* and the relationship between the two. It is a concept that for several decades has played an important role in scholarly debates in the social sciences generally (Archer 2003), and in theories of migration behavior as well (Bakewell 2010, de Haas 2010). The terms *structure* and *agency* are inherently linked, but their precise definitions can vary according to the context in which they are used. In simplest terms, *agency* refers to the degree of freedom an individual has in choosing his or her actions, while *structure* refers to the societal norms, obligations, and institutions that shape and set limits on the individual's actions (for a more detailed discussion of structure and agency, suggested readings are Hays 1994, Emirbayer and Mische 1998, and Archer 2003). Migration theories have traditionally tended to focus either on the decisions and behavior of individuals and households (i.e. agents) or on the larger forces beyond the influence or control of the household that help shape migration patterns more broadly (i.e. structure), with scholars in recent years encouraging researchers to seek out approaches that try to incorporate both (Bakewell 2010, de Haas 2010). This is easier said than done. It is an ongoing methodological challenge to find ways of conducting empirical analyses of migration events that can account

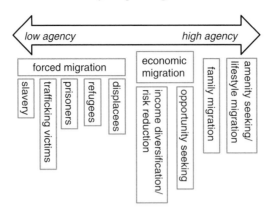

Figure 2.2. Continuum of migrant agency and migrant categories.

for the combined influences of macro- and meso-structures and link these to the deci-sions individual agents make.

In my own empirical research on climate-related migration in North America, I have tended to combine social theories developed by late French theorist Pierre Bourdieu with methodological tools used by scholars who practice grounded theory and critical realism research (Charmaz 2004, Bakewell 2010). As a methodological approach, it is far from perfect, and requires tremendous commitment to gathering qualitative data from participants in migration events and from those who could have participated in the same events but did not. However, it does shed light on how struc-tural influences and individual motivations play out on the ground, and allows for the recognition and identification of influences that are not necessarily obvious to the outsider, such as the amount of clay soil in a drought-stricken area (McLeman and Ploeger 2012) or the role of local churches in helping people adapt in situ, without migrating (McLeman et al. 2008).

2.6 Categorizing Migrants Based on Agency

Earlier sections of this chapter showed how migrants might be categorized by the dura-tion of their migration (i.e. temporary, seasonal, recurrent, continuing, indefinite, and return) and by the distance of their movement (i.e. intra-urban, intraregional, interna-tional, and interregional/intercontinental). A third parameter that may be used to catego-rize migrants is the degree of agency the migrant (or household, depending on who is the decision-making entity) has in exercising its decision. This is illustrated in Figure 2.2, which shows a continuum from a high degree of agency or freedom in choosing migra-tion options and destinations to one of little or no freedom of decision making. Against this are listed common categories of migrants described in the migration literature.

The category of migrant exercising the greatest degree of agency is the lifestyle migrant, who chooses to relocate first and foremost to enjoy lifestyle amenities of another place. This can include the young adult who migrates to an urban center for the sheer thrill and perceived glamour of it, often referred to as the 'bright lights, big city' phenomenon (McCormick and Wahba 2005). Another is the 'snowbird' migrant mentioned earlier, retired senior citizens of sufficient financial means who spend winters in sunny locations. Flows of lifestyle migrants can be considerable in number; for example, Coates, Healy, and Morrison (2002) suggest that a full 1 per cent of the Canadian population spends extended periods each winter in the U.S. Sun Belt states.

Adjacent to this is the category of family migration, which can take on a variety of forms, such as the movement of one spouse to join another, movements of people from one household to another within extended family networks, the movement of an aging parent to live with adult children, and so forth. Depending on the circumstances, there may be less agency involved in the individual migrant's decision to undertake such movements. Health considerations may oblige an aging parent to move in order to live near or with adult children. In some cultures the young are free to choose their own marriage partners and live where they wish, but in others, marriages may be arranged with or without both participants having liberty to select their potential spouse (Watts 1983, Lievins 1999). In some instances, such as rural China, economic considerations may also influence marriage-related migration choices (Fan and Huang 1998). While the majority of family-related migration likely occurs at intraregional distances or nearer, a significant international/intercontinental component exists as well. For example, between 20 and 30 per cent of international migrants to Canada each year between 2006 and 2010 were 'family class' spouses, fiancées, children, and parents migrating to join sponsoring relatives who are permanent residents (Citizenship and Immigration Canada 2011).

The next two adjacent categories in the continuum are those who migrate primarily for economic reasons. Consistent with the theories described previously, these are divided into opportunity-seeking migrants, who move to take up or seek out employment, and those who migrate as part of a broader household risk management strategy. The degree of agency among economic migrants can range considerably depending on a wide variety of factors. Certain types of occupations have disproportionate levels of participation by migrants, and these can be found at various places across the wage spectrum. Some are low-paying occupations, such as agricultural labor and domestic service, and often provide only seasonal or temporary work, making them unattractive to people with access to more permanent labor market opportunities. These jobs can also be more dangerous than other occupations. For example, it has in the past decade been estimated that America hosts between 3 and 5 million migrant farm workers, many of whom live in substandard living conditions and face a wide range of workplace hazards and health risks (Hansen and Donohoe 2003). Cross and colleagues (2008) found migrant farm workers in the United Kingdom also experience below-average health compared with cross-society norms, and note that the type of farm, organic or commercial, has no effect on physical health.[6] Ahonen, Benavides, and Benach (2007) suggest migrant farm workers in most industrialized nations experience similar conditions.

Migrants can also be disproportionately represented in highly skilled, higher-income occupations, such as health care. Rural areas in many nations find it challenging to recruit and retain adequate numbers of health care professionals, and many developing nations find themselves losing doctors, nurses, and specialists to wealthier countries (Stilwell et al. 2004, Kumar 2007, Lehmann, Dieleman, and Martineau 2008). The investment necessary from both the individual and the state to train and educate health care professionals is considerable, and provides the health care professional with a highly marketable set of skills that facilitates his or her mobility and migration destination choices. Many countries require migrant professionals, including health care workers, to undergo occupational recertification or accreditation before allowing them to practice their profession. It is not clear whether such requirements deter migration, but it can result in the phenomenon of 'overskilling', where migrants find themselves working in jobs well below their training and qualification (Mavromaras et al. 2010). It can be generally assumed that higher-skilled, higher-income workers are more commonly found in the opportunity-seeking category of migrants in Figure 2.2, with lower-income, low-security jobs more common in the household risk diversification category. However, this is not a hard and fast distinction, and what constitutes opportunity for one person might be better described as making the best of a difficult situation for another.

At this point in the continuum, agency becomes increasingly curtailed, entering the realm of what is described as forced migration (Chimni 2009). The first of these categories consists of displacees – people dislodged from their place of residence by forces beyond their immediate control. The displacing force may be environmental in nature, such as an extreme storm, fire, or riverbank erosion, or the result of a wide range of human activities from violence to land degradation to planning decisions. The International Disaster Monitoring Center (IDMC) estimated that in 2010 more than 40 million people worldwide were displaced because of sudden-onset natural hazards. Not all persons displaced by natural disasters become migrants; assuming it becomes safe and feasible to do so, many displacees will return to their place of residence (see Chapters 4 and 5). Cernea (2009) has suggested that international development projects are an important and often overlooked driver of forced migration and permanent displacement in developing countries. The largest single source of development-related displacements has been China's Three Gorges Project, which has displaced an estimated 1.3 million people (Wilmsen, Webber, and Duan 2011a,b; see also Chapter 5).

---

[6] Workers on organic farms do, however, report higher levels of short-term happiness with their employment.

The United Nations High Commissioner for Refugees (UNHCR 2012) estimates that the worldwide population of forcibly displaced people has reached 42.5 million – 27.3 million still living within their own countries and another 15.2 million living outside their countries of origin. Under international law, the former group is known as 'internally displaced persons' (IDPs), while the latter are described as refugees. This spatial distinction – the act of crossing an international boundary – is a key element in the distinction between displacees and refugees in Figure 2.2. It is also one element in the definition of a refugee under the United Nations *Convention Relating to the Status of Refugees*. The Convention also makes particular reference to the causes of displacement. A *Convention Refugee* is someone who has been singled out (or has reasonable fear of being singled out) for persecution in his or her home country on the basis of membership in some political, social, cultural, or demographic group, and is unable to return because the fear of persecution remains. In this dynamic, the role of the state can vary; it may be directly responsible for persecution or it may be indirectly responsible because of incapacity or unwillingness to protect its citizens from persecution by third parties. The term *persecution* implies something more sinister than random acts of violence that are not directed at any particular group (Steinbock 1998). It also implies a human actor being responsible; by definition, the environment cannot be an agent of persecution because it cannot make distinctions among societal groups (McLeman 2010a). The term *environmental refugees* promoted by El-Hinnawi (1985) to describe people involuntarily displaced by natural disasters, human changes to the environment, and similar causes is inconsistent with legal understandings of the term (Hugo 1996) and for this reason is best avoided, notwithstanding its use in the popular media.

Prior to the adoption of the UN Refugee Convention in the 1950s, the term *refugee* was widely used as a generic term synonymous with forced migration. U.S. government reports in the 1930s routinely made reference, for example, to 'drought refugees' fleeing the southern Great Plains (Rowell 1936). Since the advent of the Convention, policy makers are much more circumspect in the use of the term *refugee*, and stick closely to its Convention definition, as does this book. People who move across international boundaries for reasons other than persecution do not enjoy formal protection or mobility rights under international law. People who move within their country of origin, even for reasons of persecution, are also not recognized as refugees under international law. An internationally recognized document called the *Guiding Principles on Internal Displacement* defines a broad range of displacees, including ones displaced for climate-related reasons, that might be recognized and offered rights and protection, but it is legally nonbinding (Cohen 2004). The *Guiding Principles* are reviewed in more detail in the context of mean sea level rise in Chapter 7; in the meantime, it is enough to recognize here that all refugees are displacees, but not all displacees can be considered refugees. Generically, both groups fall under the term 'forced migrants', the distinctions being the reasons for displacement and whether an international boundary has been crossed.

Displacees and refugees are not entirely without agency, and can exhibit a significant range of decision making and choices with respect to their final destination, depending on their circumstances (Riddle and Buckley 1998). The final categories in Figure 2.2 are reserved for those who have no agency at all: prisoners, victims of trafficking, and slaves. Statistics for the last two categories are inherently difficult to obtain for obvious reasons, as those who engage in such enterprises operate outside the law. Overt and institutionalized slave transportation is thankfully rare today, although in a few locations, such as the West African nation of Mauritania, authorities turn a blind eye to the still-continuing practice (Ruf 1999, Bales 2004, Quirk 2006). Migrant trafficking is, however, not rare, and again, in many countries where human traffickers operate the authorities turn a blind eye (Laczko and Gramegna 2003). The most common victims of human trafficking are typically the most powerless members of society, often impoverished young women and children (Laczko 2005). In some cases the victims are forced into sexual slavery; in others, they are forced into unpaid and unwilling servitude. Note here there is a critical difference between the terms *trafficking* and *smuggling*, which are sometimes used interchangeably, but should not be. Smuggling organizations operate outside the law, and smuggler-organized migration often entails dangerous or life-threatening conditions (Peterka-Benton 2011). However, a migrant who engages a smuggling organization has not entirely surrendered his or her agency; that is, the migrant is still selecting destinations, duration of stay, and so forth. Victims of trafficking have no agency; they are entirely at the mercy of others. It is often the case that trafficking organizations pass themselves off to unsuspecting victims as smugglers or labor migration consultants. Traffickers may specialize in certain types of victims and run regular networks between particular sending and receiving regions. Unlike smuggling, which by definition assists people across borders, trafficking may occur internally within countries as well (Aronowitz 2001).

People sentenced to imprisonment are removed from their place of residence and, in many instances, may be transported over long distances to the places where they are to be incarcerated. In the days of European empires, it was a significant international phenomenon (Shaw 1977, Toth 2006). Today it remains a notable segment of internal migration in many countries, particularly for demographic and cultural groups with high incarceration rates. For example, the U.S. rate of incarceration, which is the highest among industrialized nations, was more than 7 in 1,000 in the year 2004; for African American males in their twenties and not engaged in postsecondary education or training, the figure was approximately 135 in 1000 (Western and Wildeman 2009). High rates of incarceration have significant negative impacts on the health and well-being of source communities (Thomas and Torrone 2008, Western and Wildeman 2009), with Pettit and Western (2004) suggesting incarceration is becoming a de facto stage in the life course of African American males with low education attainment. This latter conclusion may overstate matters,

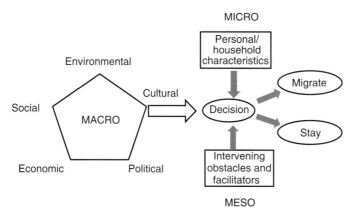

Figure 2.3. Interaction of macro-, meso-, and micro-level factors in shaping environmental migration decisions, simplified from Foresight (2011). One change made here is the substitution of 'cultural' for 'demographic' factors at the macro level. The reasons for this are described later in this chapter.

but it is clear that incarceration-related migration is a real risk for members of that social group. Aboriginal males in Australia and Canada also experience disproportionately high rates of incarceration relative to the general population. In Australia, aboriginal incarceration rates are 15.6 in 1000 versus 1.6 in 1000 for non-aboriginals (Krieg 2006); in the province of Saskatchewan, Canada, where only 11 per cent of the population is aboriginal, 81 per cent of the prison population is aboriginal (Perreault 2009).

2.7 Structural Forces that Shape Migration

Having categorized the various possible types of migrants according to agency, it is also possible to suggest basic categories of broader macro- and meso-level factors, beyond the control of individuals or households, which limit or constrain migrant agency. The various theories of migration described earlier in this chapter have alluded to many examples of these. For ease of description, they can be organized into the following categories – cultural, environmental, macroeconomic, political, and social in origin. This categorization of structural factors is similar to that suggested in the Foresight project's (2011) model of the emergence of environmentally related migration (Figure 2.3). As can be seen from Figure 2.3, none of these structural factors act in isolation; in many cases they are fundamentally linked to one another, often in a self-reinforcing fashion. The Foresight model provides a useful starting point for visualizing how climatic factors may interact with other macro-level factors in shaping migration, and is developed further in the next chapter. The remainder of this chapter describes the influence on migration of each of the macro categories of factors.

2.7.1 The Influence of Social Factors on Migration

Some types of migration are inherently driven by social motivations, such as the desire to join friends, to reunite with family members, or to marry. Beyond these immediate social impetuses for individual migration decisions, social networks' effects in initiating and perpetuating migration movements cannot be understated. Even over short distances, migration has direct costs for the migrant and his or her household, such as transportation, relocation, and the need for accommodation at the destination. Migration also brings indirect costs, such as the household's loss of the migrant's labor, the migrant's absence from participation in family life, and the opportunity cost of giving up a known economic and social system for one that is less familiar. When migration flows initially emerge between one place and another, the high costs mean that households and individuals with limited economic resources may have difficulty participating (Neto and Mullet 1998). Once migrant networks become established, *social capital* is generated and transmitted through these networks, which can reduce the cost of migration and facilitate subsequent migration and incorporation (Massey and Espinosa 1997, Nee and Sanders 2001).

The term *capital* traces back to the classical economics writings of Adam Smith, David Ricardo, and Karl Marx, and at its simplest describes financial resources above and beyond those needed for basic day-to-day living (McLeman 2007). We most commonly think of capital in terms of economic capital: money, and things that can be converted to money in a straightforward fashion (like shares in companies or home ownership). In the 1980s, social scientists suggested that alternatives to economic capital can form within certain aspects of social structures, and called these *social capital* (Bourdieu 1986, Coleman 1988). Social capital can take on a variety of shapes, such as reciprocal obligations, advantageous information, knowing who to trust, and limits on undesirable behavior (Serageldin and Grootaert 2000, Mohan and Mohan 2002). It can serve to strengthen ties between individuals within communities and social networks, and to build new bridges linking different social groups (Putnam 2000). It can be created and maintained through informal social connections, such as relations between family and friends, as well as through formal social organizations, such as churches, service clubs, and trade or labor associations (Wall, Ferrazzi, and Schryer 1998). Social capital is increasingly seen as an important factor in international development (Woolcock 1998, Portes and Landolt 2000) and in adaptation to climatic variability and change (Adger 2003, Pelling and High 2005). It has also been observed to be an important factor in the recovery of communities from natural disasters like Hurricane Katrina (e.g. Airriess et al. 2007).

Examples of social capital that are important in the context of migration include information about crossing borders, assistance in acquiring transportation over long distances, introductions to potential employers in the settlement area, and assistance in finding accommodation (Massey and Espinosa 1997, Palloni et al. 2001). Because social capital does not belong to any one individual but is instead a resource shared among members of social groups, it is not limited in terms of its potential geographical scale. Hence transnational communities can form between migrant sending and receiving areas that are separated by long distances, examples being the transnational Kurdish community connecting Western Europe to Turkey (Faist 1998) and the transnational community connecting the Dominican Republic to New York (Georges 1992). Not all migration movements necessarily give rise to strongly interconnected transnational communities (Riccio 2001). The types and nature of social connection between sending and receiving areas can vary significantly from one case to another depending on the cultural group and the degree of assimilation or incorporation into the destination culture.

2.7.2 *The Influence of Macroeconomic Factors on Migration*

A variety of macroeconomic processes and forces have been identified as influencing migration, often working in conjunction with other micro-, meso-, and macro-scale processes (Massey et al. 1993). In industrialized countries, an increase in economic growth and employment opportunities in a given location is often associated with increasing in-migration (Karras and Chiswick 1999). Differences in economic growth between locations and the resulting wage differentials are believed to influence migration patterns at intraregional and international scales (Todaro 1969, Karras and Chiswick 1999). For example, Milne (1993) observed that internal migration patterns in Canada seemed to follow regional economic performance within the country. Blanchflower and Shadforth (2009) have observed similar connections between economic performance and migration from continental Europe to the United Kingdom in the past decade, while Mayda (2009) found that OECD countries with better income opportunities have generally attracted higher levels of international migration. The difference in potential income opportunities that commonly exists between rural areas and urban centers has long been believed to be a key driver of rural-urban migration (Todaro 1969). Urban centers that develop large pools of economic and human capital may influence a stronger attraction to potential migrants than other centers (Sassen 2001).

Some economic sectors where the work is typically place-specific, such as agriculture and construction, may rely heavily on migrant or transient workers (Passel 2007). In other economic sectors, such as light manufacturing and the garment industry, companies can move production facilities to sites where low-wage workers, often female, are available. Governments in many developing regions attempt to attract such facilities by establishing special zones where offshore companies can operate with low or no taxes, so long as production is for export (Engman, Onodera, and Pinali 2007). These zones in turn draw laborers from the host country or region, and can have a significant influence on migration patterns (Ong 2006, Wang, Wang, and Wu 2009, Resurreccion 2010).

International trading agreements often include provisions that facilitate the move-ment of certain types of labor, especially in highly skilled sectors such as infor-mation technology and financial management. At a global scale, the World Trade Organization's General Agreement on Trade in Services (GATS) is a key agreement in terms of seeking to liberalize the movement of labor (Broude 2007). Signatories are in principle required to allow the entry of workers from other signatory coun-tries to perform labor pursuant to particular types of services covered under GATS. However, these provisions apply only to workers already employed for the purpose at hand; GATS does not allow unemployed workers to travel among signatory states to seek employment. Regional trade agreements such as the North American Free Trade Agreement (NAFTA) may have similar provisions in that workers already employed in prescribed sectors can move relatively freely between states, but job seekers or those seeking to establish permanent residence must typically conform to ordinary migration rules and regulations. The EU's Schengen agreement is much broader, in that citizens of member states are generally permitted free movement within the region and are not required to have employment prior to moving to another member state (Zaiotti 2011). For readers seeking more details, Dux (2008) provides a region-by-region analysis of labor migrant rights under regional agreements.

Adverse macroeconomic conditions, as experienced through such phenomena as high rates of unemployment, commodity price swings, changing interest rates, price inflation, and changing currency valuations, can have a strong influence on migration. For example, during the Great Depression of the 1930s, large numbers of unemployed North Americans migrated from city to city in search of work, with iconic images of that period including overloaded jalopies of west-bound families and transient young men known as 'bindlestiffs' or 'rubber tramps' (Figure 2.4), crisscrossing the con-tinent on railway cars or on foot in search of work (Mitchell 1996, Barden 2004). Financial downturns since the 1930s have not been as widespread across countries and economic sectors, meaning that labor migration movements have in some cases been able to divert from hard-hit areas to still-prosperous ones. What has become known as the post-2008 'Great Recession' has had its effects on labor migration within various regions around the world (Wright and Black 2011).

2.7.3 *The Influence of Cultural Factors on Migration*

Cultural norms and understandings about migrants and migration can be influential at all stages of the migration process, from the decision to migrate to incorporation into the destination population. Relevant cultural factors flow from the migrant's own culture as well as those of the culture of the dominant population at the destina-tion, assuming they differ. In many cultures and communities, undertaking migra-tion at a particular life stage, typically young adulthood, is an encouraged or at least widely accepted practice (Gabriel 2006, Geisen 2010). Pastoralist cultures in diverse

Figure 2.4. Migrant worker alongside California highway, 1935. Image source: Library of Congress Prints and Photographs Division Washington. Image no. LC-USF347–003801-ZE (b&w film neg.), Dorothea Lange, photographer. Public domain image. http://www.loc.gov/pictures/collection/fsa/item/fsa1999000001/PP/

geographical settings, from Central Asia's steppes to Sudano-Sahelian Africa to Scandinavia's Lapland practice inherently migratory lifestyles, and conflicts have emerged in situations where governments have sought to restrict their movements or force them to move into fixed settlements (Fernandez-Gimenez and Le Febre 2006). In traditional hunter-gatherer societies, such as the Inuit of the Arctic, many of Australia's aboriginal peoples, and First Nations[7] of the North American Great Plains, mobility and migration have historically been an inherent component of culture, with severe social problems sometimes occurring when outsiders have forced them to abandon such practices (Billson 1990, Memmott and Long 2005, Wishart 2007). Within cultures that outwardly seem homogeneous, particular groups may

---

[7] Aboriginal peoples in the United States are generally referred to as American Indians, while in Canada they are referred to as First Nations.

maintain very different practices with respect to migration. For example, Europe's large Roma population consists of people who prefer maintaining permanent residence in one place as well as those who prefer practicing the more itinerant lifestyle outsiders typically associate with them (Fonseca 1996). Cultures that favor migration are not confined to traditional, subsistence, or noncapitalist lifestyles. For more than a century, Chinese migrants to North American came disproportionately from Taishan County and surrounding settlements in the Pearl River Delta, where it was expected that young people would seek their fortunes abroad and remit money back to those remaining behind (Hsu 2000, Skeldon 2003).

Scholars increasingly recognize that gender is a relevant factor in migration across all the categories identified in Figure 2.2, playing out in a variety of ways too numerous to adequately summarize here (for more detailed reviews, see Hondagneu-Sotelo and Cranford 2006, Palmary et al. 2010). A number of trends have emerged in recent decades that are distinctive to female migration, some noteworthy ones bearing mention here. International migration of women has grown in certain occupations such as caregiver and domestic worker (Lutz 2008). Industrial sectors such as garment manufacturing rely heavily on female labor, providing employment opportunities and alternatives to home-based work for women, and are important employers in developing nations for female migrants from rural areas (Resurreccion 2009). It is not simply that such workers happen to be women, but that economic structures and control over them are gendered (Wright 2006). Marriages in many cultures require the bride to move to the household of the husband, and some women in countries such as Russia and the Philippines have turned to participation in the mail-order bride industry as a means of escaping poverty (Morgan 2007). Women often suffer disproportionately as victims of violence, persecution, and trafficking in many regions of the world (Hodge and Lietz 2007, Hunt 2008). These are but a small sampling of ways migration patterns observed at all scales may be gendered, with additional examples appearing in later chapters.

Education plays an important role in shaping migration behavior and patterns, again playing out in a variety of ways. Travel to attend educational institutions is a common phenomenon across many countries, often attracting migrants from rural or smaller communities to larger centers. In the United States during the late 1960s and 1970s, programs that mandated the racial integration of schools are believed in some places to have had the opposite effect, helping to drive an out-migration of whites from many urban centers (Farley, Richards, and Wurdock 1980). Educational attainment is inherently linked to internal and international labor migration; higher-skilled workers typically experience greater labor market demand, and government migration regulations tend to make their movement across borders easier than for lower-skilled workers. Studies in a range of countries from Burkina Faso (Henry, Boyle, and Lambin 2003) to China (Hare 1999) have found that opportunity-seeking migrants often have above-average literacy and education rates. However, the valuation of migrants' education

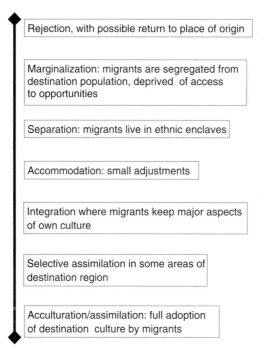

Figure 2.5. Continuum of settlement outcomes, after Segal, Mayadas, and Elliot (2010).

and skills credentials in a receiving area may be downgraded by the receiving culture or population, thereby leading to newcomers earning lower average wages than established residents (Bauder 2003, Tong 2010, Creese and Wiebe 2012).

Cultural differences play a significant role in the adjustments migrants make when settling in a new place. Segal, Mayadas, and Elliot (2010) suggest that migrant settlement outcomes occur across a continuum, and that these outcomes can have a feedback effect on future migration. The continuum (Figure 2.5) ranges from acceptance and assimilation into the resident population at one extreme, to marginalization and rejection at the other. Experts have reached no agreement as to which type of adjustment (with the obvious exception of rejection) is most advantageous to migrants or host populations, with each type having its own ramifications depending on the context in a given place and time. Where migrants feel perpetually excluded from the host culture, unrest and clashes can occur, as was witnessed during the 2005 riots in Parisian suburbs where most residents were not of European origin (Snow, Vliegenthart, and Corrigall-Brown 2007). Cultural clashes and migrant exclusion can also result from internal migration events. Californians, for example, were notoriously hostile to migrants arriving from the Great Plains during the 1930s, the Los Angeles sheriff's department going so far as to blockade the state's border with Arizona for several months in 1936 to prevent would-be migrants from entering (Giczy 2009). With the passage of time, however, it is often the case that migrants become part of the established community and the next wave of migrant newcomers must struggle for recognition and acceptance. In California's central valley, descendants of the once discriminated against 'Okie' migrants are today in positions of economic and political influence, and it is now migrants of Mexican and Central American origin struggling for acceptance (McLeman 2006).

2.7.4 The Influence of Political Factors on Migration

Political factors and processes influence migration behavior in three broad ways: through the policies and regulations implemented by states and other political actors to shape migration and citizenship; through general governance structures and processes that make a given jurisdiction more or less politically stable and economically prosperous relative to others; and through violence carried out by the state against members of its own population or the populations of its neighbors.

Government regulations on mobility and migration are the most obvious structural constraint on the agency of migrants and potential migrants. States whose citizens enjoy high degrees of freedom with respect to mobility and travel also often have high rates of participation in international migration over long distances in comparison with states where mobility and travel rights are restricted (Karamera, Oguledo, and Davis 2000). Under international law, states exercise the right to enforce entry across their borders and to make determinations with respect to citizenship and legal right of residency within their borders (Neumayer 2006). Most states maintain entry controls at land border crossings, ports, and airports. A smaller number also maintain exit controls, meaning that anyone seeking to leave the state must seek permission to do so. Two basic tools used by states to regulate the movement of people across borders are the passport and the visa. A passport is a government-issued identity document for the purpose of international travel that follows standards set by the International Civil Aviation Organization for its appearance and required contents. The passport allows the issuing state to exert some control over its nationals' ability to travel abroad, and enables receiving states to establish the identity and citizenship of those seeking entry. A visa is a document issued by a state that allows non-nationals the right to appear at its border control points and seek admission. Its effect is to enable the issuing country to prescreen those who would seek entry, keeping them at a physical distance until the traveller has demonstrated at a consulate, embassy, or authorized agent of the state that he or she meets admissibility requirements. Such controls do not necessarily prevent unauthorized migration; the International Organization for Migration suggests 10–15 per cent of global migration is irregular (i.e. unauthorized or illegal) (IOM 2010). The actual criteria for gaining admission and the length of time for which non-nationals are permitted to stay vary considerably from one state to another. In some cases, governments make special agreements to facilitate the movement of people across one another's borders, such as the European Union's Schengen

Agreement that removes border controls between participating countries except in instances of heightened national security.

States also determine questions of citizenship, which typically includes an automatic right of indefinite residence within a state's borders. Other rights and benefits accrue with citizenship, which vary according to the state (Fix and Laglagaron 2002). Common such rights include the protection of the state, access to the labor market and to state-provided services such as health and education, and, in democracies, the right to participate in the selection of political leadership. In return, citizens defer to the state's authority and undertake certain obligations, such as the requirement to pay taxes. Another obligation in some countries is military service, which can itself become a driver of migration, as witnessed by the thousands of 'draft dodgers' who fled the United States for Canada during the Vietnam War era (Kasinsky 1976). States may also use citizenship as a means of fostering nation building and a sense of national belonging and purpose (Samers 2010).

Not all people have a citizenship; the UNHCR (2011) estimates there are roughly 12 million people worldwide who are stateless, and therefore do not have a permanent right of abode in any nation. Statelessness can arise for a variety of reasons. It is a phenomenon often associated with discrimination against ethnic minorities or as a by-product of political instability, such as the situations that arose after the Yugoslav conflicts, the collapse of the Soviet Union, and the displacement of Palestinians from Israel (Pejic 1998, Gelazis 2004, Shiblak 2006). Statelessness can also result from restrictive laws on the transmission of citizenship to children, such as in the case where the identity of a child's parent is not properly documented, rendering the child stateless (Manly 2007). Some states reserve the right to revoke citizenship of individuals who violate the laws of the state, reside abroad, or marry a foreign national, thereby rendering such individuals stateless after the fact (Manly 2007).

Citizenship can be obtained through three general mechanisms, which vary from state to state (Weil 2001, Shachar and Hirschl 2007). One is consanguinity, whereby a child acquires the citizenship of its parent. Variations of consanguinity exist, with some states having broad rules that allow people with familial ties more distant than simply parent and child to claim citizenship on the basis of their ethnicity. A second way of acquiring citizenship is through place of birth, whereby countries automatically confer citizenship upon anyone born within their territory, regardless of the citizenship or residency status of the child's parents. Not all do so, however, and a child born in a country that does not confer automatic citizenship can become stateless if the parents' home country does not automatically confer consanguine citizenship. The third possibility is naturalization, whereby people who have migrated from another state may acquire citizenship according to some prescribed administrative process. Each state maintains its own rules and regulations regarding naturalization. States that allow little or no possibility of naturalization, such as many Persian Gulf states, are committed to a policy of ethnic citizenship only, having no interest in

integrating newcomers beyond the labor market. For other states, naturalization policies foster a range of integration processes from assimilation through to multiculturalism (Bloemraad, Korteweg, and Yurdakul 2008). The assimilation ideal is that newcomers and their children will adopt the language, customs, and cultural values of the
majority population and eventually become mainstreamed into the broader structure
of the society (Grosfoguel and Cordero-Guzman 1998). Multiculturalism as a policy
choice allows citizens to freely maintain or pursue membership in social groups of
their choice within the broader nation-state, and to choose the extent to which they
embrace the host culture. A considerable body of scholarship is currently debating
the merits of multiculturalism versus assimilation (Bloemraad et al. 2008); what is
relevant here is that states' immigration and naturalization policies have downstream
implications for international migration movements.

Many states impose strict controls on the entry of foreign nationals, and will
actively detain and deport those who violate immigration rules (Hyndman and
Mountz 2008). Some may also seek to impose controls on population movements
within their borders to achieve particular political or economic ends (Coutin 2010).
The People's Republic of China, for example, has since the 1950s operated a system of household registration known as *hukou* (Cheng and Selden 1994). Under this
system, the personal details of each household member are registered with the local
government registration office, along with any changes due to births or deaths (Liu
2005). Those registered in the *hukou* are entitled to basic social benefits such as education and primary health care, and are legally eligible to work in that jurisdiction
(Wang 2005). Indeed under the centrally planned economy, the state is obliged to
find employment for adult household members, although such employment, especially in rural areas, may provide only a subsistence income (Liu 2005). The *hukou*
system also historically enabled the state to enforce its one-child policy and to regulate the movement of people within China, since one could move only with the
approval of the registration offices in the source and destination locations (Cheng
and Selden 1994, Merli 1998, Zhu 2007). As the Chinese government opened up its
economy to international trade in the 1990s, the resulting demand for nonstate sector laborers in urban centers and coastal regions led to the emergence of a 'floating'
population of up to 120 million people who migrated without official permission
and without modifying their *hukous* (Zhu 2007).[8] In recent years, the central government has downloaded responsibility for the *hukou* system to local-level governments, placing the floating population in a netherworld of undetermined residential
status (Chan and Buckingham 2008).

In highly unstable states where responsible government structures are largely
absent, such as Somalia, Congo, and Afghanistan (outside the capital region), a lack

---

[8] Some Chinese newspapers have suggested the number is closer to 200 million.

of personal security and periodic episodes of violence can result in frequent internal population movements and displacements across borders (Autesserre 2008, Lindley 2008, Harpviken 2009). In others, state governments use their power to deliberately persecute their own citizens and force them into flight, as Saddam Hussein's Ba'athist regime did to the *ma'dan* ('marsh Arab') minority in southern Iraq and to ethnic Kurds in northern Iraq (Schwabach 2004, Lischer 2008). In worst-case scenarios, such as in Rwanda and the former Yugoslavia in the 1990s, the rapid breakdown of institutions and the factionalization of rival groups can spark civil conflicts that result in gruesome interethnic violence and refugee flight (Uvin 1996, Zaum 2011).

2.7.5 Demographic Factors

The original Foresight (2011) conceptualization of migration that was used to organize this discussion of macro-level influences on migration, and which is reflected in Figure 2.3, has demographic factors as a distinct category of macro-level driver of immigration behavior. In this book, demographic processes are treated as an outcome of cultural, economic, political, and social factors, and not a first-order driver of equal weight. It is, however, useful to include a few observations on the relationship between larger demographic processes within a population and migration patterns and behavior.

Zelinsky (1971) suggested that as societies become more economically developed, they experience both a demographic transition and a mobility transition. The demographic transition occurs when a population moves from a regime of high death rates and high birth rates to one of low death and birth rates, in the midst of which there is typically a period of population increase because death rates tend to fall earlier than do birth rates (Kirk 1996). Under the mobility transition, the population moves through a multistage process from low overall mobility to high levels of rural-to-urban migration, eventually reaching a 'super-advanced state' where most people live in urban centers and most migration is intra- or interurban (Zelinsky 1971: 231). While this concept greatly simplifies what is actually observed on the ground, King and Skeldon (2010) point out that the mobility transition theory is a useful reminder that migration is dynamically linked to demographic processes.

Earlier, the importance of the life course was mentioned. Migration decisions often coincide with important transition stages in the human life course, such as the end of childhood, entry into the labor force, marriage, and retirement (Sjastaad 1962, Cuba and Hummon 1993, Plane 1993). Consequently, aggregated migration patterns observed in a given region often reflect the number of people of various age cohorts. In most societies, young adults tend to be the most likely to migrate, and this applies to both internal and international migration (Weeks 2008). People in their twenties have the highest rates of migration within the United States; in Hare's (1999) study of Henan, China, the average age of migrants was around thirty years. In a study of international migration into OECD countries in the period from 1980 to 1995, Mayda (2009) found that source countries with higher proportions of their populations in the fifteen- to twenty-nine-year-old age cohort had slightly higher rates of out-migration. By comparison, older people, whose mobility is less affected by labor market forces, tend to be less likely to undertake migration over long distances (Bradley and Longino 2008). Retirees who do undertake longer-distance or international migration tend to be people returning to countries of origin, people reuniting with family members, and/or seekers of particular amenities such as a mild climate or particular health care facilities (Warnes 2008). For example, Sunil, Rojas, and Bradley (2007) found that the main reasons international migrants seek to retire in a popular Mexican community include the perceived environmental amenities, social connections, and quality of life, including available services. The aging populations of industrialized countries have created growing demand for eldercare workers (Plane 1992), which immigrants from developing nations have increasingly been filling (Browne and Braun 2007).

Researchers sometimes ask if international migration might offset divergent population growth rates between countries (Keely 2008). In most industrialized countries, rates of natural population increase have fallen significantly over recent decades, to the point that countries as culturally different as Japan and Hungary have fallen below replacement rate fertility (UN DESA 2007). China, more than a generation into its one-child policy, now exhibits similarly low levels of fertility, and India will soon overtake it as the world's most populous nation (Hesketh, Lu, and Xing 2005). Low levels of population growth and an aging population are seen by many countries as problematic in terms of maintaining sufficient labor for sustaining economic growth and providing a large enough tax base for health and social programs (UN DESA 2000, Bloom and Finlay 2009). Meanwhile, in many developing regions, particularly sub-Saharan Africa and parts of the Middle East, birth rates remain high, reinforcing ongoing challenges in terms of providing sufficient employment opportunities and basic needs such as food, clean water, sanitation, housing, and health services (Bongaarts and Sinding 2011). Greater levels of migration from high-birth-rate to low-birth-rate countries are seen by some as a policy option that could address challenges faced by both (UN DESA 2000). Coleman (2008) observed that in-migration has already become a driving factor in shaping demographic patterns in some European countries. However, the rates of migration needed to overcome the effects of very high or very low birth rates are typically much larger than most countries find politically palatable (Keely 2008).

2.7.6 Environmental Factors Influencing Migration[9]

A wide spectrum of interactions between humans and the environment can potentially influence migration decisions and behavior, of which climate-related phenomena are only one subset. Some environmental conditions can be beneficial to human livelihoods and well-being, and can thereby be seen as attracting migrants to particular locales; others can have adverse impacts on livelihoods and well-being, and thereby act as stimuli for people to leave, or in the worst cases, flee particular locales. There are various time scales over which changes in environmental conditions and events occur, such as those that occur suddenly (e.g. earthquakes, tsunamis, volcanic eruptions, tornadoes, flash floods) or those that may take years to emerge or accumulate and the full consequences recognized (e.g. drought, soil erosion, forest loss). In other cases, the environmental condition may not change, but changes in technology may make particular environments more favorable for habitation, such as irrigation of California's great Central Valley, engineered controls on flood-prone rivers, or the invention of air conditioning that made hot places like Florida and Arizona more attractive (Gutmann and Field 2010). In still other examples, human activities combine with natural processes to create conditions that stimulate migration, such as the combination of drought and farming techniques that generated dust storms across the southern Great Plains in the 1930s (Worster 1979). Migration in response to environmental conditions or events can take on most of the forms, spatial scales, and time scales described previously in this chapter, and a single environmental event can lead to multiple forms of migration simultaneously. For example, Hurricane Katrina required a large-scale evacuation of much of the population of New Orleans and surrounding Gulf Coast communities. As is further detailed in a case study in Chapter 4, some people returned almost immediately to their homes, others returned after a more extended period of months or years, and still others never returned (Fussell, Sastry, and Van Landingham 2010, Groen and Polivka 2010). Employment opportunities created by the reconstruction of the city attracted new migrants who did not live there before the storm (Donato et al. 2007).

A simple way of illustrating the range of potential migration responses to environmental phenomena is shown in Figure 2.6, in which duration of the migration event is represented on the horizontal axis and the nature of the environmental stimulus (in this case all climatic stimuli) is on the vertical axis, with known examples from the United States given for each of the four quadrants. The two quadrants above the horizontal axis reflect the potential migration outcomes where environmental conditions are beneficial or attractive. The upper right-hand quadrant describes migration undertaken on a permanent basis to take advantage of favorable environmental conditions,

---

[9] Parts of this section appeared in similar form in McLeman (2010a). 'On the origins of environmental migration'. *Fordham Environmental Law Review* 20: 403–25.

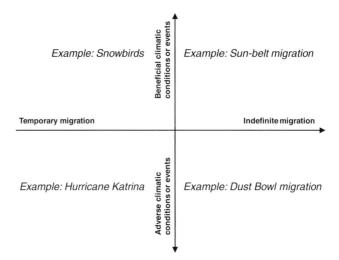

Figure 2.6. Four examples of environmental influence on migration. Adapted from McLeman (2010a).

an example being high rates of population growth in the Sun Belt states, much of it fuelled by north-to-south migration.[10] As noted earlier, each winter these permanent migrants to the Sun Belt are joined by 'snowbirds'; that is, people who maintain their nominal permanent residences in more northerly states or in Canada, but who spend the winter months each year in the south or southwest. This latter group is captured in the upper left-hand quadrant.

The lower half of Figure 2.6 captures the opposite side of the environmental impact spectrum, where environmental conditions (or changes in those conditions) have negative or potentially negative effects on livelihoods and well-being. The lower right quadrant describes long-term or indefinite migration of households away from regions of adverse environmental conditions, one of the best known examples being the 1930s Dust Bowl migration, the subject of a case study in Chapter 6. The lower left-hand quadrant describes short-term or temporary migration in response to adverse environmental conditions, such as flight from natural disasters like Hurricane Katrina, although in actuality the various types of migration triggered by Katrina would sprawl across the entire lower half of Figure 2.6.

While Figure 2.6 illustrates how interactions between environment and migration may play out in a variety of ways, it does not attempt to explain how or why. Chapter 3 picks up where this section ends, by focusing on how climatic events and conditions are understood to affect human well-being, using the concepts of vulnerability and adaptation to do so.

---

[10] According to the U.S. Census Bureau (www.census.gov), the five fastest growing states are Texas, California, Florida, Georgia, and Arizona, each of which is also among the top recipients of interstate migration.

2.8 Chapter Summary

No grand unifying theory explains human migration. However, a range of tested and relatively complementary theories and concepts may be used like a toolkit to study and interpret migration processes, behavior, and patterns. With Ravenstein's Laws of Migration as its guide, this chapter began by identifying common characteristics of modern migration, including:

- Migration flows most often from rural to urban areas
- Individuals are more likely to migrate than are complete households
- Male and female migration behavior can be quite different
- Young adults are most likely to undertake migration
- More migration occurs over short distances within countries or regions as compared with long-distance international migration
- Migration decisions are shaped by conditions and events at sending and receiving areas, and
- Because migration is a complex process, all of these statements are simply generalizations, and circumstances on the ground may be different in any given event.

Migration can take on a range of spatial dimensions (e.g. intra- or interurban; internal or international) and temporal dimensions (e.g. seasonal, temporary non-seasonal, recurrent, continuous, and indefinite). Migration is a path-dependent phenomenon; that is, past events influence present and future behaviors. The cumulative causation of various events and processes over time helps shape and perpetuate migration movements once they begin. The likelihood that an individual will participate in migration and his or her destination preferences will vary over the course of his or her life. Not all migrants exercise the same degree of agency over their migration decisions, with agency providing a general way to categorize migrants. Lifestyle or amenity-seeking migrants have the highest agency. Those who migrate for family-related reasons do so with varying degrees of agency, which are often differentiated along gender lines. People who migrate for economic reasons may do so in attempts to maximize incomes and opportunities or as part of household-level strategies to diversify their exposure to economic or other risks. Forced migrants have limited to no agency that varies by degrees, from displacee to trafficking victim, prisoner, or slave. Under international law, displacees from state-sponsored violence fall into two categories, those who are internally displaced (that is, remain within the borders of their country of normal residence or citizenship) and those who are refugees by virtue of having crossed an international border fleeing persecution. The latter group enjoy the right of international protection; the former typically do not.

Migration decisions are shaped by a range of micro-, meso-, and macro-level structures and forces, many operating beyond the control or influence of the migrant. Using a conceptual representation of migration based on Foresight (2011), the influence of cultural, economic, political, social, and environmental factors on migration was introduced, with a range of examples provided. The next chapter reviews scholarly research on human vulnerability and adaptation to climatic phenomena, and outlines how these can be combined with migration concepts and theories reviewed in this chapter to create a generic conceptual framework for analyzing climate-related migration.

3

Migration in the Context of Vulnerability and Adaptation to Climatic Variability and Change

3.1 Introduction

Much of the existing research on climate and migration has its origins in scholarly fields not traditionally associated with mainstream migration research, such as natural hazards, human ecology, and climate change impacts and adaptation research. Current studies tend to treat migration as one of a range of possible outcomes when vulnerable individuals, households, and communities adjust and adapt to climatic events and conditions or to changes in prevailing conditions. Treating migration in this way is consistent with how it has evolved within the reporting processes of the Intergovernmental Panel on Climate Change (IPCC) and the structure of the United Nations Framework Convention on Climate Change (UNFCCC). It is also conceptually logical to do so, given that the cultural, economic, political, and social forces believed to shape vulnerability and the capacity to adapt are similar to those that have a strong influence on migration behavior. The present chapter covers a considerable amount of ground, describing key theories of vulnerability and adaptation used in climate impacts research, and combining these with key theories and concepts developed in migration scholarship to show how migration occurs within the context of dynamic, adaptive, human-environment interactions.

In particular, this chapter:

- Explains the specific meanings of vulnerability and adaptation, their implications under the UNFCCC, and why this is relevant;
- Traces the origins of vulnerability and adaptation as they are presently understood and describes their development;
- Shows how vulnerability and adaptation are influenced by cultural, economic, environmental, political, and social forces similar to those that shape migration behavior;
- Details how household-level adaptation options are shaped and the place of migration within those options;
- Shows how access to economic, social, and other forms of capital is an important determinant of how adaptation processes play out;

- Creates a diagrammatic representation of how migration may emerge within dynamic processes of adaptation, which is used in later chapters to interpret migration outcomes in response to a range of climatic phenomena.

3.2 The Linkages between Climate, Adaptation, and Migration at the International Policy Level

The published literature that deals with climate and migration often comes from scholarly fields and journals where migration is not a common subject of inquiry, and often in contemplation of future migration in response to future climate change. Sometimes these studies make reference to concepts that are familiar in the natural sciences, but are less commonly used in the main body of migration research. In particular, a growing amount of literature describes climate-related migration as an outcome of human vulnerability and adaptation (Adger et al. 2003; McLeman and Smit 2006a; Perch-Nielsen, Bättig, and Imboden 2008; Mortreux and Barnett 2009; Tacoli 2009; Bardsley and Hugo 2010). The terms *vulnerability* and *adaptation* are entirely compatible with the concepts used in mainstream migration research, as reviewed in the previous chapter, but to understand how these terms came to be applied to the study of climate-related migration, it is necessary to understand international public policy pertaining to climate change. These terms have specific legal meaning and usage in the formal agreements that govern international climate policy, and so any discussion of climate-related migration that wishes to remain consistent with policy making needs to be framed in the context of adaptation. Of course, this does not preclude researchers from using other terms and concepts like *environmental refugees* or *eco-migration* or anything else for that matter, and many researchers do. However, given that adaptation and migration are logically compatible concepts, it makes sense to use them in a way consistent with the way policy makers discuss issues related to climate. It is therefore logical to begin by reviewing the origins and meaning of adaptation in the context of international climate agreements before proceeding to a more practical discussion of the concept and its linkages to migration.

3.3 Climate and Adaptation in the UNFCCC Process

The Earth's climate is constantly changing as a result of naturally occurring phenomena, including the amount of radiation received from the sun; variations in the Earth's orbit, the tilt of its axis, and its rotation on its axis; volcanic activity that emits aerosol particles into the atmosphere; and the composition of the atmosphere itself.[1] Jean

---

[1] The authoritative source on climate science is the Intergovernmental Panel on Climate Change, with a large number of reports available at its website www.ipcc.ch. These can, however, be dry and technical for the non-expert. Any number of books and other documents exist that provide detailed but accessible reviews of the functioning of the Earth's climate and human interference with it. Those I have found useful for teaching include Hardy (2003) and Mann and Kump (2009).

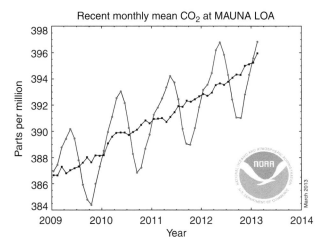

Figure 3.1. Atmospheric accumulation of carbon dioxide in recent years.
Source: US National Oceanic and Atmospheric Administration http://www.esrl.noaa.gov/gmd/ccgg/trends/#mlo_full.

Baptiste Joseph Fourier (1878, first English translation) first suggested in the early 1800s that naturally occurring gases found in trace amounts in the atmosphere influence temperatures experienced at the Earth's surface.[2] Short-wave radiation arriving from the sun passes through these trace gases unobstructed, and that which does not reflect off shiny surfaces (like the tops of clouds or snow cover) is absorbed at the surface. This energy is reradiated back into the air at different, longer wavelengths than the incoming radiation. Before this reradiated energy can escape the Earth's system and return to space, the aforementioned trace gases delay it by absorbing and reradiating some of it. The analogy of a greenhouse is often used to explain this process, the trace gases in the atmosphere playing the role of glass in a greenhouse, and so these gases have become known as *greenhouse gases* (GHGs). Beginning in the 1950s, scientific observations of atmospheric concentrations of carbon dioxide showed a steady increase that could not be attributed to natural processes (Figure 3.1). By the late 1980s, it had become widely accepted within the scientific community that these changes in GHGs were likely affecting global average temperatures and sea levels (see also Chapter 7).

In response to growing scientific concern, the UNFCCC was signed at the 1992 Earth Summit in Rio de Janeiro, coming into effect in 1994.[3] Virtually all UN member states have signed and ratified the UNFCCC, including all of the nations with high levels of greenhouse gas (GHG) emissions, such as Australia, Brazil, Canada, China,

---

[2] Fourier correctly suspected that carbon dioxide played a role; later research identified water vapor, methane, nitrous oxides, and ozone as additional GHGs. For a very readable account of the history of climate science from someone who was an influential player in it, see Schneider (2009).

[3] All information regarding the UNFCCC is taken from the Convention website (www.unfccc.int) unless otherwise noted.

the EU, India, Japan, Russia, and the United States. The opening lines state that parties to the UNFCCC:

Acknowledg[e] that change in the Earth's climate and its adverse effects are a common concern of humankind ...

and are

[c]oncerned that human activities have been substantially increasing the atmospheric concentrations of greenhouse gases, that these increases enhance the natural greenhouse effect, and that this will result on average in an additional warming of the Earth's surface and atmosphere and may adversely affect natural ecosystems and humankind ...

Article 2 of the convention, which follows the definition of terms used in its text, states that the ultimate objective of the UNFCCC is the

stabilization of greenhouse gas concentrations in the atmosphere at a level that would prevent dangerous anthropogenic interference with the climate system. Such a level should be achieved within a time frame sufficient to allow ecosystems to adapt naturally to climate change, to ensure that food production is not threatened and to enable economic development to proceed in a sustainable manner.

To achieve this goal, signatories agreed to undertake a variety of commitments, including: to report their GHG emissions; take actions to reduce GHG emissions; promote the sustainable management of GHG sinks (i.e. natural systems such as forests that absorb GHGs from the atmosphere); to promote technical, scientific, and educational cooperation; and, in Article 4.1.e, to 'cooperate in preparing for adaptation to the impacts of climate change'.

The commitment to adaptation cooperation found in Article 4.1.e was further elaborated and codified in the Kyoto Protocol, adopted at the 1997 annual meeting of signatories to the UNFCCC (also known as the Conference of the Parties to the Convention, or COP). The Kyoto Protocol is perhaps best known for setting GHG emissions reduction targets that industrialized countries were expected to meet by the year 2012. Not all UNFCCC signatories ratified the Kyoto Protocol, most notably the United States; and many countries that ratified Kyoto never came close to meeting their targets, such as Canada and New Zealand.[4] In addition to setting

---

[4] Developed countries and former Soviet bloc states agreed to GHG emissions reductions targets under Kyoto, the targets varying by country. The baseline period was each country's 1990 emissions, and success is measured by each country's average emissions over the period from 2008 to 2012. At the time of this writing, final 2012 emissions figures are not available from the UNFCCC website, but it is already evident from 2008–11 data which countries did not meet their targets, including Australia (which was late to ratify Kyoto), Canada, nine European nations (although the EU as a whole performed much better, including the larger countries like France, Germany, and the United Kingdom), and New Zealand. Countries like Japan and the United States have also likely exceeded their targets but, because of the 2008 global economic slowdown, their GHG emissions have slowed considerably and so they may not have missed their Kyoto targets by as much as had once been expected.

emissions reductions targets, in article 10(b) the Kyoto Protocol also requires signatories to

Formulate, implement, publish and regularly update national and, where appropriate, regional programmes containing measures to mitigate climate change *and measures to facilitate adequate adaptation to climate change.* (italics added)

The Kyoto Protocol also established 'clean development mechanisms' (CDMs) that facilitate countries in reducing GHG emissions, and in doing so states at Article 12.8 that a share of the proceeds from CDMs shall be used 'to assist developing country Parties that are particularly vulnerable to the adverse effects of climate change to meet the costs of adaptation'.

What specifically constitutes 'adaptation' is not specified in the Kyoto Protocol or in the convention itself. However, these two documents effectively created a dynamic whereby adaptation became the center point for the creation of programs that would transfer money from industrialized states to vulnerable ones. Subsequent COPs since 1997 have increasingly sought to identify which states are most vulnerable (and therefore entitled to financial assistance), and to determine what constitutes appropriate and adequate adaptation to climate change. At their 2010 annual COP in Cancun, UNFCCC signatories stated that adaptation must receive the same priority as efforts to reduce atmospheric GHG accumulation,[5] and through the Cancun Agreement established something referred to as the Cancun Adaptation Framework. Under this framework, signatories called for the creation of more mechanisms for transferring money and technology to assist with adaptation, and to dedicate more resources to adaptation. Section II of the Cancun Agreement explicitly mentions migration and displacement in the context of adaptation, something that is not done in the UNFCCC or the Kyoto Protocol. It states that the Conference of the Parties

14. Invites all Parties to enhance action on adaptation under the Cancun Adaptation Framework, taking into account their common but differentiated responsibilities and respective capabilities, and specific national and regional development priorities, objectives and circumstances, by undertaking, inter alia, the following:

(f) Measures to enhance understanding, coordination and cooperation with regard to climate change induced displacement, migration and planned relocation, where appropriate, at the national, regional and international levels.

Through this statement, the international community has explicitly situated climate-related migration within the broader context of adaptation policy making and adaptive capacity building. Any research on climate and migration that is intended to have influence with policy makers should therefore approach the topic in such terms.

---

[5] A cynic might find this logic flawed, because so many countries are all talk and little action on GHG emissions.

3.4 Climate, Migration, and Adaptation as seen by the
Intergovernmental Panel on Climate Change

Deliberations of parties to the UNFCCC are informed by the reporting of the Intergovernmental Panel on Climate Change (IPCC), a body charged with distilling for international policy makers the scholarship on climate change, its impacts, and opportunities for mitigating the dangerous accumulation of GHGs. The IPCC is an unusual phenomenon. It is quite rare in human history for international governments to establish a permanent, independent body with the responsibility of keeping them regularly informed of the scholarly research on a particular subject.[6] The IPCC was established in 1988 as a joint project by the World Meteorological Organization (WMO) and the United Nations Environment Program (UNEP), and under a resolution of the UN's General Assembly was instructed to 'prepare a comprehensive review and recommendations with respect to the state of knowledge of the science of climate change, the social and economic impact of climate change, possible response strategies and elements for inclusion in a possible future international convention on climate'.[7] The IPCC released its first assessment report in 1990, and this report formed the scientific backdrop against which the UNFCCC was negotiated.

Beginning with that first assessment report, the IPCC has organized itself into three working groups; the first (WGI) charged with reviewing the physical science of climate change; the second working group (WGII) charged with reviewing the impacts of climate change; and the third (WGIII) responsible for identifying and recommending strategies to respond to GHG accumulation in the atmosphere (generally referred to as *mitigation*). In the first report, WGII (Tegart, Sheldon, and Griffiths 1990) warned that the impacts of climate change may include large-scale human migrations, reporting to policy makers in its executive summary that:

Changes in precipitation and temperature could radically alter the patterns of vector-borne and viral diseases by shifting them to higher latitudes, thus putting large populations at risk. As similar events have in the past, these changes could initiate large migrations of people, leading over a number of years to severe disruptions of settlement patterns and social instability in some areas.

The impacts of climate change on migration are described in greater detail in chapter 5 of the report, section 2.2.3 of which, entitled 'Migration and resettlement', states that climate-related migration in the future may unfold for one of three general reasons:

• Loss of housing because of flooding or mudslides;

---

[6] Note, for example, there is no equivalent body named the Intergovernmental Panel on Migration and Mobility Research.
[7] All information about the IPCC is derived from its website, www.ipcc.ch, unless otherwise indicated. This particular quote is taken from its History page, last accessed 24 January 2013.

- Loss of 'living resources' such as water, energy, food, or employment;
- Loss of social and cultural resources such as community or neighborhood networks (Tegart et al. 1990: 5–9).

The report goes on to suggest that the most likely types of migration related to climate change will be the movement of impoverished people in developing countries from rural to urban areas, and from coastal zones to inland areas. The report uses the term *vulnerability* in stating that people living in areas where natural hazards are prevalent are most at risk of forced migration. It asserts that environmental refugees 'are becoming a much larger factor in many developing countries' (Tegart et al. 1990: 5–10) and that in industrialized nations the greatest risks with respect to forced migration will come from natural hazards and sea level rise.

These conclusions were based on a relatively small body of scholarship. Mortimore's (1989) World Bank study of soil degradation in northern Nigeria is cited (at pages 5–8) as evidence that drought and subsequent outbreaks of hunger may lead to migration and abandonment of land. A scoping paper on migration in developing countries published by the International Development Research Centre (Simmons, Diaz-Briguets, and Laquian 1977) contained observations that declining demand for natural rubber has influenced migration patterns in southeast Asia, and this is alluded to as an example of how changing commodity prices can influence migration in developing nations, ostensibly an analogy of how changes in living resources influence migration. The claims about environmental refugees are supported by a popular report published by the Worldwatch Institute (Jacobson 1988) and public lectures given by a British academic (Tickell 1989) and a retired U.S. military officer (Debrah 1989).

In hindsight, it may seem quite astounding that the scientific advice then given to international policy makers on the potential effects of climate change on migration did not draw on any scholarly research about migration. However, those charged with authoring the report were drawn primarily from the natural sciences, and few would have had much prior exposure to migration scholarship. One could imagine that a similarly unsatisfactory result would have been achieved, for example, had a group of migration scholars been charged with writing a report on how to reduce greenhouse gas emissions.

While the breadth and rigor of IPCC reporting has expanded dramatically since 1990, the same basic working group structure has been maintained. WGII's reports now explicitly summarize impacts, adaptation, and vulnerability. Subsequent IPCC assessment reports in 1995, 2001, and 2007 expanded their coverage of migration, but always within the context of vulnerability and adaptation. Membership in WGII has expanded to hundreds of authors and reviewers from across the academy, and its 2014 report will include approximately thirty chapters. Migration will continue to be considered within the context of vulnerability and adaptation, and is expected to comprise a substantial section of a chapter on human security.[8] As IPCC coverage of migration issues has expanded, so too has the amount of scholarship on which it is able to draw, much of which is also now cast in terms of vulnerability and adaptation. It is now time to examine these terms more closely.

3.5 Vulnerability to Climatic Variability and Change: Conceptual Underpinnings

3.5.1 Origins of Current Usage

The concept of vulnerability is used widely across the natural and social sciences, in medicine, and in specialized and technical fields like security studies and information technology management. In the context of climatic variability and change, *vulnerability* refers to the potential to experience loss or harm (Weichselgartner 2001). In the 2007 IPCC Synthesis summary for policy makers, *vulnerability* is defined as

the degree to which a system is susceptible to, and unable to cope with, adverse effects of climate change, including climate variability and extremes. Vulnerability is a function of the character, magnitude, and rate of climate change and variation to which a system is exposed, its sensitivity, and its adaptive capacity. (IPCC 2007, SPM Glossary)

It is worth noting that this definition places *vulnerability* as the antonym of *opportunity* (i.e. the potential to experience gain or benefit), something picked up again later in this chapter. Adger (2006) has provided a detailed history of the use of the term *vulnerability* in the context of climate change and environmental change, observing that the vulnerability concept is an attempt at explaining the linkages between human and natural systems – also referred to as *socio-ecological linkages* – that has mixed origins in natural hazards scholarship and in what has come to be known as *entitlement theory* (Sen 1981). Both of these scholarly fields deal with phenomena where population displacement and migration are potential outcomes of physical processes, and where much of the landmark research has been generated by scholars not associated with traditional demographic or migration scholarship.

In natural hazards research, scholars have long wrestled with how to explain the different outcomes that occur when disaster events strike. Why is it, for example, that in developing countries tropical storms typically cause higher loss of life than in developed countries? At subnational scales, why is it that the poor and marginalized are more likely to suffer during disasters? In the 1970s and 1980s, scholars in natural hazards research began looking to theories and approaches derived from social science to answer such questions, notable early examples including *The Environment as Hazard* (Burton, Kates, and White 1978) and *Interpretations of Calamity from the*

---

[8] The implications of considering climate-related migration in the context of human security are discussed in Chapter 8.

Viewpoint of Human Ecology (Hewitt 1983). Blaikie (1985) used concepts rooted in traditional political economy to bring what is alternately described as a human ecology or political ecology[9] approach to understanding human-induced soil erosion in developing countries, explaining how larger socioeconomic forces drive farmers into practices they know contribute to land degradation and potential disastrous consequences, a theme he developed further with Harold Brookfield in *Land Degradation and Society* (Blaikie and Brookfield 1987). Blaikie later went on to formally conceptualize vulnerability to natural hazards as developing when socioeconomic pressures mount in the presence of a natural hazard, eventually reaching a point where the hazard releases the pressure, creating adverse consequences for those exposed (Blaikie et al. 1994, later updated as Wisner et al. 2004).

Adger (2006) traces the other key scholarship to the famine literature of the 1980s and early 1990s, a period when popular and scholarly attention focused on widespread hunger, loss of life, and distress migration occurring in Sudano-Sahelian Africa (Watts 1991, Ezra 2001). Over the course of history, semiarid and dry land regions have periodically experienced famines during times of drought, but scholars like Sen (1981) and Watts and Bohle (1993) showed how modern-day hunger and deprivation are not solely caused by food production shortfall, but by its combination with acute socioeconomic inequity. Sen (1981, 1999) demonstrated empirically how society's most powerless people are vulnerable to disasters because they lack the social, political, and economic wherewithal to ensure their entitlement to the basic resources they require. The entitlement approach has been highly influential in studies of human security and food security, discussed in Chapter 8.

3.5.2 Current Conceptualization of Vulnerability

From these origins, climate change researchers and the IPCC have adopted a basic conceptual representation of vulnerability that looks like this:

$$V = f(E, S, A)$$

where vulnerability (V) is seen as the function of

E = *exposure* to conditions or events that may lead to loss or harm
S = the inherent *sensitivity* of a given system, population, or place to the particular events or conditions to which it is exposed
A = the capacity of said system, population, or place to *adapt* to the given exposure.

Although this representation looks neat and tidy, there is some debate whether exposure, sensitivity, and adaptation truly function as independent variables. While

---

[9] See Neumann (2005) for a detailed review of the political ecology field.

exposure is here meant to refer only to climatic stimuli and biophysical conditions that may affect human systems, the reality is that settlements, infrastructure, and live-lihood assets can be located in areas of higher or lesser exposure depending on social, economic, political, and cultural processes that unfold over time (McLeman and Smit 2006b).

As an example, many urban centers in North America are located in floodplains, where the risk of damage to buildings and infrastructure from periodic flooding has been a long-standing concern (i.e. where exposure is continuous). One might imagine that in such cities, abandonment of the most flood-prone neighborhoods and imple-mentation of flood prevention measures and insurance regimes would be the norm. Yet studies have shown that residents of such communities have remarkably low par-ticipation rates in flood insurance plans when it is not required by law (Browne and Hoyt 2000). Those who do purchase flood insurance tend to take few other steps to mitigate the risk of flood damage (Blanchard-Boehm, Berry, and Showalter 2001), and the availability of insurance acts as a disincentive to local planning initiatives that might reduce the number of properties exposed to floods (Burby 2001). It is very rare in present-day North America for a flood-prone settlement to be entirely abandoned or relocated (McLeman 2011a), the largest recent example being that of Pattonsburg, Missouri, a flood-prone settlement of a few hundred people relocated in the 1990s (Greenberg, Lahr, and Mantell 2007). It can consequently be seen that exposure to the physical hazards of climate is not simply the result of natural processes, but of human decision making as well.

Sensitivity refers to the reality that some types of human livelihood systems are inherently more affected by particular climatic stimuli than others: agricultural sys-tems being inherently at risk of drought, coastal settlements of storm surges, and so forth. It is widely held that populations in developing countries are especially vul-nerable to climate change, partly because of the disproportionate number of people participating in climate-sensitive livelihood systems (IPCC 2007). However, this does not mean that urban systems or the capital-intensive land use systems of developed countries are not sensitive to climate. For example, Schindler and Donohoe (2006) have documented how stream flows in several large rivers in western Canada are declining, meaning that region's fast-growing urban centers, which depend on them for drinking water and wastewater treatment, could face water shortages in coming decades because of climate change. Rural households in western Canada, which typ-ically get their water from wells and not surface sources, are less sensitive to these stream flow trends.

3.5.3 *Adaptive Capacity and Adaptation*

The third element in the V=*f*(E, S, A) representation of vulnerability is *adaptive capac-ity*, which describes the potential for adaptation and works opposite to exposure and sensitivity (Smit and Wandel 2006). Populations with high levels of adaptive capacity can better manage high levels of adversity before experiencing any notable change in vulnerability; those with lower adaptive capacity are more likely to be vulnerable when in a similar situation. *Adaptation* is a term widely used across the natural and social sciences, where it has historically referred to physiological or behavioral changes in organisms that, when successful, enhance survival chances and reproductive success (Darwin 1859 (2004)).

In contemporary climate change research, adaptation is seen as a 'process by which initiatives and measures [are taken] to reduce the vulnerability of natural and human systems against actual or expected climate change effects' (IPCC 2007, Glossary). Adaptation is therefore a response to a stimulus, with adaptive capacity being the ability to recognize the need for adaptation and to take action (Smit et al. 2000). Adaptation can occur in anticipation of potential events or in reaction to those already experienced, and can be initiated at any scale, from the individual or household to multilateral international engagements (IPCC 2007). Examples of adaptation to climatic variability and change are numerous (Berrang-Ford, Ford, and Peterson 2011). Some forms of adaptation are planned, such as the building of dykes or sea walls to prevent against flooding (IPCC 2007). Other types of adaptation occur spontaneously or autonomously, such as the processes whereby farm operators adjust the selection and rotation of crops so as to maximize productivity over time. While it is tempting to think about adaptation as a process enacted by rational decision makers, various limits and constraints exist on the agency of those who would adapt (Inderberg and Eikeland 2009). These limits manifest themselves in forms such as institutional barriers, access to financial markets and resources, access to technology, social cohesion and coordination, gender relations, local ecological limits, past experience and knowledge, and perceptions of risk, to name but a few (Mendelsohn 2000, Denton 2002, Ikeme 2003, Thomas and Twyman 2004, Adger et al. 2007, Peterson 2009, Westerhoff and Smit 2009, McLeman et al. 2011). If these sound similar to the types of factors identified in the previous chapter as influencing migration behavior, it is because they *are* similar. Just as cultural, economic, environmental, political, and social factors operating at macro-, meso-, and micro-scales affect migration options, decisions, and behavior, as seen in Figure 2.3, they also affect adaptation options, decisions, and behavior.

3.6 Dynamic Interactions Shape Vulnerability and Adaptation

Given that environmental conditions and human systems are continually changing, the fundamental elements of vulnerability – exposure, sensitivity, and adaptive capacity – are also continually changing. Moreover, the nature of such changes varies from one place to another, as does the rate of change itself. Adaptation to specific manifestations of a changing climate consequently takes place within a dynamic of moving targets and shifting baselines. In some cases, this dynamic plays out in such a

Figure 3.2. Tapped maple trees at Wheeler's Sugar Bush near McDonald's Corners, Ontario. The plastic tubing connects the trees to a vacuum pump that collects the sap. Raw sap is mostly water and must be boiled extensively to make syrup. The timing of the sap collection period is linked to a particular range of spring temperatures, and so sugar producers' records provide a useful data source for understanding spring temperature trends. Photo by author.

way that adaptation occurs seamlessly. For example, in rural eastern Ontario, Canada, a trend toward earlier spring thaws has emerged over the last fifty years (McLeman 2008). It is during the spring thaw – when daytime temperatures are above freezing and nighttime temperatures are below it – when maple trees awaken from their winter dormancy and their sap begins to flow. Producers of maple syrup – an iconic Canadian product and an important rural livelihood in the region – collect this sap each spring from taps inserted into the trees and boil it down to make syrup, sugar, and other maple products (Figure 3.2). Since the 1980s, the period during which these temperature conditions occur has arrived earlier than it did in the 1950s and 1960s, so sugarbush operators have adapted by advancing their collection dates (Figure 3.3). No one had to tell them how or when to adapt, they just did so autonomously, with ongoing success. The climate trends they are experiencing have emerged at a rate with which they could keep pace, falling within their capacity to recognize and make adjustments. Maple sugar continues to be a thriving livelihood, and has many ancillary sociocultural and environmental benefits that may enhance the capacity of the

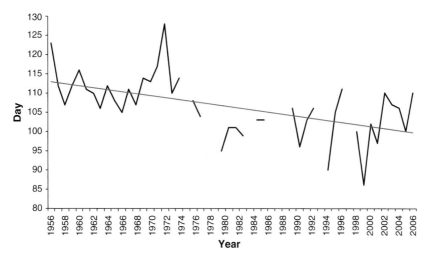

Figure 3.3. End of sap collection period, maple sugar bush near Flinton, Ontario, Canada. Dates on the vertical axis are Julian dates (i.e. January 1 = day 1, December 31 = day 365). Dates are when taps are pulled from the trees, signifying the end of the collection season. Gaps in the data reflect years when sap was not collected. Data courtesy of J. Hasler.

rural population to adapt to future socio-ecological changes in the region (Clark and McLeman 2012).

In the Canadian Arctic territory of Nunavut, a very different story is emerging. There, changes in land and sea ice conditions are occurring rapidly, placing considerable strain on the adaptive capacity of Inuit communities (Prowse et al. 2009). Environmental conditions are in many cases beyond the range of those previously experienced, and the hunting and fishing skills developed over centuries by the region's indigenous Inuit population are not always sufficient to meet these new conditions. This has placed considerable strain on the social fabric of Inuit communities, altering relations among families and across generations. These climatic changes are coinciding with rapid social, political, and economic changes in the north, creating conditions of mounting vulnerability in traditional Inuit communities (Ford et al. 2008). One outcome has been high rates of urbanization, as young adults migrate from smaller settlements to the territorial capital of Nunavut (McLeman and Ford 2013).

The case of the Nunavut also shows that within any given population there will be differences at individual and household levels in terms of the wherewithal to recognize, anticipate, and adapt to emergent changes in climate (Adger 2006, Smit and Wandel 2006). Within Inuit communities where hunting is still practiced, there are differences between households in their ability to adapt to changing ice conditions. For example, hunters with access to more expensive equipment increasingly have an advantage over those who do not in terms of accessing the best hunting and fishing locations, and in being able to travel more safely (Ford et al. 2007). Better-equipped, more successful hunters find their socioeconomic status rising within the community, while others face the opposite trajectory, which generates a self-reinforcing socioeconomic gulf and differential vulnerability within the community.

3.7 Migration in the Context of Vulnerability

3.7.1 Migration and Changes in Exposure

Many of the best-known studies of climate and migration, at least in terms of popular attention and citations by other scholars, focus principally on the relationship between exposure to climatic risks and migration. As noted in Chapter 1, for many years Norman Myers's 1993 and 2002 studies were among the few peer-reviewed articles that offered forecasts of future environment-related migration, and researchers have cited them hundreds of times since. Myers used very general assumptions that increases in exposure to adverse climatic and environmental conditions lead to increases in population movements. The 2007 Christian Aid report also described in Chapter 1 is based on a similar assumption that as exposure increases, so will migration. The availability of relatively inexpensive and powerful geographical information systems (GIS) in recent years has provided researchers better tools for matching climate information to specific locations, and allows them to combine these with population data to identify populations with high levels of exposure to particular climate risks, as seen in CARE International's *In Search of Shelter* (2009) report. Scholars have used similar techniques to identify populations highly exposed to mean sea level changes, with McGranahan, Balk, and Anderson (2007) providing worldwide estimates of the number of people at risk, and Byravan, Rajan, and Bangarajan (2010) identifying exposed populations and infrastructure along India's Tamil Nadu coast. These types of approaches, sometimes referred to as *vulnerability mapping* exercises, are used in other fields such as natural hazards and groundwater management, where they can serve as useful tools for planners and policy makers (Clark et al. 1998; Cutter, Mitchell, and Scott 2000; O'Brien et al. 2004; Dixon 2005).

Nothing is fundamentally wrong with the assumption that increased levels of exposure to adverse climatic conditions may stimulate increased levels of migration, especially in areas where livelihoods and locations are inherently sensitive to climate. Indeed, the second section of this book (Chapters 4–6) is deliberately organized according to types of climatic conditions (i.e. exposure) known from past experience to influence migration. Exposure is, however, only one aspect of vulnerability generally, and only one part of the puzzle in understanding the climate-migration relationship specifically. For example, the results of studies by Easterling and colleagues (1992) that modelled the impacts on crop yields in the American Midwest under various scenarios of future climate change varied wildly depending on what assumptions the authors made in terms of farmers' adaptive behavior. Describing these assumptions as 'smart farmer/dumb farmer scenarios', in the 'dumb farmer' scenarios, the modellers assumed that farmers did not recognize that climatic conditions were changing and so made no changes in their farming practices and crop choices. Unsurprisingly, crop yields would fall dramatically in such scenarios. In 'smart farmer scenarios', the modellers assumed that farmers were able to fully recognize climatic changes as they occurred and always made the appropriate adjustments in their farming strategies so as to maximize yields.[10] In these scenarios, crop yields were actually expected to increase in the future. In other words, under the same degree of exposure, the future outcomes for farmers could be positive or negative depending on the adaptation of those exposed. The same thing applies to understanding how climate affects migration: the same climatic phenomenon will generate a range of possible migration outcomes depending on how people adapt (McLeman and Smit 2006a).

3.7.2 Migration as Part of the Adaptation Process

3.7.2.1 Migration as One of Many Adaptations

Migration scholars have long used the term *adaptation* to discuss the ability of migrants to integrate into destination communities (e.g. David 1969). Here, however, we are talking about adaptation as the underlying rationale for the act of migration itself, something that traditional migration scholarship has not commonly done. Migration is a possible strategy by which those facing adverse climatic conditions may act to reduce the potential for loss or harm (or take advantage of new opportunities), and fits well within the broader context of vulnerability and adaptation to climate as described to this point. However, it is very rare that migration is the first act of adaptation individuals or households undertake when exposed to change or variation in climatic conditions (McLeman and Smit 2006a, Tacoli 2009). This is not surprising. Migration entails uncertainty, disruption, financial cost, and emotional distress. Regardless of the stimulus, climatic or otherwise, it is not something people enter into lightly. Understanding migration in the context of climate therefore also requires considering the broader range of adaptation options available in a given situation, including those that do not lead to migration; the constraints on adaptation possibilities; and the processes by which individuals and households adapt.

Most past and current migration undertaken for climate-related reasons is the result of decisions made by individuals and households. We can point to some past examples when governments and institutions have actively engaged in resettling households and communities exposed to climate-related risks. During the 1930s, provincial governments in Alberta and Saskatchewan, Canada, sought to reduce the number of farms in drought-stricken areas by paying for the rail shipment of household effects

---

[10] An assumption that would mean they were not just smart, but clairvoyant (Smit, McNabb, and Smithers 1996).

Table 3.1. *Typology of adaptation options in agricultural systems*

Level of adaptation	Adaptation Option	Examples
Farm level	Production choices	Crop choices, land use, improving soil and drainage, irrigation, timing of operations...
	Farm finances	Participating in crop insurance programs, investment in crop shares and futures, seeking off-farm employment, entrepreneurship...
Government, institutional, industry	Technological developments	Crop science, improvement of weather and climate information systems, resource management innovations, new farming technologies...
	Government programs and insurance	Agricultural subsidy and support programs, private insurance, resource management programs

Source: Adapted from Smit and Skinner (2002).

for families willing to leave (Marchildon et al. 2008, McLeman and Ploeger 2012). In more recent decades, the Ethiopian government also implemented programs to relocate people living in drought-stricken areas (Adugna and Thrift 1989). In practice, however, organized resettlements reflect just one segment of migration directly attributable to climatic variability and change.[11]

To better understand how household-level adaptation processes play out and where migration fits into them, the example of the farm is again useful. Farmers are continually faced with ever-changing weather conditions. Over time, farmers and farming systems adapt to the range of climatic conditions experienced in their home region. Some of these adaptations happen at the farm level and are initiated by individual farmers themselves, such as decisions made with respect to production methods and decisions related to the financial management of the farm business (Table 3.1). Adaptation of production methods can include making choices with respect to crop types and livestock stocking rates, implementing technologies such as irrigation, and adopting tillage practices that reduce the chance of crop losses during poor conditions. For example, grain farmers in semiarid areas have various choices of crops to plant, common ones being barley, rye, sorghum, and wheat. Each has its strengths and weaknesses. Sorghum plants are very drought tolerant, making them an excellent choice for drought-prone areas, but sorghum typically has a lower market price than wheat, which is slightly less drought

---

[11] For discussion and other examples of organized resettlements, see Cernea (2009), de Sherbinin and colleagues (2011), Hugo (2011), and McLeman (2011a).

tolerant.[12] Even within a given grain type, there is typically a choice in varieties that provide different yields depending on soil and climatic conditions. Through experience, farmers learn which combinations provide them the best chances of maximizing income from their land in a typical year. Because income from farming typically fluctuates from one year to the next, farmers often adopt wherever possible a variety of management strategies for reducing their risk and diversifying income sources. These can include such things as finding off-farm wage employment, joining producers' associations, and seeking out other opportunities through entrepreneurship or accessing government programs. In some cases, finding off-farm employment may entail short-term labor migration, a process detailed in Chapter 6.

Farmers' adaptation options are shaped not only by past experience, local environmental conditions, regional employment opportunities, and so forth (i.e. micro- and meso-level factors); they are also shaped by macro-level forces over which the farmer has no influence or control, such as commodity markets, fuel prices, land tenure systems, currency values, interest rates, and institutional policies, to name just a few. Institutions can provide opportunities for building adaptive capacity on farms, with Smit and Skinner (2002) identifying as examples government programs, crop insurance, enhanced weather forecasting systems, and improved production technologies. Depending on the circumstances, institutional policies and programs can also hinder farmers' adaptation prospects (Hazell et al. 2010). The combined effects of factors operating at the farm level and those operating at higher levels consequently generate a range of climatic conditions to which a farm or farming system is capable of adapting without disruption, as represented in Figure 3.4. Assuming that the y-axis represents the amount of precipitation received in a given year, the grey shaded area shows the range of rainfall conditions that is beneficial to an unspecified farm or farming system, or at least causes it no great loss or harm. Above and below this range are amounts of precipitation to which the system is vulnerable, which in Figure 3.4 consist of one excessively wet year and two very dry ones, plus one wet and one dry year that were just at the margins of adaptive capacity. These are the years in which the vulnerability of the system is realized.

A broad aim of individuals and institutions within the system is to attempt to expand that range of adaptive capacity over time. However, because extremes by definition occur infrequently, the financial benefits relative to the costs may be prohibitive.[13] So long as climatic conditions generally remain within the range of adaptive capacity shown in Figure 3.4, with extreme events remaining infrequent, changes in existing migration patterns are unlikely to occur – at least not for climatic reasons. Even in the

---

[12] For grain price comparisons, see U.S. Department of Agriculture Economic Research Service annual crop reports at http://www.ers.usda.gov.

[13] Readers interested in pursuing questions relating to the economics of adaptation – farm-related or otherwise – may wish to consult, among others, Fankhauser (2010), Mendelsohn and colleagues (2007), Stern (2007), and Yohe and Tol (2002).

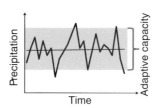

Figure 3.4. Capacity to adapt to precipitation variability in a hypothetical farming system. Based on Burton (1997). Note that although the top and bottom margins of adaptive capacity are depicted here as straight horizontal lines for ease of presentation, they, too, will vary over time as the factors that influence adaptive capacity change and evolve.

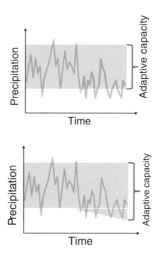

Figure 3.5. (a) Changing precipitation trend that exceeds adaptive capacity, (b) adaptive capacity adjusts in concert with precipitation trend.

infrequent years when precipitation levels fall outside the range of adaptive capacity, farmers are unlikely to abandon their farms entirely and relocate elsewhere, unless other factors are at work. They might increase their participation in short-term labor migration as a means of tiding over until favorable conditions return. As shown in greater detail in Chapters 5 and 6, short-term migration is just one of many adaptation options farmers might employ as they to adjust to severe droughts or excessive rainfall, and not until they have exhausted these do they contemplate permanent relocation.

Many climate scientists express concern that anthropogenic climate change will alter precipitation patterns in many parts of the world (IPCC 2007). This scenario is represented in Figure 3.5a, where a downward trend in average precipitation emerges, creating an increased frequency in the number of dry years as compared with Figure 3.4. So long as farmers and farming systems can adjust their adaptive capacity accordingly (Figure 3.5b), the effects on migration patterns will be moderate, with those that do occur experienced primarily as changes in short-term labor migration, with migrants exerting some degree of agency. But, should adaptive capacity not keep pace (i.e. the situation represented in Figure 3.5a persists), events to which the system is vulnerable become more frequent, and in these situations, there is increased potential for changes in migration patterns.

The processes just described do not apply solely to farms or farming systems, but are reflective of the relationship between climate and adaptation processes more generally. So long as climatic events and conditions to which a given population is exposed occur within or close to the capacity to adapt by other means, migration patterns are not affected. Households and individuals act in response to a particular climatic event or condition according to their own adaptive capacity. Actions that do not entail migration can be referred to as *in situ adaptation*. When migration does occur, the type, duration, and destination choices are shaped by the same types of cultural, economic, political, and social factors that influence adaptive capacity more generally.

3.7.2.2 The MESA Function

A simple shorthand can be used to capture the relationship between migration and adaptation as developed previously. Earlier in this chapter, a basic conception of vulnerability to climatic phenomena was introduced, $V = f(E, S, A)$, which suggested that the potential for loss or harm is a function of the nature of the climatic event or change, the sensitivity of the system in question to that particular event/change, and the capacity of those exposed to adapt. Because migration is one possible outcome of adaptation, we can use the vulnerability function in a modified form to reflect that the potential for migration in response to extreme events is a function of the nature of the event, the characteristics of the population exposed to that event, and its capacity to adapt in ways other than migration. Expressed a different way:

$$M = f(E, S, (A-M))$$

where

M = migration in the context of vulnerability

is a function of

E = exposure to a climatic stimulus
S = sensitivity of the population to that stimulus
A-M = adaptation options other than migration.

The potential for migration increases with the severity of the event and with the sensitivity of the exposed population (i.e. is positively related to these factors), and decreases as a population's in situ adaptive capacity becomes stronger.

3.8 Conceptual Representation of Migration within
an Adaptive System

The MESA function given in the preceding paragraph offers no information about
spatial or temporal scale, and gives no more than a simple indication of the relationship between migration potential and other components of vulnerability. It is possible to begin combining that which has come before in Chapters 1 through 3 to create
a generic, process-style representation of an adaptive human-environment system
of which migration is a component, and to do so in a way consistent with existing
research in migration and climate impacts and adaptation. The first step is shown in
Figure 3.6, which has a generic population X in the box at its center. Population X is
subject to a range of cultural, economic, environmental, political, and social forces
operating at higher (macro) scales, represented by the pentagon to its left. At the
same time, a range of similar forces operates within the population itself and the surrounding region, represented by the smaller pentagon within the population X box
and labeled *meso-scale factors*. The combination of macro- and meso-scale factors
influences the livelihood opportunities and strategies of households within population X, as represented by the house-shaped icon to the right side of the diagram.[14]
In a system with no great or sudden perturbations, it is here at the household or
sub-household level where most migration decisions are made and carried out. In
this simple representation, households continually and autonomously adapt their
livelihood strategies to the changing conditions around them, and migration may or
may not be a viable or necessary part of those strategies, as shown by the two dark
decision arrows pointing out to the upper left and to the right from the house icon.
Some households may have the option of employing migration as part of their livelihood strategies but choose not to, while others find migration a preferred option;
this latter group is shown by the arrow in the upper right-hand corner pointing out
of the diagram.

This is not, however, the end of the story, for the decisions households make have
implications for the larger population. People who leave the population take with
them their skills, attributes, and capital, which are no longer immediately available
to be shared with those left behind. At the same time, population X does not exist in
isolation, and so it is reasonable to expect there will be in-migration from other locations, bringing new skills, attributes, and capital to the population. Former residents
may also return, depending on the circumstances. Thus, the characteristics of population X in aggregate continually change as a result of the feedback effects of household
adaptation and migration.

---

[14] For sake of simplicity, the diagram does not drill down to the individual level, but the reader is reminded that households have within them their own social dynamics, often falling along lines of gender, age, and health. It would also
be possible to add other intermediate levels to the diagram, such as extended family, neighborhood, community,
state, and so forth.

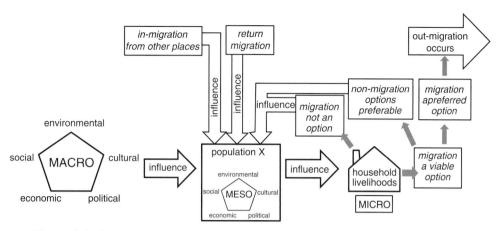

Figure 3.6. General representation of an adaptive system. Incorporates some elements from a model used in Foresight (2011).

Two short examples illustrate the dynamic nature of an adaptive system. In northern coastal Vietnam, rural household vulnerability to current climate-related risks, such as extreme weather events and floods, and to future risks associated with sea level rise, is closely linked to household-level poverty and income inequality across communities (Adger 1999). One way households try to get out of poverty is having young adults migrate to inland regions where they work in forestry, or to urban centers where they seek wage labor. In both cases, these households expect migrants to send remittance money home once they get established. Adger and colleagues (2002) sought to find out what effect these remittances had on the sending communities, and learned they are most often used to pay for education of younger family members, to purchase food or consumer goods, or to invest in additional livestock or shrimp ponds for aquaculture. Individual households able to capture remittance income have better prospects for economic and social advancement, and their adaptive capacity grows. For the sending area's population as a whole, the net effects in terms of adaptive capacity may be mixed. Income inequality between remittance-receiving and non-remittance-receiving households grows, meaning that the latter group may find itself increasingly marginalized both economically and socially. Thus internal dynamics within the population change because of migration, and vulnerability gets redistributed. Figure 3.6 is consistent with this.

A second example comes from rural eastern Ontario, Canada, where there has been a steady outflow of young people from highland rural communities for many decades, leaving a base population that is aging considerably (Figure 3.7). The relatively isolated rural settlements in the region have incomes well below the provincial average, few social services, and limited access to information and communications technologies (McLeman 2008, 2010b; McLeman and Ford 2013). They also face a climate characterized by cold winters, difficult spring and fall shoulder seasons that

Migration

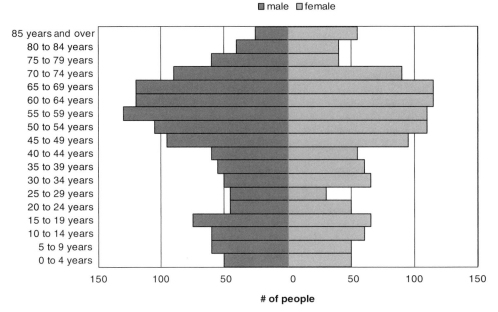

Figure 3.7. Demographic profile, Addington Highlands, Ontario.
Data source: Statistics Canada (2012).

often feature freezing rain events, and hot summers that bring windstorms and fire
risks. Over the generations, residents adapted to these conditions through a mix of
household self-reliance and strong informal social networks through which neighbors
look out for one another. The steady loss of young people, who move away primarily
to seek economic opportunities, undermines the capacity of those who remain behind
to cope with the climate. As residents age and become physically weaker, their individual self-sufficiency wanes, and they become more dependent on local social networks, which are in turn no longer replenished by young adults and so, too, become
weaker.

As eastern Ontario's highland population ages, a new migration phenomenon has
emerged in recent decades: the in-migration of retirees from urban centers to establish homes on waterfront properties. Some previously vacationed in the region, while
others are complete newcomers. Either way, they are outsiders with different cultural
and social values, and find it difficult to become accepted and incorporated into local
social networks. The newcomers have skills and experience very different from those
of lifelong residents, and these skills do not necessarily prepare them for the isolation and physical rigors of rural life. Further, they reinforce the trend toward a general aging of the area's population and create additional demand for public services
such as health care, which are already in short supply. Without any change in current
demographic trends or intervention from higher-scale actors, the capacity of the population as a whole to adapt to future stresses, climate-related or otherwise, looks poor,

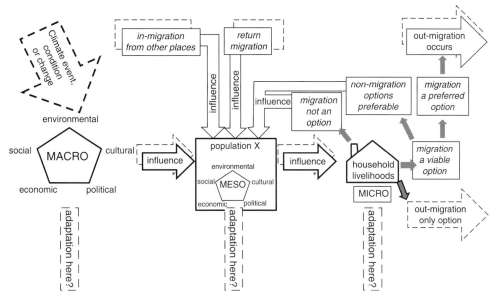

Figure 3.8. Effect of climatic event on adaptive system. In this diagram, dashed lines around boxes and arrows represent uncertainty as to the nature of the action or reaction. For example, the climatic event may be favorable or unfavorable, or adaptation may occur at some scales but not others.

and may eventually result in further changes in migration patterns (McLeman 2010b). Figure 3.6 is consistent with the eastern Ontario highlands example, and captures the interconnectedness of vulnerability, adaptation, migration, and the feedback effects in one part of the system on others.

The next step in analysis is to consider what may happen when a climatic event or condition, or a change in prevailing climatic conditions, occurs (Figure 3.8). Although it may be recognized and experienced at all or only some scales of the system, for sake of simplicity the figure starts by assuming that it is felt by all. The first step is to consider macro-level responses to the climatic event, represented by the dashed arrow at the upper left. Existing macro-level structures may be sufficiently robust and adaptive and/or the climatic event sufficiently weak that the impacts are absorbed at the macro scale without causing any significant disruptions to processes operating at lower scales. An example would be a heavy rain event that could cause serious flooding, except that national authorities have already invested in flood control engineering and emergency warning systems so that property damage is minimal and insured, and no lives are lost. This is the purpose of the dashed box below the pentagon-shaped set of macro-level processes containing the question 'adaptation here?' If adaptation is inadequate at higher levels, population *X* and its local institutions may be required to respond, again, the outcomes depending on the nature of the climatic stimulus and the internal dynamics operating within population *X*. Should adaptation at that level be insufficient, adaptation falls to individuals and households. To the household adaptation outcomes identified in the previous diagram must be added two more: the possibility of additional voluntary out-migration (represented by the additional dashed arrow in the upper right-hand corner) and the possibility that in extreme circumstances, flight might be the only option for many (represented by the dashed arrow in the lower right-hand corner). At the same time, recognizing that population X does not exist in a bubble, other populations or regions may also be experiencing the same climatic event, and population X may attract new migrants or additional return migrants from those other places (shown by the additional dashed arrows). Again, the figure shows that feedback effects and influences ripple throughout the system and across scales as actors at each level adjust, respond, and adapt to not only the climatic stimulus itself, but to the adjustments made in other parts of the system and in other systems to which it is connected.

An example that illustrates the processes described in Figure 3.8 is that of responses to drought in rural eastern Oklahoma in the mid-1930s. There, the rural population was already grappling with depressed commodity prices and high unemployment due to the Great Depression when severe droughts struck in 1934 and 1936 (McLeman 2006). Many farmers and agricultural workers in that region had long adapted to the inherent climatic and economic uncertainties of farming by participating in seasonal migration to farms in other regions when work was completed on their own farms, or seeking off-farm work with railroads, the oil industry, or other nonfarming industries. High rates of farm tenancy meant that there was also a steady movement of families within eastern Oklahoma from one farm to another. With the onset of the Depression, unemployed urban families began moving to rural areas, where they competed for access to tenant farms. The increased competition for good land worked to the advantage of those who owned land. Because of the Depression, the traditional adaptation of working off the farm was not available because of a lack of jobs. Younger families with children migrated out of eastern Oklahoma in droves to seek a new start farther afield, often in California, leaving behind a population increasingly divided into haves (landowners) and have-nots (landless poor) (McLeman 2006, McLeman et al. 2008). Formal meso-level institutions such as banks and local/county governments were largely insolvent across the region, so adaptation assistance at the meso level came through less formal institutions like merchants' credit and social networks. Funding and programs developed by the national government to deal with the much larger economic crisis proved beneficial to those who remained and likely averted an even higher level of out-migration from the region. A much more detailed account of 1930s drought-related migration in western North America appears in Chapter 6; for now, it is sufficient to observe the general consistency of the example with Figure 3.8.

Although Figure 3.8 shows the case when climatic conditions change, it might equally be used when technologies change to make given climatic conditions more

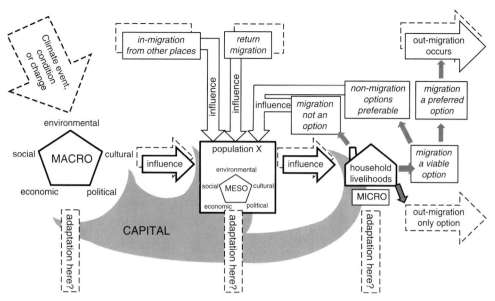

Figure 3.9. General representation of an adaptive system, with capital.

attractive (e.g. the advent of cheap air conditioning) or when individuals reach a stage in life when they desire different climatic conditions. Decisions to migrate because of such events have feedback effects on other parts of the system.

3.9 Capital: The Missing Piece of Social Theory

While Figure 3.8 does a decent job of capturing the dynamic nature of the system, its vulnerability to a climatic perturbation, and the role of migration within its adaptive processes, it is still missing something: an explanation of why the system behaves the way it does. It is a bit like drawing a schematic diagram of an automobile without making reference to the fluids – gasoline, oil, coolant, brake fluid, and so forth – that actually make the parts work together as they do. Using this analogy, Figure 3.8 needs to show the 'fluids' that help transmit actions from one level of the system to another; determine what is possible and what is not possible, feasible or unfeasible at each level; and shape how actors within the system decide to pursue one option over another when multiple options are available. What is needed is social theory – in this case, social theory well suited to understanding migration behavior. Chapter 2 briefly touched on many possibilities from the toolkit of available migration theories and concepts; my own empirical research has found that migration theories that make use of the concept of *capital* are a very useful 'fluid' for this purpose. This does not mean they are the only ones suitable for this purpose, or that they are applicable to every possible circumstance. Rather, what it does mean is that to move beyond simply describing climate-migration interactions to understanding how and why they occur in the ways that they do, forms-of-capital theories work reasonably well much of the time.

The idea that economic and social capital can influence adaptation and migration behavior was introduced in the previous chapter. As a reminder, *economic capital* – that is, money and those things quickly convertible to it, like real estate or investments – is seen as both a stimulus for migration and as a factor that limits the agency of would-be migrants. Economic capital is also seen as a key factor in adaptation to climate change – those with more money tend to have more adaptation options, other things being equal. Scholars have used *social capital* – which refers to elements of social networks that may be of economic benefit – in explaining how to build adaptive capacity at the community level and how migration becomes facilitated and perpetuated (Palloni et al. 2001, Pelling and High 2005). Other forms of capital, including human capital, cultural capital, natural capital, even religious capital (i.e. economic benefits stemming from religious involvement), have also been implicated in migration and adaptation behavior (Berkes and Folke 1994, Myers 2000, Reilly and Schimmelpfennig 2000, Marger 2001, Waters 2006, McLeman 2007). Capital is one of the few concepts regularly used in both migration and climate research that easily makes linkages across spatial, structural, and temporal scales. It is indeed like a fluid that moves throughout the system, transmitting the effects of actions taken at one part of the system onward, enabling certain actions and discouraging others. By identifying the distribution and valuation of capital, it becomes possible to see, interpret, and anticipate migration behavior within the adaptive system.

Capital does not explain all distinctions and differentiations in social behavior and social outcomes. Pierre Bourdieu, arguably the social scientist most responsible for the advancement of the use of capital as a means of explaining social behavior, saw capital as only one of three elements influencing societal structures and behavior within them, the others being habitus and social field (Bourdieu 1984). *Habitus* is the set of behaviors and worldviews learned over the course of a lifetime and leads individuals to acquire certain tastes, to value certain things over others, and to judge and interact with others in particular ways. *Social fields* are subsets of society where individuals sharing similar habitus and with access to similar endowments of capital connect and mix with one another. Such concepts also have relevance to understanding the relationship between climate and migration, but their use is less developed than that of capital in existing scholarship that considers climate and migration together. They will, therefore, not be pursued at any greater depth in the present book.[15] The various forms of capital are, however, accepted and used across both fields, and taken on their own are sufficient to build theoretical rigor into the process shown in Figure 3.8.

The availability and distribution of capital in its various forms helps shape adaptation choices and outcomes, as shown in Figure 3.9. The adaptation options available

---

[15] This presents a promising opportunity for future research.

to an individual or household, and the actions taken in response to a climatic risk or opportunity, are to a significant extent a function of the capital possessed by that individual or household and its value. By definition, capital links the individual through the property, financial resources, connections, skills, and abilities he or she possesses to the macro- and meso-level forces that shape vulnerability and adaptation. It is not the farmer who determines the market price of crops at harvest, or the homeowner who determines the value of a home; larger economic forces do. The wage commanded by a particular type of training or education is similarly set by larger cultural and economic forces, as are attitudes toward gender or race that can exclude some people from opportunities available to others, regardless of their qualifications. Knowing the right combinations of people or being a member of the right social network are forms of social capital that can make a tremendous difference in a household's adaptive capacity (Adger 2003, Pelling and High 2005). But the value of the social capital possessed by an individual depends not only on the nature of his or her direct social interactions with other people, but also on the social interactions of the people he or she knows with third parties he or she does not know. So the extent to which social capital can be mobilized through adaptation, whether it is to facilitate out-migration or to resist migration and remain in situ, is a product of collective action and interaction across scales. All of these examples simply highlight the fact that capital is a valuable resource for the individual, but its utility and value are set at other scales of the system. Consequently, capital is depicted like a grey web in the background of Figure 3.9, a fluid that courses through the system to regulate its behavior.

Figure 3.9 is consistent with the basic elements of vulnerability (exposure, sensitivity, and adaptive capacity) and the MESA function introduced earlier; reflects the dynamic interaction across scales of factors believed to influence vulnerability and migration behavior; and brings these together in a systems diagram to show how climatic phenomena and human processes may combine to give rise to migration. By identifying the movements and distribution of capital within the system, it is possible to understand and potentially anticipate how particular adaptation and migration outcomes might arise. In the next three chapters, past examples of known climate-related migrations are plugged into Figure 3.9 to check on its utility.

3.10 Chapter Summary

Scholars increasingly treat climate-related migration as a possible outcome of processes through which vulnerable individuals and households adapt to climatic events and conditions or changes in those conditions. Treating migration in such terms is consistent with the reporting of the IPCC on the human impacts of climate change and with the framing of international responsibilities under the UNFCCC. In addition to these pragmatic reasons, it is also conceptually logical and consistent to do so. Vulnerability, understood as a function of exposure, sensitivity, and adaptive capacity, is shaped by cultural, economic, political, and social forces operating at multiple spatial, structural, and temporal scales similar to those shown in Chapter 2 to shape migration behavior. Environmental refugee-type research has tended to connect migration with changes in exposure to climatic phenomena, overlooking the effects of adaptation processes, especially those operating at the level of households and individuals, where most migration decisions are made. The MESA function captures how migration is related to exposure, sensitivity, and in situ adaptive capacity. This chapter ends by constructing a process diagram of a generic adaptive system to show how a population and households within it may be affected by and respond to changes in climatic conditions, and how those responses in turn have feedback effects on other parts of the system. Access to economic, social, and other forms of capital helps determine the adaptation options available to actors within the system and shapes their choices, including migration (or lack thereof).

4

Extreme Weather Events and Migration

4.1 Introduction

Extreme weather events comprise a range of phenomena, including tropical cyclonic storms (hurricanes, cyclones, and typhoons), tornadoes, other types of intense storm events (e.g. windstorms, hailstorms, blizzards, thunderstorms), unusually heavy precipitation associated with monsoons, and periods of extreme heat or cold. Extreme storm events are typically accompanied by strong winds and large amounts of precipitation, meaning that they may also lead to flooding, mudslides, storm surges, and other dangerous impacts. Especially severe storms can cause destruction of houses and businesses; damage critical infrastructure such as water supplies, transportation networks, and electrical utilities; disrupt livelihoods; cause large numbers of injuries or loss of life; and lead to displacement and out-migration from the affected area. Wealthy and poor populations alike are at risk of experiencing loss, harm, and displacement as a consequence of extreme weather events, although research reviewed in this chapter shows that it is the poor, the physically weak, and the socially marginalized or isolated who are often most vulnerable.

As suggested in the MESA function in the previous chapter, the potential for migration increases with the severity of the extreme event and with the sensitivity of the exposed population, but decreases when the exposed population has strong adaptive capacity. In regions where extreme weather events are already common and expected to remain so, such as the southern United States, the Caribbean, and coastal south and southeast Asia, human population numbers are increasing rapidly. Population growth in these regions has often been accompanied by removal or degradation of natural features that act as buffers to storm impacts, such as coral reefs, barrier islands, coastal mangroves, wetlands, and upland forest cover. The combined effects of climate change, population growth, and landscape modification suggest a future trajectory of growing human vulnerability to extreme events and increased potential for associated migration. Actual future outcomes in terms of migration will depend heavily on the continued development of proactive measures to reduce

exposure (through such things as emergency preparedness, improved advance warning and communications systems, and protection of natural buffers) and improving
institutional and household-level capacity to respond effectively to these events when
they occur (through, for example, improved housing and infrastructure standards,
disaster recovery assistance, and greater overall socioeconomic well-being).

This chapter explores the connections between physical and human processes that
create vulnerability to extreme weather events, with particular attention to those interactions that hold the greatest potential to stimulate migration. The severity and spatial
scale of tropical cyclones, and their potential for destroying housing, makes them the
type of extreme event most capable of stimulating large-scale migration. Tornadoes
and other types of storm events may also lead to smaller-scale population movements,
and there is considerable room for more scholarly research in this area. As seen in
Chapter 6, where extreme heat events are associated with drought, they increase the
potential for migration. Shorter-term heat waves and extreme cold spells pose significant public health concerns, but little research has been done to determine if they may
also influence migration.

In particular, the remainder of this chapter:

• Describes the general characteristics of extreme weather events, their spatial distribution,
  and human exposure to them
• Identifies processes that increase the sensitivity of human populations and systems to
  extreme weather events
• Explains how migration emerges in response to extreme weather events as a consequence
  of adaptation processes, and how a range of migration responses may emerge from a single
  event depending on socioeconomic and political factors
• Provides case studies of migration outcomes from hurricanes Katrina and Mitch, illustrating the interplay of causal factors and the various forms internal and international migration
  may take as a consequence
• Checks the utility of the process diagram of migration in an adaptive system (Figure 3.9)
  through comparison with the case studies.

4.2 General Characteristics of Extreme Weather Events

Although it is popular to treat extreme events as exceptions from normal weather
patterns, describing them, for example, as 'Acts of God' (Steinberg 2000), they are
an inherent part of climatic systems (Hewitt 1983). Extreme weather events simply occur less often than do benign conditions. Researchers in the broader scholarly
field of natural hazard research have long recognized that extreme weather events
become hazardous to human well-being through interactions of physical processes
and human behavior that put people in places at risk (Burton, Kates, and White 1978;
Blaikie et al. 1994). Indeed, the concepts of vulnerability and adaptation introduced

in the previous chapter owe much of their origins to the study of extreme events by researchers in the natural hazards field (Adger 2006).

For organizational purposes, we may place extreme weather events into three general categories, according to their most characteristic attributes:

- Extreme wind events (e.g. tropical cyclones, tornadoes, gales, microbursts)
- Extreme precipitation events (rain, snow, freezing rain, hail)
- Extreme temperature events (heat waves, cold snaps)

These categories are not mutually exclusive. Tropical cyclones typically bring large quantities of rain, tornadoes are often spawned as part of intense thunderstorm events, and blizzards combine heavy snow, strong winds, and frigid cold. Extreme events vary in terms of the spatial area they affect, from thunderstorms that have intense local impacts to tropical cyclones that may sweep across huge swaths of an entire continent. The duration of extreme weather events can also vary, from the momentary touchdown of a tornado that causes tremendous local destruction in a matter of seconds, to the weeks-long duration of extreme heat events, such as the 2003 event that contributed to the deaths of tens of thousands of Europeans (Kovats and Kristie 2006). Extreme events can also be precursors to events like floods and droughts (treated separately in the next two chapters) that in turn lead to population displacements.

No universal definition exists of what makes a given event 'extreme'. Most definitions tend to focus on the rarity of the event, the intensity of the event, and/or its destructiveness as compared with some set of relative norms and thresholds (Beniston and Stephenson 2004). What is considered extreme in one setting may not be in another. For example, in Ottawa, Canada, the average daily temperature in January over the past three decades has been about minus eleven degrees Celsius (Environment Canada 2012). Infrastructure is designed accordingly, and residents know how to ensure their personal comfort out of doors.[1] The same winter temperatures occur occasionally in the United Kingdom, but create emergency situations when they do. A January 2010 cold snap in the United Kingdom led to school closures, flight delays at major airports, the shutdown of motorways, and many burst water pipes. Death rates in Scotland increased by roughly 20 per cent over similar periods in previous years (Bingham, Hough, and Carter 2010). By comparison, July temperatures of thirty degrees Celsius are considered extreme heat events in Ottawa, triggering the implementation of emergency measures such as the opening of community cooling stations where residents lacking air conditioning can go to get relief. In other national capitals like New Delhi or Bangkok, people are much less likely to get excited by thirty-degree heat (although Londoners would).

---

[1] Indeed, I can say from personal experience that a sunny minus-eleven day makes for a great day of skating on Ottawa's Rideau Canal.

While very diverse in their physical manifestations, extreme weather events share a common potential to inflict considerable loss or harm on populations exposed to them. This loss or harm can be experienced in a variety of ways, including direct impacts on health and well-being through injury, sickness, or loss of life; damage to critical infrastructure including housing, roads, electricity, and water supplies; economic losses, including damage to crops, livestock, personal property; and loss of present or future income or livelihood opportunities. The potential for people to be exposed to extreme weather events and the degree of harm they may suffer is a function of the physical conditions in the regions in which they live and the human cultural, economic, political, and social processes that influence where and how people live (Wisner et al. 2004). The loss of housing, loss of livelihoods, and disruption to social networks that can accompany extreme events are all factors that can potentially predispose people to migrating elsewhere. Whether migration actually happens depends on the combined effects of the adaptive capacity of institutional actors and household-level economic, social, and cultural capital during the post-event recovery period. Where these are robust, where people's displacement from their homes is temporary, and where resumption of livelihoods is quick, out-migration is unlikely (Paul 2005). Where institutional responses are feeble and/or households lack adaptive capacity, the chances of permanent displacement and migration elsewhere rise. Prior experience with extreme events can have an important influence on responses to and preparation for subsequent ones, making it possible for institutional actors to reduce the number of people exposed through contingency planning and to improve future post-event recovery (Comstock and Mallonnee 2005).

Information derived from general circulation models[2] suggests that the frequency and/or intensity of some types of extreme weather events may increase in some regions in coming decades (IPCC 2007). The intensity of tropical cyclones is expected to rise, although their frequency of occurrence may not (Emanuel 2005, Knutson et al. 2010). There is little evidence to suggest the areas where tropical cyclones are generated will change in the foreseeable future. Other types of extreme wind events and storms may increase in frequency in many regions (Gastineau and Soden 2009), although there is no evidence of any current increase in tornado frequency, especially the more violent tornadoes in the United States (Simmons and Sutter 2011). Extreme heat events are expected to become more common over many continental areas because of rising average temperatures over land, with extreme cold events becoming less common (Meehl and Tebaldi 2004, Cattiaux et al. 2010). The response of monsoons to anthropogenic climate change remains uncertain, but recent modelling efforts suggest monsoonal precipitation becomes more intense as average global temperatures and sea surface temperatures rise (Schewe, Levermann, and Meinshausen 2011; Shin, Sardeshmukh, and Yeh 2011).

---

[2] A general circulation model is a mathematical model that simulates the behavior of the atmosphere, oceans, or both. Scientists commonly use this tool to understand climate and human modification of it.

4.3 Exposure to Extreme Weather Events

All inhabited areas may be subject to extreme weather events of one type or another, but certain types of events tend to strike particular regions more often. Consequently, the potential for extreme weather-related migration is not equally distributed across the globe. The physical processes that give rise to each of these types of events and their resulting spatial distributions are now described briefly.

4.3.1 Exposure to Extreme Wind Events

4.3.1.1 Tropical Cyclones

Each year, between eighty and ninety tropical cyclones form on average, although the number varies considerably from one year or decade to another (Pielke et al. 2003, Tory and Frank 2010). Tropical cyclones are given different names depending on the region in which they form: they are called *hurricanes* in the Atlantic and Caribbean region, *cyclones* in the Indian Ocean and the southwestern Pacific Ocean, and *typhoons* in the rest of the Pacific and the South China Sea. The destructive effects of tropical cyclones result from their tremendous wind speeds, the enormous sheets of precipitation that may accompany them, the large waves they generate over water, and the surge of water that builds up before the storm and floods inland if the storm makes landfall. Tropical cyclone wind speeds are capable of exceeding 250 kilometers per hour on a sustained basis; one of the most intense tropical cyclones to ever strike the United States, 1969's Hurricane Camille, had sustained wind speeds of eighty-five meters per second near the eye of the storm (Neumann 1993). The amount of rainfall that accompanies tropical cyclones can be quite remarkable. For example, Typhoon Morakot in 2009 delivered more than two meters of rainfall to locations in Taiwan over the course of forty-eight hours, triggering multiple landslides that killed more than 600 people (Hong et al. 2010). Cyclone Bhola, which struck the Bay of Bengal region in 1970 and killed hundreds of thousands in Bangladesh, is believed to have driven ashore a storm surge ten meters high (Karim and Mimura 2008), one of the highest recorded storm surges of the past century.

Tropical cyclones form when (1) sea surface temperatures are above twenty-seven degrees Celsius and (2) where the sea surface is overlain by low-pressure air that is relatively still and moist (Terry 2007). Under such conditions, parcels of warm, moisture-laden air close to the sea surface can begin to rise rapidly, causing moisture to condense and forming a convective cell of circulating air. If such conditions persist, an air pressure gradient forms that causes air to be drawn rapidly toward the center of the convective cell, generating increasingly faster wind speeds. The rotation of the Earth, through what is known as the *Coriolis effect*, causes the air to begin rotating

Tropical cyclone frequency

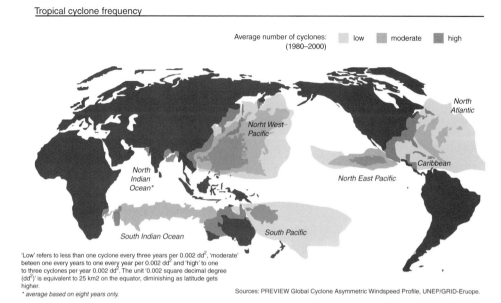

Figure 4.1. Map of regions with high physical exposure to cyclonic storms, E. Bournay, designer. Reproduced with permission from UNEP/GRID-Arendal, http://maps.grida.no/go/graphic/tropical-cyclone-frequency.

around what emerges as the eye of the storm, giving cyclonic storms their unmistakable appearance (Tory and Frank 2010).

Tropical cyclones tend not to form immediately at the equator, where the Coriolis effect is weakest (Terry 2007). They also tend not to form in regions where sea surface temperatures do not become sufficiently warm, such as higher latitudes and areas where cold ocean currents upwell. Once formed, the cyclonic storm will continue to grow and persist only so long as the key inputs of moisture and heat are available; this is why tropical cyclones begin to lose strength as they move out of lower latitudes to cooler waters, or pass over large land areas. This combination of causal factors means certain parts of the globe are more likely to experience tropical cyclones than others (Figure 4.1), with coastal populations in these areas of frequent storm genesis having the greatest level of exposure. Figure 4.2, which shows the tracks of tropical cyclones that formed in 2009, further illustrates this point.

Tropical cyclones can travel across long distances. The chances of being in the path of a particular cyclone decrease with distance from the location where it is generated. Even within cyclone-prone regions, certain locations are more likely than others to experience one. For example, Pielke and colleagues (2003) suggest that in the Caribbean region, southernmost Florida has the highest chance of experiencing a hurricane in a given year (15 per cent), while Trinidad and Tobago and the Caribbean coast from Venezuela to Nicaragua have a lower annual risk of between 1 and 5 per cent. Along the U.S. Caribbean-Atlantic coast, the frequency of hurricane strikes

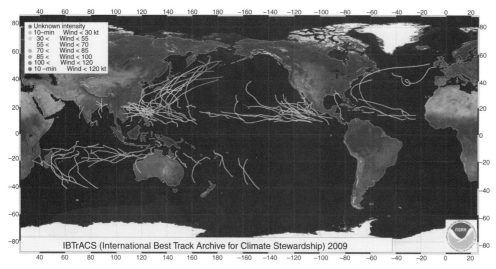

Figure 4.2. Tracks of tropical cyclones that formed in 2009. Map generated from NOAA Climatic Data Center IBTrACS data set [online], accessed 25 January 2012, from http://www.ncdc.noaa.gov/oa/ibtracs/index.php?name=browse. For complete scholarly details about IBTrACS, consult Knapp and colleagues (2010).

varies from one every two years along the North Carolina outer banks to one every three years along the U.S. Gulf of Mexico coast from Texas to Florida (Keim, Muller, and Stone 2007). As one travels farther north along the U.S. Atlantic coast, the frequency of hurricane strikes drops significantly, to an average of one every ten to fifteen years along the New England coast. Tropical cyclones remain dangerous even as they move inland and/or away from the tropics and weaken. For example, 1954's Hurricane Hazel caused widespread flooding, infrastructure damage, and loss of life from the southern Caribbean to south-central Canada (Robinson and Cruikshank 2006) (Figure 4.3).

4.3.1.2 Extreme Storm Events and Tornadoes

Extreme thunderstorms occur frequently in spring and summer over the south-central United States, Argentina, and parts of Sahelian Africa and the Congo, while intense convective storms often occur just prior to the monsoon seasons in India and Bangladesh, or in conjunction with short monsoon seasons in other parts of Asia and Australia (Zisper et al. 2006). In Europe, extreme wind events are a relatively frequent and costly winter occurrence in terms of damage to infrastructure, especially in central and northern Europe and Scandinavia (Schwierz et al. 2010). In arid and semiarid regions, especially in western China and the Saharan region, strong winds can generate dust storms that present significant risks to human respiratory health and to livestock (Goudie 2009). Hailstorms can occur on most continents, and are especially damaging to agricultural crops. There is considerable variability in terms of the

Figure 4.3. Personnel of the Canadian Army clearing away debris in the aftermath of Hurricane Hazel, near Toronto, Ontario, 1954. Image source: Gordon Jolley/ Canada. Dept. of National Defence/Library and Archives Canada/PA-174540 (http:// data4.collectionscanada.gc.ca/netacgi/nph-brs?s2=&s4=&s3=&s1=&s8=93517&S ect4=AND&l=20&Sect1=IMAGE&Sect2=THESOFF&Sect4=AND&Sect5=FOT OPEN&Sect6=HITOFF&d=FOTO&p=1&u=http://www.collectionscanada.gc.ca/ archivianet/02011503_e.html&r=1&f=G).

spatial distribution of hailstorm occurrence between and within regions. For example, in the United States, hailstorm events are most common on the Great Plains, in the central Rocky Mountains, and in the southeast (Chagnon and Chagnon 2000), while in the United Kingdom, severe hailstorms occur most often in central and eastern England (Webb, Elsom, and Meaden 2009). In China, several regions regularly experience hailstorm events, with the southwestern province of Guizhou experiencing the most severe events in terms of hail size (Xie, Zhang, and Wang 2010). Rosenfeld and Bell (2011) have presented evidence that hailstorms occur more often on weekdays when emissions of air pollutants are highest, these acting as seeds for hail formation when conditions are amenable for storm genesis.

In mid to high latitudes, a mixture of hazardous weather phenomena, including heavy snowfall, freezing rain, high winds, and rapid temperature fluctuations, can

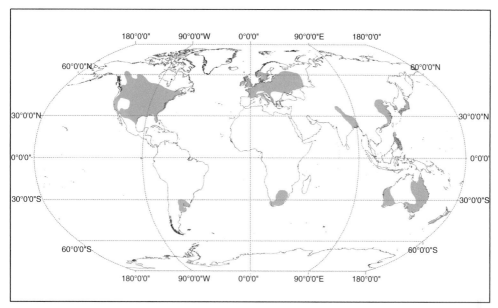

Figure 4.4. Regions exposed to tornado risks. Redrawn from data retrieved from U.S. Tornado Climatology page, Climate Services and Monitoring Division, NOAA/ National Climatic Data Center, Asheville NC http://lwf.ncdc.noaa.gov/oa/climate/ severeweather/tornadoes.html#alley.

accompany extreme winter storm events (Martin 1998). The risk of blizzards (storms with high winds and blowing snow) increases under conditions where warm and moist air masses collide with colder ones, when air masses are pushed up by increased terrain elevation, or when the passage of cold, dry air masses over large water bodies creates 'lake-effect' snow (Martin 1998, Morin et al. 2008). Blizzards increase the risk of accidental death and heart attacks, and can cause severe damage to infrastructure, bringing down power lines and causing roofs to collapse under heavy snow loads (Schwartz and Schmidlin 2002).

Extreme thunderstorms can generate tornadoes. The specific dynamics of tornado genesis are the subject of ongoing study, and while it is possible to recognize the types of weather systems that can potentially generate tornadoes, it remains difficult to predict reliably in advance if a particular storm will indeed do so (Markowski and Richardson 2009). Tornadoes can form on any continent where conditions for the genesis of extreme thunderstorms are present, but particular regions tend to have a more elevated risk than do others (Figure 4.4). The majority of the world's tornadoes occur in North America, especially in spring and early summer around the 'tornado alley' of the southeastern and midwestern United States. Since 1950, the United States has experienced approximately 875 tornadoes annually, affecting an average area of roughly 335 square miles in aggregate (Simmons and Sutter 2011), much less surface area than that which a single tropical cyclone might affect.

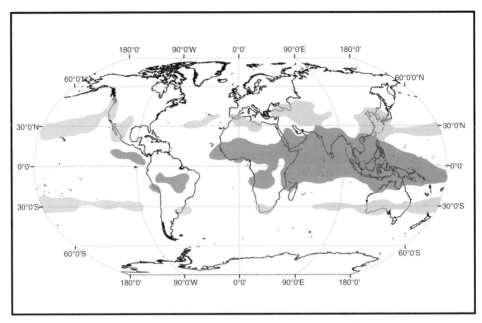

Figure 4.5. Map of world tropical (dark grey) and subtropical (light grey) monsoon regions. Based on Li and Zeng (2003).

4.3.2 *Exposure to Extreme Monsoon Precipitation*

Monsoonal climates are highly seasonal, characterized by a distinct wet period during which most annual precipitation is received. Abnormally high amounts of rainfall in monsoon regions can trigger floods, landslides, riverbank erosion, and other events that displace people (see the next chapter for more on river valley flooding in monsoon regions). Roughly half the world's population lives in monsoonal climates (Cook et al. 2010) (see Figure 4.5). Within a given rainy season, precipitation may not fall uniformly, but in a series of heavy rain events interspersed with periods without any precipitation (Pattanaik and Rajeevan 2010). The actual amount of precipitation received and the pattern in which it falls is influenced by a mix of factors, including sea surface temperatures, fluctuations in solar radiation, wind patterns, and existing soil and moisture content on land surfaces (Wahl and Morrill 2010). The complexity of these interactions means that reliable modelling and forecasting of monsoon behavior remains difficult (Cook et al. 2010). When monsoons deliver amounts of precipitation that are well above average, they are typically associated with anomalous sea surface temperatures and climatic oscillations like El Niño-La Niña (Wang, Wu, and Li 2003). Because monsoonal regions receive most or all of their precipitation in one season, years when the precipitation received falls well below average can be a precursor to droughts (see Chapter 6).

4.3.3 Exposure to Extreme Temperature Events

Extreme temperature events are generally associated with anomalous patterns in large-scale atmospheric circulation processes (Cassou, Terray, and Phillips 2005). As noted earlier, what constitutes 'extreme' temperatures depends on prevailing temperature norms at a given location. Meteorologists typically devise locally relevant indices to classify extreme temperature events, which can include non-meteorological measures, especially measures of the physiological stress of temperature extremes on the human body (e.g. see Robinson's 2001 definition of a heat wave). Even here, what constitutes a temperature extreme is case specific. For example, those most at risk physiologically to extreme heat are the elderly, young children, and people with respiratory or cardiologic conditions (Basu and Samet 2002), so a temperature that is extreme for someone of this description might not be extreme for a healthy young adult. Further complicating clear definitions is that the nature of the built environment has an influence on both absolute temperature (e.g. the urban 'heat island' effect (Stone and Rodgers 2001)) and the physiological effects. For example, certain types of residential construction, particularly older multistory apartment buildings with poor ventilation and no air conditioning, can reach unbearable inside temperatures during hot weather, as evidenced by the hundreds of deaths of residents of such accommodations during Chicago's 1995 heat wave, and the thousands of deaths during France's 2003 heat wave (Klinenberg 1999, Kovats and Kristie 2006, Vandentorren 2006). Such accommodations can, however, be made less dangerously hot through installation of fans and air conditioning, but these simple technologies may be inaccessible to the very poor. Studies have found that temperatures inside the informal and self-built housing typical of poorer parts of developing country cities can reach physiologically dangerous levels in both hot and cold periods (French and Gardner 2012).

The physiological impacts of extreme heat and extreme cold events are different. The effects of extreme cold on mortality are more immediate, especially among older people with cardiovascular disease (Huynen et al. 2001, Medina-Ramón et al. 2006). Extreme heat can cause mortality directly, though not as rapidly as exposure to extreme cold; heat may also have longer-lasting health effects by damaging the respiratory system (Huynen et al. 2001). The importance of extreme heat to overall mortality rates is relative to other risks to health, and appears to be highest in developed country populations. For example, Hajat and colleagues (2005) found the relationship between heat and additional deaths is much more identifiable in London, England, than it is in New Delhi, where infectious diseases and childhood illnesses play much greater roles in mortality rates. Extreme heat events are reported as being the leading weather-related cause of death in the United States (Luber and McGeehin 2008). However, this may in part be due to demographic trends that see slower growth and higher rates of out-migration in colder states as compared with hotter ones (Deschenes and Moretti 2007).

4.4 Processes that Increase the Sensitivity of Human Populations and Systems to Extreme Weather Events

The human impacts of extreme weather events vary considerably from one time and place to another. Part of this is due to differences in adaptation, discussed shortly. Cultural, economic, political, and social processes also increase the number of people exposed and make human systems more sensitive to disruption by extreme weather events. These include:

- Population growth
- Landscape modification
- Residential location
- Housing quality
- Social inequality.

The effects of each on increasing exposure and/or sensitivity are discussed in turn.

4.4.1 Population Growth in Areas of High Physical Exposure

Many regions with high levels of physical exposure to extreme weather events have also experienced rapid population growth over recent decades, driven by the combined effects of high rates of natural population increase, urbanization, labor migration, and amenity migration. For example, approximately 2.25 billion people live in coastal regions where there is a moderate to high risk of tropical cyclone occurrence, a number that has increased by roughly 10 per cent over the past decade (Table 4.1). Of these, the rate of population increase is greatest in countries along the east African coast and along the U.S. coast, and lowest in Oceania. In absolute terms, the largest number of people presently exposed to tropical cyclone risk live in coastal Asia, from India to the China coast, including Indonesia and the Philippines. With ever larger numbers moving to coastal cities in south and southeast Asia, China, and the United States, Lall and Deichmann (2011) suggest that by 2050 approximately 600 million urbanites will live in high-risk areas; this may be a conservative estimate given present urbanization and population growth rates in Asia. Pielke and colleagues (2003, 2008) have warned that, given population trends in the United States, Central America, and the Caribbean, property damage and numbers of people harmed by hurricanes in those regions will continue to climb. While the United States as a whole has a relatively moderate rate of population increase by global standards, states along America's hurricane coasts – from the Carolinas to Texas – are among the leaders in population growth within the United States (U.S. Census Bureau 2012). States in the U.S. Tornado Alley have varying rates of population change, with all experiencing at least moderate growth (U.S. Census Bureau 2012).

Table 4.1. *Population growth in areas of high exposure to extreme weather events*

Region	2001 population (in thousands)	2010 population (in thousands)	% change
Caribbean basin & Central America (1)	193,051	216,781	12.3
Coastal Asia (2)	1,710,358	1,876,443	9.7
East Africa (3)	69,490	82,619	18.9
Oceania (4)	15,833	16,898	6.7
USA (5)	49,079	57,956	18.1
TOTAL	2,037,811	2,250,698	10.4

Notes: (1) Does not include USA; (2) Includes Sri Lanka, coastal states of India, SE Asia, coastal states of China, Japan and Koreas; (3) Madagascar, Mozambique, Tanzania; (4) Includes Pacific Island states, Papua New Guinea and Australia's Queensland and Northern Territory; (5) from Texas to North Carolina; for Texas, only coastal county populations are included. For more detailed explanation of calculations and breakdowns by country, along with a list of data sources, see Appendix I.

4.4.2 Landscape Modification

Human alteration of the landscape can exacerbate the impacts of extreme weather events by removing natural features that store precipitation, slow erosion and surface runoff, and blunt the effects of storm surges. The filling of wetlands removes storage for excess precipitation, accelerates precipitation drainage into rivers and other watercourses, and increases flood risks (Opperman et al. 2009). Clearance of forest cover from hill slopes, whether for agriculture or settlement, increases the risk of slope failure when soils become saturated by high levels of precipitation, creates the potential for flash flooding, and allows high levels of sediment to erode into watercourses (see Hurricane Mitch case study later in this chapter). Coastal wetlands that absorb storm surges in the world's large, low-lying delta regions are shrinking in size because of human activity, with sea level rise related to climate change expected to exacerbate wetland losses (Nicholls 2004; Coleman, Huh, and Bruad 2008). Mangroves – a mix of tree and shrub species that thrive in tropical intertidal zones – protect inland settlements from the impacts of storm surges associated with tropical cyclones and tsunamis. Das and Vincent (2009) demonstrated that villages protected by mangroves experienced much lower death rates during a 1999 tropical cyclone than did unprotected settlements along India's Orissa coast. Worldwide, mangroves are in rapid decline because of pollution and active clearance by human populations to make way for aquaculture or urban development (Duke et al. 2007). Coral reefs and offshore barrier islands perform similar functions of sheltering landward areas from large waves and storm surges, and human activity is also degrading these in many settled coastal areas (Munday 2004; Grzegorzewski, Cialone, and Wamsley 2011; Zhang and Leatherman

2011). As these and other natural features that offset the impacts of extreme events disappear from heavily populated areas, the risk of property damage and loss of life from extreme events grows.

4.4.3 Residential Location

Cultural, social, and economic processes within highly exposed landscapes can influence residential location patterns. In some areas, wealthy people deliberately choose to live in highly exposed areas; in others, the poor are relegated to doing so. In the United States, coastal waterfront property is considered highly desirable for residential, commercial, and recreational accommodation, notwithstanding the known weather-related risks of occupying such areas (Bin et al. 2008). Similarly, the cyclone-prone Queensland coast has seen an influx of amenity-seeking migrants from other parts of Australia where cyclones are not common (Anderson-Berry 2003). In some cases, people may not even be aware their homes are situated in at-risk locations until after an event occurs, as Bin and Polasky (2004) observed in a U.S. study of Hurricane Floyd's impact on the Carolinas. Coastal property values are pushed upward by trends such as these, and when a tropical cyclone strikes, undamaged housing becomes scarcer and even more valuable (Murphy and Strobl 2009).

In other places, poor populations may from lack of choice be obliged to live in locations such as steep hillsides and coastal flats that are highly exposed to the physical impacts of extreme weather events. Although inherently dangerous, the landless poor accept such risks in order to live near employment opportunities (Sanderson 2000). In such places, the poor often live in informally built accommodations on land to which they hold no legal title (Prevatt, Dupigny-Giroux, and Masters 2010). When extreme weather events occur, the contrast in impacts between rich and poor neighborhoods can be quite stark. For example, in 2006, heavy rains caused flooding in the El Paso-Ciudad Juarez region along the U.S.-Mexico border. Of the twenty thousand left homeless, a disproportionate number were the poorest of the poor, migrants who lived in informal settlements along *arroyos* (intermittent watercourses) on the Mexican side of the border (Collins 2010). Similar dynamics occur in other regions as well. In crowded Jakarta, flood-prone watercourses are often the site of slum housing occupied by rural migrants (Texier 2008), while in Jamaica it is the steep slopes around coastal cities where large informal settlements are built (Ishemo 2009). This pattern of marginalized people occupying marginal and unsafe land areas is not unique to these examples, which are indicative of the challenges faced in many developing regions.

4.4.4 Housing Quality

Damage to infrastructure and housing stocks is a key first-order outcome of extreme storm events, with urban centers especially at risk of post-event housing crises, especially when damage to housing stocks is concentrated in particular neighborhoods (Comerio 1997). People whose homes are lost or damaged irreparably by extreme events are de facto more likely to relocate elsewhere in search of new, permanent shelter. Not all types of housing are equally susceptible to storm damage. A variety of models exist to gauge the structural integrity of housing stock in the face of high winds and hail, and the investment necessary to reduce risks to specified levels (e.g. Stewart, Rosowsky, and Huang 2003). In developed countries, prefabricated houses and mobile homes are the most susceptible to storm damage, and their occupants face a much greater risk of harm during tornadoes and tropical cyclones than do occupants of more robustly constructed homes (Schmidlin and King 1995, Schmidlin et al. 2009). Tornado-related death rates in the United States are especially high when tornadoes occur at night, when mobile homes are most likely to have people inside (Sutter and Simmons 2010). Often, damage to housing stocks from extreme storms is not distributed equally across an affected area, but is concentrated in places where the buildings have similar structural design, and the debris from one damaged building is hurled against its neighbors to create a chain reaction of damage (De Silva, Kruse, and Wang 2008).

Where they exist, building codes have an important influence on the resilience of buildings in the face of tropical storms. In many at-risk areas, planning for infrastructure and housing could be greatly improved to reduce the potential for loss or harm during extreme events (Guikema 2009). Too often, short-term interests and anemic policy-making processes confound wise construction and development practices. For example, Fronstin and Holtmann (1994) found that a deliberate lessening of minimum residential construction standards beginning in the 1950s meant that older houses in Dade County, Florida, better withstood the impacts of Hurricane Andrew (1992) than did newer, more shoddily built houses. In surveying damage to housing following a 1999 tornado in Moore, Oklahoma, Marshall (2002) found that certain housing designs that complied with local codes had high rates of damage, namely wooden frame houses with attached garages built on poured concrete slabs. This particular design had a characteristic sequence of destruction, whereby the garage door and/or windows failed, allowing winds to enter and create a pressure differential inside the house, which in turn lifted the roof off its relatively weak attachments. Remarkably, the author found on a return inspection months later that houses being rebuilt were of no better construction than those that had been destroyed, there having been no modifications of the building code since the tornado. Even basic safeguards like roof tie-down straps had not been made mandatory. When a large tornado struck Moore again in 2013, the results were tragically similar to those of 1999.

In less developed nations, informally built homes and settlements are typically at greatest risk of damage. Given that they are often situated on land to which the occupant has no legal title and from which he or she could be forcibly removed, informally built houses are usually not constructed robustly enough to withstand storm damage. Anderson and colleagues (2010) estimate that 60 per cent of houses in hurricane-prone eastern Caribbean nations have been built in the absence of build-ing regulations. In Jakarta, collections of self-built homes (*kampongs*) in flood-prone areas typically have no second story, meaning that residents cannot escape the path of floods by running up (Texier 2008). Despite this risk, *kampongs* continue to be rebuilt in similar fashion in similar locations (Tunas and Peresthu 2010). Lall and Deichmann (2011) point out that this dynamic is common across developing regions, and can in part be resolved by providing the urban poor access to land to which they enjoy clear title; this in turn typically leads to improved building quality and pro-vides the occupants collateral that gives them access to credit with which to finance improvements to their homes.

4.4.5 Social Inequality

A recurrent theme in the preceding pages and in the case studies that follow is that poverty and social marginalization increase the risk of physical harm and loss of shel-ter during extreme events. This should not surprise. The poor and marginalized tend to be the ones living in less sturdy housing, who have less access to communications and transportation, and who lack resources to draw upon to improve their housing to withstand an extreme event or to rebuild it after one (Clark et al. 1998; Cutter, Mitchell, and Scott 2000). Ethnic minorities, children, the elderly, and those in poor health or with physical disabilities are often disproportionately represented among those most vulnerable to extreme weather events (Cutter 2010; Bjarnadottir, Li, and Stewart 2011; Emrich and Cutter 2011). Women, especially those who head house-holds, tend to experience higher rates of poverty than men, and so they, too, may be at elevated risk of loss of life and displacement (Morrow 1999). These are broad-brush assertions, however, and within any given population there will be patterns of wealth distribution, access to opportunity, and social justice norms particular to that place. Furthermore, the degree of loss and harm experienced during an extreme event does have a potential influence on migration patterns, but this relationship is not a simple stimulus-response effect. As later shown in the example of the Vietnamese commu-nity in New Orleans, socially and economically marginalized groups can potentially mobilize sufficient social capital in the wake of an extreme event to quickly reestab-lish and resume occupancy of their neighborhoods and communities.

4.5 Adaptation to Extreme Weather Events

The human impacts of extreme weather events vary considerably from one location to another, even between areas where the physical and climatological conditions are similar. The contrast in impacts of tropical cyclones in the United States as compared with those in a less developed country like Bangladesh highlights the role of adapta-tion in the creation or moderation of vulnerability. In 1991, a tropical cyclone killed an estimated one hundred thousand people in Bangladesh, while the following year a much more severe cyclone, Hurricane Andrew, killed only twenty-three people in the United States (but caused an estimated $23 billion in property damage) (Adger et al. 2005). Both Florida and Bangladesh are low-lying, heavily populated coastal areas where tropical cyclones are common. Why was there such a marked difference in outcomes?

Part of the reason relates to the differences in housing stocks, which are much more variable in Bangladesh in terms of their robustness in the face of storms, and the larger number of poor Bangladeshis who live in highly exposed places like unstable slopes and flood-prone locations. The difference in resources available for emergency preparedness and response also had much to do with the stark contrast (Lindell, Kang, and Prater 2011). The United States has for many decades operated highly sophisticated meteorological systems that watch for tropical storm genesis and seek to provide as much advance warning as possible to exposed populations. Most Floridians have access to information and communications technologies (ICTs), such as television, radio, telephones, and, in the years since Hurricane Andrew, Internet and cell phones, meaning that storm warnings and instructions can be disseminated quickly and easily. U.S. state and federal governments have emergency management plans that include establishing evacuation routes and emergency shelters, allowing most people the opportunity to get out of harm's way. Only in more recent years have storm monitoring technologies, emergency planning, and access to ICTs in Bangladesh started to catch up with those in the United States. As they have done so, the death toll from tropical storms has dropped accordingly (Paul 2009). In other words, proactive adaptation is of tremendous importance in reducing the loss of life during extreme events and, by reducing the amount of disruption to people's lives and livelihood, reduces the likelihood that migration will follow.

Even at its best, proactive adaptation cannot entirely eliminate deaths, injuries, damage to buildings and infrastructure, displacement of people from their homes, and disruption to their livelihoods. Safer buildings can reduce the loss or damage to housing stocks, but a direct hit from a tornado or a hurricane is still going to cause damage and harm. Advance preparation and evacuation can save lives, but are not always possible. Slower-onset events like cold spells and heat waves can most easily be recognized and planned for, with accommodations made for those most at risk. Tropical cyclone tracking is continually getting more sophisticated, and so it is possible to get at least a few days warning in most cases; the challenge is less in the prediction than in making sure systems are in place for spreading word efficiently and ensuring people know what steps to take. Sudden-onset, localized events like tornadoes present more of a challenge. Residents of exposed areas can be advised what general precautions and preparations to take in case of a tornado, but there is often little or no time to give any more advance warning than simply that tornadoes are possible given the weather conditions. The result is that people typically do not evacuate because of tornadoes, but can seek local emergency shelter where it exists (Nigg, Barnshaw, and Torres 2006). Where advance evacuation is possible and is carried out, as it was in the case of Hurricane Katrina, an extra dynamic is created in that, by physically removing people from their place of residence, they are dislocated from social networks and other place-specific assets that must be mobilized for post-disaster recovery when they return.

In the previous chapter, the MESA function was introduced, suggesting that the potential for migration in response to a climate event or condition is a function of the nature of the exposure, the sensitivity of those exposed, and the capacity of the affected population to adapt through ways other than migration. When an extreme weather event occurs, the likelihood that people will continue living in the affected location (or return if they have evacuated) or choose to migrate elsewhere is positively related to the aggregated adaptive capacity of actors at all scales (macro-, meso-, and micro-) in the affected area. If the livelihoods of those affected return swiftly and successfully to some degree of normalcy, people are less likely to migrate away from the affected area. They are even less likely to leave if their place-specific economic capital, such as homes or businesses, survives the event, or if they have strong, local social capital. This helps explain why certain types of extreme climate events, like tropical cyclones, are much more likely to have a direct effect on migration patterns than less sudden, less physically destructive events like heat waves or blizzards.[3]

From an institutional perspective, successful adaptation to extreme events means having the capacity to get those affected back to living in suitable, permanent homes as quickly as possible, and restoring their means of household income. This is not a simple process, especially in the wake of large-scale events like tropical cyclones. Following an extreme event there is a range of potential sheltering needs, including emergency shelters, intermediate temporary housing, and permanent replacement housing (Nigg et al. 2006). Meeting these needs means mobilizing a broad range of resources at multiple scales: from governments and institutions at regional, national, and (potentially) international levels; the savings and resources of individuals and households; financial networks, through mechanisms such as insurance; community-level organizations; and informal social networks. The greater the resources an affected population can mobilize, the lesser the chance members of that population will be obliged to relocate elsewhere for lack of other options. Even in a poor nation with weak formal government institutions, such as Bangladesh, prompt responses and assistance from other sectors of society, such as nongovernmental organizations (NGOs) and social networks, enable communities to recover quickly from extreme

---

[3] This does not mean to say that temperature extremes could not have indirect effects on migration patterns of some households or individuals. For example, someone whose respiratory condition is aggravated by extreme heat may decide to move to a new home closer to health care facilities or to relocate to a cooler climate. Researchers have conducted few scholarly studies on this topic, creating an opportunity for future research.

events without large-scale displacement or permanent out-migration (Paul 1998, 2005; see also the Bangladesh case study in the next chapter).

Any life-changing event has the potential to stimulate thoughts of migration, and experiencing an extreme weather event is certainly a significant moment in the life of a community and its members. It is very rare that a settlement will be entirely abandoned following an extreme event, even in absolutely dire situations (McLeman 2011a). In most cases, the majority of people who lived in a given area prior to an extreme event will continue to live there afterward. Those who do leave may be sizeable in number, but are likely to be a minority of the overall population just the same. The question therefore becomes, what distinguishes those who adapt and remain from those who adapt by leaving? And among those who do leave, where do they go, for how long, and for what purposes? Recalling the continuum of migrant agency shown in Chapter 2 (Figure 2.2), it can be expected that different types of migration may emerge from a single extreme event, from distress migration to opportunistic labor migration, reflecting different degrees of migrant agency. The most noticeable will be those left homeless by the first-order impacts, the ones whose faces populate TV screens and newspaper photos following extreme events. However, the longer-term impacts on livelihoods and well-being may stretch out much longer than the immediate days after the fact, and so too may the migration effects. To pursue these questions further, two case studies of relatively recent hurricane-related migration are now used to help tease out the particular interactions that give rise to migration and the characteristics of subsequent migrations.

4.6 Case Study: The Impacts of Hurricane Katrina on Population Movements in New Orleans

The best-studied extreme event of recent years is Hurricane Katrina, which struck the Gulf of Mexico coast of the United States in August 2005. The storm is believed to have killed more than eighteen hundred people (almost one thousand people in the state of Louisiana alone (Brunkard, Namulanda, and Ratard 2008)) and caused an estimated US$125 billion in damage (Melton et al. 2009). Approximately one million people were evacuated or displaced from their homes (Elliott and Pais 2006), half of them from the New Orleans metropolitan area. Over two hundred thousand homes were damaged or destroyed in the state of Louisiana, and the City of New Orleans alone experienced an estimated US$23 billion in damage to private property and public infrastructure (Pistrika and Jonkman 2009). Images of tens of thousands of mostly African American residents sheltering in the Superdome sports stadium were broadcast around the world, iconic reminders that even the wealthiest of nations are vulnerable to natural hazards. The impacts of Hurricane Katrina on migration and population dynamics in New Orleans are the particular focus of this case study.

The low-lying coastal delta within which New Orleans is situated experiences extreme weather events and flooding on an ongoing basis. Kates and colleagues (2006) suggest the city's 300-year history can be read as a long process of recurrent losses, recovery, and reconstruction. The first hurricane to hit the European settlement at New Orleans occurred in 1717, while the twentieth century brought particularly severe hurricanes in 1915, 1947, 1965, 1969, and 1979. Between 1978 and 2000, the New Orleans metropolitan area[4] experienced nineteen flood events and eighteen hurricane events, an average of one a year (Burby 2006). After 1965's particularly destructive Hurricane Betsy, which displaced three hundred thousand people and destroyed twenty-seven thousand buildings, the federal government began investing heavily in levees and other physical infrastructure to reduce the risk of storm surge–related flooding of the city (Kates et al. 2006). A by-product of this program was the stimulation of additional housing development in especially low-lying areas that had previously not been built upon. By 2005, the City of New Orleans could be described as three shallow bowls holding a half million people at or below sea level (Kates et al. 2006). As population and economic growth expanded in the Mississippi Delta region during the twentieth century, many of the naturally occurring barrier islands that sheltered the region from storm surges had been developed or channelized, reducing their protective capacity (Grzegorzewski et al. 2011).

Hurricane Katrina formed east of the Bahamas in August 2005 and travelled westward into the Gulf of Mexico, at times reaching category 5 wind speeds (i.e. 250km/h), the highest of the categories used to classify tropical cyclones on the Saffir-Simpson scale (Graumann et al. 2005). By the time it reached the U.S. Gulf Coast on August 29, the storm had sustained wind speeds of more than 200 kilometers per hour, making it a category 3 storm. The most serious damage to the City of New Orleans was caused not by the winds, but by the combined effects of heavy rains (as much as 350 millimeters received within twenty-four hours) and a massive storm surge that at some points along the coast approached nine meters in height (Kates et al. 2006, Melton et al. 2009). Within hours of the storm's arrival, protective flood walls began to fail, overwhelming the pumps used to drain water into Lake Pontchartrain, allowing rain and flood water to pool in the lowest-lying parts of the city. In some neighborhoods, flood waters reached up to four meters, and not until forty days after the storm was the city finally drained (Jonkman et al. 2009). Drainage of the city was complicated by a second failure of the protective levees on September 23 during a new storm surge that

---

[4] A variety of spatial areas are regularly used to describe 'New Orleans', including the City of New Orleans (consisting of Orleans Parish and its contiguous parishes); the Metropolitan Statistical Area (MSA), which consists of seven parishes; the Combined Statistical Area, consisting of eight parishes; or Greater New Orleans, which consists of ten parishes. A parish in Louisiana is roughly equivalent to a county in other states. In the case of Katrina, out-migration was higher from the City of New Orleans than from parishes in the larger areas. Although it may appear repetitive, for sake of clarity the case study will refer explicitly to *the City of New Orleans* when referring to that unit, and *the metropolitan area* when referring to any of the larger units.

accompanied Hurricane Rita as it passed the city to its landfall along the Texas coast (Graumann et al. 2005).

On August 28, the day before Katrina made landfall, the mayor of the City of New Orleans ordered a mandatory evacuation of the city. Approximately 70 per cent of the population left, but as many as one hundred thousand people did not, for reasons such as lack of transportation, health conditions, job commitments, or belief that the risk was not as high as reported (Elliott and Pais 2006, Nigg et al. 2006). When the protective levees failed, tens of thousands of residents converged on the Superdome and the Ernest Morial Convention Center, which had been designated as shelters of last resort. Across the metropolitan area, the response by governments at all levels in the immediate aftermath of Katrina was confused and disorganized (Schneider 2005). A major challenge was that U.S. emergency management systems contained many layers of bureaucracy and jurisdictional overlaps. Decision making could not be carried out quickly enough, and officials were often uncertain who was responsible for what (Sobel and Leeson 2006). Wal-Mart stores in the region were able to distribute emergency water supplies more quickly than could the U.S. Federal Emergency Management Agency (FEMA) (Rosegrant 2007).

Those who had stayed behind in New Orleans and had nowhere else to go were transferred by bus to more distant temporary shelters, particularly the Reliant Park stadium complex in Houston, Texas, 550 kilometers away. This process took most of the following week. As Reliant Park became increasingly overcrowded, evacuees were transported to temporary shelters in San Antonio and Dallas. By September 6, it was estimated that two hundred fifty thousand evacuees were sheltering in Texas, with other evacuees found in every state in the United States (Nigg et al. 2006). After Houston, the most common evacuation destinations were suburban New Orleans parishes and Louisiana's capital city of Baton Rouge, followed by Atlanta, San Antonio, and Memphis in that order (Frey, Singer, and Park 2007). A Red Cross telephone survey conducted one month following the storm found that roughly 40 per cent of evacuees were living in a private home owned by someone else, while 50 per cent were staying in commercial accommodation (i.e. hotels, rental units) or temporary shelters provided by authorities (Elliott and Pais 2006). In a study of evacuees living in temporary accommodation in Houston, Brodie and colleagues (2006) found that a disproportionate number were African American (more than 90 per cent) and had low household incomes. Half were married, with 45 per cent having children under age eighteen. More than half had no health insurance, and more than 40 per cent suffered from chronic health conditions. Roughly 60 per cent had not evacuated before the storm hit, their reasons for not doing so including not having received clear instructions before the storm, not having access to transportation, and not having fully appreciated the scale of Katrina. Some stated they would have been able to leave in advance, but were obliged to stay behind for work reasons or to care for others.

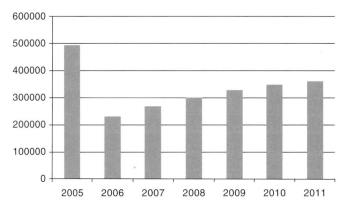

Figure 4.6. Population of New Orleans before and after Hurricane Katrina. Data source: U.S. Census (www.census.gov)

Of particular interest here is the question of who returned to the City of New Orleans and who resettled elsewhere in the months and years since Katrina. As shown in Figure 4.6, the population of the city remains well below pre-Katrina levels. Rates of return peaked approximately four months after the storm and then slowed (Fussell, Sastry, and Van Landingham 2010). The longer evacuees remained away from the city, the less likely they were to return, especially after nine months had passed. Vigdor (2008) notes that the City of New Orleans had experienced gradual population and economic decline prior to Katrina, so the storm should also be seen as having accelerated and exacerbated preexisting out-migration pressures. Pre-Katrina employment levels in traditional sectors like manufacturing had already fallen well below the average for comparable urban centers. Average household incomes and education attainment levels were also below national averages, as were average house prices.

Evacuation destinations, resettlement locations, and return rates displayed pronounced distinctions along racial lines, with black residents generally less likely than white residents to return (Figure 4.7). A year after Katrina, the percentage of African Americans within the population of New Orleans dropped from 68 per cent to 59 per cent (Vigdor 2008). Black residents tended to evacuate (either by choice or with government assistance) to more distant destinations, such as Houston, Baton Rouge, Dallas, and Atlanta, as compared with white residents, who were more likely to remain within the vicinity of New Orleans and its adjacent suburbs (Frey et al. 2007). Fussell and colleagues (2010) estimated that within three months of Katrina, half of white residents who had evacuated had returned to the City of New Orleans, but more than a year later less than half of black residents had returned. Educated white residents who were gainfully employed and/or retired, and whose home remained habitable, had the highest rate of return to New Orleans (Sastry 2009). Vu and colleagues (2009) found that residents of Vietnamese origin, who numbered approximately twelve thousand

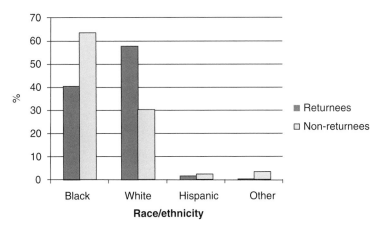

Figure 4.7. Proportion of returnees and non-returnees, by race. Data source: Groen and Polivka (2010).

prior to Katrina, also had above-average rates of return (roughly two out of three) one year after the storm.

The very different patterns of displacement and return across racial groups in New Orleans reflects important socioeconomic distinctions that existed within the population and that often fell along racial lines. One of these was differential access to housing and tenure. A year after Katrina, there were roughly one hundred thousand housing units in New Orleans, down 50 per cent from a previous count done in 2000 (Vigdor 2008). Rates of housing damage varied by neighborhood, and those that experienced the deepest flood waters had the lowest rates of return (Finch, Emrich, and Cutter 2010). These neighborhoods tended to have large black populations (Groen and Polivka 2010, Fussell et al. 2010). Return rates were particularly slow in the city's Ninth Ward, an area of below-average incomes home to approximately fifty thousand people before the storm, the vast majority African Americans (Green, Bates, and Smyth 2007). This neighborhood was one of the last to be reopened by authorities after the storm, with electricity and potable water not being widely available until fourteen months after the storm. Return rates were also strongly associated with home ownership (Landry et al. 2007, Paxson and Rouse 2008, Groen and Polivka 2010). Three-quarters of those who owned a home that was still inhabitable had returned to New Orleans within a month, while only one-quarter of those who had been renting accommodations returned (Elliott and Pais 2006). Homeowners whose properties suffered extensive damage tended to have lower rates of return than those whose homes were quickly made habitable again, with homes owned by black residents having typically experienced more severe damage than those owned by whites (Fussell et al. 2010).

A number of factors slowed the repair and replacement of the damaged housing stock. Most low-income residents did not have flood insurance, and had to await ad hoc relief payments from government (Green et al. 2007). Concerns about the future inadequacy of the city's flood defenses led to a spike in household insurance premiums for reconstructed homes, and a severe shortage of construction laborers meant that even those with the funds and insurance to restore their homes had trouble finding someone to do the work. Lack of shops, basic services, and schools persisted even a year after the storm, creating ongoing disincentives to return. The lengthy period required to rebuild critical infrastructure created a particular need for longer-term temporary housing to accommodate people awaiting the repair or replacement of their homes (Nigg et al. 2006). Consequently, housing prices and rental rates were considerably higher following Katrina, and likely constituted a significant disincentive for return to the city. Finch and colleagues (2010) found that a number of working-class neighborhoods where residents tended to be neither especially poor nor well-off experienced very slow rebuilding and return rates, and suggest this is because residents lacked sufficient resources of their own but were not so poor as to attract institutional assistance.

The post-Katrina population of New Orleans showed a number of other socioeconomic changes from the pre-Katrina population (Figures 4.8 a–e). The average age of the population was six years older after Katrina, and children formed a smaller proportion of the population (Paxson and Rouse 2008, Vigdor 2008). The average number of people per household post-Katrina was also much higher, not surprising given the housing shortage that persisted. At the same time, the rate of separation within families (in terms of an adult member leaving the household) was more than double the national average (Rendall 2011). The average level of education attainment in post-Katrina New Orleans was higher than before, reflecting the higher average education rates of returning white residents (Fussell et al. 2010). Groen and Polivka (2010) suggest older people had higher rates of return because they were more likely to own homes and were less likely to be affected by labor market conditions. People with lower family incomes were also less likely to return, likely because of the local labor market disruption and higher costs of rental accommodation. Younger people and those able to find higher-paying employment in the city to which they evacuated were less likely to return to New Orleans (Landry et al. 2007). Neighborhoods where schools, libraries, hospitals, and child care facilities quickly returned to function were also associated with high rates of population return; however, it is not evident whether this was a driver of evacuee return or an outcome of it (Groen and Polivka 2010).

There is discussion in the literature as to whether a 'sense of place' played a role in evacuee decisions to return to New Orleans (Landry et al. 2007, Sastry 2009). In their qualitative research among residents of the lower Ninth Ward, Chamlee-Wright and Storr (2009) found that a sense of place did factor into decision making, but that there was no one set of clearly defined characteristics that captured it. Rather, decisions to return were influenced by a suite of amenities such as strong local family and social networks; cultural attributes specific to New Orleans like the food, music, and

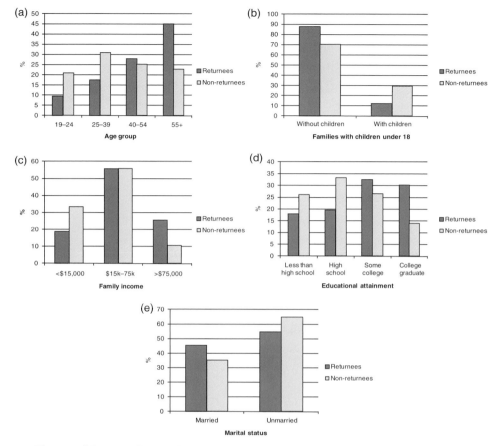

Figures 4.8. a–e: Selected demographic and socioeconomic characteristics of returnees/non-returnees. Data source: Groen and Polivka (2010).

funeral traditions; and the ability to socialize out of doors with neighbors. Evacuees who chose not to return to New Orleans despite having similar 'sense of place' sentiments cited additional reasons for not returning, such as lack of employment, lack of homeownership, poor-quality schools in New Orleans, and the sense that the quality of life in New Orleans had changed irrevocably.

Although much of the literature focuses on the distinctions between blacks and whites in terms of their likelihood of return, other racial groups did not necessarily follow similar patterns. The Vietnamese community had a relatively high rate of return. This is notable because members of that community tended to be among the more economically disadvantaged in New Orleans and lived on the city's badly damaged east side (Vu et al. 2009). Within this group, rates of return were highest among married couples and families with dependent elders and/or children under eighteen – the opposite of the broader citywide trend. For the Vietnamese community, especially strong social capital appears to have been a key factor distinguishing them from the larger groups within the city's population. Airriess and colleagues (2007) documented how the Vietnamese community was able to mobilize local, regional, and national social networks to acquire resources needed for recovery and rebuilding, with the church community playing an important coordinating role. New Orleans has seen steady growth in its Vietnamese population in subsequent years, suggesting the community is now well reestablished (Plyer 2011).

The Latino population underwent a dramatic transformation in the wake of Katrina. Prior to Katrina, the metropolitan area of New Orleans had a Latino population of just under sixty thousand of diverse national origins, half of whom had been born in the United States, and nearly three-quarters of whom were American citizens (Drever 2008). In the City of New Orleans proper, Latinos made up roughly 4.5 per cent of the total population (Fussell 2007), and their numbers grew very slowly in comparison with the national rate of increase in the Latino population (Plyer 2011). In the immediate aftermath of Katrina, there was an urgent need for workers in the demolition and construction sectors, attracting thousands of Latino laborers, who make up roughly one-fifth of the workforce in the construction industry nationwide (Fussell 2007). In the rush to get the reconstruction under way, much of the government-funded work was subcontracted, with authorities turning a blind eye to the fact that many of these workers were undocumented migrants (Gorman 2010). The city's Latino population quickly doubled with the new arrivals, many of them young, unmarried, non-English speaking men from Mexico and Central and South America (Fussell 2007, 2009a). Their movement to New Orleans was typically supported by their employers, and few of the new arrivals had any strong preexisting social connections to the city. Despite exploitative practices of employers, often hazardous work conditions, inadequate shelter and health care, and prevalent drug abuse within the casual laborer population, these young workers came because the wages on offer were better than the wages offered in other U.S. cities (Fletcher et al. 2007, Fussell 2009b, Weil 2009, Valdez et al. 2010). Few arrived with any intention of settling permanently in New Orleans or the surrounding area, but intended to remain only so long as it made economic sense (Vinck et al. 2009). The net effect of Katrina is that New Orleans has emerged as a gateway city for Latino migration to the United States (Plyer 2011).

Although much is made of race in scholarly and public discussions of postmigration population patterns in New Orleans, race is a coarse and nonexplanatory distinction between those who returned to New Orleans and those who resettled elsewhere, and does not explain the influx of new migrants to the city. Blacks are not biologically or psychologically predisposed to migration any more than whites or Asians or Latinos, in New Orleans or anyplace else. How race matters is that in pre-Katrina New Orleans, inequities in terms of wealth, education, and housing closely followed racial lines, a legacy of the historical socioeconomic trajectory of the city and the American South more generally (Fussell 2007). These socioeconomic inequalities were manifested geographically within the city, with the most economically margin-alized people (disproportionately black) occupying the neighborhoods most exposed to flood damage. The poor were most heavily dependent on disorganized and inad-equate government assistance, which for many resulted in being transported hundreds of miles away from their homes and social networks. Conversely, better educated and wealthier residents (disproportionately white) lived in better situated, less-damaged neighborhoods, and were less dependent on government for assistance. Being more likely to have an undamaged home to return to and being less exposed to the tightened rental market, they were more likely to return, and did so relatively quickly. The expe-rience of Vietnamese residents, a relatively small and tightly knit group who were more recent entrants to the socio-economy of the city, shows that the ability to mobi-lize social capital can overcome economic shortcomings and institutional ineptness. The influx of young Latino workers speaks to the inequities of the U.S. immigration system and unwillingness of authorities to enforce labor laws, the net result being the creation of an easily exploitable, rapid-reaction workforce of migrant workers that flows to wherever there is a sudden-onset need for labor (Fussell 2009a).

The key lessons from Katrina with respect to the potential for internal migration in response to extreme weather events can be summarized as follows:

- Damage to housing is a key determinant of whether people return (or stay, if evacuation does not occur) or migrate elsewhere
- The competency of institutional authorities to provide relief and recovery assistance is an important influence on how people adapt, especially the poor and marginalized
- Adaptation and migration decisions strongly exhibit path dependency
- Wage labor opportunities exist in the aftermath of the event, and these can influence migra-tion patterns
- Strong social capital can overcome institutional inadequacy and economic adversity in help-ing people adapt in situ

The case of New Orleans is fully consistent with the MESA[5] function introduced in the previous chapter. All residents of the city were sensitive to the impacts of Katrina, but groups that had the highest level of exposure, as experienced through housing damage, and had limited economic or social capital to help them adapt, did indeed have higher rates of non-return. The outcomes witnessed in post-Katrina New Orleans can also be used to check the reliability of the migration process diagram introduced at the end of Chapter 3, which is done through a marked-up version here (Figure 4.9). With one exception, the process diagram is a good fit, the exception being that because New Orleans was evacuated, the question was not whether to leave but whether to return.

---

[5] Potential for migration is a function of exposure, sensitivity, and in situ adaptive capacity.

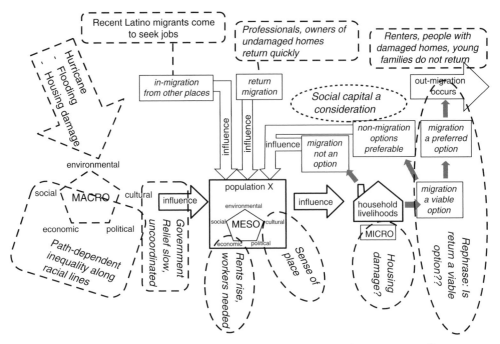

Figure 4.9. Migration outcomes of Hurricane Katrina mapped onto process diagram (Figure 3.9).

4.7 Case Study: International Migration following Hurricane Mitch

The second case study looks more closely at how extreme weather events can influence international migration patterns. Hurricane Mitch was a category 5 storm that made landfall in Central America on October 26, 1998, bringing high winds and heavy rains to much of Honduras and Guatemala, as well as parts of Belize, El Salvador, Nicaragua, and southern Mexico. The storm was a relatively slow-moving one. Rains fell for a full week, saturating soils and making slopes across this rugged area highly susceptible to failure (Bucknam et al. 2001). Extensive deforestation and vegetation clearance had taken place for many decades, enabling the storm to cause widespread landslides and flash flooding in rural and urban areas (Hellin, Haigh, and Marks 1999). Central America had been experiencing significant rural-to-urban migration in the years prior to Mitch. Poor rural migrants arriving in the region's cities had found it difficult to find accommodations in safe places, leading to the development of extensive areas of poor-quality housing on steep slopes or hilltops on the outskirts of urban centers (Pielke et al. 2003). These informal settlements made the slopes unstable and were very dangerous places to be during Mitch.

Mitch was one of the deadliest hurricanes in the history of the Caribbean. Honduras suffered the worst effects, with an estimated seven thousand killed (some reports have suggested as many as seventeen thousand killed (Glantz and Jamieson 2000)), over twelve thousand injured, and more than six hundred thousand people displaced from their homes (UN ECLAC 1999a). Over one hundred thousand people were left home-less in Guatemala, with up to seven hundred fifty thousand experiencing significant harm or livelihood losses (UN ECLAC 1999b). An estimated six thousand dwellings were lost and twenty thousand damaged in Guatemala, while thirty-five thousand were destroyed and fifty thousand damaged in Honduras (UN ECLAC 1999a,b). A disproportionate number of those affected are believed to have lived on or at the base of unstable slopes or in flood-prone parts of river valleys (UN ECLAC 1999a,b).

The storm caused widespread damage to infrastructure and agricultural cropland across the region. Roughly one-half of the affected population lived in rural areas (UN FAO 2001). Livelihoods of the rural poor were severely disrupted, with one-third of rural households in one Honduras-based study reporting lost income due to crop damage (Morris et al. 2002). In Honduras, 90 per cent of the country's infrastructure was damaged, as were many large export-oriented banana and coffee plantations (Glantz and Jamieson 2000). Total losses in the agricultural sector of Honduras were estimated at more than US$960 million (UN FAO 2001). The distribution of economic losses differed across Honduran society. Although in absolute terms the value of economic losses per family unit was greatest among wealthier households, economic losses expressed as a percentage of total household assets were highest among the rural poor (Morris et al. 2002).

The scale of the loss of life, damage to housing stock, and loss of livelihoods due to Mitch reflected the region's high rates of poverty and lack of proactive adaptive capacity on the part of governments and institutions (Comfort et al. 1999). In many parts of the region, people received little advance warning of the storm, and dangerous areas were not evacuated. The countries affected by Mitch had much less in the way of financial resources or institutional capacity to direct at recovery efforts as compared with the United States post Katrina. Although the international community pledged large amounts of financial assistance, much of it never arrived, and that which did was slow in coming, meaning that those affected by Mitch had to rely heavily on family resources and social networks (Cupples 2007). One study found that the average rural Honduran household received less than US$10 of post-disaster assistance, primarily in the forms of food, clothing, and medicine (Morris and Wodon 2003). After the hurricane, more people were seeking employment locally than before, particularly women, even though wage income opportunities were scarce (World Bank 2001).

Out-migration from rural areas slowed temporarily as people immediately engaged in rebuilding homes, replanting crops, and repairing basic infrastructure damaged by the storm (e.g. Carr 2008). After this initial recovery period, migration became a key form of adaptation in the months and years following Mitch for many rural and urban households. Remittances from relatives abroad had already been an important source of household income and security for Central Americans, and their importance grew after Mitch. In 1999, it was estimated that Hondurans received US$400 million

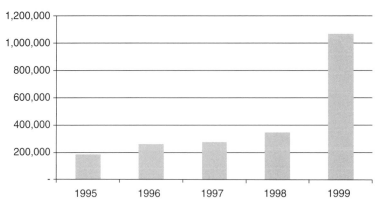

Figure 4.10. Estimated migration out of Honduras. Data source: UN FAO (2001).

in remittances from abroad, primarily from the United States; a decade later, total annual remittances were believed to exceed US$2 billion (UN FAO 2001, McKenzie and Menjivar 2011). Migration out of Honduras in particular spiked in the year following Mitch (Figure 4.10); how much of this was temporary as opposed to permanent migration is not clear from the available statistics.

Intranational migration (from rural areas to urban centers), intraregional migration (from one country to neighboring ones), and long-distance international migration to the United States all increased in the wake of Hurricane Mitch. Costa Rica, an economically and politically stable neighbor of the Mitch-affected countries, and the United States were key destinations. Studies have found notable distinctions in the socioeconomic characteristics of those who migrated to Costa Rica as compared with those who left for the United States. In a study of Nicaraguan migrants, Funkhauser (2009) found that those destined for Costa Rica tended to come from the poorest households in Nicaragua, and their migration often resulted in a rapid, observable improvement in the sending household's economic well-being. Migration to Costa Rica was facilitated by the presence of well-established social networks between the two countries, Nicaraguans having long travelled to Costa Rica in search of seasonal employment in agriculture, construction, and domestic service (Murrugarra and Herrera 2011). Migration to Costa Rica provided a low-cost, quick way to boost a Nicaraguan family's financial assets after Mitch. The majority of migrants going from Nicaragua to Costa Rica originated in urban centers, but there was also a large component of rural out-migrants given the seasonal agricultural work available there.

The characteristics of migrants bound for the United States differed in a number of ways. In the case of Nicaraguans, these migrants were overwhelmingly from urban centers and came from less destitute households (Funkhauser 2009). In Honduras, it quickly became common practice in the post-Mitch era for households to send the member with the highest earning potential to the United States in search of wage

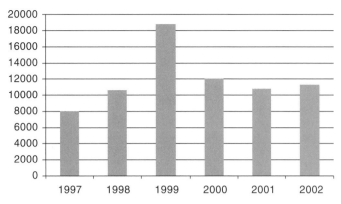

Figure 4.11. Deportable Honduran nationals apprehended by U.S. authorities, by year. Data source: U.S. INS Statistical Handbooks 1997–2002.

employment (Schmalzbauer 2004). The distance and difficulty in getting to the United States and across the border made this an expensive undertaking. Many migrants had to hire migrant smuggling organizations (known colloquially as *coyotes*), with the family members remaining behind responsible for paying off incurred debts that averaged US$5,000 (McKenzie and Menjivar 2011). It is therefore not surprising that migrants destined to the United States tended to come from less destitute and overwhelmingly urban households, as the household needed to have access to local wage labor markets to finance the migration debt. Unlike intraregional migration to a destination like Costa Rica, the economic benefits of sending a family member to the United States were less immediate. While social networks were important in both cases, the longer, costlier journey to the United States meant that household financial assets and the skills of the migrant himself or herself figured much more prominently in this undertaking (Murrugarra and Herrera 2011).

Post-Mitch migration placed new pressures on the U.S. immigration system, at that time run by the Immigration and Naturalization Service (INS). A sudden increase was observed after Mitch in the number of apprehensions of illegal migrants arriving from Honduras (Figure 4.11). Given the already sizeable population of Central American origin living in the United States, the American government granted to El Salvadoran, Guatemalan, Honduran, and Nicaraguan nationals who were in the United States prior to 30 December 1998 Temporary Protected Status (TPS), a provision of U.S. law that allows a group of persons temporary refuge in the United States when conditions in their home country pose a danger to personal safety because of ongoing armed conflict or an environmental disaster (US INS 2002). The program was originally scheduled to last eighteen months, at which time it was cancelled for El Salvadorans[6]

---

[6] TPS would be reinstated for El Salvadorans in 2001 following severe earthquakes.

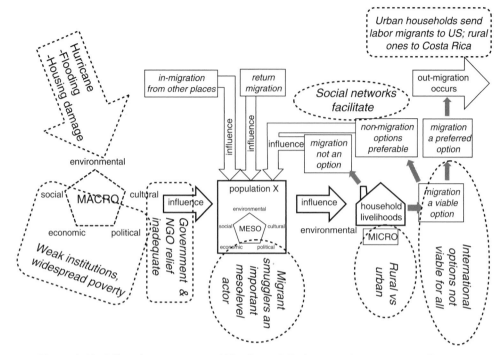

Figure 4.12. Migration outcomes of Hurricane Mitch mapped onto process diagram.

and Guatemalans but left in place for Hondurans and Nicaraguans for more than a decade. The practical implications of TPS were that nationals of these two countries would not face deportation until such time as the TPS program expired. By 2003, five years after Mitch, approximately one hundred fifty thousand Hondurans and Nicaraguans were living and working in the United States under TPS (Kugler and Yuksel 2008). Most migrants arriving from Central America in the two years following Mitch settled in states bordering Mexico or situated along the Gulf of Mexico (Kugler and Yuksel 2008)).

Post-Mitch migration patterns highlight the importance of access to capital as an important moderator of adaptation and migration decisions after an extreme event. Labor migration and remittances were important ways for households to acquire essential financial capital to rebuild their homes and livelihoods, given the inadequacy of government and NGO assistance. For households of limited financial means, the most affordable option was short-term, short-distance labor migration within the region. Migration to the United States took resources beyond the means of the poorest, because it required the household to mobilize social networks, to have enough money to finance the trip (or be willing to go into debt to smugglers), and to forego the migrant's labor and earning potential for an extended time. The costs and risks of international migration were thus borne not just by the migrant, but by the household and family network.[7] Post-Mitch migration patterns can also be successfully mapped onto the process diagram introduced in the previous chapter, marked up here in Figure 4.12.

4.8 Chapter Summary

A number of general conclusions can be drawn from the case studies and the discussion of the literature that preceded them. A first is that the sheer size of injuries, deaths, damage to property and livelihoods, population displacements, and migration after a large-scale, sudden-onset extreme event can be considerable. The number of people exposed to the threat of extreme events around the world is growing because of general population trends and landscape modification. The types of extreme events to which populations are exposed varies by region, and within a given region residential location and housing quality further influence exposure. These latter factors are closely tied to social, economic, and political processes that over the course of time create inequalities that play out spatially, with the poorest and least adaptable often living in more exposed locations. Damage to housing has a critical influence on whether people adapt through migration or via other means. Those who lack homeownership are at risk of inflated post-event housing costs that may create an impetus for resettling elsewhere.

The importance of institutions in preparing and warning people in advance and in assisting those affected in recovering from extreme events is critical. The less capacity institutions have, the more adaptation falls to households and meso-level actors. Access to housing after an extreme event is a critical determinant of migration potential. Note the use here of the word *access*. Homeownership is a significant reason not to migrate, so long as the home is not destroyed. Homeownership and the quality of home construction being lowest among those least well-off financially helps explain why the poor are most likely to become migrants.

Households' adaptation choices, including migration, are strongly influenced by the economic and social capital they have accumulated prior to the event. Although the poor are often at great risk of displacement from extreme events, their limited financial means may limit their migration choices. The cost of long-distance, international migration being extremely high (especially if it requires clandestine movement across borders), the largest amount of migration is likely to be intraregional, to destinations where wage labor is available and migration networks are already in place.

Elements of many of the main theories of migration reviewed in Chapter 2 are present in the examples cited in this chapter, with the MESA function and the process

---

[7] Winkels (2012) provides a useful essay on how migration risks are shared across social and family networks, using the example of internal migration in Vietnam.

diagrams from Chapter 3 shown to be useful tools that illustrate the connections. It is also evident from the examples that a range of migration patterns can emerge from the same event depending on the interplay of social, economic, political, and cultural processes within the exposed population. These in turn transform the longer-term characteristics and dynamics of the affected population, as witnessed by the emergence of post-Katrina New Orleans as a gateway city for Latino migration to the United States.

5

River Valley Flooding and Migration

5.1 Introduction

Of the various types of natural hazards to which human settlements are exposed, flooding affects the greatest number of people worldwide (Jonkman 2005). The Millennium Ecosystem Assessment suggests as many as 2 billion people worldwide may live in areas exposed to flooding risk (Millennium Ecosystem Assessment 2005). The vast majority of the world's nations – an estimated 85 per cent – have experienced significant flood events in recent decades (Bakker 2009). Like droughts and extreme storms, floods are inherent, regularly occurring outcomes of climatic processes. In some regions, flooding is an annual risk because of high seasonal variability in precipitation. In others, floods occur irregularly. The size and scale of the human impacts of extreme floods can be tremendous. There are the immediate risks of death from drowning or injury from flowing debris, outbreaks of waterborne and insect-borne diseases generated by standing waters, and the longer-term mental health effects of experiencing such a crisis (Ohl 2000, Ahern et al. 2005). Housing, businesses, and critical infrastructure may be destroyed or damaged, creating enormous financial costs and requiring much time and effort to repair and replace. Yet, while floodplains are inherently hazardous, they also tend to make especially suitable locations for human settlements, providing easy access to fertile soils, potable water, hydraulic flow for irrigation and powering turbines, and the potential to transport goods and people by boat. Researchers estimate floodplains provide more than a quarter of all ecosystem services consumed by humans, despite representing a small fraction of the Earth's surface (Tockner and Stanford 2002). It is therefore not surprising that human population numbers continue to rise in many of the world's most flood-prone river valleys and deltas despite the risks.

Scholars expect anthropogenic climate change to increase the physical risk of flooding in many river valleys in coming decades (Kundzewicz, Hirabayashi, and Kanae 2010). Cultural, economic, political, and social processes all figure heavily

111

into determining the relative degree of exposure to flooding within a given population and the access to and utilization of adaptation (McLeman and Smit 2006b). Institutional capacity to manage and control flood risks varies considerably from one country or region to another. In places where institutional capacity is weak and flooding is a recurrent risk, households typically develop over time a range of adaptive livelihood strategies. Especially in rural areas in less developed countries, these adaptation strategies may include temporary or seasonal labor migration. Extreme floods can generate increases in more permanent out-migration from affected areas, but existing research suggests that people are more likely to rebuild and reoccupy the same flood-prone locations than to migrate away from them.

This chapter:

- Reviews the characteristics and the physical and human causes of river valley flooding
- Describes common institutional measures taken to manage and reduce people's exposure to floods, as well as those implemented after a flood event
- Identifies differences in migration responses to annual, seasonal flooding as compared with more irregular, extreme flood events, and
- Uses case studies from Bangladesh and China to analyze in greater detail the interactions of environmental and human forces across scales that influence migration patterns and behavior in the wake of floods

5.2 Physical and Human Dimensions of Vulnerability to River Valley Floods

5.2.1 General Characteristics

In simple terms, a flood occurs when water flows onto land that is not ordinarily under water, a definition adapted from Ward (1978). Douglas and colleagues (2008) identify four general categories of floods human settlements and habitations may experience:

(1) Inundations of buildings due to poor drainage
(2) The rapid rise of water in small catchments and watercourses within a settlement
(3) Inundations from rivers and larger watercourses along which a settlement is located, and
(4) Flooding of coastal settlements

The first two categories of floods are localized phenomena that can occur in virtually any settlement, and can be triggered by even relatively brief precipitation events. The frequency and location of the second two categories of larger flood events are more closely linked to prevailing regional climatic patterns and conditions.

Rivers and other inland watercourses flood when high volumes of water cause them to overspill their banks or channels onto surrounding lands, typically described as the *floodplain*. Floodplains are estimated to cover somewhere between eight hundred thousand and 2 million square kilometers of the Earth's surface (Tockner and Stanford 2002). A number of climate-related factors, such as heavy rains, rapid melting of snow or ice, ice jams, and landslides, may cause river flooding. In arid and semiarid regions, dry or intermittent channels may be subject to flash flooding when rare precipitation events occur. In these latter cases, the water may not actually overflow its ephemeral channel, but people unaccustomed to the presence of water in such channels may find themselves in harm's way when a flash flood occurs.[1] River flooding can also be caused by deliberate human actions, such as decisions to build a dam and flood upstream lands, or by the unintended consequences of human actions, such as downstream flash flooding caused by the failure of a dam or other water containment structure.

Coastal floods occur in low-lying areas adjacent to oceans, such as coastal plains, estuaries, deltas, and low-lying islands. The forces that cause ocean water to overflow coastal lands may be geotechnical in origin, such as tsunamis caused by offshore earthquakes, or be linked to climatic events, such as tropical cyclones and their accompanying storm surges. Coastal flooding typically takes place when events occur that are beyond the usual range of tides, surf, and currents to which a given coastal area is exposed (Smith and Ward 1998). Having just dedicated a chapter to tropical cyclones, whose impacts include coastal storm surges, the remainder of this chapter turns to the impacts of inland watercourse flooding on migration behavior.

5.2.2 Frequency and Severity of Past Floods

Drawing on a number of existing disaster databases, Adhikari and colleagues (2010) estimate 2,900 significant flood events took place during the period from 1998 to 2008, with four countries – the United States, China, India, and Indonesia – each experiencing at least 100 such events. Overall, they found 84 per cent of floods were associated with heavy rain events (including intense monsoons); of the remaining 16 per cent, snowmelt figured in 7 per cent of flood events, tropical cyclones in 6 per cent, failure of dams or levees in 2 per cent, and ice jamming in 1 per cent.[2] The geographical regions most prone to flooding are Southeast Asia, China, Central America, and the Caribbean, regions which have large populations living in geographically exposed locations and where monsoonal precipitation patterns and tropical cyclones are common. Asia in particular, with its many large, densely populated river valleys and deltas, hosts the greatest number of people at risk of being affected by floods (Jonkman 2005).

The scale of human displacement, fatalities, and damage to property and infrastructure during flood events can be tremendous. A 1998 flood event in China's densely

---

[1] See Collins (2010) for examples from Mexico's Paso del Norte region.
[2] The authors note the possibility that some heavy rain events may have been associated with tropical cyclones but not categorized as such in the original databases.

populated Yangtze Valley affected more than 200 million people, destroyed almost 10 million homes, and caused an estimated US$420 billion in damage (Zong and Chen 2000, Yin and Li 2001). That same year, more than 60 per cent of Bangladesh was inundated by floods for more than two months, affecting 30 million people, damaging 5 million homes, and requiring the evacuation of more than a million people (Kunii et al. 2002, Kundzewicz et al. 2010). In Pakistan, summer flooding in 2010 affected an estimated 20 million people (Houze et al. 2011). The scale of human fatalities from a single flood event can easily number in the thousands, with the worst fatalities in recent decades experienced in the region around Caracas, Venezuela, in 1999, when thirty thousand people were killed (Jonkman 2005). Flash floods affect fewer people in aggregate than do other types of floods, but have a much greater potential for causing high fatality rates (i.e. the ratio of people killed to people affected) given the difficulty in providing advance warning and evacuating those in harm's way (Jonkman 2005).

From 1950 to the end of the twentieth century, the number of major flood events varied considerably from one year to the next, and did not show any particular trend in terms of frequency (Berz 2000). However, the number of people living in flood-exposed areas and the value of property and infrastructure in those areas has grown considerably in recent decades, in developed and developing countries alike, and continues to do so (Schultz 2001, Mitchell 2003). Combined with the effects of climate change on precipitation patterns and extreme storm events, the potential for greater damages and displacements due to floods will grow. Kundzewicz and colleagues (2010) have estimated that with a two degrees Celsius warming in global average temperatures, roughly 200 million people worldwide would be exposed to floods in river valleys; that estimate rises to more than 500 million people with a four degrees Celsius warming (Hirabayashi and Kanae (2009) arrive at similar estimates).

5.2.3 Physical and Human Processes that Increase Exposure to Riverine Flood Hazards

From a physical standpoint, river valley flooding results from the combination of climatological events and the physical characteristics of a given river basin. Most river valley floods are triggered by excessive precipitation – 'excessive' meaning either large volumes arriving all at once or accumulation over a prolonged period of time (Smith and Ward 1998). In higher latitudes, rapid melting of snow and the formation and sudden failure of ice jams may also trigger river valley flooding, especially in late winter or early spring. In mountainous environments, landslides (often triggered by heavy precipitation) may create temporary dams on rivers that subsequently fail and cause a flash flood downstream (Bonnard 2011). The physical characteristics of the catchment basin are also important. Generally, the larger the upstream catchment area, the greater the potential amount of water to flow past a given point downstream.

The nature of the upstream landscape also matters; steep slopes and impermeable or saturated surfaces hasten the movement of precipitation into river channels and increase the risk of flood surges, while heavy vegetation, wetlands, and permeable surfaces delay the movement of water into channels and reduce the likelihood of downstream flooding (Smith and Ward 1998).

Scientists have long known that human modification of catchment basins affects the likelihood and severity of flooding (e.g. Shank 1938, White 1945; see Gregory 2006 for a detailed review of the literature). Human activities that exacerbate the physical risk of flood occurrence include the clearance of forests, drainage of wetlands, construction of impermeable surfaces (e.g. rooftops, paved roadways), building of storm drains, and the straightening and narrowing of channels. Bradshaw and colleagues (2007) studied flood events that occurred in fifty-six developing nations between 1990 and 2000 and found that high rates of deforestation have a positive correlation with flood frequency and severity. Soil eroding from deforested areas and from agricultural fields can collect in stream channels, thereby constraining or blocking them (Poesen and Hooke 1997); this has been an ongoing challenge in the loess uplands of China's great river basins (Fu 1989). The magnitude of 2004 floods along the Soliette River of southern Hispaniola, which killed an estimated fifteen hundred people and destroyed more than three thousand houses, was likely exacerbated by extensive deforestation on the Haitian side of this international watershed, and by unregulated urbanization on the Dominican Republic side, which saw large numbers of people living in high-risk areas (Brandimarte et al. 2009).

Calder and Aylward (2006) caution that the relative contribution of human modification of the landscape to flood causation can be overestimated in the case of very large catchment areas. They critique claims that human modification of the upper Ganges-Brahmaputra basin has increased the frequency and severity of flooding in Bangladesh, citing Hofer's (1998) work that shows Bangladesh has always been subject to flooding, and that there are no discernible trends in flood frequency or severity. Other scholars have noted that river channel modification and construction of levees, embankments, and artificial flood defenses can create a false sense of security for nearby residents. When these are poorly or inadequately designed or maintained, they can fail catastrophically when overwhelmed by exceptionally strong water volumes (Burton and Cutter 2008). In some cases, levees or flood defenses constructed at one location without consideration for downstream consequences have put other communities at greater risk, as has been the case in the Poyang Lake region of China's Yangtze basin (Shankman, Davis, and Leeuw 2009).

5.2.4 Flood Prediction and Identification of At-Risk Locations

The degree to which a given settlement is exposed to flooding, and the relative risk of particular locations within that settlement, can be identified fairly accurately. Historical records and geomorphological evidence provide information on the frequency and extent of past flood events, enabling watershed management organizations to create flood outline maps. In China, written flood records date back two thousand years for some watersheds, with people in many areas having had a tradition of inscribing high water marks on rock faces, allowing scholars to recreate detailed historical return rate and maximum discharge estimates (Luo 1987). Floodplain managers often use a *probability of return* vocabulary when discussing floods, with terms like *five-year floods*, *hundred-year floods*, *thousand-year floods*, and so forth (Smith and Ward 1998). This does not mean that a 'hundred-year flood' is expected to occur only once every 100 years; rather, it implies there is a 1 in 100 chance in any given year of experiencing a particular level of inundation. The city of Peterborough, Ontario, Canada, for example, experienced hundred-year floods in 2002 and 2004 because of sudden rainstorms that overwhelmed city sewers, the second flood occurring even as residents were still recovering from the first (Oulahen and Doberstein 2012).[3]

The ability to identify at-risk locations does not necessarily eliminate the occurrence of flooding, as the Peterborough case shows. The experience of Peterborough is common to many well-established urban settlements. Until the second half of the twentieth century, development in floodplains was often unregulated (in many places it still is). Land use and settlement in floodplains reflects historical trade-offs between the economic opportunity presented by waterside locations versus the damage caused by flood events. The oldest part of Peterborough – the downtown core – was established more than a century ago in a low-lying area close to a small lake. It today features a high density of impermeable surfaces, has older drainage infrastructure, and hosts a relatively high concentration of residences and commercial property. As in other cities, once economically valuable location-based property rights are created, their owners are unlikely to relinquish them without receiving commensurate financial consideration in return. More often, they look for public investment in flood defenses and drainage improvements that will maintain or even increase economic development and property values in flood-prone locations (Hartmann 2009). The consequence is that people and property continue to be exposed to flood risks despite the fact that the province of Ontario has implemented a variety of land use regulations, watershed management procedures, and flood planning arrangements in the century following Peterborough's establishment.[4]

---

[3] I selected this example on the basis of first-hand experience, having spent the rainstorm that triggered the 2002 flood camped in a tent east of Peterborough and attempting unsuccessfully the next day to enter the flooded city. For video footage of the Peterborough floods taken by the Canadian Broadcasting Corporation, visit http://www. cbc.ca/player/Digital+Archives/Environment/Extreme+Weather/ID/1487879864/.

[4] For a history of Ontario flood-planning measures, see Robinson and Cruikshank (2006). The classic diagnosis of vulnerability to flooding is Gilbert White's 1942 doctoral thesis at the University of Chicago, entitled 'Human adjustment to floods: A geographical approach to the flood problem in the United States'; it is remarkable how closely examples like Peterborough fit the model described in White's work and how relatively little has changed since the 1940s.

5.2.5 Institutional Measures to Reduce Exposure to Flooding

A common strategy in reducing the exposure of settlements to flooding is the construction of physical structures like dams, levees, and spillways to contain high flow levels within existing channels or to create diversions. In doing so, governments must sometimes make conscious decisions as to which locations along a river system will be protected and which will be left exposed to flooding. Experience shows that the preferred choice is to protect the most densely populated areas, especially urban centers, even when they are situated at highly exposed locations. The city of Winnipeg, Manitoba, Canada, with a metropolitan area population of over seven hundred thousand, is a good example of the bias toward reinforcing the continued occupation of flood-prone urban centers.

Situated at the confluence of the Assiniboine and Red Rivers, which collectively drain approximately 180,000 km², Winnipeg has experienced frequent and often catastrophic flooding since its establishment in the early 1800s (Stunden Bower 2010). Nonetheless, political and economic interests have continually pressed for investment and intensification of development. After a severe flood in 1950 displaced one hundred thousand people (Figure 5.1), governments began constructing massive spillways to channel floodwaters around the city (Stewart and Rashid 2011). Even with these defenses, the city and surrounding areas experienced tremendous flooding in 1997 (Siminovic and Carson 2003). In 2011, flooding again threatened Winnipeg; in this case, government authorities deliberately breached a dyke upstream of Winnipeg, flooding farms and rural communities to spare the city (Government of Manitoba 2012). Water was simultaneously diverted into Lake Manitoba north of Winnipeg, so much so that many shoreline residences and entire aboriginal settlements were destroyed (Kusch 2012). As of summer 2013, many aboriginal people displaced by the floods remained in temporary accommodation.

The prioritization of urban settlements over rural ones in floodplain management, and choices to protect and reinforce occupation of land with the highest economic valuation at the expense of other lands, are not unique to Winnipeg (see, for example, Tariq and Van de Giesen (2011) on institutional flood management practices in Pakistan, and Erdlenbruch and colleagues (2009) in France). The accumulation over time of economic wealth and opportunity in urban locations means that residents are often loath to migrate away from them, even after floods that cause displacement and loss of homes and property. Flood-prone urban settlements, especially large ones, are almost never entirely abandoned or relocated (McLeman 2011a). More often, other measures are pursued, such as investing in water-level monitoring and flood forecasting, construction of engineering measures to reduce the frequency of inundations, creating flood insurance schemes, and developing incentives or regulations to discourage higher-value construction in higher-risk areas (e.g. Burby 2001, Calder and Aylward 2006, Demerritt et al. 2010, Hartmann 2011). While these measures

Figure 5.1. Floodwaters at Winnipeg, Manitoba, 1950. Source: *Winnipeg Tribune* Photo Collection, University of Manitoba Archives no. PC 18/3060/18–6482–015. http://umanitoba.ca/libraries/units/archives/tribune/photographs/display_photo. php?id=1530&UML_wpgtrib=9006d0473005939fa60fb62a63e78490.

can indeed reduce the physical risk of inundation, redistribute the financial risks, and facilitate continued occupancy, they are expensive. Less affluent countries or populations (or less affluent members of otherwise affluent populations) may not be able to implement or access them. It is consequently in less affluent areas (especially rural areas) and among less affluent populations (especially those who do not have secure land tenure or private property rights) where migration is most likely to emerge as a strategy for coping with and adapting to flood risks.

5.2.6 The Poor are often most Exposed

It is not by random chance that the poor and marginalized are disproportionately exposed to flood risks. In urban and peri-urban settings, where market prices for private land and housing strongly influence who lives where within the landscape, the poorest people often occupy the most flood-prone locations, which have the least economic value (Pryce and Chen 2011). In many developing regions, rapid urban population growth has driven housing prices upward and caused many cities to expand outward in an unplanned fashion, thereby increasing the number of people living in flood-prone locations. For example, Manila grew from a population of 200,000 to approximately 10 million during the twentieth century, driven by natural increase and large-scale in-migration from the countryside (Zoleta-Nantes 2002). Manila's poorer residents, including many new arrivals to the city, often occupy housing built in areas prone to flash flooding and slope failure or on land reclaimed from low-lying coastal wetlands. These groups tend to have little opportunity to participate in community politics and decision-making processes, further enhancing their vulnerability (Zoleta-Nantes 2002). A similar dynamic exists in peninsular Malaysia, where rural-urban migration caused many cities to expand into flood-prone parts of their surrounding river basins, the poorest residents occupying highly exposed land to which they have no formal title (Chan and Parker 1996). As Malaysia's urban settlements became more densely packed, the traditional *kampong* style of construction, whereby houses are built on stilts to raise them above flood waters, was abandoned (often with official encouragement) for less flood-resistant housing designs. In Jakarta, Indonesia, self-built *kampongs* often spring up in flash-flood-prone areas where they house large numbers of rural-urban migrants unable to afford housing in safer, tenured locations (Texier 2008, Tunas and Peresthu 2010). Unplanned settlement growth in a number of African cities has also increased the number of people at risk of flooding (see Di Baldassarre et al. (2010) for a review).

Not only do the urban poor tend to be disproportionately exposed to flood hazards and be more likely to occupy houses that are not flood resistant, they also often suffer disproportionately adverse consequences when flooding occurs (Few 2003). The ability to recover from flooding often differs significantly between those who own their houses, those who rent homes to which there is clear title, and those who occupy homes constructed on untitled land. For example, in flood-prone Georgetown, Guyana, owners of homes in exposed locations can experience significant loss of personal wealth and equity when floods occur, but they also have a greater ability to absorb these financial losses (Pelling 1999). Conversely, those who rent property and those who occupy squatter residences also experience very high levels of damage, but have few resources to draw upon after the event. Households headed by single women of mixed Indo- and Afro-Guyanese origin are especially at risk, being less likely to take part in community-based activities organized to proactively reduce flood exposure.

Access to housing after a flood event can be a significant challenge for the poor, as was seen in the wake of 1998 floods in Dhaka, Bangladesh, where rent for even the lowest-quality slum housing increased, leaving many urban poor more deeply indebted (Rashid 2000). In their study of five African cities, Douglas and colleagues (2008) observed that, in addition to destroying homes, floods disrupt the income-earning opportunities of the urban poor, whose livelihoods are often based on small, place-specific activities such as local trading in goods and services or operation of artisanal businesses. Floods may also lead to increases in waterborne and insect-borne diseases, further hurting the health and well-being of the poorest households (see Few and Matthies (2006) for a detailed review of the health impacts of floods).

5.2.7 *Institutional Capacity to Facilitate Post-Flood Recovery Varies*

Adaptation to flood risks and strategies to recover after flood events can occur at all scales, with the role of institutional actors proving very important in determining the extent and type of responses needed on the part of actors at lower scales. In wealthier nations, governments typically can develop standing emergency plans and implement ad hoc response and relief measures to assist the recovery of those affected by floods. As seen in the Hurricane Katrina case study in the previous chapter, such measures may be far from perfect, and those affected must still often rely heavily on their own financial resources and social networks during the recovery process. Nonetheless, the discrepancy between developed and developing nations in terms of institutional resources and capacity to recover from floods can be quite significant. In countries where governments lack the financial wherewithal to provide substantive assistance to those affected by floods, recovery comes largely through individual and community-level resources, sometimes supplemented by contributions from nongovernmental organizations (NGOs) (e.g. Rashid 2000, Douglas et al. 2008, Dun 2011). A compounding factor in some cases is that powerful vested interests may appropriate limited institutional resources for their own use. In the Pakistani Punjab, for example, a relatively small number of politically connected, economically powerful families openly use their influence to construct spillways and flood diversions that protect their own considerable landholdings (Mustafa 2002).[5] The poor, who occupy the most marginal, flood-prone lands, have traditionally received little assistance or support from authorities during floods. Following the major flood event of 2010, Pakistan's

---

[5] These individuals also use their influence to extract a disproportionate amount of surface water for irrigation purposes during the dry season (Mustafa 2002).

rural poor received meager relief from government institutions, with both the international donor community and many Pakistanis expressing frustration with government incompetence and corruption (Burki 2010). International assistance to Pakistan may have been hindered because the 2010 floods occurred when donor assistance and UN agencies were still helping Haitians recover from an earthquake earlier that year (Great Britain House of Commons 2010).

Floodplain residents in developed countries often have access to flood insurance provided through public, private, and/or combined public-private programs (Pryce and Chen 2011). Depending on local circumstances and regulations, participation in such programs may be voluntary, mandatory, or requested by lending institutions prior to issuing mortgages for floodplain properties (McLeman and Smit 2006b). When not obligatory, participation in such programs can often be surprisingly low even in higher-risk areas, with floodplain residents often expecting that ad hoc relief measures from government will be forthcoming in the event of a flood (Browne and Hoyt 2000; Blanchard-Boehm, Berry, and Showalter 2001; McLeman and Smit 2006b). Researchers have generated a sizable literature on how people perceive flood risks that suggests individuals' willingness to undertake anticipatory adaptation is influenced by a wide range of cultural, economic, political, psychological, and social factors that may be completely unrelated to any quantitative measure of frequency of flooding at a given location (e.g. Mustafa 2002, Ali 2007, Douglas et al. 2008). The perceptions of flood risks and the appropriateness of potential adaptive responses often differ considerably between individuals and institutions, further impeding efforts to get people to participate in institutionally led flood adaptation (Slovic, Kunreuther, and White 2000; Calder and Aylward 2006).

5.3 Migration as Adaptation to River Valley Floods

5.3.1 Exposure to Frequent Flooding as Compared with Infrequent, Extreme Floods

To better understand how flooding can shape migration, it is useful to make a distinction between floods that happen on a frequent basis, such as those that occur as a consequence of monsoonal precipitation regimes, and the less frequent extreme flood events that arise from precipitation events or weather conditions that fall outside the usual norms. As described in this section, in areas where flooding is a common occurrence rural populations may incorporate temporary or seasonal labor migration as part of a wider set of ongoing adaptations. Extreme flood events can generate tremendous temporary population displacements, especially in the geographically extensive and densely populated river valleys of Asia. While displacement in and of itself is not an act of migration, being displaced increases a person's potential to become a migrant. However, the scale of migration that results from extreme floods is not always as great as might be expected, with those affected often seeking for economic and social reasons to resettle in or near the same place. The migration outcomes from these two different types of flood scenarios are now discussed in turn.

5.3.2 Seasonal Migration as an Ongoing Rural
Adaptation to Regular Flooding

Floodplains are more biologically productive than upland areas, with the ongoing deposition of soils and nutrients from run-off and periodic over-spilling of channels beneficial from an agricultural perspective (Tockner and Stanford 2002). Agricultural practices in large river basins in Africa and Asia have over generations adapted to take advantage of seasonal flooding of river valleys through the widespread production of rice, a grain traditionally grown in fields that are flooded for part of the growing season to prevent competition from weeds. It is estimated more than 140 million rice farms exist worldwide, most of them in Asia, with rice the leading source of calories in areas where it is produced, especially for the poor (Dawe, Pandey, and Nelson 2010). Regular floods have other potential benefits for food producers as well, such as recharging lakes and wetlands used for dry-season irrigation, or filling ponds used for fish and shrimp farming. Southeast Asia's lower Mekong river system is an example of an integrated and extremely productive food production system based on rice growing, fish farming and wild-capture fishing, with seasonal flooding critical to maintaining the system (Berg 2002). The health of Cambodia's Tonle Sap Lake ecosystem, which supports a human population of 1 million, depends on annual pulses of Mekong floodwaters (Kummu and Sarkkula 2008). The rotation of wheat and rice crops in heavily populated river valleys of Bangladesh, India, Nepal, and Pakistan is timed to coincide with the monsoon rains (Bhushan et al. 2007). Seasonal flooding is also critical for livelihoods in the dry Sheeb region of Eritrea, where farmers divert flash floods from intermittent channels to spate irrigate[6] low-lying lands (Tesfai and De Graaff 2000). These are just a few brief examples of areas and livelihood systems that benefit from flooding.

Inevitably, occupation of regularly flooded areas also exposes agriculturalists to occasional extreme flood events that cause short-term harm, but over the long run the benefits of living in such locations often outweigh the risks. Consequently, in rural areas where flooding is common, a regular seasonal movement of people and/ or livestock, timed to coincide with the flood cycle, may form part of local livelihood strategies that reduce risks and maximize potential opportunities (Ellis 2000). This is not universal across all regions; for example, many rural populations in Ghana perceive seasonal floods as too short-lived for there to be a significant advantage or

---

[6] *Spate irrigation* refers to the diversion of water from intermittent or seasonal watercourses for farming purposes, and has been widely practiced in dryland regions for millennia (Mehari et al. 2011).

opportunity to gain from temporary migration (Tschakert et al. 2010). In other African watersheds, however, temporary migration is a common coping strategy by which the rural poor, especially the landless, routinely deal with floods. For example, crop farmers in Somalia's Juba and Shabelle river valleys have traditionally migrated to regional urban centers during the rainy season (Le Sage and Majid 2002). In Eritrea's Sheeb region, farmers migrate to upland areas where they tend livestock while awaiting the next flash floods in the lower valleys, which they capture for spate irrigation. Importantly, not all the farmers migrate at the same time, but do so on a rotating basis so that someone is always on hand to organize water diversions during sudden rains and to rebuild any structures damaged by flash floods (Mehari et al. 2005).

Seasonal migration in annually flooded areas is not exclusive to Africa. For example, residents of islands in the lower reaches of the Brazilian Amazon have traditionally moved during the annual floods to higher ground, where they keep cattle and grow vegetables for market (Winklerprins 1992). Seasonal migration timed to annual flood cycles is especially pronounced in rice-producing areas of Asia, where large numbers of seasonal workers migrate in concert with key stages of rice production – first to do the labor of transplanting seedlings to the paddies and later to harvest (e.g. Kikuchi and Hayami 1983, Bhushan et al. 2007, De Brauw 2010). Unlike other grain crops, where commercially intensive production tends to reduce labor requirements, commercial rice production has in some parts of Asia increased the demand for casual wage labor, which has in turn been met by greater seasonal labor migration (Otsuka, Cordova, and David 1990; Upadhyaya, Otsuka, and David 1990; Rogaly et al. 2001). At the beginning of the present century, researchers estimated that half a million people engage in seasonal migration in India's West Bengal state, with migrants drawn from a variety of locations and a range of social and religious backgrounds (Rogaly et al. 2002). In southern Vietnam, poor farmers who do not have access to irrigation, and are thus able to grow only a single rice crop each year during the flood season, have high rates of seasonal outmigration as they seek out income opportunities during the rest of the year (Paris et al. 2009).

5.3.3 Rural Migration in Response to Extreme Floods

Migration is one of a range of possible responses to extreme floods. When heavy flooding occurs in rural areas, residents may experience loss of shelter and loss of livelihood through crop damage and livestock deaths. Floods may also destroy stored food reserves and seeds saved for future planting (Armah et al. 2010). In less developed countries, the rural poor typically lack access to insurance plans or ad hoc government compensation schemes that might assist them in overcoming the double impact of lost shelter and income, making them particularly predisposed to migration when extreme flood events do occur. Whether they do so, and whether that migration is likely to be temporary or indefinite in duration, is highly dependent on local socioeconomic dynamics. Rural populations are not homogeneous, and within any given group there will be differences in livelihood strategies, land tenure, and household-level access to financial resources, social networks, and other forms of capital (see also Brondizio and Moran 2008). The following brief examples from Asia and Africa illustrate some of the potential outcomes.

In Pakistan's Indus River basin in 2010,[7] unusually heavy monsoonal rains triggered widespread flooding that killed an estimated two thousand people, caused widespread disease outbreaks, and affected the livelihoods of an estimated 20 million people (Webster, Toma, and Kim 2011). It is believed as many as 2 million homes and more than 500 health care clinics were damaged or destroyed (Warraich, Zaidi, and Patel 2011). Rural households made up 90 per cent of the affected population, and government relief assistance was generally slow and inadequate (Kirsch et al. 2012). A large proportion of those households that sustained damage to housing were a year later still unable to secure adequate shelter (Kurosaki et al. 2012). Female-headed households, the elderly, ethnic minorities, and people with physical disabilities found it especially difficult to recover from loss of housing (Shah 2012). A study by Kirsch and colleagues (2012) found that after six months had passed, 18 per cent of the rural population displaced by floods, and 12 per cent of the urban population displaced by floods, had migrated away from their home district. Local case studies suggest that wealthier households recovered faster than others, and that poorer ones turned to short-term borrowing from family networks and informal lenders to restart their livelihoods (for example, by replacing lost livestock (Kurosaki et al. 2012)). Reconstruction efforts created a short-term increase in the availability of wage labor opportunities, with irrigation systems a focus of infrastructure replacement. By 2012, the socioeconomic characteristics of villages in some areas were beginning to resemble those that existed prior to the flood, namely, a small number of households of reasonable wealth and a much larger number of families living in poverty (Kurosaki et al. 2012).

In neighboring India's West Bengal state, the year 2000 'millennium flood' affected 4.4 million people (Rafique 2003). The following months saw a large upswing in the number of rural landless undertaking seasonal migration. Government relief was minimal, and the few options available to the rural poor were to borrow money from moneylenders to rebuild or to leave in search of wage employment in Kolkata or in unaffected agricultural areas. The responses in this example parallel those in the more detailed Bangladesh case study presented later in this chapter.

In southern Vietnam, where the Mekong delta floods annually during the wet season, the rural population makes distinctions between 'nice floods' (those where water levels rise by less than four meters and are beneficial for farmers) and 'high floods' (where water levels increase by more than four meters and become destructive) (Dun

[7] Some parts of the country experienced heavy monsoonal flooding again in 2011.

2011). A common adaptive response by rural Vietnamese to high floods is temporary migration to upland farms or cities in search of wage labor (Nguyen 2007, Chinvanno et al. 2008). In recent years, Vietnamese government authorities have actively organized the resettlement of dispersed Mekong delta households into denser settlements for a variety of reasons, including service delivery, infrastructure creation, and as a strategy to reduce future displacements due to floods and erosion (Dun 2011). Those targeted for government resettlement are the rural poor living in erosion-prone locations, many of whom are quite resistant to relocating for fear of losing their social networks and being forced to live farther from wage labor opportunities. In a questionnaire survey of a small sample of Vietnamese migrants living in Phnomh Penh, Cambodia, Dun (2011) found that a number of respondents cited crop loss due to floods as a reason for leaving their former rural homes. Within Cambodia, seasonal migration has been a long-standing livelihood practice for rural residents of the Tonle Sap region, but permanent out-migration to urban settlements is growing because of the combined effects of flood-damaged rice crops, droughts, declining water quality, land scarcity due to high rates of natural population increase, and growing rates of poverty (Heinonen 2006).

Extreme flooding is also an ongoing risk in China's major river valleys, where impacts on rural migration patterns can be significant. For example, those affected by severe floods in the Beijiang district of southern Guangdong in 1994 received immediate assistance through friends, relatives, and social networks, along with relief donations raised in Hong Kong, Macau, and Taiwan (Wong and Zhao 2001). The Chinese government also provided emergency relief and began an active campaign to rebuild villages and homes in the same locations and to create new embankments and other infrastructure to reduce the future physical risk of flooding. Nonetheless, so many people migrated to the regional urban centers of Guangzhou and Shenzhen in search of wage labor, it became difficult to resume agricultural production the following season. China is also the site of the world's largest recent example of flood-related displacement and migration, the 1998 Yangtze River floods, an event that merits its own more detailed case study later in this chapter.

Extreme floods also influence migration patterns in rural sub-Saharan Africa. In northern Ghana, for example, severe flood events causing loss of income, loss of seed stock for future seasons, and increased risk of disease outbreaks have contributed to growing rates of rural-to-urban migration (Armah et al. 2010). Remittances from friends and families living outside the flood-stricken area provide immediate help in household recovery efforts, but they also encourage more people to migrate out of affected areas. Many poorer households displaced by floods who elect to remain in the affected area resettle on lands close by watercourses. Although this decision renews their physical exposure to future floods, land in less exposed areas is typically beyond the economic means of Ghana's rural poor. In Botswana's Okavongo delta region, rural livelihoods are based on agricultural activities that vary according to cultural group (Motsholapheko, Kgathi, and Vanderpost 2011). Floods in 2004, 2009, and 2010 displaced many villagers, damaging crops and leaving roads impassable for an extended period. The floods did not result in significant increases in permanent migration away from the area, but influenced many to undertake temporary or seasonal migration in search of wage employment. In Mozambique, severe floods have caused several large-scale population displacements in recent years. In the year 2000, floods in the Limpopo River basin affected more than 4 million people, while floods in the Zambezi River basin in 2007 and 2008 displaced an estimated one hundred thousand and eighty thousand people respectively (Stal 2011). In the Zambezi watershed, having fields close to the river reduces the potential for crop loss due to droughts – an ongoing risk – but at the same time increases farmers' exposure to flooding. Government programs were created following the 2007 floods to actively establish new settlements for the displaced, although this led to new environmental challenges, such as localized water scarcities and deforestation as those resettled sought wood for fuel (Stal 2011).

5.3.4 Urban Flooding and Population Movements

Few modern examples exist of large numbers of people migrating autonomously out of river valley urban settlements, even in the wake of repeated, severe flooding. The examples that do exist have typically involved relatively small settlements, where economic decline and out-migration for other reasons was already under way, an example being the Meridean Islands settlements of Wisconsin in the United States (Barnes 1989; see McLeman 2011a for other examples). In some instances, governments have organized the abandonment and relocation of settlements that suffered particularly severe flood damage. For example, in 1937, catastrophic flooding struck the Ohio River valley of the United States, inundating thousands of square kilometers and causing an estimated $400 million in damages (which would equate to more than $6 billion today) (Shank 1938). Officials initially believed half a million people living in affected areas might need to permanently relocate. Instead, most areas were quickly reoccupied once the waters receded, and great public investment was made (and continues to be made) in engineered flood defenses. Shawneetown, the oldest settlement in Illinois, with a population of one thousand, was the largest of the affected settlements to be entirely relocated, to a location on higher ground three miles away. In another example, the Alberta, Canada, town of Slave Lake was relocated several kilometers to higher ground upriver following a major 1935 flood event (Government of Alberta 1993). In 2011, Slave Lake's sixty-seven hundred residents evacuated after a severe fire followed by a major flood event destroyed much of the new town. At the time of this writing, many of those who evacuated had not returned.

Instead of complete abandonment or relocation, a more common response is for governments to expropriate or otherwise prevent the (re)occupation of the most heavily flooded lands within an urban settlement and to protect the remainder through engineered defenses. Persoons, Vanclooster, and Desmed (2002), for example, reviewed options proposed for the Meuse basin of Belgium following two severe floods in the 1990s. These included avoiding the issuance of building permits in highly exposed areas, the strategic expropriation of waterside commercial and residential properties, and a variety of engineered defenses and land use change regulations. Large-scale relocation of people was not considered an option. Strategic expropriation and conversion of floodplain land to nonresidential and/or noncommercial use have been relatively common practices in the Netherlands and in Ontario, Canada (Robinson and Cruikshank 2006, Kuks 2009). However, land expropriation in developed countries is financially very expensive and entails potential legal conflict over private landowners' rights, and consequently tends to be done as sparingly as possible.

In urban settlements where people occupy floodplain lands without any legal title, as in several of the Asian and African examples given earlier, the financial costs of expropriation and removal of housing may be less costly, but such actions may still be very contentious, especially when done for reasons not directly related to flood risk reduction. In Jakarta, for example, authorities frequently seek to remove residents of informally built *kampongs* situated in flash-flood prone locations, but residents tend to resist strongly and the *kampongs* often reappear soon after (Tunas and Peresthu 2010).

5.3.5 Abandonment of Settlements due to Dam Construction

Since the early twentieth century, large numbers of people, especially in Asia, have been forcibly relocated following the construction of large dams, which are sometimes (though not always) built with flood management in mind. The World Commission on Dams (2000) estimated that dam construction projects have displaced between 40 and 80 million people worldwide, with China and India accounting for a large portion of these. The commission further noted that in many countries, the number of people forcibly relocated is often understated, and in many instances those forced to relocate are evicted without any assistance or compensation. Displacement can occur upstream from the dam, where land is permanently inundated, and downstream, when reduced stream flow affects river-based livelihood resources like fish stocks. Indigenous groups, the elderly, the poor, women and children, and other vulnerable groups are most likely to be adversely affected and to receive inadequate compensation or support (World Commission on Dams 2000). Scudder's (2012) study of fifty large dam projects that necessitated resettlements found that those resettled likely lived in greater poverty after their involuntary relocation. Cernea (1997) summarized a range of impacts experienced by households subject to forced resettlement programs, including:

- Loss of land that generates household incomes and livelihoods
- Loss of wage employment opportunities

- Loss of housing
- Economic marginalization and declining standard of living
- Declining food security
- Increased rates of illness and/or death
- Loss of common property resources
- Disruption of social networks

Tilt, Braun, and He (2009) suggest that resettlement programs can better meet the needs and interests of those displaced when authorities engage in a transparent process that respects basic rights, and act early to encourage affected residents to participate in the resettlement planning process. Several of the impacts listed above were experienced by those forcibly displaced by China's Three Gorges dam project, and contributed to knock-on migration as people struggled to adjust to their new homes. The Three Gorges project – which has been anything but a transparent or participatory process as recommended by Tilt and colleagues (2009) – forms part of the Yangtze River case study that appears in the next section of this chapter.

5.4 Case Studies of Asian River Valley Flooding and Migration Patterns

A closer look at two relatively well-known examples from Asia will better connect the linkages between river valley flooding, adaptation, and migration. Bangladesh's Ganges-Brahmaputra-Meghna delta region and China's Yangtze River valley make for compelling case studies, being sites of considerable population growth that are also highly exposed to both seasonal and extreme flood events. In Bangladesh, lack of institutional capacity means adaptation to flooding falls mainly to individual households; at the other extreme, the Chinese government has undertaken the world's largest engineering project to manage water flows in the Yangtze. The population movements that have occurred in each example provide useful insights for reflecting on how flood-migration dynamics play out more broadly.

5.4.1 Case Study: Brahmaputra-Ganges-Meghna River Basin, Bangladesh

Bangladesh has become somewhat of a poster child for 'environmental refugee' research, given its past experience with floods, cyclones, and droughts that have caused tremendous loss of life and population displacement, plus fears that sea level rise will make things much worse in the future. Scholars have conducted a considerable amount of research on the Bangladeshi experience with natural disasters, including tropical cyclones and storm surge–related flooding;[8] the focus here will be on riverine flooding triggered by the East Asian monsoon. Situated at the mouth

---

[8] See Paul and Routray (2010) for an overview of recent literature.

of the Brahmaputra (or Jamuna), Ganges (or Padma) and Meghna rivers, much of Bangladesh consists of deltaic and floodplain land no more than a few meters above sea level (Figure 5.2). Each year, an average of 20 per cent of the total land area of Bangladesh is flooded, typically between the months of June and September, when South Asia receives its monsoon rains (Paul and Routray 2010). This annual flooding delivers organically rich sediments to the delta, and agricultural productivity rises significantly on land after it has been flooded (Banerjee 2010). In the lowest-lying areas, the river channels and the lands between them, referred to as *char* lands, are regularly shifting and reshaped through erosion and accretion caused by floods.

The majority of the Bangladeshi population lives in rural areas, where farming and, to a lesser extent, fishing have traditionally been the main livelihood activities. Shrimp farming has become increasingly important to the rural economy. The types of crops produced at any given location depend on local conditions, with rice the most common crop, followed by wheat, groundnuts, and vegetables (Banerjee 2010). Farmers grow different varieties of rice at different times of year. Lower-yielding *aman* varieties are transplanted to newly flooded paddies during the wet season and harvested late in the calendar year; higher-yielding *boro* varieties are grown during the dry season; and *aus* rice is sown in March or April and harvested early in the wet season (Del Ninno and Dorosh 2001). The rural population distinguishes between 'good' floods that benefit rice and shrimp farming and 'bad' floods that damage or destroy crops, housing, livestock, and shrimp ponds. Bad floods can be defined as those where more than one-third of the country is inundated and/or the flood waters have not receded by late September (Banerjee 2010). In a very bad year, more than half the country may be inundated, with particularly severe floods experienced in 1955, 1987, 1988, 1998, and 2004.

Bad floods hurt food production. In the 1998 'flood of the century', domestic rice production fell short by more than 2.2 million metric tons, and the government and NGOs provided emergency food relief (Del Ninno and Dorosh 2001). In addition to the damage done directly to land and property, severe or prolonged flood events are often accompanied by outbreaks of diarrhea, cholera, and other waterborne diseases, especially where sewage contaminates surface waters (Schwartz et al. 2006). The duration of inundation is often more important than the actual depth of inundation, with the extent of damage, disruption to livelihood activities, and health impacts worsening the longer the flood waters remain (Paul and Routray 2010). Death rates associated with bad floods have declined steadily over the past several decades as systems for advance warning and preparation improve, but the economic and social costs of bad floods remain high (Penning-Rowsell, Sultana, and Thompson 2012).

Household and community-level exposure to flooding in Bangladesh is shaped not simply by the physical aspects of flooding, but also by the socioeconomic dynamics that lead particular groups to occupy highly exposed locations and make land use choices that increase their exposure. In both urban and rural areas, the poorest and

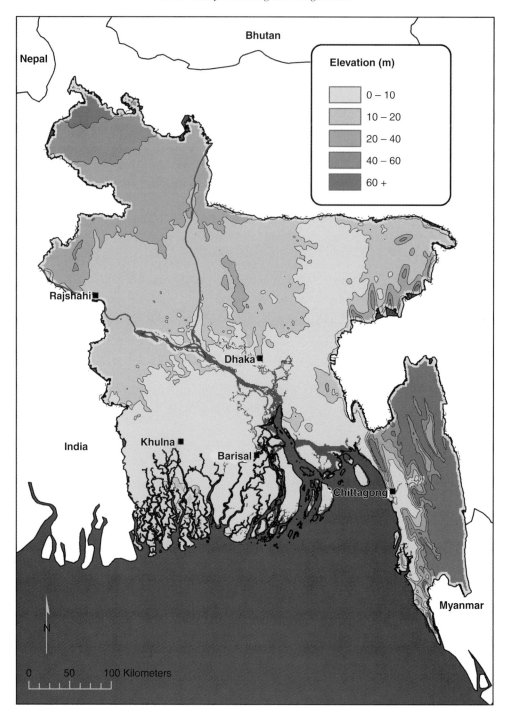

Figure 5.2. Map of Bangladesh, showing main rivers, elevations.

most socioeconomically marginalized tend to occupy the most flood-prone locations, while wealthier groups tend to occupy higher ground. In aggregate terms, wealthier groups experience the greatest value of economic losses due to floods, which is not altogether surprising given that they also possess the greatest amount of land and assets generally (Brouwer et al. 2007). The economic impacts of flooding hit the poorest people hardest, because their household incomes are less diversified and more dependent on farming. In the low-lying *chars*, the rural poor may own small parcels of land of no more than a few hectares, or may be completely landless and reliant on agricultural wage labor to survive (Siddiqui 2003, Lein 2009). Poor farmers tend to plant the rice varieties that are most susceptible to damage from above-average floods, the higher-yielding dry season *boro* rice being too expensive to grow because of the need for supplementary fertilizers and irrigation (Banerjee 2010). Given the physical risks, *char* lands may from the outside seem like desperate places or refuges of last resort, but they offer opportunities as well as hardships. People living there often form strong social networks and communities. Even after extreme flood events such as those caused by tropical cyclones, few *char* residents give any serious consideration to leaving (Lein 2009).

In a country where flooding is endemic and institutional capacity is limited, one would expect that people have developed a range of adaptation strategies, and this is indeed the case. Migration has its place within the suite of household-level adaptation options. During the flood season, once the *aman* rice has been transplanted to the paddies, young men from poorer households often go to nearby urban centers or other rural areas in search of temporary wage income (Rabby et al. 2011, Penning-Rowsell et al. 2012). Even after the flood waters have receded, there is often little work for agricultural laborers until the *aman* rice crop is ready for harvest in November. This period, known as *monga* or *mangha*, which roughly translates as the 'lean season', can also see significant numbers of the rural poor on the move in search of short-term employment. Traditionally, men participate in seasonal migration, especially those from large families, although in recent years larger numbers of young women have sought work in garment factories (Lein 2009, Ahamad et al. 2011). The loss of men from migrant households creates additional burdens for women, who must look after the household in their absence and whose diets and health often suffer.[9] The destination choice of seasonal migrants depends on the availability of employment, the distance as it relates to travel costs, and the presence of social networks that help offset the costs of travel and accommodation (Ahamad et al. 2011, Farhana, Rahman, and Rahman 2012). Those who would like to participate in this seasonal migration but do not typically cite the costs and a lack of social connections as the main barriers (Khandker, Khalily, and Samad 2012).

---

[9] See Cannon (2002) for a more detailed study of the gender dimensions of flooding and other natural hazards in Bangladesh.

Bad flood events do not cause particularly significant changes to existing migration patterns within Bangladesh or from Bangladesh to international destinations (Barman et al. 2012, Gray and Mueller 2012a). This may seem surprising given the high rate of urbanization within Bangladesh, the large number of Bangladeshi labor migrants who travel to India and to the Middle East, and the large communities of Bangladeshi migrants residing permanently in the United Kingdom and the United States. The lack of any change in participation in long-distance international migration can be fairly easily explained in that most migrants leaving for abroad are higher-skilled, higher-educated workers from urban centers (Siddiqui 2003), who are less likely to be significantly affected by flooding. Yet, even the rural poor, who typically suffer most from extreme flooding, are unlikely to undertake anything more than the short-term, short-distance migration that already characterizes rural life, because of the strong economic and social ties that anchor them to their homes (Lein 2009, Gray and Mueller 2012a). People maintain legal tenure to the land they own even when it becomes inundated because of river channel movement, so those displaced by floods tend to remain close by (Lein 2000, 2009). Only once it becomes evident that their land has been permanently lost to erosion do those displaced by floods begin seeking out new *char* land to occupy or consider moving farther afield (Siddiqui 2003, Iqbal 2010, Barman et al. 2012). Even then, the distinction between the impacts of the flood on the household and the impacts on the community is important (Gray and Mueller 2012a). Where the community as a whole can recover quickly, even households that have suffered considerable losses are less likely to migrate away and will instead draw upon local social and employment networks. It is when the community as a whole has suffered significant losses that new or additional out-migration is likely to occur (Gray and Mueller 2012a).

Droughts and tropical cyclones are much more likely than floods to stimulate rural-to-urban distress migration, for households and communities often lack the capacity to recover from those types of events (Lein 2000, Kartiki 2011). Further, the financial costs of accommodation, food, education, and other services are relatively higher in the city, and moving there requires severing beneficial social networks at home, making permanent migration less viable or attractive in the aftermath of a flood (Kartiki 2011). Seasonal food insecurity during *mangha*, especially during years when *mangha* is followed by poor harvests (more often due to a lack of rain than flooding), is cited by rural migrants as a reason for resettling in Dhaka, as is the permanent loss of land due to erosion (Farhana et al. 2012). Overall, though, most people who permanently resettle in the city cite economic factors – the lack of permanent land of their own, the search for employment, the desire to take advantage of new economic opportunities, and so forth – as their main motivations (Lein 2000, 2009). Escaping chronic poverty, rather than recovering from riverine flood impacts, will likely remain the greatest driver of permanent rural-to-urban migration in Bangladesh for the near future, with seasonal or temporary labor migration remaining a useful coping strategy for those who stay in rural areas.

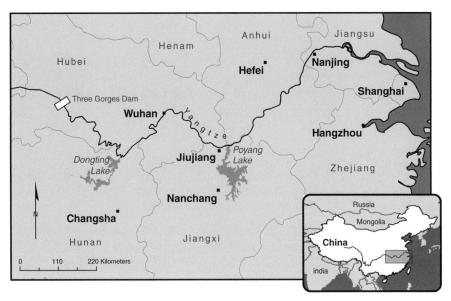

Figure 5.3. China, showing Yangtze river basin, major cities, and location of Three Gorges project.

5.4.2 Case Study: Yangtze River Basin, China

An estimated 400 million people live in the Yangtze River basin, a vast region of 1.8 million km² in south central China (Zong and Chen 2000). The river, which flows sixty-three hundred kilometers from its headwaters in the Tibetan Plateau to its outlet at Shanghai, experiences high flow rates in spring, when it receives melt water from its upper reaches, and again in summer when seasonal rains arrive (Yu et al. 2009; Bing, Shao, and Liu 2012) (Figure 5.3). Severe floods have been an ongoing but irregularly occurring risk in the middle and lower reaches of the Yangtze, with 300 significant flood events recorded in the past thousand years (Gu et al. 2011). The past century saw major flood events in 1931, 1935, 1954, 1996, and 1998 (Yu et al. 2009).

Overall flood frequency in the Yangtze basin appears to have increased since the 1950s, but this is likely due as much to anthropogenic factors as climatic ones (Yu et al. 2009). In the upper reaches of the Yangtze basin, land use and land cover changed considerably in the last decades of the twentieth century (Yin and Li 2001). Population growth and better access to markets for food producers led to an expansion in the area devoted to crops and livestock, which in turn increased soil erosion and the sediment load of the river (Cui and Graf 2009, Yin et al. 2010). In more recent years, government programs have taken less productive land in the upper reaches out of agricultural production and encouraged reforestation to reduce soil erosion rates (Wei, He, and Bao 2011). Despite these efforts, in its middle and lower reaches where the Yangtze's embankments are up to fifteen meters high, the bed of the channel has silted upward to the point that it is often higher than the surrounding land (Yin and

Li 2001). Consequently, when the embankments are breached during a flood, the water cannot drain back to the main channel. In the river's lower reaches, large urban developments are exacerbating flood risks by accelerating run-off through creation of impermeable surfaces and removing natural drainage channels (Xu et al. 2010). A further challenge in the deltaic region, home to more than 90 million people, is that heavy rates of groundwater extraction have caused the land to subside, further increasing the impacts of flooding (Gu et al. 2011).

Approximately thirteen thousand reservoirs and other human-built water storage structures sit in the Yangtze basin (Wei et al. 2011). The most famous and largest of these is the massive Three Gorges Dam that spans the river in Hubei province. Construction began in 1992; the barrage was completed in 2012, with the full range of hydroelectric turbine installations and ship lifts still under construction. The purpose of the Three Gorges project is to control downstream flooding, generate electricity, and facilitate navigation upstream (Tan and Yao 2006, Guo et al. 2012). Two significant displacement and migration events occurred during the construction of the dam: the deliberate removal of more than a million people to make way for the reservoir, and a catastrophic 1998 flood event that occurred before the dam was operational, which displaced millions of people in the middle and lower reaches of the basin.

Planned population displacements to make way for the Three Gorges reservoir began in the early 1990s, with a dozen cities and sixteen hundred eighty smaller settlements in twenty counties having since been inundated (Wilmsen, Webber, and Duan 2011a, b). Estimates of the total number of people displaced vary, with the most recent figure suggesting it was somewhere between 1.1 million and 1.35 million people (Duan and Wilmsen 2012). Of the displaced rural population, an estimated two hundred thousand moved to urban centers, while another three hundred forty thousand to four hundred thousand relocated to other rural areas (Wilmsen et al. 2011a, b). Displaced urbanites relocated to other urban centers. In the early years of the project, the government's preferred method of organized resettlement was to relocate rural populations from the valley floor to uphill locations in the immediate vicinity (Tan, Hugo, and Potter 2003). This soon proved problematic, as the new land was typically much less fertile and more erosion prone than valley bottomland. Those resettled to upland farms were often obliged to seek off-farm employment, leading subsequent rural displacees to demand resettlement to cities or to other regions, while others took matters into their own hands and migrated away independently (Li, Waley, and Rees 2001, Wilmsen et al. 2011a, b).

In the midst of the Three Gorges dam construction and its organized relocations, the summer of 1998 saw a pronounced El Niño event generate unusually heavy rainfall across central China (Ye and Glantz 2005; Wang, Song, and Hu 2010). The rains arrived in early June, even as the Yangtze was still carrying a considerable load of snowmelt from the Tibetan plateau (Zong and Chen 2000). From June through August, water levels in the main channel were very high, especially in the vicinity of Poyang Lake and Dongting Lake (Ye and Glantz 2005). Flooding occurred at various locations across the watershed that summer, with rural areas especially hard hit (Zong and Chen 2000). In August, the main dykes were breached upstream of the cities of Wuhan and Jiujiang (X. Wang et al. 2010).[10] Many flooded areas were under water for over two months, and by the end of the summer an estimated thirteen hundred people had been killed and 13.2 million people were left homeless (Zong and Chen 2000, Ye and Glantz 2005). By late September 1998, 2.9 million home-less people were still living on dykes in makeshift shelters, waiting for floodwaters to recede (UN DAC 2000). Over the following three years, the Chinese government began a program to relocate 2 million people living in the flood-affected areas of Hubei, Hunan, Anhui, and Jiangxi provinces, most of whom had been occupying land close to embankments and flood defenses (*People's Daily* online, 2002). Most of these people were resettled in new construction within the same region (Pittock and Xu n.d., Wan 2003).[11]

Because clearance of upland areas for farming was seen as contributing to the 1998 flooding, the government put a halt to it, and began forcing subsequent Three Gorges displacees to resettle in more distant areas to the east and south (He and Jiao 2000, Tan et al. 2003, Tan and Yao 2006). Many of those resettled to distant loca-tions (an estimated one hundred sixty thousand in total by 2005) soon returned to the Yangtze River valley, having found it difficult to integrate socially and economically elsewhere (Tan and Hugo 2011). Although early in the resettlement process most rural displacees preferred to remain close to their original homes where they enjoyed strong social connections, it appears that as time passed increasing numbers wanted to resettle in urban areas because of the better housing, education, and employment opportunities (Li et al. 2001). Despite these advantages, rural displacees often strug-gled in the city, and many complained about government corruption and failure to deliver on promised relocation benefits (Li et al. 2001). Those who complained too loudly sometimes earned a reputation with local authorities for being troublemakers (Xi and Hwang 2011).

China's tradition of collective landownership complicated the formal process of relocation, especially because of a concurrent government initiative to provide farmers small plots of land for their own use and tenure (Tan, Bryan, and Hugo 2005). While the government officially claimed to subscribe to what is known as *resettlement with development* – the idea that resettlement provides an opportunity to improve the well-being of those resettled – results were clearly mixed and highly variable at the county level (McDonald, Webber, and Duan 2008). Evidence of this was seen in a 2006

---

[10] In the case of Wuhan, this breach was done deliberately in an unsuccessful attempt to save the city from flooding.

[11] Despite much effort, I have not been able to uncover any information as to whether China's 'floating' population of people who migrate without official permission spiked in the wake of the 1998 floods. It is reasonable to assume that unofficial labor migration did increase in the wake of the floods, based on the Beijiang example cited earlier in this chapter, which saw a spike in labor migration to Guangzhou and Shenzhen following a flood event (Wong and Zhao 2001).

study of Yunyang County, at the heart of the resettlement area, where one-third of rural displacees between the ages of twenty and forty-nine migrated independently to coastal cities, seeking work in factories, shops, and restaurants (Jim and Yang 2006). Researchers estimated these migrants would typically remit half their earnings, which helped to alleviate poverty in Yunyang county, but at the same time inspired others to undertake migration.

It is unlikely that a deliberate displacement and resettlement exercise of the scale or magnitude of the Three Gorges project will ever be attempted again in China or elsewhere; at least, not in the foreseeable future. Only in a situation where private property rights are minimal could such an initiative even be contemplated. Were the Chinese government to consider a similar project today, its execution might now be impeded by recent policies that somewhat relax restrictions on private ownership of land and physical assets.

5.5 Lessons from Bangladesh and China

Bangladesh's Brahmaputra-Ganges-Meghna delta region and China's Yangtze River basin present similar physical challenges. Both have highly variable flow levels influenced by drainage of snowmelt at higher elevations and by seasonal fluctuations in basin-wide precipitation. Both contain valuable agricultural land and are home to very large populations. But while the environmental conditions share similarities, the cultural, economic, political, and social conditions differ considerably between Bangladesh and China, thereby making for differences in the way people adapt to flooding, including through migration.

In the case of Bangladesh, the relationship between flooding and migration outcomes is mediated through a number of factors; those which stand out include gender, food security, land tenure, private wealth, and social networks. Government institutions in Bangladesh being generally weak, the burden of adapting to flood risks falls primarily to local communities and households – the meso and micro levels of the adaptive system introduced in Chapter 3, and now marked up in Figure 5.4 to illustrate the Bangladesh case. Within the rural population, seasonal migration out of flood-affected areas is a common adaptive strategy that helps the household adapt not only to flooding, but to the *mangha*, or hungry season. However, the ability to participate in migration is mediated by having access to social capital in the form of migrant networks, and gender relations, in that working-aged men have traditionally undertaken migration. This leaves segments of the rural population trapped in chronic poverty and food insecurity, reinforcing a cycle of gender inequity at the household level (where many rural women and their children must suffer through the hungry season on their own) and socioeconomic inequity within communities (between households that have migrant members and those that do not). Migration remains mostly seasonal in nature because those who have clear tenure to their land

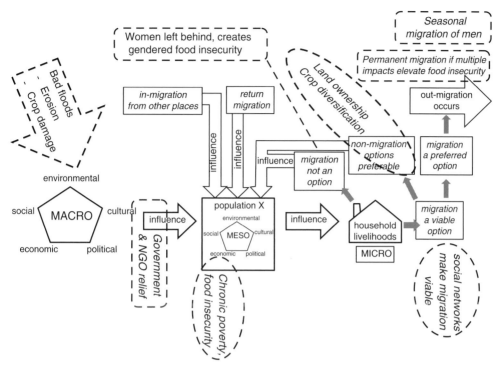

Figure 5.4. Flood-related adaptive migration outcomes in rural Bangladesh.

wish to retain it, and because rural communities have strong local social capital that their residents value highly. 'Bad' floods in and of themselves tend not to stimulate higher levels of permanent out-migration from rural areas, but when accompanied or followed by other events that exacerbate chronic poverty and food insecurity, the cumulative effects can affect participation in indefinite rural-to-urban migration. Not all that might participate in migration, seasonal or permanent, do so; wealthier land-owners tend not to occupy the most flood-exposed lands, and are able to diversify their crop production so that they do not suffer during the *mangha*. For them, migration is not a necessary adaptation.

At the risk of oversimplifying a complex process, it is possible to offer a general classification of who migrates and who does not during periods of bad floods in Bangladesh. As shown in Table 5.1, those who do not migrate tend to be at the upper and lower ends of the socioeconomic spectrum: people with sufficient wealth that they are less exposed to flood risks and food insecurity and can adapt through in situ means; and those poorest members of the rural population who lack either the economic capital or the social capital to migrate. Although more women in Bangladesh are participating in labor migration, in the flood-affected countryside migration is still a disproportionately male undertaking, and women suffer disproportionately from the food insecurity and other hardships created during flood events.

Table 5.1. *Floods in rural Bangladesh: Who migrates? Who does not?*

Seasonal migrants	Non-migrants
Owners of smaller landholdings	Wealthier landowners
Men of working age	Landless poor
	Those lacking access to social networks
	Many women

In contrast with Bangladesh, China has a government that exerts much more command and control over all aspects of society, including management of and adaptation to flood risks and households' ability to migrate. Indeed, the government's ambition to manage the river through the Three Gorges project has become as great a driver of population movement as the flood events the project is intended to prevent. Although China's institutional arrangements are unique, several useful lessons nonetheless might be taken away from the Yangtze River example. A first relates to the observation that many people displaced by the project and resettled by the authorities have since re-migrated of their own accord. This suggests that, at least for many people, the planned relocations did not achieve their supposed development aims, and is a reminder that people will adapt in such situations through independent labor migration, even in a country where migrating without official permission entails extra costs and risks. Second, it highlights the importance of social connectivity in decisions to migrate, and in the process of migrant integration. Early on in the relocation process, most people preferred to stay within the region they knew best and where their social connections were strongest. The absence of social connections made government-organized resettlements in more distant locations less successful, and many returned on their own. At the same time, the presence of independent labor migrants in coastal cities, combined with the economic promise those cities held, encouraged people to take the risk of joining their friends, neighbors, and family members in the floating migrant population.

Third, it showed a remarkable lack of foresight or willful blindness on the part of the Chinese government in thinking that farming communities could be successfully relocated from fertile bottomland soils to rough upland areas. There were obvious ecological reasons farmers had occupied the Yangtze floodplain for millennia, in spite of the regular flood events they experienced there, and avoided farming in upland areas. By relocating people to ecologically unsustainable and economically less profitable farming locations, authorities simply created a new dynamic whereby those they resettled would subsequently undertake further, less controllable migration. Indeed, hundreds of thousands of people will likely still migrate (voluntarily or through further planned relocations) as a result of the knock-on ecological consequences of the dam project itself and poor initial choices for resettlement (Duan and Wilmsen 2012). In short, this case is a reminder of Cernea's (1997) description of the perils of forced resettlement, a topic that comes up again in Chapter 7 in the context of low-lying island states and mean sea level rise.

5.6 Chapter Summary

Flooding is a price people must pay for living in the otherwise highly desirable environment of a river valley. The frequency and nature of flooding varies from one watershed to another depending on a range of climatic and geomorphologic factors. Virtually all watersheds are potential sites of irregularly occurring, extreme floods. In regions where monsoonal precipitation conditions prevail, flooding is an ongoing, annual risk. In dryland areas, flooding can be a highly unpredictable and localized phenomenon associated with infrequent extreme precipitation events. El Niño/La Niña events are sometimes associated with extreme flood events. Human modification of watersheds can exacerbate flood risks considerably.

Despite the heterogeneity in the origins and manifestations of river valley flood events across the globe, several common themes relevant to the study of climate and migration emerge from the literature. A first is that, while large floods may cause temporary population displacements in just about any river basin, migration as an adaptation to flooding is primarily a rural phenomenon practiced in lower- and middle-income countries. In urban centers, government authorities may act to evict residents of informal settlements built in high-flood-risk locations, or mobilize funds to expropriate private property in particularly exposed areas. The priority interest of households, communities, and officials alike is to make investments in systems and infrastructure to protect urban settlements from risks and to facilitate reoccupation after a flood event. In some cases, these infrastructure investments increase the risk of flooding for rural settlements elsewhere.

Rural migration in response to flooding tends to take the form of short-duration, short-distance labor migration. This is particularly the case when flooding is an ongoing occurrence, such that temporary migration becomes incorporated into the livelihood practices of rural households as a means of diversifying household income sources, offsetting temporary hardship, and taking advantage of potential opportunities. Additional spikes of temporary labor migration may occur in the wake of unexpectedly severe flood events. The destination choices of labor migrants are shaped by nonclimatic factors such as the availability of wage labor opportunities, the presence of social networks, and other factors that influence the cost of migration.

There is little evidence to suggest river valley flooding has any great influence on international migration, except where cross-border labor migration already occurs on an ongoing basis over relatively short distances, such as that between Bangladesh and India. Especially severe floods where the loss of housing is widespread, such as in the case of Pakistan in 2010, can be followed by an increase in permanent rural-urban migration. Even in that example, however, where the damage was tremendous and the institutional response was inadequate, over 80 per cent of the rural population remained in its home districts (Kirsch et al. 2012). The role of floods in stimulating changes in patterns in indefinite migration should consequently be seen within the broader context of the nonenvironmental factors that influence rural household livelihood choices and well-being.

It makes sense that in flood-prone watersheds, only the most severe events cause significant changes to established migration patterns. Livelihood systems in such environments must include in situ strategies for adapting to flood events if floodplain settlements are to remain viable over the long term. Even in the seemingly tenuous environment of Bangladesh's *chars*, the long-term benefits of occupying a flood-prone location have traditionally outweighed the costs, and residents have their own place-specific social and cultural capital that they value highly. Consequently, only the most extreme floods that damage the well-being of the community as a whole are likely to prompt households into leaving permanently. What is more likely to draw permanent migrants from the *char* or countryside to the city is some other type of climatic event for which the community lacks adaptive capacity or, more often, the desire to escape grinding poverty. The same logic helps explain why people who are cleared from flood-prone informal settlements in large Southeast Asian cities often return to rebuild as soon as they can: their existing social networks and economic opportunities are linked to those locations, and the costs of finding and developing new ones elsewhere are great.

6

Drought and Its Influence on Migration

6.1 Introduction

Droughts are a regularly occurring phenomenon in many parts of the world, and have had adverse impacts on more than a billion people in the past century (Below, Grover-Kopec, and Dilley 2007; see Table 6.1). Most migration that occurs because of drought, or as a means of mitigating the impacts of it, takes place as temporary labor migration, especially in rural populations where household livelihoods and incomes are closely tied to agricultural productivity. Extreme cases, such as distress migrations in dryland Africa of recent decades, tend to occur when the impacts of drought combine with political or economic crises, and are rarely the outcome of drought alone. Although drought-related migration originates primarily in rural areas, a number of urban centers have come perilously close to running short of water during droughts in recent years, presenting a potential future risk for which greater planning and preparation is needed. Droughts are expected to become more frequent and/or severe in many parts of the world in coming decades because of anthropogenic climate change. Recent years have seen global food prices spike in part because of droughts in key grain-exporting areas, suggesting that we are entering an era when droughts will have greater impacts on human well-being generally, even for populations not living in drought-prone areas.

Employing concepts and theories developed previously in this book, this chapter provides insights into how drought influences human migration processes by:

- Explaining the causes, general characteristics, and types of drought
- Identifying regions most exposed to drought and how human activities can exacerbate exposure
- Describing the sensitivity of agricultural, pastoralist, forestry, and urban systems to drought
- Outlining various ways exposed populations may adapt to general seasonal dryness and drought events, including through migration
- Using specific examples to show how migration patterns respond and change when droughts occur

Table 6.1. *Twentieth-century drought events and their impacts*

Region	# drought events	deaths	# people affected	Estimated economic losses (in thousands US$)
Africa	139	1,129,000	243,268,000	5,271,000
Americas	90	73*	61,003,000	18,378,000
Asia/Middle East	113	9,663,000	1,541,783,000	24,027,000
Europe	33	1,200,000	19,866,000	17,889,000
Oceania	17	660*	8,028,000	13,303,000
Total	392	11,993,000	1,873,948,000	78,867,000

* With exception of these entries, figures for deaths and people affected have been rounded to nearest thousand.
Source: Below and colleagues (2007).

- Analyzing a case study of Depression-era drought migration on the North American Great Plains to generate lessons on how nonclimatic factors can constrict adaptive capacity and magnify the impacts of drought, and how household adaptation and migration decisions within a drought-affected population are distinguished by access to particular forms of capital

The Depression-era drought case study also provides an opportunity to consider how government and institutional actions may influence household adaptation and migration behavior. As shown at the conclusion of this chapter, the conceptual diagram of migration in an adaptive system introduced as Figure 3.9 provides a useful way of capturing the interactions of processes across scales that influence migration behavior in times of drought.

6.2 Physical Characteristics of Drought

6.2.1 Causes of Drought

Drought is a natural and regularly occurring phenomenon common to many inhabited regions, including those not always associated with dryness, such as Amazonia (Zeng et al. 2008). In its simplest terms, drought occurs when precipitation falls below expected levels for a period of time sufficiently long for adverse effects on natural or human systems to be noticed.[1] There is no one specific cause or set of causes of droughts, which are exacerbated when they coincide with high average temperatures (Nagarajan 2009). At larger scales, researchers believe, droughts are linked to periodic fluctuations in tropical sea surface temperatures (SSTs) and their influence on

---

[1] For a more detailed overview of the drought phenomenon from an interdisciplinary perspective, readers are encouraged to consult Kallis (2008).

air currents (Cook et al. 2007). Such SST fluctuations include the well-known El Niño and La Niña events that originate in the tropical Pacific and occur in two- to seven-year cycles, but scientists have identified other SST fluctuations that also have a significant influence on global precipitation (Cook et al. 2007). What in turn causes SST fluctuations is not well known. They may simply be the product of regular ocean-land-atmosphere interactions that scientists as yet poorly understand. They may be influenced by fluctuations in incoming solar radiation received from the sun, or by volcanic activity that releases fine particulate matter (known as *aerosols*) into the atmosphere and thereby affecting the amount of energy received at the Earth's surface. In larger dryland regions, especially the North American Great Plains, the Indian subcontinent, and Africa's Sudano-Sahelian region, there is a strong feedback effect between soil moisture and precipitation, so that once drought conditions begin they tend to be self-reinforcing (Koster et al. 2004, Legates et al. 2011). At local scales, the onset, severity, and duration of droughts are influenced by an additional number of biophysical conditions, such as topography, vegetative cover, soil type, winds, local evapotranspiration rates, and surface water availability. Human modification of the landscape also plays an influence, through such things as the removal or alteration of vegetative cover, modification of drainage patterns, livestock grazing patterns, crop selections, and shape and form of the built landscape. For these and other reasons, droughts are very difficult to predict in advance, meaning that those living in drought-prone regions must over the long term develop a capacity to adapt to a wide range of highly variable conditions.

6.2.2 Types of Drought

Scientists make reference to three general categories of drought: meteorological, hydrological, and vegetative/agricultural. *Meteorological drought* refers to a significant shortfall in precipitation levels as compared with some predetermined average (Burke and Brown 2008). What constitutes a 'significant' shortfall in precipitation is relative to a particular location; a deviation of five centimeters of precipitation from one year to the next may go unnoticed by people living in a wet tropical environment, but may have a critical influence on livelihoods in a dry continental area. Scientists have developed a variety of indices that use relative and cumulative measures of precipitation to create quantitative descriptions of meteorological drought, with no one index fitting all circumstances (Smakhtin and Hughes 2007). Common indices include the Palmer Drought Severity Index (PDSI), which is widely used in North America to translate meteorological drought into a measure of agricultural drought, and which also has a variant for measuring hydrological drought; the Drought Area Index (DAI), which is used to calculate cumulative moisture shortfalls in a monsoonal climate (specifically the Indian subcontinent); and, a relatively new Standardized Precipitation Index (SPI), which has gained popularity in a number of countries (Kentayash and Dracup 2002). It is not essential to understand the workings of these various drought indices to investigate the influence of droughts on human migration, but a familiarity with them is helpful for those seeking to take model-based projections of future droughts under climate change and assess their potential impacts on food supplies, population movements, and other aspects of human well-being.

Hydrological drought refers to shortages in the available supply of water in all potential locations across a given area, including natural features on the surface (e.g. streams, rivers, and wetlands), in the ground, and in human-constructed features like canals and reservoirs (Nalbantis and Tsakiris 2009). Precise measures of the amount of water present in a watershed at a particular time are virtually impossible given the enormous amounts of data and sampling points required. The availability of ground-water is especially challenging to measure, and shortfalls in groundwater often linger well after precipitation and surface water levels have returned to normal (Shahid and Hazarika 2010). Hydrological drought is typically recognized by observing changes in stream flow over time, by using gauges situated at critical points within a water-shed, and by monitoring water levels in storage reservoirs. The ability to recognize and generate future predictions of hydrological drought is particularly important for areas of chronic water stress (i.e. where the size of the population is very high rela-tive to available potable water supplies). In recent years, cities including Atlanta, Mumbai, and Sana'a (Yemen) have come perilously close to exhausting their water supplies during hydrological droughts (Associated Press 2007, *Deccan Herald* 2012, IRIN 2012).

Vegetative drought refers to conditions where shortfalls in available moisture cause stress on the ability of plants to photosynthesize and grow (Thurow and Taylor 1999). Shortfalls in moisture can result from low levels of precipitation, prolonged high tem-peratures, or combinations of both. Vegetative drought can have impacts on human socioeconomic systems in a variety of ways. One is by reducing forest productivity, increasing the potential for damage or death of healthy trees, and rendering forests more susceptible to pest outbreaks (Billings and Phillips 2011). This in turn can have negative effects on forest-based activities like timber extraction or food collection and raise the risk of forest settlements being threatened by fire (Westerling et al. 2006, Marengo et al. 2008). Vegetative drought also affects the productivity of agricultural and grazing lands, and it is this type of drought, *agricultural drought*, with which most people are familiar (Quiring and Papakryiakou 2003). In severe cases the availabil-ity of drinking water for livestock may also be affected. Again, no universal standard exists for measuring agricultural drought nor is there any single cause. Agricultural drought conditions at a given location are shaped by the combination of climatic fac-tors, local physical characteristics (such as the local topography, soil conditions, and availability of ground or surface water) and the characteristics of local human systems (such as crop choices and land management practices). Common agricultural crops have widely varying soil moisture requirements and heat tolerance, and so conditions that constitute drought for one cropping system may not do so in another. For example, sorghum and cowpeas have relatively low moisture requirements, whereas corn (maize) and potatoes have comparatively high demands for soil moisture. Wheat's moisture requirements fall between those of sorghum and corn, while rice has difficulty growing in dry conditions without irrigation.

Three important dimensions of agricultural drought are the general availability of moisture in a given region, the timing of moisture shortfalls within the growth cycle of the crops, and temperatures during the growing season. For example, in the northern hemisphere's key grain-exporting nations like Canada, Russia, and the United States, large areas of wheat are seeded in the spring, once the ground is workable and the risk of a late frost is past.[2] There needs to be sufficient moisture in the soil to enable the germination of seeds and to maintain the plant through a rapid period of growth that cumulates in the formation of the seed head by mid-July (Robertson 1974). A lack of soil moisture during this critical six-week to eight-week period has a much more significant effect on crop yields[3] than it does later in the summer. The moisture available in the soil for use by the plant comes from the combination of unused moisture from the previous growing season, the melting of snow that accumulated over the winter, and spring precipitation. A shortfall in any one of these three contributors to soil moisture can have a negative impact on crop yields. Soil moisture levels are further affected by air temperatures, with hot temperatures causing evapotranspiration rates to rise and accelerating the rate of soil moisture depletion; hence farmers worry more about a 'hot drought' (i.e. low rainfall and high temperatures) than a 'cool drought' (low rainfall but cool temperatures). All this goes to say that the amount of crop harvested is the result of many interconnected factors, and that it may be well into the growing season before farmers know for certain they are in the midst of a drought.

An important distinction needs to be made between seasonality of precipitation and drought. Many regions experience a high degree of seasonality in precipitation, with areas described as having monsoonal climates experiencing distinct wet and dry seasons (see map of the world's monsoonal climates, Figure 4.5). Annual dry seasons are not droughts. In seasonal precipitation regimes, droughts occur when low amounts of precipitation are received during the wet season. For example, in late 2009 and the first half of 2010, much of India experienced severe drought conditions because rain during the June to September 2009 monsoon was more than 20 per cent below the expected mean, a shortfall that was compounded by long gaps between rainfall events during the monsoon period (Neena, Suhas, and Goswami 2011). While Indian agricultural and urban systems are adapted to highly seasonal precipitation regimes,

---

[2] In areas with mild winters, wheat may be seeded in the fall, allowing it to sprout and then go dormant before resuming growth in the spring. This is generally referred to as *winter wheat*.

[3] The term *crop yield* simply refers to the amount of a crop harvested as compared with the area sown, and is measured in units of volume or weight of harvested crop per unit of area.

this particular event had significant impacts on agricultural yields and left municipal water supply reservoirs in Mumbai dangerously close to empty.

6.3 Exposure to Droughts Past, Present, and Future

Droughts are believed to have had a significant influence on past human settlement and migration patterns, and scholars have included drought among the factors that led to the fall of classical civilizations in Mesoamerica, Africa, and Asia (Fagan 2004, 2008, 2009). In China, where written records extend back a millennium, there are numerous examples of large-scale population movements and political unrest occurring during periods of extended drought and longer-term precipitation regime changes (Gottschang 1987; Smit and Cao 1996; Fang, Ye, and Zeng 2007; Zhang et al. 2007; Lee, Fok, and Zhang 2008; Huang and Su 2009; Kim 2010). For other parts of the world, instrumental records for precipitation vary, but typically do not extend much farther back than the mid-nineteenth century. Scientists therefore use proxy data to estimate past drought occurrences, which are acquired from tree rings, ice cores, corals, and lake sediments (Laird et al. 2003, Mann et al. 2008). Such data suggest that, notwithstanding events like the North American Dust Bowl of the 1930s, severe African droughts of the 1980s and 1990s, or Australia's recent 'Big Dry', the twentieth century was a relatively 'wet' century in terms of precipitation received in most continental regions. Drought events of living memory and in more recent recorded history pale in comparison with those of past centuries in terms of duration and severity (Sauchyn, Stroich, and Beriault 2003; Cook et al. 2007).

Climate scientists believe that the frequency and intensity of droughts will increase in many continental regions in coming decades as a result of anthropogenic climate change (Solomon et al. 2007). If so, this presents a number of concerns regarding future population movements, especially distress migration. Of seventy-six famine events documented during the twentieth century, sixty-eight were associated with drought events (the others were mostly associated with armed conflict (Below et al. 2007)). The International Disaster Database at Belgium's Centre for Research on the Epidemiology of Disasters (CRED) identified a total of approximately 400 multiyear drought events worldwide during the twentieth century, linking these to approximately 12 million deaths, affecting 1.8 billion people, and leading to nearly US$80 billion in economic losses (Table 6.1). While disaster reporting data is inherently variable,[4] Table 6.1 provides a good general picture of the implications droughts hold for human societies, especially in less-developed regions. In addition to the direct impacts on

---

[4] Table 6.1 suggests that only seventy-three deaths can be directly associated with droughts that occurred in the Americas during the twentieth century. Great Plains droughts are suspected of having significant health impacts on residents (Smoyer-Tomic et al. 2004), and so the figure of seventy-three deaths likely underreports the actual number of premature deaths that occurred in drought-stricken areas of North America during the 1930s alone. See Egan (2006) for a description of the phenomenon of dust pneumonia in the southern Great Plains.

lives and livelihoods, droughts are also associated with other environmental risks to human well-being, including desertification, soil erosion, and declining availability of water in underground aquifers (Nagarajan 2009).

6.4 Sensitivity of Human Systems to Drought

6.4.1 Rural System Sensitivity

All human systems require water to function, and so all populations are sensitive to droughts directly or indirectly to some extent. Rural populations are particularly sensitive given how closely rural livelihoods, land use systems, and incomes are linked to vegetative productivity. The degree and nature of this sensitivity varies from one place to another according to local environmental conditions and local socioeconomic systems, the latter including land use, land occupancy and tenure systems, and the structure of local rural labor markets. These are now considered in greater detail.

6.4.1.1 Impacts of Crop Losses on Incomes and Livelihoods

Crop-based agricultural systems, even those with irrigation, are inherently susceptible to the possibility of reduced crop yield due to drought-induced moisture deficit. Precisely how drought-related crop losses translate into changes in household well-being depends on such factors as the type and orientation of production, cropping practices, and tenure systems. Subsistence and small-hold farmers are especially vulnerable to drought. They make up the largest share of the global population directly dependent on agriculture; they also make up a disproportionate share of the world's poorest people, perhaps as much as three-quarters of the more than one billion people who live on less than a dollar a day (Morton 2007). The percentage of subsistence and small-hold farmers varies by country and region, with the largest concentrations found in sub-Saharan Africa.

Subsistence farmers' objectives are to produce sufficient food for direct household consumption plus enough surplus to sell or exchange for goods and services that cannot be self-produced. When hit by drought, subsistence farming populations can experience a decline in the food calories available to household members and an inability to purchase or trade for basic necessities. Where drought conditions persist across multiple growing seasons, severe hunger or famine may ensue. Where subsistence producers operate the land as tenants, they may be structurally predisposed to displacement and migration during drought conditions because their residency and land occupancy rights depend on generating sufficient yield to pay the following season's rent (see case study later in this chapter). Landless agricultural laborers, indebted subsistence farmers, or those who occupy land in jurisdictions where tenure is unclear or disputed may also be at higher risk of displacement during drought (Unruh 2004, McLeman et al. 2008).

The economic, mobility, and land use patterns of subsistence swidden agriculturalists (also described as slash-and-burn agriculturalists) are also sensitive to drought, which can lead to changes in swidden locations, crop choices, and seasonal wage labor migration. Such changes were documented by Wadley (2002) among Indonesia's Iban people following the drought-triggered forest fires of 1997 (where the haze caused by fires had a greater influence on crop yields than dryness itself), while Conelly (1992) described Napsaan swidden agriculturalists in the Philippines experimenting with more sedentary, irrigation-based systems following a 1981 drought.

For crop farmers whose production is market oriented as opposed to subsistence oriented, droughts translate into lost farm business revenues and smaller household incomes. Farm incomes are variable from one year to the next because of a wide range of production and market factors; droughts tend to exacerbate the negative periods in this inherent variability. For example, in a recent study of Australian farmers, Edwards, Gray, and Hunter (2009) found that those who had experienced drought conditions in the previous three years were nearly twice as likely to be experiencing financial hardship as farmers who had not experienced a drought (47 per cent versus 25 per cent).[5] Where drought conditions persist for extended periods, farmers can become trapped in a downward economic spiral of reduced ability to purchase farming inputs for future seasons or update equipment; increased indebtedness; seeking greater off-farm employment; and other situations that reinforce or increase future vulnerability to the inherent variability of farming incomes (Pandey and Bhandari 2007). Droughts may also reduce the need for agricultural labor, thereby causing a drop in the availability of wage labor opportunities in the rural area and creating hardship for farm workers and their families (e.g. Edwards et al. 2009). For example, a 1987–92 drought in the Fresno area of California led to one-quarter of farms ceasing operations (most of them small-hold operations); the closure of three of seven produce-packing facilities; overall decline in farm and produce-packing incomes; increased unemployment; and a decline in retail sales at area businesses (Villarejo 1996).

6.4.1.2 Effects of Drought on Livestock Production and Pastoralism

Livestock production – whether done on farms or by pastoralists – is also highly sensitive to drought. Livestock need regular access to drinking water to ensure survival, with cattle particularly sensitive to lack of water. When droughts cause the disappearance of surface water on grazing land, water must be obtained from other sources or livestock must be moved to other locations. Prolonged drought conditions can also lead to a degradation of soil and vegetation quality on grazing lands (Thurow and Taylor 1999). Decreased quality or availability of fodder over even short periods causes a rapid decline in animal weight and health, reducing the commercial value

---

[5] The authors also observed that out-migration was a few per cent higher in rural areas that had experienced a drought in the preceding three years as compared with areas that had not experienced drought.

of the herd. If animals must be sold during drought, the owner is often selling from a position of weakness relative to potential buyers, and may be competing with other distress sellers of livestock (Rass 2011). In extreme situations, animals may be exterminated or left to waste and die.

Depending on the country and economic system, livestock production may be carried out by commercial livestock operators using private or public grazing lands; by small-hold farmers as part of specialized livestock or diversified crop-livestock operations; by pastoralists; or by combinations of some or all of these. In some regions, smaller livestock (e.g. goats, pigs) and poultry may be kept by households living in urban and peri-urban areas as a means of supplementing household income and food supplies. Livestock production is governed by market mechanisms that also vary from one country or region to the next.[6] Of the various types of livestock operations, pastoralists stand out as being those where drought sensitivity and livestock loss has the most direct linkage to changes in mobility and migration behavior. Pastoralism is by its nature an adaptation to highly variable climates. Pastoralists can be *nomadic*, moving their herds across large regions in search of fodder and water, or practice *transhumance pastoralism*, whereby herd owners living in settlements move their herds between set destinations on a seasonal basis.[7] The world's estimated 100–200 million pastoralists typically live in dryland and upland regions, the largest concentrations found in the drylands of Asia and Africa (Davies and Hatfield 2007).

Drought conditions can translate rapidly into severe economic and livelihood losses for livestock-dependent populations. The experience of Kenyan pastoralists over recent decades provides a good example. Ariaal pastoralists in north central Kenya reported losses of cattle of up to 50 per cent during a 1984 drought, which led to a deepening of socioeconomic inequality among households and increased out-migration to urban centers (Fratkin and Roth 1990). In the Baringo district, a nine-month drought in 1985 led to herd losses of up to 50 per cent, (Homewood and Lewis 1987). That same year in the Maasailand, herd losses of over 40 per cent were experienced in some areas, especially where less drought-resistant cattle were kept because of their higher market value (Nkedianye et al. 2011). In that particular drought event, the movement of cattle from extremely dry areas to less hard-hit ones led to over-grazing of pasture and exacerbated the loss of animals. Drought conditions in Kenya in 2008–9 led to the deaths of an estimated 57 per cent of cattle and 65 per cent of sheep in Samburu District, with even higher death rates in the Laikipia North District (International Livestock Research Institute 2011). It is not only drought that can cause large-scale deaths of pastoralists' livestock; unusually heavy rains in east Africa following an El Niño event in the 1990s caused widespread loss of herds.[8]

---

[6] See, for example, Turner and Williams (2002) for an analysis of livestock markets in the African Sahel.
[7] Such as those who live in mountainous environments moving herds to higher elevations in summer and to lower ones in winter.
[8] See Galvin 2009 for a more detailed review of present-day stresses on pastoralist livelihoods.

Institutional regimes that govern grazing and water rights in a given region strongly influence the degree of sensitivity of pastoralists to drought. Where rights are constrained or restricted, the search for water during drought can bring pastoralists into conflict with other groups. In western Sudano-Sahelian Africa, for example, pastoralists tend to move their cattle along established routes between Chad, Niger, and Nigeria, which governments reserve for them as grazing corridors (Nyong, Fiki, and McLeman 2006). During droughts, fodder and water within these corridors can become scarce, leading herders to move their animals to more distant areas and bringing them into competition and conflict with resident farmers. Traditional conflict resolution systems involving local elders have historically kept such conflicts from becoming violent, but state governments seeking to impose their authority have begun undermining these systems (Nyong et al. 2006). In Darfur and in the Somalia-Kenya border regions, competition between pastoralists and other groups has led to violence in the past decade (Meier, Bond, and Bond 2007; UNEP 2007). In these and other regions, the mobility of pastoralists is being curtailed because of fragmentation of traditional grazing lands (due to settlement of non-pastoralist farmers and/or changes to land tenure systems instituted by governments) or through the decision of pastoralists themselves to settle in permanent locations so as to engage in more diversified livelihoods and to gain access to health, education, and other services (Galvin 2009). Because pastoral mobility is itself an adaptation to highly variable environmental conditions, grazing fragmentation and greater levels of sedentarism heighten pastoralists' sensitivity to drought in the absence of other livelihood system adjustments.

6.4.1.3 Sensitivity to Drought in Forest-Based Livelihood Systems

In forested regions, drought conditions place stress on trees, causing temporary decline in growth and productivity and rendering them more susceptible to pests and disease. Persistent drought conditions may eventually lead to tree death, although trees in intact and healthy forests are generally resilient to drought (Saleska et al. 2007). Droughts also elevate the risk of fire. In some forest ecosystems, such as the mixed coniferous and boreal forests of western North America, fires are a regular and naturally occurring disturbance. Trees there are consequently highly adapted to fire, and species like jack pine (*Pinus banksiana*) and some ponderosa pines (*Pinus ponderosa*) actually require periodic fires to propagate (Viegas 1998). In tropical forests, fires are less common and often associated with severe droughts, which are in turn associated with El Niño events like the one in 1997–8 that caused large fires in Indonesia and the Amazon (Harrison 2000, Laurance and Williamson 2001). De Mendonca and colleagues (2004) compared forest losses due to fire in the Brazilian Amazon during the 1998 El Niño event to a non-El Niño baseline year of 1995, and found the losses were over fourteen times higher in the El Niño year. Anthropogenic climate change is expected to create hotter, dryer conditions and more frequent drought events in both tropical and nontropical forest regions that will exacerbate fire risks (e.g. Aragão et al.

2007, Flannigan et al. 2009). Wildfire activity in the U.S. southwest already appears to be rising because of a combination of spring warming, which brings on an earlier snowmelt, and hotter summer temperatures in that generally arid region (Westerling et al. 2006).

The impacts of drought and fire on forest-dependent communities are experienced through local impacts on incomes, on human health and safety, and property damage. The loss of harvestable timber to fire has direct economic implications for forestry workers and their dependent families, although these are challenging to quantify on a standardized basis across large scales (Silva et al. 2012). Settlements situated adjacent to forests are also at risk of loss or damage during fire. In 2003, twenty-six thousand people evacuated from homes in Kelowna, British Columbia, Canada, in the face of severe fires that destroyed nearly 250 homes and caused significant financial losses to the area's tourism industry (Hystad and Keller 2006). In Amazonia, pasturelands adjoining forests are particularly susceptible to damage from fire, with de Mendonca and colleagues (2004) valuing the average losses in any given year during the mid-1990s at between US$20 million and $40 million. Estimated annual hospitalizations for respiratory illnesses in Brazil's Amazonian region tripled during the El Niño fire seasons of 1997 and 1998 (de Mendonca et al. 2004). Even short-duration fires can pose significant risks for people with preexisting respiratory conditions, as measured by hospital emergency visits (e.g. Duclos, Sanderson, and Lipsett 1990). A 2005 drought caused widespread forest fires in Brazilian Amazonia, and led to falling water levels in many lakes and tributaries. This meant that some settlements within the forest could not bring in supplies by boat (the main transportation method in the region) nor get their own produce to markets, while other settlements found their drinking water poisoned by large fish die-offs (Marengo et al. 2008). The impacts of fire on livelihoods and well-being in Brazilian Amazonia are reminiscent of the late nineteenth and early twentieth century in frontier settlement areas in North America, where forest fires in Montana's high country mining region and Canada's Upper Ottawa Valley led to the abandonment of some small settlements and localized population loss (Currie 2009, Egan 2009).

6.4.1.4 Urban Sensitivity to Drought

While agriculture tends to be the highest sectorial user of water, especially where irrigation is practiced, there is concern that urban growth is exacerbating the rapid depletion of surface and groundwater supplies in many already water-scarce regions across South and Central Asia, large areas of Africa, and China's lower Yellow River valley, thereby increasing the risk of urban drought (Postel 2000, Yang and Zehnder 2001). McDonald and colleagues (2011) estimate that more than 150 million people worldwide live in cities with perennial water shortages, primarily in the Middle East and North Africa, and another 800+ million in cities with seasonal water shortages, found across Asia, Africa, and Latin and South America. Urban water scarcity is not, however, simply a developing world challenge. On the Canadian Great Plains, water flow levels are steadily declining in rivers that service several large cities (Schindler and Donohue 2006). Growing competition between rural and urban users is emerging in many parts of the Mediterranean region (Iglesias et al. 2007). Most Australian urban centers face very real limits on the availability of water, with drought conditions of recent years highlighting the need for increasing supplies and raising prices charged for municipal water (Grafton and Kompas 2007).

The sensitivity of a particular urban population to drought is highly dependent on local climatic conditions; the accessibility and reliability of surface and groundwater supplies; human-use patterns and related demand; and the nature of the built water system and sewerage infrastructure. Urban populations consume water for domestic, commercial, and industrial purposes, and with economic development, water demand for all three purposes typically grows. In developing regions, urban water scarcity is typically caused by high rates of population growth, under-investment in water infrastructure, and the physical limits of water availability in the surrounding area (Van der Bruggen, Borghgraef, and Vinckier 2010). Cities also require large amounts of surface water to accept and transport wastewater. Not all cities have sanitary sewerage or waste water treatment, and not all areas within a city that does have sewerage infrastructure have access to it, especially informal settlements. The volume of water required to accept incoming waste varies according to the nature and volume of the waste stream. Where the waste stream overwhelms the capacity for naturally occurring microorganisms to break it down, dissolved oxygen is depleted and the water becomes septic (APHA 1992). When drought reduces surface water availability, the impacts of urban waste on water quality are compounded.

In the face of local scarcity or seasonal variability in water supplies, cities with sufficient financial resources typically invest in water storage and transportation infrastructure. In southern California, for example, the Metropolitan Water District collects, stores, and transports water via aqueduct from the Sierra Nevada mountains and the Colorado River basin to 19 million people in Los Angeles and surrounding areas. On average, the amount of water delivered via this system is nearly 7 billion liters (over 1.8 billion U.S. gallons) each day to an area that could never begin to meet its water needs from local surface supplies (Metropolitan Water District of Southern California 2012). The city of Mumbai, India, which receives most of its annual precipitation in bursts of summer monsoonal rains, also has an elaborate infrastructure for capturing, storing, and delivering water. This infrastructure is stretched increasingly thin by rapid population increase and demand, and in 2009 the city's water reserves ran dangerously low following a poor monsoon season (Gandy 2008). At the time of this writing, Mumbai is again struggling with low water supplies. On a global basis, African urban centers tend to have the least amount of investment in supply infrastructure, relying heavily on ground and surface water supplies in their immediate vicinity (Showers 2002). This renders them particularly vulnerable not only to drought but to water supply contamination from industrial, agricultural, and human waste.

6.4.1.5 Sensitivity of Global Food Systems

A particularly notable indirect impact of drought on urban and rural populations alike is its influence on food prices, which hits poor households especially hard. Up until the mid-twentieth century, the diets of most people in developed and developing regions alike were based primarily on foods produced in the regions where they lived. When droughts caused declines in local or regional production, the effect on food prices was felt most strongly at the same spatial scale. Today, agricultural products are exchanged and shipped internationally in ever-growing amounts, with more and more of the world's agricultural regions becoming incorporated into a global food system. Many basic food staples are produced not just for direct consumption, but for other purposes as well, such as food processing inputs and biofuel feedstocks, with market prices reflecting this range of demands (McMichael 2009a). While global food production has risen steadily over the past several decades, these productivity gains have been matched by global population growth and rising per capita food consumption by increasingly affluent populations in China, India, and other middle-income countries. Two important outcomes emerge from the combination of these trends. First, we now live in a world where food prices are becoming very volatile (Figure 6.1), and global food production must increase year over year simply to maintain price stability. It is no longer enough to simply produce the same amount as last year, for that may lead prices to rise. Second, given the interconnectedness of the global food system, the impacts of drought are no longer constrained to food prices in the regions where the drought occurs; instead, they ripple outward across the globe. This is especially the case when drought hits one of the world's key food-exporting nations such as Australia, Brazil, Canada, Russia, or the United States.

For example, severe droughts hit the main grain-producing areas of Kazakhstan, Russia, and the Ukraine in 2009 and again in 2010. Normally this region is a significant exporter of grain, but crop yields fell from the previous year by as much as 60 per cent for crops in some areas, with Russia's overall grain production dropping by 30 per cent (USDA 2011). The Russian government consequently placed restrictions on grain exports (McMichael 2009b, Wegren 2011). Between 2006 and 2010, many parts of Australia also suffered through drought, significantly curtailing grain exports in some years. In 2011, wheat-producing areas of China experienced drought, prompting the Chinese government to begin purchasing large quantities of grain from global markets (Sternberg 2012). These events combined to cause significant volatility in global food prices, which is in turn believed to have spurred urban riots on several continents over recent years, and contributed to broader political unrest in food-importing nations such as Tunisia, Egypt, and Syria (Cohen and Garrett 2010, Joffé 2011). Johnstone and Mazo (2011) argue that the link between food prices and

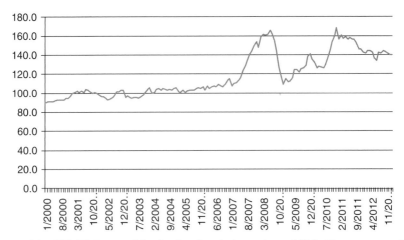

Figure 6.1. UN FAO monthly food price index, since 2000. Data source: UN FAO World Food Situation Database, February 2013 (http://www.fao.org/worldfoodsituation/wfs-home/foodpricesindex/en/). 100 on the vertical axis = average of 2002–4 food prices.

the Arab Spring is an example of how climate-change-related impacts on food production will have greater influence on international security, a topic discussed further in Chapter 8. At the time of this writing, Syria is engaged in a violent civil war; it is probably not coincidental that Syria experienced severe drought conditions from 2006 until 2011, when the current conflict began to take shape (IRIN 2009).[9] In 2011 and 2012, drought-stricken Iran purchased wheat from the United States, even as the two nations' governments were having a war of words over Iran's nuclear ambitions (Plume 2012).

6.5 Adaptation in Response to Drought

6.5.1 Urban Adaptation is Primarily In Situ

Past centuries saw a number of notable examples of settlements abandoned for reasons related in whole or in part to water scarcity and droughts, such as Fatehpur Sikri, briefly the capital of the sixteenth-century Moghul Empire in India (Biswas 1979), cities of the classic Mayan empire of Central America (Haug et al. 2003), and the twelfth-century to thirteenth-century Anasazi cliff settlements of the U.S. southwest (Benson, Petersen, and Stein 2007). In more recent living memory, a number of urban water shortage events have occurred in various regions, but these have typically not led to large-scale out-migration or settlement abandonment. The first decade of the twenty-first century saw severe droughts lead to worryingly low municipal water in

---

[9] This is not to say that the drought caused the civil conflict in Syria, only that it likely exacerbated the political and economic tensions within that country. For more on links between climate and security, see Chapter 8.

Atlanta, Mumbai, and several Australian urban centers. Local protests and isolated acts of violence accompanied water rationing measures in Mumbai, but in none of these cases did shortages cross the threshold from scarcity to absolute supply failure. The seaside town of Tofino, British Columbia, popular with tourists and surfers, in 2006 had to cut off water supplies to businesses following an unusual two-month dry spell along notoriously rainy Vancouver Island (Dodds 2012). This may have affected the number of visitors and prompted some residents to temporarily relocate elsewhere.

For the most part, however, urban adaptation to drought tends to be in situ as opposed to migration related. Cities with strong institutional capacity adapt through increasing investment in water supply infrastructure and through direct and indirect measures such as water pricing, regulation, and public education to encourage water conservation. Where institutions are weak, individual and household adaptations can include the purchase of household water from private suppliers, reducing consumption, and the drilling of private wells, among others. Ensuring adequate and reliable water supplies is an ongoing challenge for many urban centers in Africa and parts of Asia and Latin America, typically as a result of the combined effects of growing demand, underinvestment in supply infrastructure, and physical limits on local surface and groundwater resources (Showers 2002, Van der Bruggen et al. 2010). Anthropogenic climate change and rapid urbanization in these regions will likely increase the number of urbanites facing severe water shortages in coming decades, testing the limits of in situ adaptation (McDonald et al. 2011).

6.5.2 Rural Adaptation to Seasonal Dryness and Drought

Because rural populations, regardless of geographical setting, may encounter agricultural drought at one time or another, they over the course of time typically develop a range of adaptive responses tailored to the characteristics and frequency of drought in their particular region. Most of the drought-related migration events observed in living memory have involved rural populations; however, it is important to recognize that not all droughts lead to migration, and that migration is just one of a wide range of adaptation possibilities. The role that migration plays (or does not play) in drought adaptation processes in a given region or population is a function of the availability of institutionally led adaptations, the economic well-being of exposed communities and households, the functioning of social networks, land tenure arrangements, and other factors identified in the MESA function in Chapter 3 and which fit within the conceptual diagram of an adaptive system (Figure 3.9).

6.5.2.1 Institutional Adaptation

Chapter 3 also provided in Table 3.3 a simple typology of rural adaptations to climate that consisted of those guided or enacted by institutions, governments, corporations, and other macro- or meso-scale actors, and those that are undertaken at the household or micro level. This distinction between macro- and micro-level adaptation is especially relevant in discussing rural adaptation to drought. Some macro-scale adaptations are ongoing and preemptive in nature, such as the development of drought-tolerant crop varieties, the implementation of weather forecasting systems, creation of irrigation infrastructure in drought-prone areas, and micro-financing systems targeted at rural populations. Others, such as insurance, exist to lessen the impact of crop or livestock losses once drought or some other damaging event occurs. Governments may also create ad hoc programs to provide financial assistance to distressed rural populations in the wake of severe droughts. Lower-income or conflict-torn countries may lack the financial or institutional wherewithal to create and deliver these or other types of adaptation assistance to rural populations.

In countries where reliable institutions have broken down or are entirely absent, the international community through multilateral government action, UN agencies, and/or humanitarian nongovernmental organizations may intervene to provide emergency assistance, although this often does not occur until conditions are quite desperate (see, for example, the case of Somalia (Cabrol 2011)). Occasionally, governments and institutions may actively organize the movement of people out of drought-stricken rural areas on a temporary or permanent basis. Examples include government-supported abandonment of drought-prone farms in Canada and the United States during the 1930s (see case study later in this chapter) and rural population resettlement in Ethiopia during the 1980s (see Ezra 2001). In these examples, relocation was encouraged only following periods of protracted droughts, when the impacts on rural households had become particularly severe.

Where institutional adaptive capacity is strong, droughts are likely to have a relatively mild influence on rural migration decisions initiated at the household level (McLeman and Smit 2006a). However, access to institutional adaptation measures is rarely universal or equitably distributed across or within populations. For example, the latest developments in drought-tolerant crop varieties may be beyond the financial means of poorer farmers, as seen, for example, in the varieties of rice grown by Bangladeshi farmers in the case study from Chapter 5. Crop insurance programs typically depend on robust government subsidies (Smith and Glauber 2012), with developing nations often unable to implement these without external support (Linnerooth-Bayer et al. 2009). Private sector crop insurance, where it is available, is often beyond the means of poorer farmers.[10] Access to institutional programs to enhance drought prevention, protection, and recovery may be limited to people with certain categories of land tenure, or may target particular sectors of the rural economy such as farmers but neglect other sectors, such as service providers. Where institutions invest in infrastructure such as irrigation projects, benefits in terms of increased productivity and

---

[10] See Hazell and Hess (2010) for how access to crop insurance might be improved in developing regions.

fewer crop losses may follow; a question is whether such benefits are equitably distributed throughout the rural population (Khandker and Koolwal 2010). Experience shows that, where land rights are uncertain or unequally distributed, the introduction of large-scale irrigation infrastructure can exacerbate income inequality and reinforce the poverty and vulnerability of the rural poor (Hussain and Hanjra 2003).

6.5.2.2 Household Adaptation

In situations where institutional adaptations to drought are inadequate or inaccessible, adaptation takes place primarily at the household level through adjustments to existing livelihood systems and methods, seeking access to additional resources, or engaging in new or additional livelihood practices and methods. Examples of adjustments to livelihoods can include farmers changing their crop choices, reallocating land on the farm to different uses, terracing slopes to reduce run-off, or acquiring irrigation equipment (Smit and Skinner 2002, McLeman et al. 2008). The extent to which responses such as these are adopted is often determined not simply by their relative efficacy, but also by nonclimatic macro-level influences, such as prevailing commodity prices and interest rates; meso-level factors, like access to credit from lending institutions; and micro-level factors, such as the health of household members.

As an example, sorghum is a drought-tolerant grain crop that can be used as human food (e.g. bread and couscous), for livestock feed, or for ethanol production, and has a market price similar to corn. Choosing sorghum over corn would at face value seem a logical adaptation for farmers to reduce their exposure to drought. Yet in North America, even in areas where droughts are known to occur, so long as the land is viable for both corn and sorghum, farmers will plant many times more area in corn. There are two key reasons. First, a healthy corn crop yields anywhere between two and three times more grain than the same acreage planted to sorghum.[11] In non-drought years, which will be the majority, the farmer earns more income per acre growing corn instead of sorghum. When selecting crops to plant, farmers make decisions based on what is most likely to generate a good economic return, so even following a drought that drastically reduces corn yields, farmers in traditional corn-growing areas are just as likely to plant more corn than sorghum in subsequent years. A second reason is that North American farmers have access to a variety of crop insurance and other institutional programs that help stabilize farm incomes, meaning most can afford to take some crop losses due to drought in a given year. However, even before such programs were in place, such as in the 1930s, corn was still a much more popular crop choice than sorghum among U.S. farmers, and was still just as likely to be planted in years

---

[11] See, for example, U.S. Department of Agriculture Economic Research Service annual feed crop reports at http://www.ers.usda.gov/data-products/feed-grains-database/feed-grains-yearbook-tables.aspx (last accessed August 2012). For international readers, North American farmers invariably describe land area in units of acres and not hectares. One acre is approximately 0.4 hectares. There is a logical reason for this beyond tradition: land in North America was surveyed according to the imperial measurement system, and so a farmer's landholdings are still easily measured in blocks of acres.

following droughts. The development of increasingly drought-tolerant corn varieties – which appear to have fared reasonably well during the severe 2012 drought in the U.S. Corn Belt (Stecker 2012) – may further reinforce farmers' decisions to favor corn over sorghum in the absence of any changes in the prices of the two crops.[12]

Irrigation is another obvious adaptation to drought, and can be done using water available at the surface (i.e. streams, ponds, rivers) or using water drawn from wells. Farmers face a range of potential physical, institutional, technical, and financial impediments to implementing irrigation systems. The most obvious physical one is the availability of a water source near where it is needed. Where an irrigation water source is not present or immediately accessible to a farmer's land, he or she must work through institutional actors and/or collectively with others to gain access to water. Institutionally operated irrigation schemes can be found in developed and less-developed countries alike, from central California to central Mali, each presenting their own particular user needs, water-sharing arrangements, competing interests, and management challenges (Vandersypen et al. 2006). In areas where individual farmers make their own decisions about irrigation, their ability to implement small-scale irrigation depends in part on their personal financial resources or their ability to borrow money at reasonable interest rates to acquire the necessary equipment (such as through micro-finance schemes). Creditors may be less willing or able to lend to farmers during times of drought for fear of default, and households' own financial resources may be stretched. Consequently, farm-level capital expenditures on things such as irrigation systems are adaptations more likely to be successfully pursued in good times rather than after drought conditions strike (McLeman et al. 2008).

It is also important to note that irrigation is not a perfect adaptation. There is growing concern, for example, that groundwater is overexploited in the western United States, and in the absence of better management a water crisis may emerge there in coming decades (Scanlon et al. 2012). In rural northern Iraq, the drilling of private boreholes wells, encouraged by international donors as a means of helping rural populations adapt to drought, is lowering local water tables and affecting the reliability of traditional communal water systems called *karez* (Lightfoot 2009). In dryland areas, overuse of irrigation can lead to the salinization of soil, reducing its long-term productivity, and increase the salinity of water running off the land, reducing the quality of water received by downstream users (Isidoro and Grattan 2011).

Other household-level adaptations to drought can include a range of actions that are not directly related to production, such as seeking off-farm employment; participating in farm or community support programs; selling off livestock or assets; or sharing equipment, labor, and resources with neighbors (Skinner and Smit 2002, McLeman et al. 2008). Some of these responses entail a certain degree of mobility or

---

[12] Sorghum is, however, able to grow in areas too dry for corn, and is a more effective feedstock for ethanol than is corn, explaining why sorghum remains within the mix of crops American farmers grow.

temporary migration on the part of household members, while others do not. In most cases, permanent migration out of a drought-stricken area is a last resort response not undertaken unless and until the household has exhausted all of its other adaptation options. For example, in interviewing farm families in a particularly drought-prone area of rural northern Burkina Faso, Barbier and colleagues (2009) found very few who considered permanent out-migration an attractive adaptation option for drought. Respondents instead cited better access to credit, irrigation, short-term food aid, local off-farm employment, better seeds, insurance, and income diversification as more preferable options. This case is especially noteworthy because temporary and seasonal migration are relatively common adaptations for drought in the study area, and permanent out-migration for reasons other than drought (typically economic reasons) is also common. For readers interested in exploring further the range of non-migration rural household adaptations to drought, a number of useful studies and reviews are available for Africa (e.g. Mortimore and Adams 2001, Thomas et al. 2007, Barbier et al. 2009, Eriksen and Lind 2009, Eriksen and Silva 2009, Mertz et al. 2009, Stringer et al. 2009), Latin and South America (e.g. Liverman 1999, Eakin 2005, Nelson and Finan 2009), and South Asia (e.g. Selveraju et al. 2006; Prabhakar and Shaw 2008; Ghimire, Shivakoti, and Perret 2010).[13] The remainder of this chapter focuses on adaptive migration specifically.

6.6 Migration as a Rural Adaptation to Seasonal Dryness and Drought

In considering the linkages between drought and household migration, it is useful to make a distinction between migration used as an ongoing adaptation to seasonal dryness, and cases where exceptional drought conditions are experienced, especially those that have an impact on food security.

6.6.1 Seasonal Migration as an Ongoing Adaptation to Uncertain Precipitation in Dryland Regions

Rural households have long used seasonal labor migration to maximize incomes and diversify risks, independent of any concerns of drought. Participation in seasonal labor migration is still strong among rural populations in many developing countries, especially in dryland regions. Agricultural systems tend to have fluctuating demands for labor throughout the year. The timing of busier and less busy periods is determined by climate (e.g. seasonality of rainfall) and by the natural growth cycle of crop and fodder plants. With the mechanization and commercialization of agriculture in developed countries over the past 100 years, the need for a large stock of resident

---

[13] Given that the number of English-language peer-reviewed studies on household-level adaptation to drought outside of Africa is rather low, this suggests an opportunity for future research in an increasingly important field.

labor in the countryside has dwindled. Rural populations in developed countries have become smaller and, on average, older, and participation in seasonal rural migration has dwindled.[14] Instead of hosting a large resident labor base that looks elsewhere for work during slack times, rural areas in developed countries are today more likely to import seasonal migrants from elsewhere to perform agricultural work during busy times. In the United States, for example, three-quarters of farm workers were born in Mexico, and it is estimated slightly more than half of them are not legally authorized to work in the United States (U.S. Department of Labor 2005). By contrast, in developing countries in Africa, Asia, and Latin America, where agriculture and other rural activities still operate on smaller scales, seasonal migration of residents within the region remains a particularly important adaptation strategy for rural households. Several examples help illustrate how seasonal migration works in the context of dryland agricultural adaptation and some of the challenges that go along with it.

In India, dryland regions exhibit much lower agricultural productivity and higher rates of household poverty and indebtedness than other regions (Rao 2008). Seasonal migration has long been incorporated into the livelihood strategies of dryland Indian households as an ongoing adaptation (Haberfeld et al. 1999). The reasons for migrating, destination choices, and numbers and types of people undertaking seasonal migration vary significantly depending on the particular environmental conditions and crop systems of the source area; the nature of labor migration networks already established; labor market conditions in the receiving area; the caste to which the household belongs; the ability of the household to do temporarily without the labor of the migrant (i.e. family size and health of members); and other factors.[15] In recent years, participation in seasonal migration in Madhya Pradesh state has been growing, not because of a change in climate or other push factors in the countryside, but because growth in employment opportunities and wages in the city has helped improve the financial well-being of many rural households (Deshingkar et al. 2008). At the sub-household level, research from Andhra Pradesh shows that because seasonal off-farm employment opportunities are greater for men, there is a growing gender gap in income and earning potential between men and women (Garikipati 2008).

In Sudano-Sahelian Africa, dry season migration is commonplace across sedentary farmer and pastoralist populations in many countries. In his study of seasonal migration in Niger, *Eaters of the Dry Season*, Rain (1999) described how the regular,

---

[14] In my ongoing research in rural Ontario, Canada, I still occasionally encounter small-operation farmers who move to the city during winter to work in construction. These are few and far between, however, and in many cases are people who originally lived in the city and took up farming as a second career. A more common seasonal movement phenomenon is for young people to go to the city to attend college/university and return home on weekends and holidays to perform chores as needed; once their education is completed, however, they tend to remain in the city and have increasingly less contact with the old rural home. I suspect this phenomenon is not unique to Ontario.

[15] See Deshingkar and Start (2003) for a broad-based study of seasonal migrants in Madhya Pradesh and Andhra Pradesh.

circular movement of people from rural villages to cities or more prosperous agricultural regions and back again through the seasons is critical to maintaining the long-term economic security of rural households in the drylands. Villagers Rain interviewed during his study indicated explicitly that they placed great value in the social networks created through migration, and that these were to some extent as valuable as the land itself; in other words, their choice of migration as an ongoing adaptation strategy is deliberate. Similar to Deshingkar's commentaries on India (Deshingkar and Start 2003, Deshingkar et al. 2008), Rain argues that seasonal migration must not be seen as undesirable, but a very logical behavior that should not be restricted.

Northern Ghana provides another example of adaptive dry season migration. There, the northern dry savannah experiences only a single rainy season, from May to August (Codjoe and Bilsborrow 2011). Subsistence rain-fed agriculture is the most common rural livelihood in that region, but in many years farmers are unable to produce for themselves a full twelve-month food supply (Quaye 2008). Members of northern households have long engaged in dry season migration to more humid areas to the south to find wage employment, which increases household food security and provides one of the few ways of gaining access to money and consumer goods (Van der Geest 2010; Owusu, Abdulai, and Abdul-Rahman 2011). Seasonal migrants may be destined to both rural and urban areas. In some cases, rural-to-rural migrants may extend their stays in the south to work as sharecroppers, saving money in hopes of acquiring their own land in the south while simultaneously remitting food to family members back in the north (Luginaah et al. 2009). By doing so, they reduce pressure on the family's farmland in the north and, where successful, the cumulative effect is to enable household members at sending and receiving ends to achieve higher living standards (Van der Geest 2010). The household-level outcomes of north-south labor migration are not always positive. Van der Geest (2010) notes that sometimes migrants are not successful at finding work, or simply lose interest in their sending community and fail to make their remittances. Should they return home empty-handed, they become a burden to the household. A study by Karamba, Quinones, and Winters (2011) found that remittances are not necessarily spent on food by receiving households, and when they are, they are often spent on eating in restaurants or on low-quality junk foods. As in India, there are gender implications of seasonal labor migration in northern Ghana, with responsibility for operating the northern farmland in the hands of women, but land management decisions and tenure still reserved for male household members, placing women food producers in a difficult social dynamic (Bugri 2008). For many young people, the physical demands, limited mobility, and lack of alternative opportunities make northern farm life unappealing, leading them to remain longer in the urban centers of the south (Porter et al. 2011). Especially for younger men, migrating to the city has become more than simply a socioeconomic adaptation, and personal motivations of gaining status within their own peer group may provide a greater motivation for migrating than any interest in providing for family members during the dry season (Ungruhe 2010).

Recent decades have seen pastoralist groups in dryland West Africa adopt temporary wage labor migration as a means of diversifying their livelihoods. For example, in research carried out among the Fulani people of Burkina Faso, Hampshire (2002; with Randall 1999) found seasonal out-migration of young men to cities began in the 1970s and 1980s and grew in importance for maintaining the socioeconomic well-being of rural communities. Hampshire observed that poorer households, as measured by the number of able-bodied workers and/or wealth in cattle, were less likely to participate in rural-to-urban seasonal migration. This is due to two factors. First, the costs involved in transportation to and accommodation in the city are not affordable for all. Second, because most Fulani typically keep cattle, even among more sedentary households there is still labor to be performed at home during the dry season, so the ability to do without household members is a consideration, and smaller families with few able-bodied men might not be able to do without labor even during dry periods. As might be expected, a considerable differential in household wealth emerges between those that can afford to participate in seasonal labor migration and those that cannot. Again, as in India and Niger, social networks are critical to making seasonal migration possible, and there are gender implications from the fact that it has traditionally not been culturally acceptable for women to participate in seasonal migration. Within the broader Fulani population, for whom raising cattle has long been seen as the most important economic and cultural practice in which households might engage, social acceptance of seasonal migration varies within and across communities. In groups primarily engaged in transhumance pastoralism, labor migration may be seen as shameful, done only out of desperation; in those with more sedentary livelihoods, the migrant may be judged by the status of the occupation he performs while away. Younger people are more likely than older generations to view migration and the economic prospects it brings as desirable and a more 'modern' way of life.

6.6.2 Severe Drought and Labor Migration

The relationship between precipitation seasonality and population movements described in the previous section reflects what might be described as *background migration* – that is, migration that goes on as part and parcel of life in less developed dryland regions, as rural households adapt to make the best of generally challenging conditions. When severe drought conditions emerge in such areas, migration patterns may change as households deviate from their normal migration practices, the most common change being increased levels of participation in temporary labor migration. This makes intuitive sense. During drought, less labor is required on farms, but household members still must eat. Even if the labor migrant is unable to earn enough wage income to remit money back to the household, his or her absence reduces the pressure on the household's food reserves during a time of relative scarcity. The increased participation in labor migration is also often accompanied by short-term changes in prevailing spatial and temporal patterns of migration. The nature of the changes varies according to region, reflecting the preexisting migration patterns, the availability of off-farm labor opportunities, and the geographic distribution of social networks. Again, a few examples help illustrate.

Tobert (1985) traced in detail the progression of adaptation among the Zaghawa people of northern Darfur, Sudan, who were in the fifth year of a severe drought by 1984. Cattle were the basis of wealth in Zaghawa society. When they were not tending to their own subsistence crops, members were variously engaged in pastoral migration and in seasonal migration to local centers to sell pottery and other handcrafted items. After a failed 1983 harvest, members of the population travelled to larger urban centers farther afield to sell their goods, where the market for them would be more reliable. The Sudanese government meanwhile began sending grain to northern Darfur for relief purposes. By the following year fewer cattle remained, many having died or been traded for more resilient goats. Despite repeated plantings, millet crops failed for lack of rain, and people relied increasingly on stored supplies from past years and government-supplied grain. As drought persisted, the remaining cattle, and later goats, were sold off in such numbers that their market price dropped substantially. Having learned from past droughts to save and utilize everything, people began making porridge out of stores of watermelon seeds. Families began talking of migrating to Khartoum, which they had heard promised greater chances of earning a wage. Eventually, entire villages moved to regional centers, selling off even the thatch from their roofs to support their journey. Cities became overcrowded with people seeking work, and many ended up dependent on food relief, much of it coming from international donors.

In Ethiopia, short-term labor migration increases during droughts, especially among members of landless households and those whose landholdings are small enough in size that they must supplement their household income through wage labor, whether or not there is a drought (Meze-Hausken 2000, Gray and Mueller 2012b). Seeking off-farm employment is only one of a range of short-term strategies households attempt when confronted by droughts, others including changing their consumption patterns, drawing upon food reserves, and selling off livestock or other assets (Meze-Hausken 2000). Gray and Mueller (2012b) estimate that a 10 per cent increase in the number of communities experiencing drought leads to a corresponding 10 per cent increase in the number of people on the move. Most of this additional movement is by men; the authors found that women with children are less likely to move during drought. The number of newly married women moving to join a husband's family (the cultural norm in Ethiopia) also decreases. This is likely related to cultural practices whereby marriages typically involve an exchange of financial assets between families, and these assets become scarce during drought. The likelihood of a household having a member participate in drought-related labor migration is influenced by the average family size, with larger households more likely to send migrants.

In West Africa, droughts also lead to increased participation in short-distance rural-to-urban migration, accompanied in some cases by the temporary relocation of children to homes of extended family members living outside drought-stricken areas (Findley 1994; Pedersen 1995; Rain 1999; de Haan, Brock, and Coulibaly 2002; Hampshire 2002; Nyong et al. 2006; Bassett and Turner 2007). In research in Burkina Faso, Henry, Boyle, and Lambin (2003) observed that drought-related migration tends to be short-term, cyclical, and intranational or intraregional in nature, consistent with results reported by Pedersen (1995) in his review of historical drought migration in northern Mali. Seasonal labor migration among the Fulani likely first began in response to a drought in the early 1970s, creating the networks through which subsequent seasonal labor migration continues to this day (Hampshire 2002). Political and economic conditions in potential destination areas are an important consideration. Barbier and colleagues (2009) observed that during a 2004 drought, roughly half of rural households in northern Burkina Faso sent a migrant to Cote d'Ivoire, but that political stability that began in Abidjan the following year meant far fewer migrated to Cote d'Ivoire during the 2006 drought.

While long-distance, indefinite migration from West Africa to more distant regions like Europe is well established, movement along these intercontinental migrant networks does not necessarily increase during droughts; if anything, it may slow. For example, Findley (1994) observed that migration patterns in northern Mali switched significantly during a 1982–5 drought, even though the overall number of people participating in migration changed very little. Before the drought, half of migrants were destined to France and another quarter to destinations outside Mali; once drought struck, only one-quarter of migrants went to France, while one-half stayed within Mali. The percentage of women and children participating in migration also increased during the drought, as they became incorporated in movements designed to increase income or reduce the number of household members dependent on local food reserves. Henry and colleagues (2003) similarly found that participation in long-distance migration in Burkina Faso did not go up during drought, but that most migration was over relatively short distances. The explanation is straightforward. Long-distance migration has significant economic costs for the household, including the direct financial costs of travel and accommodation as well as the opportunity cost to the household of doing without the migrant's labor. A drought-induced period of scarcity and financial hardship is not a suitable time to make such a risky investment; instead, it is when climatic and economic conditions are good that a household is more willing to take on the financial costs and risks associated with sending a migrant farther afield. Henry and colleagues (2003) note that environmental conditions or events can influence decisions to participate in long-distance, long-term migration, but these are more likely connected to more persistent environmental challenges in the sending area, such as soil erosion or land degradation, than they are with drought.

In rural India, short-term labor migration is a widespread practice by which millions adapt to droughts that occur when monsoon rains are inadequate (Haberfeld et al. 1999, Mosse et al. 2002, Rogaly et al. 2002, Deshingkar and Start 2003, Halli et al. 2007, Jülich 2011). In the Marwar region of Rajasthan, severe droughts in the 1970s and 1980s led to growing participation in nomadic pastoralism and seasonal migration among the Marwari (Robbins 1998). This reliance on pastoralism remained strong in subsequent decades, even though the severity of the impact of droughts was lessened by rural electrification and digging of deep wells. The patterns of Marwari pastoral movements change during periods of extreme drought, leading them to seek to migrate farther afield. In the 2002 drought, neighboring states imposed a ban on movements of livestock from Rajasthan in attempts to restrict such migration (Samra 2004). In rural Orissa state, Jülich (2011) identified a progression of adaptations villagers attempt as drought conditions take hold. They begin by reducing the amount of food they consume, followed by taking out small loans using livestock or household items as collateral, which may later be sold off entirely if drought conditions persist. Once these responses have been exhausted, temporary migration to a nearby urban center may be undertaken by the male household head and older sons, or the entire household, depending on the household's circumstances. Venot, Reddy, and Umapathy (2010) and Prasad and Rao (1997) have observed a similar suite of adaptations undertaken by farmers and villagers in rural Andhra Pradesh when severe droughts strike.

In China, droughts have played an influential role in rural migration for centuries, indeed millennia (Gottschang 1987; Fang et al. 2007; Lee et al. 2008; Huang et al. 2010; Ye, Fang, and Khan 2011). Teasing out the contribution of drought to more recent migration patterns is difficult. Population growth and mobility under the communist government have been controlled through the *hukou* system, whereby every household is required to register its members with its nearest local government office. The *hukou* entitles household members to a variety of state-provided social benefits, but it also allows the state to impose its one-child policy and control movements of people. The relaxation of economic controls in the early 1990s and the rapid expansion of China's export economy helped create a 'floating' population of workers who do not reside where their *hukou* indicate. By 2000, their numbers were estimated at 79 million (Liang and Ma 2004), and more recent reports from Chinese newspapers like the *China Daily* have pegged the floating population at more than 200 million. To what extent the floating population fluctuates according to drought is not clear in the available English-language scholarship; it is, however, evident that their numbers do fluctuate and that migrants do move back and forth between rural and urban areas in large numbers (e.g. Connelly, Roberts, and Zheng 2011). West (2009) has provided evidence that droughts combined with economic reforms led rural-to-urban migration in Inner Mongolia to increase (West 2009). Chinese authorities have cited drought conditions as a justification for a program to resettle thousands of ethnic Tibetan pastoralists to newly created settlements (Wang, Song, and Hu 2010). This program is situated within a broader government plan to enhance economic growth in western China (Tan and Qian 2004), so it is not clear whether drought is a valid concern or merely a convenient pretext to seize pastoralists' traditional lands. In all, the available evidence seems to suggest that drought is a factor in modern-day migration patterns in China, but should be seen as a factor that is periodically layered on top of much stronger, ongoing political and economic forces shaping China's internal migration patterns.

Recent studies suggest drought conditions in Mexico influence migration to the United States (Feng, Krueger, and Oppenheimer 2010; Hunter, Murray, and Riosmena 2011; Nawrotzki, Riosmena, and Hunter 2012). In this case, the researchers benefit from a large body of population and environmental data through the Mexican Migration Project[16] that will likely lead to a growing number of relevant studies in coming years. The work published so far does not indicate to what extent the duration of migration may have been short-term labor migration or longer-term, indefinite relocation. Past experience suggests that Mexican migration to the United States is heterogeneous, with the purpose of migration and duration of stay likely varying considerably from one migrant household and one area of origin to the next (Lindstrom 1996). The fact that so many Mexican migrants live or work in the United States without legal status further complicates questions of the migrants' intended duration of stay.[17] Using evidence from recent drought events, Feng and colleagues (2010) calculated that a 10 per cent decline in crop production in rural Mexico due to drought is associated with a 2 per cent increase in migration to the United States. Hunter and colleagues (2011) and Nawrotzki and colleagues (2012) also found an association between drought and rural out-migration in Mexico, mostly from states that are chronically dry, and from communities that already have established migrant networks. Economic factors remain the dominant force influencing migration within Mexico and to the United States (Fussell and Massey 2004), with social networks facilitating migration (Massey and Espinosa 1997). Following the 2008 financial crisis, Mexican migration to the United States tailed off considerably (Passel, Cohn, and Gonzalez-Barrera 2012), so it remains to be seen if drought will have the same degree of influence on future cross-border movements as it has in the past.

6.6.3 Permanent or Indefinite Migration Resulting from Drought

A recurrent theme in preceding sections is that permanent relocation is typically a last resort response to drought. Even under severe, persistent drought conditions, such as

---

[16] http://mmp.opr.princeton.edu/

[17] The Pew Hispanic Center estimates there are more than 6 million Mexicans living in the United States without legal authorization (Passel and Cohn 2011).

those experienced in northern Darfur in the 1980s (Tobert 1985) or Ethiopia in the 1980s and 1990s (Meze-Hausken 2000), people tend to resist leaving their home regions permanently until all other forms of adaptation have been exhausted. In one of the few published studies to explicitly ask people exposed to drought about their adaptation preferences, Barbier and colleagues (2009) found very few families in rural northern Burkina Faso who viewed permanent relocation as an attractive option. There is a very understandable logic behind this, which can be explained in terms of housing, the speed of onset of drought, and the nature of capital.

Unlike tropical cyclones, floods, and similar climatic phenomena described in preceding chapters, droughts cause no immediate or direct damage to housing stock. There is consequently no sudden-onset displacement of people from their homes that might predispose them to permanent relocation. The relatively slow onset of drought means those exposed have time to attempt in situ adaptation strategies and/or temporary migration strategies before having to resort to permanent out-migration. The slow onset also allows time for institutional actors to become involved in providing adaptation assistance, assuming there is the will and capacity to do so. In other words, drought does not quickly turn people out of their homes the way many other climatic events do.

In periods of drought, the nature of capital often creates a strong disincentive to engage in permanent migration. With the exception of money and financial instruments, capital is often place specific and not easily transportable. In agricultural systems, the most immediate impacts of drought are on the crops and livestock fodder households need to meet their basic needs and generate cash income. To offset these losses, households dip into their household savings, draw down their reserves of stored food and seed stock, sell off animals, and/or seek short-term, off-farm wage opportunities. In doing so, they mobilize their most readily convertible capital assets – their cash, their food reserves, their livestock, and their labor. This leaves them with their less portable, less easily converted economic capital – tools, equipment, household furnishings, and their house and/or land.[18] The household needs to retain these if it is to resume its livelihood after the drought ends and, in any event, the amount of money others are willing to pay for such assets is often lower in the midst of a drought. As money becomes scarce, social capital becomes increasingly important in helping people get by, and this, too, is often local in nature: friends, neighbors, relatives, community groups, and so forth. As capital dwindles to place-specific assets, permanent relocation (which requires portable capital to ensure success) may become increasingly less appealing.

---

[18] The strength of the tie to house and land is related to land tenure, with households that own their land privately or who are members of a communal landholding system typically having much stronger ties in this respect than tenant or sharecropping households. The importance of land tenure arrangements is developed in more detail in the case study that follows.

It is consequently in situations where in situ adaptation options and place-specific capital have been exhausted that permanent migration is likely to emerge during times of drought. Even then, drought is unlikely the sole cause, but is more likely to exacerbate or interact with other economic, political, or social factors. Indeed, in the examples noted earlier – Darfur, Ethiopia, and northern Burkina Faso – political instability, weak institutions, and economic underdevelopment were contributory factors that shaped migration behavior. To better illustrate, the following case study of Depression-era drought migration on the North American Great Plains is offered. Not only does the case study describe the permanent relocation of hundreds of thousands of people, it also describes other adaptation and migration outcomes that occurred and highlights how cultural, economic, political, and social processes operating at multiple scales helped shape the migration patterns that emerged. Despite having taken place more than seventy-five years ago, this case represents one of the best-studied examples of drought migration, providing a rich amount of knowledge and detail to draw upon as a learning analog.

6.7 Case Study: Depression-Era Migration on the North American Great Plains

In the midst of the economic turmoil of the Great Depression of the 1930s, the North American Great Plains and bordering areas experienced severe, multiyear droughts accompanied by tremendous dust storms, soil erosion, crop failures, and farm abandonments. Hundreds of thousands of people migrated out of the Plains, with many more migrating internally within the region, making it the largest climate-related migration event in North America in living memory.

6.7.1 Overview of Events

The Great Plains are a semiarid grassland ecosystem spanning parts of ten U.S. states and three Canadian provinces (Figure 6.2). The region is characterized by hot summers, cold winters, and relatively low amounts of annual precipitation. In the second half of the nineteenth century and the first decades of the twentieth century, family farmers settled large areas of the Plains, with the encouragement of the American and Canadian governments (Webb 1931, Friesen 1984). Most farmers ran a mixed operation based on maintaining small herds of cattle and other livestock; poultry keeping; and cash cropping of wheat and other grains, with corn entering into the mix in wetter areas (Cunfer 2005). Tractors and other mechanized equipment began appearing on Plains farms after World War I, although even into the 1930s draft animals still played an important role on many farms (McWilliams 1942). World War I triggered a global spike in commodity prices, which in turn drove a massive expansion in wheat production and investment in farming on the Plains (Hewes 1973). Many farmers took

Figure 6.2. Map showing the Great Plains, with arrows indicating general directions of out-migration during the 1930s.

advantage of relatively easy credit during the boom time to purchase new equipment (Rajan and Ramcharan 2012). By 1920, commodity prices began to steadily drop (Figure 6.3), reducing farmers' incomes, increasing foreclosure rates, and prompting remaining farmers to further intensify production.

In 1929, stock markets around the world crashed, pushing the Plains along with the rest of North America into the Great Depression, from which it would not emerge until World War II. This had several important effects on the Plains' agricultural economy. First, demand for commodities and commodity prices collapsed to record lows, further lowering farm incomes (Figure 6.3). Second, farmers and small businesses had difficulty accessing credit, especially in the United States, where many banks across the Plains closed (e.g. Moore and Sanders 1930). Third, many nonfarm employers (e.g. railways, mines, oil companies) stopped hiring (McLeman 2006). Fourth, local governments became increasingly cash-strapped as local economies slowed and property owners and businesses became unable to pay their taxes (Great Plains Committee 1936, Marchildon 2005).

Perhaps counterintuitively, the onset of the Depression stimulated an increase in the number of people seeking to enter farming (McLeman 2006, McLeman et al. 2008). Although life on farms was difficult, life for unemployed urbanites was often more

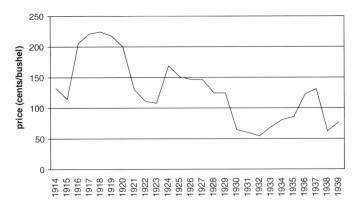

Figure 6.3. Historical average wheat prices in Canada, 1914–39. Data source: Statistics Canada, Historical Statistics of Canada, Wholesale market prices for selected agricultural products, 1867 to 1974, Series M228–238. Prices are adjusted to 1971 dollars. A version of this figure originally appeared in McLeman and colleagues (2010). Reprinted with permission of the *Journal of Historical Geography*.

so. On a farm, a family could at least produce its own food and meet its basic needs. Urbanites with previous farming experience consequently started moving back to the land (Boyd 2002), especially in places like Oklahoma where, for historical reasons, there were large numbers of tenant farms (see Sellars 2002).[19] Farm tenancy in that era was often done on a handshake basis (i.e. without any formal contract), with the tenant agreeing to either pay cash or to share a portion of the harvest with the landowner in exchange for use of the farm and/or draft animals and equipment (Southern 1939, Coleman and Hockley 1940). In this way, a family of relatively little financial means could participate in farming. The influx of people seeking tenant farms drove up the rental rates, further squeezing household incomes.

During this period severe droughts began to occur (Burnette and Stahle 2013). The exact timing of the droughts varied across the region, starting in the 1920s in southern Alberta and northern Montana, and occurring with regular frequency across most of the Plains region by the mid-1930s (Cook, Miller, and Seager 2009, McLeman et al. 2010). Droughts have always occurred on a periodic basis on the Plains (Sauchyn et al. 2003), but many of those farming on the Plains during the Depression were experiencing them for the first time. As crops began to fail, the exposed soil began to drift and blow, creating tremendous dust storms that swept across the continent and out to the Atlantic Ocean (Wheaton 1992, Schubert et al. 2004). Farming practices of the period exacerbated the problem, it being common for crop farmers to repeatedly till their land before leaving it bare and fallow (Smika 1970). Few farmers had irrigation systems, and many farm families struggled simply to produce enough food for themselves and to keep their livestock healthy (Hurt 2011).

---

[19] Farm tenancy was much more common in the southern Great Plains and bordering areas than it was in the northern U.S. Plains states and Canada.

During that era on the Plains, landless workers often engaged in seasonal labor migration to perform farm and nonfarm work, as did many tenant farmers and small landholders, a pattern somewhat similar to seasonal labor migration seen in rural Africa and Asia today (McLeman 2007). The Depression had made nonfarm wage employment scarce, and the drought was affecting such a large area there was little farm work to be had anywhere on the Plains (Bond, McKinley, and Banks 1940). As a result, farm households were left with far fewer adaptation options than were available to them prior to the Depression. A trajectory of rapid socioeconomic descent began for many farmers and for the communities and small businesses that depended on agriculture (McLeman 2006). There was high turnover on tenant farms, as tenants struggled to pay their landlords and found themselves evicted (McMillan 1943). Indebted landowning farmers and those operating on marginal lands began to abandon their farms (Riney-Kehrberg 1989). Shantytowns sprang up on the outskirts of urban centers across the Plains, the squalid conditions comparable to those in developing country slums today (McWilliams 1942). Money began to disappear from the rural economy, and families bartered with one another and with local businesses for essential goods (McLeman et al. 2008). Writer Timothy Egan has since referred to this period as 'the worst hard time' (2006).

By the mid-1930s, large-scale out-migration was in progress across the Great Plains (Figure 6.4). The states of Kansas, Nebraska, North Dakota, Oklahoma, and South Dakota and the Canadian province of Saskatchewan all experienced net population losses by the end of the decade (University of Virginia Geospatial and Statistical Data Center 2012, Dominion Bureau of Statistics 1936). California received an estimated three hundred thousand migrants from southern Plains states and surrounding areas during this period, one-third of them from Oklahoma alone (Gregory 1989). Tens of thousands more left the northern U.S. plains states for Oregon and Washington, while in Canada drought-stricken farmers moved west to British Columbia, northwest to the Peace River region (that spans Alberta and northeastern British Columbia), or due north to the Aspen Parkland of central Saskatchewan (Hoffman 1938, Dewing 2006, Gilbert and McLeman 2010, McLeman et al. 2010, Laforge and McLeman 2013). Smaller numbers migrated east out of the Plains. This was not temporary labor migration, but instead consisted disproportionately of intact nuclear families headed by working-aged parents seeking to establish new homes at their destinations. Their destination choices were typically made on the basis of preexisting social connections, with friends and relatives often providing assistance in getting established (McLeman 2007). Although poor by the standards of existing residents at their destinations, the migrants were often not entirely destitute. Those migrating from the southern Plains to California – immortalized as the 'Dust Bowl migrants' by John Steinbeck's 1939 novel *The Grapes of Wrath* – consisted of migrants from both rural areas and urban centers, with migrants of rural origin comprised of large numbers of displaced tenant farmers and landless farm workers (Holzschuh 1939, Gregory 1989).

Figure 6.4. Waving goodbye to migrant family bound for California, Muskogee, Oklahoma, 1939. Russell Lee, photographer. Image source: U.S. Library of Congress, Farm Security Administration/Office of War Information Black-and-White Negatives, LC-USF33–012310-M5, public domain image http://www.loc. gov/pictures/collection/fsa/item/fsa1997026646/PP/.

The case of migration to California provides a rich study of the impacts of climate-related migration on the receiving community. Unlike the rain-fed family-operated farms of the Plains, Californian agriculture had many mechanized, commercially operated farms that employed irrigation technologies. Before the 1930s, Californian farmers relied heavily on seasonal migrant labor, especially from Mexico, much as they do today. With the onset of the Great Depression, the U.S. government began excluding and deporting Mexican workers (and in many cases, their American-born children), ostensibly to protect jobs for U.S. workers (Hoffman 1974), thereby creating a farm labor shortage in California. This in turn attracted large numbers of displaced farmers from the southern Plains, whose general farming experience, familiarity with common California crops like cotton, and ability to work with draft animals made them highly suitable workers (Rowell 1936, Taylor and Rowell 1938). However, many Californians did not desire having Oklahoman migrants as residents, having been accustomed to Mexican migrant workers, who came for a temporary period, worked for a low wage, and then moved on elsewhere until the following agricultural season. Residents complained about newly arrived migrants wanting to school their children, use medical clinics, and draw unemployment relief payments in periods when there was no work available (McWilliams 1942,

Haslam 1977, Gregory 1989). Conflicts began to emerge between Plains migrants and California residents, and at one point in 1936, the Los Angeles police began patrolling the state's borders with Arizona and Nevada, trying to prevent would-be migrants from entering the state (Taylor 1938, McWilliams 1942, Giczy 2009). A consequence of the hostile reception migrants received was that they formed tightly knit communities, within which strong social capital formed (McLeman 2007). This in turn facilitated further migration from the Plains, and helped new arrivals become established, if not integrated into Californian society. In the agricultural communities of central California, the cultural traits of the Great Plains – like cowboy hats, country music, and biscuits and gravy – are still commonplace today, a result of the 'Dust Bowl' migrants having not been allowed to integrate in the 1930s (Gregory 1989, La Chapelle 2007). Descendants of the 1930s migrants are now among the political and economic elite in those communities, having benefited from that strong social capital generated by their parents and grandparents (McLeman 2006).

The 1930s also saw governments implement a variety of programs, some directly targeted at the Great Plains, others aimed at addressing rural poverty and unemployment more generally, and these had identifiable effects on migration patterns. In the United States, programs administered under the federal Resettlement Administration and Department of Agriculture sought to take marginal Plains farmland out of production and resettle those farmers on lands elsewhere (Bonnifeld 1979, Hurt 1986, Lewis 1989, Sylvester and Rupley 2012). Similar programs were implemented in southeastern Alberta through a program known as the Special Areas, while both the Alberta and Saskatchewan governments offered to pay the relocation expenses of any farmers willing to leave drought-stricken areas (Jones 1991, Marchildon 2005, Marchildon et al. 2008, McLeman and Ploeger 2012). On the other hand, the U.S. Agricultural Adjustment Act (AAA) and the Canadian Prairie Farm Rehabilitation Administration sought to improve the lot of those who continued farming through programs that sought to stabilize commodity prices, offer financial support to farmers, provide crop insurance, and promote soil conservation (Bonnifeld 1979; Hurt 1981; Skopcol and Finegold 1982; Bowers, Rasmussen, and Baker 1984; Marchildon et al. 2008). Federally funded infrastructure projects under the U.S. Works Progress Administration provided much-needed off-farm employment opportunities that helped many farmers remain on the land, and in many areas likely reduced the amount of out-migration that might have otherwise occurred (McLeman et al. 2008). In the United States, the Great Plains Committee (1936)[20] was struck to develop recommendations on how to avoid similar events in the future, while Congress's Lafollette Commission toured the country to gather information on interstate migration. These latter initiatives were largely forgotten during World War II, which revived agricultural and

---

[20] See White (1986) for a detailed reflection on the Great Plains Committee.

manufacturing economies and brought an end to the Depression.[21] At the same time as war broke out in Europe, droughts subsided on the Plains, not returning on any large scale until the 1950s.

6.7.2 Lessons from the Case Study

A good number of scholars have studied the Depression-era Great Plains as an analog for understanding migration behavior in times of social and ecological turmoil, and their findings are too many to enumerate them all here.[22] Several stand out as good illustrations of dominant themes of this chapter. The first concerns the question of the relative contribution of drought vis-à-vis other factors in stimulating and shaping the migration patterns observed. One reading of that period on the Great Plains is that a transition from small, family-operated farms to more mechanized, less labor-intensive farms was inevitable, and the droughts helped accelerate that process. Worster (1979, 1986) suggested this case has as much to say about agricultural capitalism as it does about drought, while McDean (1978) argued that depopulation in rural Oklahoma was not just inevitable but necessary, given the poor living conditions and low productivity on smaller farms. Structural explanations of this type are sometimes offered for why rural out-migration occurs in developing regions today.

Other scholars have argued that drought played very little role in rural out-migration relative to political and economic forces, some suggesting that many rural people were inherently transient and migratory by nature, human 'tumbleweeds' that could not stay in one place for any length of time (Manes 1982, McDean 1986, Whisenhunt 1983). Such suggestions are inconsistent with research reported in the migrant source regions at the time of the events (e.g. Duncan 1935, 1940; McMillan 1936, 1943), and are inconsistent with the fact that most migrants who left the Plains were typically quick to settle and establish roots at their destinations (e.g. Haslam 1977, Gregory 1989, Laforge and McLeman 2013). There was high turnover on farms, but this is indicative of families trying to advance economically or deal with uncertain land tenure. Drought did have an important influence on migrant decision making, but drought migrants were not somehow predisposed to transiency. The best empirical evidence comes from a detailed survey of six thousand six hundred fifty-five mainly rural migrant households receiving federal assistance upon arrival in California. Holzschuh's findings refute the 'human tumbleweed' theory, stating, 'The migrants studied were found to be a stable group, with long years of residence in their home

---

[21] The active engagement of governments in North America's agricultural economy has, however, persisted to this day; see Libecap (1988) for a detailed overview of the transformation of U.S. government agricultural policies in the post–Great Depression era, and Skogstad (1987) for Canadian agricultural policy.

[22] Examples include Gilbert and McLeman (2010), Goffmann (2006), Gutmann and Field (2010), Gutmann and colleagues (2005), Laforge and McLeman (2013), McLeman (2006, 2007, 2009), McLeman and Hunter (2010), McLeman and Smit (2006a), McLeman and colleagues (2008, 2010), Reuveny (2008), and Riebsame (1986). See McLeman and colleagues (2013) for a detailed literature review.

states prior to migration' (1939: 35). One-third of respondents explicitly gave drought as a reason for migrating, and many of the other reasons relating to income, poverty, and unemployment can be seen as potentially influenced by drought. This is a reminder of the utility of seeing migration in times of drought within the context of adaptation and not as some unrelated behavioral process with its own origins. The labeling of lower-income groups as inherently transient is a problematic value-laden judgement. Mobility and migration are logical behavioral strategies in challenging environmental and socioeconomic situations and should not be disparaged.

In the 1930s, drought and economic crisis reinforced one another synergistically, the droughts and collapsed commodity prices driving household vulnerability, and the high unemployment and inability to access credit reducing their capacity to adapt via in situ methods. This multidimensional causal dynamic is consistent with other examples identified in this chapter, and in part helps explain why subsequent droughts on the Plains have not triggered large-scale migrations: none has been accompanied by economic conditions comparable to the Great Depression. Further, the agricultural system itself has changed since the 1930s, with farms having become larger, more mechanized, and less labor intensive. Longer-term, nonclimatic processes have been the dominant forces shaping population patterns on the Plains since World War II. Drought can still potentially stimulate changes in migration patterns in rural North America, but the changes are much more subtle today than they were during the Depression.[23] In the future, the risk of drought causing large-scale changes in permanent migration patterns, whether on the Great Plains or other regions seems low, except in places and times when significantly disruptive political or economic events happen concurrently.

Household access to economic, social, and economic capital distinguished those who did not migrate from those who were internally displaced within the Plains region, and from those who left the Plains altogether (McLeman and Smit 2006a, McLeman et al. 2008). These distinctions are summarized in Figure 6.5, and in a generic sense are similar to those observed in other examples of migrations related to drought and to other climatic events and conditions reviewed in this book. Land tenure was an important factor, with those who owned land much less likely to migrate than landless people or tenant farmers.[24] As money grew scarce and credit became obtainable only from private merchants, local social capital in terms of being seen by the community as trustworthy was important. Church groups, community organizations, family networks, and neighbors became critical adaptation resources for those who had access to them. People who were not well established in the local community, who came

---

[23] Using statistics from recent decades for the U.S. Corn Belt, Feng, Oppenheimer, and Schlenker (2012) have calculated that a 1 per cent reduction in crop yields stimulates a 0.17 per cent population decrease through net outmigration, principally of young adults.

[24] Holzschuh (1939) found that less than 4 per cent of respondents in her survey of California-bound migrants owned land prior to migration. McMillan (1943) also emphasizes the high rate of tenancy and landlessness among those who migrated.

More likely to migrate:	Less likely to migrate:
People with portable capital	People with place-specific capital:
• Cultural capital: Young, families, healthy, good farming skills	• Landowners, owners of fixed assets
• Economic capital: landless, operated tenant farms, or farms on poor land; not destitute	• People with strong local social networks
	People with little or no capital
• Social capital: Connected via social networks to places outside the Plains	• Poor, elderly, infirm, broken families, people without social connections

Figure 6.5. Summary of distinctions between migrants and nonmigrants.

from broken homes, were in poor health, or were otherwise not active participants in local social networks were at much greater risk of becoming displaced and homeless, but with less ability to migrate out of the region. These were the types of people who populated informal settlements around the region. Those who migrated to the Pacific coast or elsewhere did so with the assistance of preexisting social connections to the destination areas, and were able to leverage their cultural capital – that is, their youth, labor skills, and ability – to successfully establish upon arrival. Their capital was portable and leant itself to mobility.

Out-migration from the Plains had consequences for the people and communities left behind. Another way of describing those who left the Plains is that they were the rural middle class: young, working families of modest means, neither wealthy nor destitute, and striving for economic advancement. Such people are the bedrock of successful communities. Their departure created a growing socioeconomic disparity within the remaining rural population in many parts of the Plains, and started many a community on a trajectory of population decline from which it would not recover (McLeman 2007, McLeman et al. 2008). Once rural families left the Plains, they did not go back even after the droughts had passed, for there was little social or economic advantage in returning. Scholars increasingly recognize that greater research needs to be done on the effects of climate-related out-migration on the adaptive capacity of sending areas, with particular attention to the challenges faced by those for whom migration and mobility are not viable adaptation options (Adger et al. 2002, McLeman 2010b, Black et al. 2012, Winkels 2012).

Another important lesson concerns the role and actions of governments and institutions. Programs that actively sought to resettle U.S. Great Plains farmers from drought-prone, easily erodible lands seem to have had middling results (Bonnifeld 1979). Although provincial governments offered to assist drought-stricken Canadian farmers in relocating, it appears most who migrated did so without government assistance (Gilbert and McLeman 2010, McLeman and Ploeger 2012). Financial incentives for U.S. farmers to reduce crop acreages (thereby lowering production and stabilizing prices) may have had the indirect effect of displacing some tenant farmers, because the payment went to the landowner and not to the tenant (Lange and Taylor 1939; Fishback, Horrace, and Kantor 2006; McLeman 2006). Overall, the programs that appear to have had the most beneficial influence were those aimed at stabilizing household incomes, creating employment, and improving farming conditions more generally. This makes intuitive sense, because such programs provided households with an expanded range of adaptation options and increased the agency of households when making migration decisions. This seems a useful lesson for present-day policy makers worried about the potential for future distress migration due to climate change: worry less about crafting specific, targeted strategies and focus more on general adaptive capacity building.

As was done in the preceding two chapters, this case study can be wrapped up by returning to the diagram of adaptive migration introduced in Chapter 3 and incorporating key events of the 1930s into it (Figure 6.6). Even greatly simplifying the events that took place, the diagram quickly becomes cluttered. Nonetheless, it becomes evident that Depression-era drought migration can be understood in the context of a dynamic, adaptive system, and the case study reinforces key themes in this book with respect to the interconnectedness of climatic and nonclimatic events and factors across scales, and the utility of capital as a means of interpreting how migration behavior plays out within this context. Such themes are critical in understanding future challenges with respect to climate-related migration, which are subjects for the remaining chapters.

6.8 Chapter Summary

Drought and human migration are most closely connected in rural settings, where household incomes and livelihoods are closely tied to activities like crop farming and raising livestock, and are thus inherently sensitive to vegetative drought. The ability to reliably predict and forecast droughts is still a scientific work in progress. Their occurrence appears to be connected to fluctuations in sea surface temperatures, but what in turn drives these remains to be fully understood. As land and sea surface temperatures rise in coming decades because of anthropogenic climate change, there are concerns that many continental areas will become dryer and that droughts may occur with greater frequency and/or intensity in coming years. It is therefore reasonable to be concerned that greater numbers of drought-related migration events may occur in coming decades.

The impacts of drought are experienced by rural systems through declines in crop yields and stress on livestock, which in turn reduce rural incomes. In recent years, crop failures in key exporting regions have contributed to spikes in global food prices

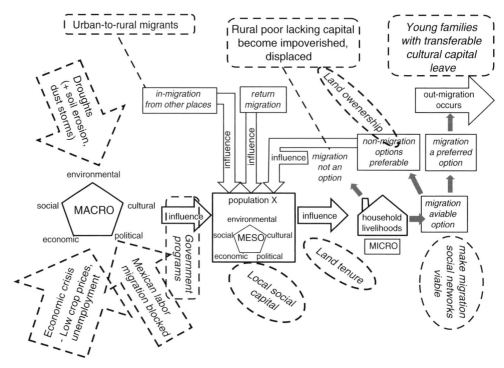

Figure 6.6. Migration in an adaptive system, 1930s Great Plains.

that affect people far from the drought-stricken areas, including urban populations. The municipal water supplies of some urban centers have been directly affected by droughts in recent years, a phenomenon that merits much closer monitoring and proactive capacity building given future climate dynamics and the continuing growth of dryland urban populations.

A wide range of potential proactive and responsive adaptation strategies exists for dealing with drought, which may involve actors at the macro, meso, and micro levels. The feasibility of adaptation options depends on climatic and other factors, with the example of sorghum showing why nonclimate considerations may dictate against farmers' selecting the most drought-resistant crop choice as an adaptation. Migration is a common form of adaptation employed by rural populations in dryland and drought-prone areas, and is often an integrated component of ongoing livelihood strategies. Small-hold crop farmers and landless agricultural workers may engage in temporary seasonal migration as a means of generating income and reducing household exposure to risks. Pastoralism is a livelihood that is highly adapted to climates with seasonal precipitation and temperature regimes.

When droughts occur, they can trigger changes in existing migration patterns, such as increasing the number of people participating in short-term labor migration and reducing participation in costlier, long-distance migration. Drought may push pastoralists into wandering farther afield with their herds in search of water and grazing, bringing them into conflict with resident populations. Permanent migration out of a drought-stricken area is generally seen as a last resort adaptation. Unlike other climatic hazards, drought does not usually cause damage to houses or buildings and has a slower onset, meaning that populations have more time to implement less disruptive, in situ adaptations. Even a severe drought may not be sufficient to stimulate large-scale permanent out-migration unless it is accompanied by political or economic instability, the synergistic effects causing a contraction in the range of adaptation options available to those exposed. Differential access to capital distinguishes those who migrate permanently in response to drought from those who do not. Nonportable capital, such as land ownership and place-specific social capital, serves as a disincentive to migration (or more precisely, provides incentives to adapt through in situ means). Portable or migration-supporting capital, such as valuable labor market skills and connections to an existing migrant network, facilitate adaptation via migration (both temporary and permanent). Vulnerability to drought is greatest among members of an affected population who have little capital of any type.

7

Mean Sea Level Rise and Its Implications for Migration and Migration Policy

7.1 Introduction

Sea levels are presently rising by approximately three millimeters per year as a result of anthropogenic climate change, with the thermal expansion of ocean water and melting of Greenland and Antarctic ice being key contributors. A few millimeters may not sound like much, but over the course of this century the cumulative effects will present significant challenges for populations living in low-lying coastal plains, deltas, and on small island states. In recent years the popular media has identified communities in Alaska, Papua New Guinea, and Vanuatu as the first climate change refugees, by virtue of having to relocate because of coastal erosion and encroachment of the sea. In the scholarly community there has been a recent surge in the number of publications on the question of what to do – legally and practically – about people displaced by rising sea levels. Such questions are difficult to answer for a number of reasons, not the least being that we have few direct precedents to draw on. A particularly difficult problem will be what to do if entire sovereign states become uninhabitable as a result of mean sea level rise.

In suggesting answers to these and other related questions, this chapter:

- Reviews the physical processes that affect the relative locations of coastal settlements and the sea, and identifies current and projected rates of change
- Describes the impacts of sea level change on coastal settlements
- Provides rough estimates of the number of people exposed
- Identifies options in adaptation, including migration
- Explains the challenges faced in dealing with people who may become internally displaced within their own countries by rising sea levels
- Considers the situation of citizens of states that may cease to be habitable
- Analyzes international legal arrangements that may be somewhat applicable to the protection of displacees
- Suggests pathways for action by a concerned international community

7.2 Physical Processes that Lead to Mean Sea Level Rise

The level of the world's oceans relative to land is continually changing. Part of this is due to geological and geomorphological processes that affect the position of the land vis-à-vis the ocean; another part is due to climate-related processes that affect the volume of water in the ocean. The geological processes affecting land include the gradual movement of the continental plates on the Earth's mantle, typically measured in timescales of millions of years or more (Conrad and Husson 2009); the isostatic rebound of northern regions of the continents as they decompress and rise after having been weighed down by snow and ice during the last ice age twenty thousand years ago, a process measured in units of thousands of years (Lambeck and Chappell 2001); and sudden-onset geological events like volcanoes and earthquakes that can cause changes in coastal areas at local or regional scales (Gorntiz 1995). Added to these are geomorphological changes, such as the ongoing erosion of the continents by heat, weather, chemical, and mechanical processes, which convert rock to sand to ever smaller particle sizes, with wind, moving water, and gravity continually transporting and depositing these. When deposited at or near sea level, such as in river deltas or coastal plains, these sediments compact and compress under their own weight, and gradually subside. They are then subject to further erosion by water currents. The combined effects of subsidence and erosion are important factors that influence the position of sea level relative to the rapidly growing human settlements built in many of the world's river deltas and coastal plains (Syvitski et al. 2009, Seto 2011). Human activities, such as the creation of artificial drainage and extraction of groundwater or fossil fuels, can increase subsidence rates (Mazzotti et al. 2009).

The volume of water in the oceans is continually changing over time. Sea levels today are at least six meters lower than they were one hundred twenty-five thousand years ago, the warmest interglacial period between the two previous ice ages, when average global temperatures were between 3 and 5°C warmer than they are today (Kopp et al. 2009). After the most recent ice age, global sea levels rose by 120 meters, and stabilized about two thousand to three thousand years ago at just below the levels we are familiar with today (IPCC 2007). Since the mid to late nineteenth century, sea levels have been rising at an average rate of 1.7 millimeters per year throughout the twentieth century, a process that will be referred to as MSLR (mean sea level rise) for the remainder of this chapter. The rate of MSLR has accelerated in recent decades, with average annual rates of increase of approximately three millimeters per year recorded since the 1990s (IPCC 2007). Changes in contemporary sea level are measured directly through data collected from tide gauges maintained at approximately two thousand sites worldwide, some of which have records dating back a century or more, and through satellite-collected altimetry data, which date back several decades (Cazenave and Llovel 2010). These data sets are also used as inputs for ocean general circulation models that estimate sea level changes at regional scales for which data do not exist.

Two climate-related phenomena account for recent trends in MSLR (Cazenave and Llovel 2010). The first of these is thermal expansion. While the calculation of the specific thermophysical properties of seawater is quite complex, it can generally be said that as the temperature of seawater increases, so does its volume. Over the course of the past 150 years, sea surface temperatures have increased by a global average of one degree Celsius, thereby leading to a coincident thermal expansion of sea surface waters (IPCC 2007). The rate of sea surface temperature change is not uniformly distributed across the globe. Waters off Eurasian and North American coastlines exhibit relatively high rates of increase, while those off Antarctic coastlines show some cooling (Lima and Wethey 2012). The second process contributing to sea level rise is the melting of glaciers and icepacks on land, which is driven by increasing average air temperatures. The largest permanent ice caps are found in Greenland and Antarctica, with smaller ice caps and glaciers found at higher latitudes and higher elevations in the Americas and Eurasia. There is considerable scholarly debate over the amount of melting of Greenland and West Antarctic ice sheets and consequent contribution to MSLR. Recent studies have estimated that since the year 2000, the world's ice caps and glaciers have cumulatively contributed anywhere from 0.6 to 1.5 millimeters per year to MSLR (Jacob et al. 2012, Shepherd et al. 2012).

There is little scientific doubt that sea levels will continue to rise throughout the coming century, but it is not known by how much. Projections for future MSLR depend considerably on several factors. A first important factor is future change in the atmospheric concentration of greenhouse gas (GHG) emissions, which in turn depends on future human economic, technological, and consumption patterns. Because these are inherently unknown, scientists work on the basis of standardized emissions scenarios that come from the Intergovernmental Panel on Climate Change (IPCC)'s Special Report on Emissions Scenarios (SRES). These include scenarios where GHG emissions are quickly stabilized and controlled by the international community (very unlikely in the present global political-economic climate); where GHG emissions continue to grow at current rates; and runaway scenarios where global GHG emissions accelerate. A second factor that contributes to future uncertainty is the question of how air and sea surface temperatures might respond to GHG levels even higher than they are at present, and a third factor is the difficulty of predicting future rates of thermal expansion and melting of ice caps (Meehl et al. 2012). In its 2007 assessment, the IPCC offered a range of estimates for sea future MSLR, suggesting an increase of anywhere from twenty to sixty centimeters by the end of the twenty-first century (Figure 7.1). More recent research suggests that the IPCC may have been too conservative in those estimates, and that even with stabilization of GHG emissions and global temperatures, there would be a centuries-long lag effect before sea levels

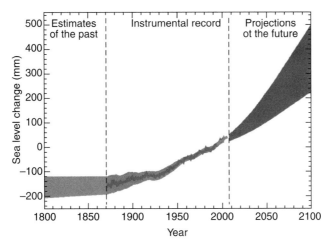

Figure 7.1. Projections of future sea level change, from IPCC (2007).

would restabilize (Vermeer and Rahmstorf 2009; Nicholls et al. 2011; Meehl et al. 2012; Rahmstorf, Foster, and Cazenave 2012).

Because of the various physical and human processes that contribute to the relative location of land and sea at a given place, the extent to which coastal populations will be exposed to MSLR in the future vary by location (Milne et al. 2009). In certain parts of the world, such as along Hudson Bay and the northern Baltic Sea, the rate of isostatic rebound is high, and so the relative change in sea levels experienced in such places will be lower than the global average (Nicholls and Cazenave 2010). Conversely, the land in many densely populated deltas is subsiding from natural processes and human activities, and so the relative increase in sea levels experienced in such locations can be expected to be higher than the global average (Syvitski et al. 2009).

7.3 Impacts of Sea Level Rise on Human Settlements, Land Use, and Infrastructure

Most coastal and island environments will experience MSLR in coming decades, with the potential impacts falling into five main categories:

- Greater rates of flooding or inundation
- Loss or change of coastal wetlands
- Erosion
- Intrusion of saltwater inland into surface water and into groundwater
- Poorer drainage of coastal soils, salinization, and higher water tables (after Nicholls 2011)

The specific ways these impacts will affect human populations living in such environments will vary from one location to another, depending on the nature of local physical geography, land use, economic systems, built infrastructure, and other factors affecting local populations and their capacity to adapt to change. The increased risk of flooding, for example, will come from the simple increase in the height of the sea relative to the land as well as the increased ability of storm surges to penetrate inland, which will be further exacerbated should MSLR cause changes in the health of natural barriers such as coastal marshes and mangroves. The resilience of these ecosystems to withstand MSLR in turn depends on the rate at which sea level changes, the local inland topographical features, and human pressure (Kirwan et al. 2010, Craft 2012). In deltaic environments, MSLR may cause seasonal floodwaters flowing down from higher elevations to overspill banks farther upriver than before. In all coastal areas, MSLR can be expected to increase the landward penetration of extreme high tides (FitzGerald et al. 2008). Sea level change itself does not directly cause erosion, but facilitates greater action of waves on erodible materials. The specific effects of MSLR on sediment deposition and erosion at a given location will depend on local coastal geomorphology, but it is safe to assume that many regions will experience unfavorable changes.

Rural and urban populations are sensitive in different ways to these risks. Rural populations are vulnerable not only to flooding (as seen in Chapter 5), but in coastal areas are also sensitive to the inland penetration of salt water and the waterlogging of soils, which can potentially harm agricultural productivity and rural livelihoods. Such concerns are particularly worrying in important agricultural areas such as Egypt's Nile delta, lowland Bangladesh, and the Mekong delta (Frihy and El-Sayed 2012, Ruane et al. 2012). Chen, McCarl, and Chang (2012) estimate that under a one-meter MSLR, Vietnam would lose more than 5 per cent of its rice crop, and Egypt 1.75 per cent of its. This is not good news for farmers in those regions, nor is it good news for nonfarmers and urban populations in those regions in an era of highly volatile food prices. Saltwater intrusion can also contaminate ground water in coastal and small island aquifers, the degree to which it does depending on the underground stratigraphy and human management of groundwater (Werner and Simmons 2009).[1]

Coastal zone urban centers host large concentrations of buildings and infrastructure that will be at increased risk of damage from storms, flooding, and erosion. The economic value of these assets and their strategic importance to the wider economy make it essential to protect coastal urbanized areas. At the time of this writing in late 2012, the direct financial costs to the state of New York of repairing damage caused by tropical storm Sandy, which struck in October 2012, are estimated at US$33 billion (Kaplan and Hernandez 2012). Note this does not include losses incurred in neighboring states nor does it count all the private losses. Sandy, which may end up having greater financial costs than Hurricane Katrina, has spurred a considerable flurry of discussion among politicians and media about the need to prepare the New York-New Jersey region for MSLR with better seawalls and similar defenses. This seems wise.

---

[1] For a collection of studies of saltwater contamination of coastal aquifers, see Volume 18, Issue 1 of the *Hydrogeology Journal* (2010).

For days following that single storm, millions of people were left without electricity, public transportation did not function, and the entire metropolitan area (and much of the northeastern U.S. seaboard) ground to a virtual standstill. Sandy should serve as a reminder for all, not just New Yorkers, that even the most economically powerful city in the most economically powerful nation is vulnerable to MSLR, and anticipatory planning is needed.

7.4 How Many People Will Sea Level Rise Affect?

Estimating how many people MSLR will affect is not a straightforward task, even if the rate of change ends up falling somewhere within the expected range. A logical place to start is to identify how many people presently live in areas relatively close to sea level. McGranahan, Balk, and Anderson (2007) estimated, using year 2000 figures, that 634 million people live within ten meters of sea level, three-quarters of them in Asia. China has by far the largest number of people living in low-elevation coastal zones at 143 million, followed by India, Bangladesh, Vietnam, and Indonesia. Five small island states – the Maldives, Marshall Islands, Tuvalu, Cayman Islands, and Turks and Caicos – each have more than 90 per cent of their populations living less than ten meters from sea level. Residents of lower- and middle-income countries are disproportionately represented in the global population living near sea level. The authors selected ten meters as their definitional boundary to accommodate the reliability of their data, acknowledging that the degree of risk is much greater for people living one meter above sea level than for those living ten meters above it. A subsequent study by Dasgupta and colleagues (2009) estimated that a one-meter MSLR would affect 56 million living in developing countries, the greatest numbers at risk living in Vietnam, Egypt, Mauritania, Suriname, Guyana, French Guiana, Tunisia, the United Arab Emirates, the Bahamas, and Benin. In the event of a two-meter MSLR, which would be a plausible scenario for the year 2100 were average global temperatures to rise by four degrees Celsius or more, Nicholls and colleagues (2011) estimated up to 187 million people worldwide would be displaced in the absence of preemptive adaptation.

Such projections do, however, need to be taken with caution. The number of people living in highly exposed areas and their distribution within those areas is continually changing (Hugo 2011), and it is not possible to make reliable estimates of coastal zone populations more than a few decades into the future. Recognizing this, Curtis and Schneider (2011) took projected population and demographic changes in counties situated along the U.S. coastline for the year 2030, and compared these with a scenario in which MSLR increased by one meter by the year 2100 (the adjusted MSLR for 2030 would therefore be somewhere between four and fourteen centimeters). The authors found that 200 of the 254 counties contained areas that could conceivably be at least partly inundated by 2030 under this scenario, and focused in on particular counties in California, Florida, New Jersey, and South Carolina that would have the largest percentage of land exposed. By 2030, the authors estimated, 19.3 million people would be living in these highly exposed areas, considerably more than the 13.7 million people recorded in the 2008 census. Southeastern Florida alone would host an estimated 9.9 million exposed people, 2.6 million of them over the age of sixty-five. The authors note, however, that these estimates of population increase assume the counties in question do not experience any sudden-onset natural disasters in the meantime, occurrence of which could be expected to stimulate out-migration and divert in-migration from elsewhere. Given the variable quality of national-level population change data in other countries, especially lower-income ones, it would be challenging to reproduce this type of study at a global scale. Nonetheless, this type of approach is necessary to enhance the reliability of projections of the number of people exposed to risks associated with future MSLR.

It is also necessary when making future projections of the impacts of MSLR to make assumptions about the adaptation measures exposed populations might potentially take. Nicholls and colleagues (2011) point out that their 187 million displaced by 2100 estimate is based on high-end assumptions of MSLR and assumes that little or no adaptation takes place. It is unlikely that coastal populations will in the future do nothing but watch idly as the risk of inundation grows. However, as was seen in earlier chapters, their capacity to adapt will vary according to their means. The difference between assuming no adaptation and assuming completely successful adaptation is significant. For example, a study that looked at the impacts of MSLR in Europe for the year 2080 estimated that in the absence of any adaptation, between 4.3 and 5.6 million people would be exposed to annual flooding under the IPCC's higher MSLR scenarios; with effective adaptation, that number was estimated to be as low as twenty-eight thousand (Bosello et al. 2012). The actual future outcome will likely fall somewhere between these two extremes.

7.4.1 Sensitivity of Populations Living on Atoll Reef Islands to MSLR

Tropical regions of the Pacific and Indian oceans contain many inhabited atoll reef islands, all of which are to varying degrees exposed to significant risks associated with MSLR. Each atoll is different in its physical characteristics. Generally, atolls develop from extinct oceanic volcanoes, the flanks of which host coral reefs (Woodroffe et al. 1999). As the volcano subsides lower into the sea, the reef builds itself upward. Eventually the volcanic material sinks below the ocean surface, leaving the characteristic ring-shaped crown standing only a few meters high, encircling a central shallow lagoon (Figure 7.2). Underneath the island is typically found a small lens of fresh water, which is filled and recharged by rainwater.

These characteristics make atolls and the populations that live on them particularly sensitive to MSLR. So long as the underwater coral reef remains healthy, the

Figure 7.2. Satellite image of Nukuoro Atoll, Micronesia (3.85° North, 154.9° East). This atoll, approximately six kilometers in diameter, exhibits the classic characteristics of an atoll island. The inhabitants live in the forested area in the lower right of the image. Image source: NASA Earth Observatory, http://earthobservatory.nasa. gov/IOTD/view.php?id=6732.

island remains above sea level. However, coral is very sensitive to changes in ocean temperatures, ocean acidity, and human disturbance. Scientists have raised concerns that even small changes in conditions can stimulate coral bleaching events which, if persistent, can cause reef die-offs (Pandolfi et al. 2011).[2] Contamination of the underwater lens by saltwater intrusion, which can be caused by human overuse or by events like tropical storm surges, can render the groundwater unusable (Terry and Falkland 2010). While atolls are widely believed to be especially at risk of inundation and erosion under MSLR projections, evidence gathered from twenty-seven Pacific atolls by Webb and Kench (2010) shows that only 14 per cent lost any land area over recent decades, the rest either remaining stable or adding land area. They therefore caution that sweeping assumptions about MSLR and the disappearance of atolls should be avoided, with more attention paid to the local processes characteristic to each island. In a related example, the Torres Islands atolls that form part of the Pacific island nation of Vanuatu have been cited in the popular media as the source of the world's first climate change migrants, after a settlement needed to be abandoned because of an incursion of sea water. However, scientific research has found that tectonic subsidence in recent years has been occurring at the same rate as MSLR, thereby doubling the rise of water levels relative to the settlements (Ballu et al. 2011).

---

[2] Healthy reef-building corals typically live in a symbiotic relationship with tiny photosynthesizing organisms called *zooxanthellae*. When these die off because of disturbance, the coral loses its pigmentation and becomes ghostly white, hence the term 'bleaching'.

7.5 Adaptation Options for MSLR

7.5.1 Engineered Infrastructure

Chapters 4 and 5 reviewed a variety of adaptation options commonly used by people exposed to seasonal or occasional flooding in river valleys and to storm surges caused by tropical storms. Coastal populations will continue to use such adaptations in the future, with MSLR likely increasing the number and geographic range of people and settlements obliged to do so. MSLR poses the additional dilemma of how to adapt to inundation that is more frequent or permanent. Apart from doing nothing but hoping for the best, there are few in situ adaptation options that do not entail considerable investment in the building and maintenance of engineered structures like sea walls, groynes, dykes, and other barriers. The costs of such structures vary considerably depending on the nature of the construction, but easily range from hundreds of dollars to thousands of dollars per linear meter, meaning they are most likely to be deployed in locations where the value of what is to be protected greatly exceeds the cost of defenses; that is, urban settlements (Cooper and McKenna 2008). As an example of the costs that may be entailed, the Thames Barrier, which protects the city of London and surrounding low-lying lands from floods, cost £535 million (approx. US$810 million) by the time it became operational in 1983, and costs £8 million (approx. US$12.4 million) annually to operate and maintain (UK Environment Agency 2012). The annual costs of shoreline protection from MSLR in Singapore have been estimated at US$3M annually (in 2005 dollars, Ng and Mendelsohn 2005). For wealthier societies like the United Kingdom and Singapore, such costs are manageable, but for a small island state like Tuvalu, which has twenty-four kilometers of exposed shoreline to protect and an annual gross domestic product (GDP) of about US$36 million (CIA 2012), the costs may be prohibitive without outside financial assistance. Nicholls and colleagues (2011) have suggested annual costs for shoreline protection infrastructure could eventually range as high as US$275 billion globally. This amount is modest in comparison with the overall size of the global economy, but the reality is that the greatest infrastructure needs are in Africa, Asia, and low-lying coastal states where less-developed countries unable to afford such investments are disproportionately at risk. There is the option of 'soft engineering' solutions, such as preserving and encouraging the formation of salt marshes and similar natural features to protect inland areas (Cooper and McKenna 2007). This type of response is best suited to areas with lower density and lower-value economic assets immediately adjacent to the shoreline, and may require a managed retreat to implement.

7.5.2 Managed Retreat

The larger the area requiring protection and the longer the time horizons over which protection must be maintained, the more prohibitive investment in engineered protective structures becomes. In such cases, the next least disruptive response is planned or managed retreat from the most exposed areas. There are relatively few examples of managed retreat from coastal areas in recent decades, and these have tended to involve small populations and areas (Cooper and McKenna 2009). A number of logistical challenges exist, one being the staggering financial costs of relocating even a small population. For example, the cost of relocating erosion-prone Alaskan coastal villages inland has been estimated as being as high as $1 million per resident, begging the question of where the funding is supposed to come from should more and larger planned retreats be necessary (Huntington, Goodstein, and Euskirchen 2012). Another challenge is the physical availability of suitable land to which a population may be relocated, with a related challenge being the ability to acquire legal title to such land. In some Pacific Island nations such as Fiji and Samoa, the majority of land is owned communally (Powell 1998), making it in principle administratively easier for people to shift inland, as compared with regimes where most property is privately owned. In areas with strong private property regimes, a relocation site might need to be purchased, which would discourage anticipatory actions to relocate were it to be done at residents' expense (Healy and Soomere 2008). In such situations, residents likely would prefer to wait until the risk is actually realized, when insurance and/or government funds might become available.

Because it is so expensive and disruptive, managed retreat is rarely implemented for large areas or for large numbers of people (Healy and Soomere 2008). Even in jurisdictions where a relatively significant amount of thought has gone into advance planning for MSLR, such as northeastern Australia, there can be a lack of institutional will to proceed with managed retreat preparations given the economic, political, and administrative challenges (Niven and Bardsley 2012). Managed retreat seems a particularly unlikely option for urbanized areas as a response to MSLR. For example, in the San Francisco bay area US$99 billion worth of property, thousands of kilometers of roads and railways, 30 power plants, 137 schools, 55 health care facilities, and 2 major airports presently are situated in areas at risk of inundation in a 1.4 meter MSLR scenario (Heberger et al. 2011). The scale and value of the infrastructure at stake essentially commits San Francisco to hard infrastructure solutions at all costs, with full abandonment or large-scale retreat likely to occur only in the most catastrophic of future scenarios. Furthermore, if managed retreat is to be a viable response to MSLR generally, government policy and planning must change from promoting occupancy and investment in low-lying coastal areas to discouraging it (Abel et al. 2011). As seen in the case study of Hurricane Katrina in Chapter 4, even when an inhabited location is proven by repeated disasters to be situated in a highly exposed location, government reaction is typically to rebuild and reinvest rather than retreat. In short, if past experience is any indication, planned retreat from MSLR is not likely to be implemented except for small populations living in highly exposed areas, and probably then only after a flooding event necessitates it.

7.5.3 Migration as Adaptation

Barring fundamental and far-reaching behavioral changes by governments and individuals alike – changes that have yet to begin on any significant scale – coming decades are likely to see rising GHG emissions, a growing rate of MSLR, further growth of population and property in coastal zones, and continued inability and unwillingness to implement meaningful proactive adaptation. Given these dynamics, it seems inevitable that later this century people will have to move from low-lying coastal plains and small islands, and the less we do to mitigate emissions or build adaptive capacity, the greater their numbers will be. In some instances, their movements will be planned and considered ones facilitated by governments; in other instances, households will take it upon themselves to undertake adaptive migration. There will also be future cases like Katrina, where the impacts of sudden-onset events are exacerbated by MSLR, and the resulting migration will take place under circumstances of distress. Previous chapters have outlined in considerable detail how migration processes work in the context of adaptation to floods and storms past and present. Next it will be considered how these processes might play out in the future, and what, if anything, the international community might legally be compelled to do should whole communities or, indeed, whole island nations become no longer viable because of MSLR.

7.5.3.1 Internal Displacees

The largest number of people who undertake migration because of MSLR will be people who relocate within the borders of their own countries. Although it is the potential disappearance of small island states that grabs the headlines, the entire population of the Pacific islands (including those not at risk of MSLR) is only about 10 million (Secretariat of the Pacific Community 2011), less than half that of the city of Shanghai, which is very much at risk. It is the densely populated 'mega deltas' of Africa and Asia where resides the largest number of people who are exposed to MSLR, and who would seek internal resettlement options. Consistent with examples from previous chapters, not all can be expected to enjoy the same degree of agency in terms of their resettlement options. Those households that have greater access to economic capital, social networks, and similar resources will have more migration options, and better chances of successful reestablishment elsewhere, than those who do not. Those who do not have the necessary means to relocate independently – sometimes described as *trapped populations* (Black et al. 2012) – will need to rely on the assistance of the state and other institutions. This does not bode well for them, for past experience shows that state governments do a poor job of caring for internally displaced persons (IDP).

People can become internally displaced for a wide variety of reasons. If violent conflict is eliminated, many of the most common reasons relate to economic development, such as the construction of large dams and infrastructure projects, or to environmental conservation, such as the establishment of parks and wildlife refuges (Cernea 2000, Dowie 2009). In the last two decades of the twentieth century, an estimated 200 million people were internally displaced worldwide in the name of economic development, the largest number of people affected living in China and India (Cernea 2000). Although none of these were related to climate change or MSLR, de Sherbinin and colleagues (2011) suggest the experience of development-induced displacees serves as a useful analog for understanding the fate of those displaced by climate change in the future.[3] The majority of those displaced for development reasons end up more socioeconomically marginalized and disadvantaged than before their relocation, often struggling to find employment and shelter, feeling socially isolated, suffering from food insecurity, and experiencing poorer long-term health (Cernea 2000, Connell 2012). Many of these adverse outcomes were identified in the Chapter 5 case study of internal displacements caused by China's Three Gorges Project, which led to knock-on migration as those relocated with state assistance sought to overcome the decline in well-being they experienced. A few additional examples provide further insights of the experiences IDPs may face in coming decades from MSLR.

7.5.3.2 *Three Cases of Internal Displacement from Islands*

A first example is that of the smaller islands of large and shallow Chesapeake Bay, in the eastern United States. Beginning in the seventeenth century and continuing well into the late nineteenth century, many of these small islands supported small towns and villages whose residents based their livelihoods on a mix of fishing and subsistence activities (Cronin 2005). The islands are highly exposed to the impacts of storms, storm surges, and erosion. Many are also subsiding at relatively fast rates. In a study of Holland Island, home to more than 250 people in the year 1900, Arnestam Gibbons and Nicholls (2006) documented how sea level rose by twenty centimeters relative to the island's main settlements in the seventy years prior to 1920, the year the island was abandoned. The authors observed that, although its land area was steadily shrinking, the island was abandoned long before it ceased to be habitable. The abandonment process appears to have been triggered by a small number of events that crossed critical thresholds. The first was the need to abandon a number of houses on the shoreward side of the main settlement because of erosion. These residents did not remain on the island, and as a result, there were no longer enough people to support the school, church, and businesses. This triggered a secondary out-migration, further hastened by a storm event in 1918 that damaged many remaining buildings. Out-migration from Holland Island was not coordinated or facilitated by outside institutions, but was instead the result of independent decisions of individual households. The decision of one household had social consequences for others, creating a

---

[3] Note that the authors write not only of displacements to accommodate MSLR, but the possibility that rural people might be displaced should countries attempt to mitigate greenhouse gas emissions through forest reserves and other programs that require reducing the economic use of natural resources.

Figure 7.3. Last remaining house on Holland Island, 2010. Image reproduced under Creative Commons 2.0 license; original source: http://www.flickr.com/photos/baldeaglebluff/5193166145/in/photostream.

synergistic effect once out-migration began. Those who left tended to resettle within the Chesapeake Bay area, where they continued to pursue similar livelihoods. The authors note that former residents and their descendants retained an emotional attachment to Holland Island for decades to follow, travelling there for picnics and occasional reunions (Figure 7.3).

A second example of island abandonment is that of St Kilda, the western-most habitable islands of Scotland, occupied for centuries by tenants who subsisted by raising sheep and capturing seabirds. The main settlement of St Kilda, Hirta, was not abandoned for reasons of erosion or subsidence, but is included here because of the role government played in hastening its abandonment (Figure 7.4). The population, which had probably numbered as many as 180, began to decline in the late nineteenth and early twentieth century as younger male residents began to migrate elsewhere in search of economic opportunity (Steel 1975). Their out-migration was likely stimulated by growing numbers of tourists visiting the island, and facilitated by the improvement in connections and communications with the mainland spurred by World War I. The remaining residents descended into deeper poverty. Scottish officials, including the island's nurse, had for a number of years felt Hirta needed to be abandoned and, following particularly difficult weather conditions in the winter of 1929, the remaining families collectively agreed to leave. The government paid for the relocation of residents and their livestock, albeit with the continuous aim of minimizing the financial costs. A few relocated residents found their situation improved on the mainland, but most found themselves more impoverished and isolated. St Kildans spoke Gaelic, were used to living communally, and were unaccustomed to wage labor

Figure 7.4. Abandoned homes of Hirta, St Kilda. Image by Mike Cookson, reproduced with permission. For additional images of St Kilda, visit http://www.mike-cookson.com/st-kilda.

or a cash economy. They struggled to hold unfamiliar jobs in forestry offered to them by government officials, and were looked upon with suspicion by neighbors. The elderly and widows fared particularly poorly.

A third example is that of the Carteret Islands, six tiny Pacific atoll islands (similar to Figure 7.2), north of Kuveria (also known as Bougainville) and administered by Papua New Guinea. The inhabited area of the islands, only about eighty hectares in size, was occupied by approximately 600 people in the 1980s (Connell 1990). Beginning in the 1960s, inhabitants recognized that the islands were slowly subsiding, and began unsuccessfully to construct their own sea walls. Their livelihood system, which depended on subsistence production of taro, bananas, and coconuts, suffered when storms damaged crops, and islanders began to rely increasingly on food imported from Kuveria. Younger islanders began to migrate to Bougainville seeking wage employment or better educational opportunities, and those remaining began to request government assistance in relocating to Bougainville. A first group of families was relocated through a government resettlement scheme to unoccupied land on Kuveria in 1984. Although they immediately experienced challenges with an unfamiliar language and unfamiliar employment in their new community, the resettlement scheme was initially perceived as successful as they started to adjust, particularly the children, and their health and population numbers increased (Connell 1990). In

1989, unusually high tides destroyed crops on the Carterets, leading more islanders to seek relocation. In the 1990s, however, Carteret Islanders became frustrated with the government resettlement program and their inability to acquire clear title to land on Kuveria, with many returning to the Carterets to stake their claims to what land remained there (Connell 2012). Civil violence that broke out on Kuveria (unrelated to the Carteret resettlement scheme) likely did not enhance its attractiveness as an alternative to the Carterets. In 2009, new schemes were proposed to resettle Carteret residents on Kuveria, but these met stiff opposition from Kuverian landowners. In 2011, another resettlement scheme was launched and a small number of families relocated to a different site on Kuveria, but again, progress has been slow because of residents' opposition and difficulty in acquiring land rights.

These three examples contain a number of potentially useful insights for understanding what internally displaced people may experience in coming decades because of MSLR. The example of Holland Island, where residents independently and autonomously relocated elsewhere, will likely be repeated in many regions in the future, especially those where residents have little confidence in the ability of governments to assist them. It is, however, important to observe that the adjustments they needed to make to integrate into the communities to which they relocated were relatively mild. They shared the same culture as people in surrounding areas, were able to pursue similar livelihoods, and were already participating in a capitalist economy. In other words, thinking back to the theories of migration reviewed in Chapter 2 of this book, the economic, social, and cultural capital of Holland Islanders was valuable elsewhere, and facilitated their migration without outside assistance, and without great upheaval. This case also reminds us that the decision to leave has feedback effects on the adaptive capacity of those left behind, and in this case triggered a chain reaction that saw the island abandoned fairly quickly once out-migration began.

The other two examples are of people who pursued traditional, subsistence livelihoods in the face of challenging environmental conditions, and who did not possess large amounts of economic, social, or cultural capital that was readily transferable elsewhere. The pursuit of such capital by younger members of the population through labor or education-seeking migration elsewhere precipitated an interest among remaining residents in relocating. In both cases, residents needed government assistance and, in both cases, this was found wanting. In the case of St Kilda, records show the primary interests of government officials were to minimize their own expenses and inconvenience, and to get St Kildans to fend for themselves as quickly as possible (Steel 1975). For residents, the relocation decision was the most important decision of their lives; for officials, it was but one administrative task among many others. St Kildans' lifestyles were so tightly bound to a particular place and livelihood system that many were unable to integrate quickly into a larger, alien community without external support. Their relocation decision was made under conditions of duress, and was almost immediately regretted by many. In hindsight, this is not surprising.

Many Carteret Islanders similarly regretted their decision to leave, but in their case were able to return, and did so to maintain their claims to land there (unlike St Kildans, who were simply tenants). While they enjoy clear title to land on the Carterets, that has not been the case on Kuveria, and the continuing inability to obtain resettlement locations with clear land title remains an impediment. Those who have resettled on Kuveria have met with resistance and resentment from established residents, as did the St Kildans (and as did 1930s Oklahoman migrants to California, described in Chapter 6). Connell (2012) observes that the fitful and, so far, largely unsuccessful effort to resettle residents of the Carterets reflects the experience from other government-sponsored resettlement projects in the Pacific region of recent decades.

Overall, these three examples suggest that the future for those who may be internally displaced by MSLR is not promising. Even in cases where a relatively tiny population must be relocated over a short distance, and at a cost that is trivial relative to the financial wherewithal of the government responsible, the results have not been encouraging. Those relocated have found themselves more isolated and socially marginalized than before relocation. It is doubtful that any governments – especially those already unable to ensure the basic needs of those they govern – would have the capacity to provide competent future assistance should the numbers requiring internal relocation be in the thousands or hundreds of thousands. A better outcome was had in the case of those who had the social, economic, and cultural capital to make their own migration decisions without institutional support. Assuming this relationship holds true in the future – and there are many examples in this book to suggest it will – MSLR will create streams of internal displacees differentiated by their household-level access to (or lack of) migration-specific capital. Socioeconomic gaps within highly exposed populations will be further increased, with the most mobile people adapting through migration to more promising situations, and those left behind descending into poverty and insecurity. The political risks associated with such a dynamic are discussed in the next chapter.

7.5.3.3 Does a Legal Obligation Exist to Assist IDPs Resulting from MSLR?

A question arises whether the international community might be willing, able, or compelled to provide assistance in worst-case scenarios to countries unable to provide meaningful support for their own citizens. States generally loathe to intervene in one another's internal affairs, even when it is clear that a country is committing violence against its own citizens, much less failing the lesser task of providing them with relocation assistance. Nonetheless, under international law a legal norm has emerged that people have a right to protection when their own government is unwilling or unable to do so (Arbour 2008). International conventions and agreements explicitly create obligations for outside states to intervene, for example, in cases of war crimes and genocides, and provide for an international criminal court where the perpetrators may be tried. Throughout the 1990s, the UN Security Council invoked and expanded upon what has come to be known as the *responsibility to protect*, a term formalized in 2001 on the basis of recommendations from a UN-mandated commission on intervention and state sovereignty (Barber 2009). In most instances the responsibility to protect has been invoked to intervene in acts of civil violence or persecution and, with the exception of threatening to invoke it in 2008 in the aftermath of Cyclone Nargis (see below), it has not been invoked to protect people displaced by climatic events. In any event, the responsibility to protect is not a formally codified or binding agreement among UN member states, but simply a customary legal norm interpreted and implemented on an ad hoc basis (Bellamy 2005).

No internationally binding agreement obliges countries to assist citizens of another nation displaced because of weather or climate-related disasters, even when the home nation is unwilling or unable to assist them itself. There is a nonbinding document called the *Guiding Principles on Internal Displacement* that was developed in the 1990s at the request of the UN High Commissioner for Human Rights, and which makes explicit reference to people displaced by environmental factors when describing those who have a right to protection and assistance. Specifically, section 2 of the preamble to the *Guiding Principles* reads:

2. For the purposes of these Principles, internally displaced persons are persons or groups who have been forced or obliged to flee their homes or habitual places of residence, in particular as a result of or in order to avoid the effects of armed conflict, situations of generalized violence, violations of human rights or natural or human-made disasters, and who have not crossed an internationally recognized State border.

It is difficult to imagine anthropogenic climate change and resulting MSLR as anything other than a natural or human-made disaster, so the *Guiding Principles* would seem to apply to those displaced by MSLR. The *Guiding Principles* outline a range of various rights and obligations, with several relevant to the present topic. These include Principle 3, which says that national authorities have the primary responsibility to care for and assist IDPs; Principle 15, which says that IDPs have the right to seek asylum in another country; Principle 25, which says that international humanitarian organizations and 'other appropriate actors' have the right to intervene to assist IDPs when the national government is unwilling or unable to assist; and, Principle 29, which says that if IDPs cannot return to their homes or recover their property, 'competent authorities shall provide or assist these persons in obtaining appropriate compensation or another form of just reparation'.

Because it is not a formal treaty or convention, the *Guiding Principles* do not impose any obligations or requirements upon the international community. Various UN and international agencies (especially those concerned with international development assistance and disaster relief) have adopted the *Guiding Principles*, and a small number of countries have incorporated them into laws and policies.[4] The

---

[4] Visit the Internal Displacement Monitoring Centre website for examples, www.internal-displacement.org.

African Union (AU) drew upon the *Guiding Principles* in creating its own *Convention for the Protection and Assistance of Internally Displaced Persons in Africa*, which came into effect in late 2012. The Kampala Convention, as it is also known, is binding upon fifteen AU member nations at the time of this writing, with another twenty-two in various stages of ratification, and is the only multilateral agreement on IDPs that creates mandatory obligations for signatories. The Internal Displacement Monitoring Centre has estimated that 40 per cent of the world's IDPs are found in Africa, numbering approximately 9.7 million as of 2011 (IDMC 2012a). The majority of these have been displaced by violence and other activities unrelated to environmental factors; only about 4 per cent of the global population of people displaced by natural disasters is found in Africa (IDMC 2012b). This implies that it may be some time before the Kampala Convention is fully tested in its ability to afford assistance to climate-related IDPs.

Situations have arisen in recent years where it would have been appropriate for the international community to invoke the *Guiding Principles* in the protection of people displaced by climatic events. For example, in May 2008, Cyclone Nargis struck Myanmar, with 190 km/h wind speeds and a 3.5 meter storm surge, leaving an estimated one hundred forty thousand people dead or missing (Selth 2008, Barber 2009). Although international humanitarian organizations were willing and ready to provide assistance, the paranoid and repressive military junta that controlled Myanmar refused to allow aid agencies to enter the country, even though it was plainly obvious the regime was incapable of assisting its own citizens adequately. Through direct negotiations, the secretary-general of the UN managed to persuade the regime to accept donations of assistance from sources the regime considered friendly (primarily its Southeast Asian neighbors), but millions of dollars in assistance from Western powers were rejected. Several EU nations and Australia argued that the aid should be delivered by force if necessary. The French government raised the issue of the 'responsibility to protect' at the UN Security Council, but other member states made it clear they would not support forced interventions in such circumstances.

Given the inability of the international community to successfully invoke the *Guiding Principles* or responsibility to protect in a painfully obvious case such as post-Nargis Myanmar, there is little reason to hope they would be more successfully invoked in less immediate cases related to future MSLR. However, it is important to note that relatively few nations are entirely incapable of assisting their own IDPs, and so the number of cases where other countries might need to invoke the *Guiding Principles* or responsibility to protect is relatively small. Countries like Myanmar are the problem children of the international community, states whose governments are corrupt, incompetent, repressive, or otherwise hopeless. Some of these countries – Somalia and Myanmar stand out – also contain large areas highly exposed to MSLR, tropical cyclones, and other coastal hazards. So long as such governments are in place, residents of those countries are doomed to having reduced adaptive capacity and heightened vulnerability to becoming internally displaced by climate change and MSLR because of their incompetent leaders and institutions.

There are no examples where governments have explicitly invoked the *Guiding Principles* to ask the international community for help in caring for their own environmentally induced IDPs. This could conceivably change in coming decades as MSLR progresses, but again, because the *Guiding Principles* are not legally binding, whether such assistance would ever materialize would be entirely at the discretion of others. The absence of any binding agreement on IDPs does not, of course, preclude nations from engaging voluntarily in bilateral or multilateral efforts to assist with caring for and resettling IDPs, which happens quite often in times of environmental crises or natural hazard events. In some cases the assistance will go so far as to aid in the temporary or permanent relocation of IDPs from one country to another. One recent example of this occurred following the Haiti earthquake when Canada, which hosts a large Haitian diaspora, implemented special immigration initiatives to assist Haitian displacees in coming to Canada to join their relatives (D'Aoust 2012).[5] Although the earthquake was not a climate-related disaster, the example suggests that special bilateral arrangements could conceivably be developed between countries that have strong transnational communities to facilitate relocations in the face of MSLR.

7.6 Abandonment of Sovereign Territories and the Implications of MSLR-Induced Statelessness

The examples given in subsection 7.5.3.2 were deliberately chosen for having been cases of island abandonment, making them useful analogs for reflecting on the effects of MSLR on population displacement. However, in each of those examples, the state of which island residents were citizens continued to exist. Indeed, the land mass of the islands involved and the number of people on the move in each case represented a very tiny fragment of the overall land mass and total population of the states in question. But future MSLR in coming decades holds the prospect of something for which no direct modern-day analog exists – the disappearance of the habitable land mass of an entire nation, and the rendering of its population physically stateless.

7.6.1 A New Way of Becoming Stateless?

The United Nations High Commissioner for Refugees estimates there are presently 12 million stateless people in the world; that is, people who do not have the right of citizenship to any sovereign nation. Although the right to a nationality or citizenship is proclaimed in the Universal Declaration of Human Rights, some groups or

---

[5] It is worth noting that many countries expedited international adoptions of children from Haiti following the earthquake, an initiative that might seem beneficial on the surface, but which is fraught with concerns that it may not be in the longer-term interest of the child, or worse, create the possibility of child trafficking (Selman 2011).

individuals live generation after generation without any citizenship. There are various ways by which statelessness can happen, including:

- The country of one's nationality ceasing to exist politically, which happened in many parts of the world during the era of European empires and subsequent decolonization period of the twentieth century
- Changes in the way countries administer their citizenship laws, or an administrative error, such as a parent neglecting to properly register the birth of a child
- Persecution by the state
- Membership in a group, such as nomadic pastoralists, that has traditionally inhabited a territory that spans national boundaries, and being unable to acquire the citizenship of either state (Goris, Harrington, and Köhn 2009)

Note that none of these examples is entirely like the scenario in which a small island state becomes uninhabitable because of MSLR. In the traditional process of becoming stateless, the ground does not disappear beneath the very feet of the person rendered stateless; the land persists and continues to be occupied, governed, and administered by a state. People made stateless in the traditional fashion may be excluded from that land and forced to live elsewhere, or they may be allowed to occupy the land but are denied the basic rights and privileges others enjoy. The main point is that the process by which the individual is currently made stateless is a political, economic, or administrative process that denies citizenship. MSLR will alter the process and implications of becoming stateless. Tuvaluans will not cease to be citizens of Tuvalu because of MSLR, but Tuvalu itself may physically cease to be habitable, becoming a sort of modern Atlantis.

   Is it possible to be a citizen of a state that physically does not exist? There is no universally agreed upon set of criteria for statehood; the closest thing to an international definition of statehood comes from a 1933 agreement among states in the Americas, known as the Montevideo Convention, which says that a state should have a defined territory (Yamamoto and Esteban 2010). Most subsequent international law and policy suggests that possession of physical territory is indeed a key criterion for statehood (Gagain 2012). But for a moment, let us assume that it *is* possible to be a state without land and ask the question: What would the citizenship of that state be worth? Although it is entirely unrelated to environmental change, the case of Hong Kong provides some useful insights. It also happens to be one with which I am intimately familiar, having been a Canadian immigration officer based in Hong Kong in the early 1990s. In 1984, the UK government reached an agreement with the People's Republic of China (PRC) – known as the *Joint Declaration* – to return the British colony to Chinese rule in 1997. In memoranda to the Joint Declaration, each party laid out its interpretation of the future citizenship of Hong Kong residents (Mushkat 1987). The PRC government declared that all Hong Kong residents would become its citizens. Up to 1984, most residents of Hong Kong had been considered by the British government as citizens of a British Dependent Territory (BDT), and it was relatively easy for

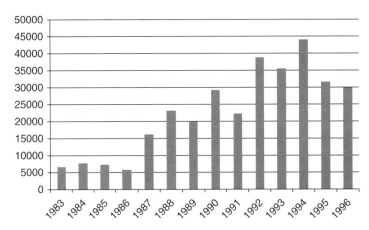

Figure 7.5. Number of immigrants to Canada from Hong Kong, by year. Data source Citizenship and Immigration Canada (1996). Note that there was typically a lag time of up to three years between time of application and time of arrival in Canada (the latter is shown in this figure). Also, Canadian immigration regulations changed in 1988 and again in 1992, and had some effect on who was permitted to migrate. The year-to-year fluctuations in the chart are therefore not entirely reflective of demand for migration to Canada. Observable are three episodes in Hong Kong-Canada migration: a pre-joint Declaration period, when migration averaged roughly six thousand people a year; a tripling of migration in the period between the Joint Declaration and Tiananmen; and, the run-up to the 1997 handover, when migration averaged approximately thirty thousand per year.

them to move to the United Kingdom and live there should they so choose. With the Joint Declaration, the UK government announced that after the 1997 handover Hong Kong BDT citizens would not have any automatic right of permanent residence in the United Kingdom (described under UK law as 'right of abode'). The British government ceased issuing BDT passports to Hong Kong residents and created a new travel document called the British National Overseas (BNO), which promised the holder the right to visit the United Kingdom without a visa and to receive British consular service while travelling in other countries. The Chinese government raised few objections because the travel document simply confirmed that the holder was a resident of Hong Kong.

With no right to live in Britain, Hong Kong residents worried about the prospects of being governed from Beijing began seeking to emigrate to countries with open immigration policies (Figure 7.5). The Tiananmen Square killings in Beijing in 1989 sparked a flood of applications at Australian, Canadian, and New Zealand immigration recruitment offices in Hong Kong. Between 1990, the first full year after Tiananmen, and 1996, the final full year before the handover, almost a quarter million Hong Kong residents migrated to Canada alone (Citizenship and Immigration Canada 1996). Had the UK government simply permitted Hong Kong residents the right to move to Britain, out-migration from Hong Kong would have likely been much lower. Despite living in a colony, Hong Kong residents enjoyed considerably greater freedoms and prosperity than residents of the PRC – especially during the 1980s – and became rightly worried about being ruled by the same individuals responsible for Tiananmen. Foreign passports became insurance policies considerably more valuable than the BNO or BDTC passports that offered no place of residence other than Hong Kong. Cities like Sydney and Vancouver, which benefited tremendously from the influx of talented, educated, English-speaking migrants from Hong Kong, would be much different places today had the UK government given residents regular British passports.[6] By way of contrast, when the government of Portugal agreed to return the colony of Macau (just down the coast from Hong Kong) to the PRC in 1999, Macanese residents were guaranteed the right to reside in Portugal. There was still some migration out of Macau in the years between Tiananmen and 1999, but it was on a proportionally much smaller scale than in Hong Kong, and the whole run-up to Macau's handover date was much less eventful. A lesson to be taken from the case of Hong Kong is that citizenship without the guarantee of a safe and secure place of residence is citizenship devalued. Being unable to reside in the place that awards citizenship relegates the individual to a netherworld of de facto statelessness. This netherworld awaits residents of states that may become uninhabitable because of MSLR.

7.6.2 What Happens When a Nation Becomes Uninhabitable?

7.6.2.1 Case Study: Montserrat

I can find no examples from recent history where an environmental phenomenon has rendered an entire nation uninhabitable. One case that is somewhat useful to consider is that of Montserrat, a small island in the Caribbean, where the administrative unit consists of that single island. In the mid-1990s, most of the island's population of eleven thousand had to be evacuated because of volcanic eruptions, and the main settlement of Plymouth was hastily abandoned (Kokelaar 2002). During the period of volcanic activity, which lasted over several years, it was questionable whether continued occupancy of the island would be possible. Montserratians resettled on neighboring islands in the Caribbean, particularly Antigua, or migrated to the United Kingdom. When the volcanic activity finally subsided, the southern two-thirds was declared a permanent exclusion zone for future settlement, and work began on building a thousand new homes in the previously sparsely inhabited north of the island. Some of those who left returned, and the population has since rebounded to approximately forty-nine hundred (Government of Montserrat 2012).

---

[6] By 2002, the UK government reversed its rules to allow nationals of current and former colonies the right to reside in the United Kingdom. The refusal to allow Hong Kong residents the right to live in the United Kingdom is easily one of the more foolish migration policy decisions made by any country in living memory. Imagine if the enormous amounts of human capital gained by nations that accepted migrants from Hong Kong had instead flowed to the United Kingdom.

Montserrat is not a perfect analog for MSLR-induced statelessness for reasons beyond the obvious one that it remains inhabited today. First, the volcanic eruptions on Montserrat were a (relatively) sudden-onset event, and the evacuation took place in several stages over several months. Even under the most rapid scenarios of MSLR, the horizon for planning and preparation will be measured in years, not months. Second, Montserrat was not a fully sovereign state, but a UK-administered territory. Even in the worst days when it seemed they might never return to their home island, Montserratians were never in a position where they lacked the protections of a state or the legal right of abode somewhere. They enjoyed the right to live in the United Kingdom or in other UK-administered Caribbean islands, and the UK government concerned itself with their welfare. Nonetheless, a few key points may be learned from Montserrat. First, Montserrat is a relatively small island, no more than forty kilometers at its widest point, and home to a relatively small number of people. The financial costs of evacuating and relocating Montserratians and then later building a new settlement for them in the north of the island were much greater than the financial means of Montserratians themselves. Adaptation was only made possible through the financial largesse of the colonial power. In the future case of independent states that may need to be evacuated because of MSLR, it is an open question where the necessary financial resources would come from.

A second useful observation from Montserrat is that, despite the physical danger posed by the volcano, many Montserratians were reluctant to leave the island until it was absolutely necessary. Skinner (2000) recalls how residents tried to go about their daily business even as volcanic ash drifted down on them. To an outsider, it may seem foolish to even consider returning to an island with an active volcano, yet it is not entirely surprising. People's economic capital is often tied up in nonportable assets such as houses, businesses, and the like. They may also form a cultural and psychological attachment to the places where they live, both individually and collectively, making it very difficult to leave or abandon them entirely (as seen in the post-Katrina New Orleans case study in Chapter 4 (Chamlee-Wright and Storr 2009)). One is best able to feel and be Montserratian when one is in Montserrat. It should therefore be assumed that residents of island states threatened by MSLR will similarly be unwilling to permanently abandon their island nations unless no other possibilities remain.

7.6.2.2 *Waiting for a State: The Case of the Palestinians*

Another useful case to consider is that of Arab Palestinians. From the sixteenth century until World War I, the area known as Palestine (today Israel and the Palestinian Occupied Territories) was ruled by the Ottoman Empire. Between 1917 and 1947, the area was governed by the United Kingdom under an internationally agreed mandate. In 1948, the UN general assembly decided to partition Palestine into a Jewish state and an Arab state; a civil war quickly ensued, and seven hundred thousand Arab

Palestinians fled as the new state of Israel was created (Bocco 2009). Wars between Israel and its neighbors in 1948 and in 1967 led to Israel gaining control over the entire original territory of the Palestine mandate. In the 1990s, international negotiations led to the creation of the Palestinian Territories of the West Bank and Gaza, administered by the Palestinian Authority and a precursor to eventual statehood for Arab Palestinians. An outcome of all of this has been the creation of the world's single largest population of stateless people, today estimated at over 4 million people of Arab-Palestinian origin (Shiblak 2006). The travel documents they hold include refugee travel documents issued by other states (typically Arab neighbors of Israel), temporary Jordanian passports, and passports issued by the Palestinian occupied territory authorities, which are not yet sovereign states.

The Palestinian experience also holds clues for what may befall people made stateless by MSLR. Palestine was not an independent state in 1948 and, like many colonized areas, its residents were de facto stateless under Ottoman and then British occupation. The emergence of Israel as the sole state exercising authority in Palestine gave it monopoly control over the determination of citizenship and the ability to restrict or control the return of Arab Palestinians. Those who fled Palestine in 1948 and their descendants are people with a long-standing social and physical attachment to a specific place who, for reason of forces beyond their immediate control, were involuntarily forced from their traditional lands. Although people of Palestinian origin may be found in many countries, the bulk of the stateless population has remained in the home region of the Middle East despite the passage of more than sixty years since their original displacement (Bocco 2009). They have not simply gone away, or somehow dissolved into other nationalities, but have continued to push for citizenship in a state of their own control. In this sense, stateless Palestinians are in a situation analogous to that which residents of small island states may find themselves in a century or less from today. However, unlike Palestinians, there will be no land to go back to, no matter how many decades they may be prepared to wait. Moreover, it is unlikely that displaced residents of disappeared small island states, whose numbers will be much smaller in aggregate than those of the stateless Palestinians, would command the same geopolitical importance and constant international attention as does resolution of Palestinian statehood.

7.6.3 Not Refugees

No international law or policy would give automatic shelter or protection to those made stateless by MSLR. Although the popular media, nongovernmental organizations, and some scholars use terms like 'environmental refugees' or 'climate change refugees', such a category of persons simply does not exist under international law. The United Nations' 1951 *Convention Relating to the Status of Refugees* provides the internationally recognized definition of what qualifies a person to be considered a refugee and the protections to which such a person is entitled. Article 1 of the Convention states:

A. For the purposes of the present Convention, the term 'refugee' shall apply to any person who:

(2) owing to wellfounded fear of being persecuted for reasons of race, religion, nationality, membership of a particular social group or political opinion, is outside the country of his nationality and is unable or, owing to such fear, is unwilling to avail himself of the protection of that country; or who, not having a nationality and being outside the country of his former habitual residence as a result of such events, is unable or, owing to such fear, is unwilling to return to it.[7]

This definition imposes an explicit requirement that anyone seeking protection under the convention must be the victim, or live in fear of becoming the victim, of persecution. The natural environment does not persecute; only humans are capable of this, and so people made stateless by MSLR or by any other effects of climate change are by definition *not* refugees under international law. There is, furthermore, virtually no interest among states that are parties to the Convention in expanding the definition so that more people might qualify for protection (McLeman 2008b). A reality is that there are already approximately 15 million people worldwide who meet the existing convention definition, and the international community is doing an overall poor job caring for them (UNHCR 2012).

   Countries are, of course, free to unilaterally offer protection or relocation assistance to people in need, even if they do not qualify for protection under the UN refugee convention. Canada alone, for example, accepts three hundred thousand immigrants from other states every year, and even people with no preexisting economic or family ties are eligible to apply as independent migrants. This is roughly equivalent to the entire population of the Maldives, the state most often cited as among the first likely to disappear from MSLR. In other words, Canada and similar migrant-receiving countries could accommodate stateless residents of small island nations within existing immigration programs without tremendous disruption. Of all the options discussed in this chapter, past experience suggests ad hoc arrangements such as these will be the most likely international response to the issue of MSLR-induced statelessness if and when it should occur (McLeman 2008b, 2010a). There currently exist a number of bilateral and multilateral agreements on the movement of people between small island states in the Pacific and regional or former colonial powers. For example, citizens of the Marshall Islands, the Federated States of Micronesia, and Palau have the right of visa-free entry and residency in the United States, while residents of Niue enjoy similar relations with New Zealand (Dema 2012). Other Pacific island countries participate

---

[7] The original 1951 Convention applied only to people who met the definition because of events that occurred prior to 1951. In 1967, parties to the convention agreed to a protocol that removed the reference to events before 1951, and maintained the remainder of the definition.

in agreements that facilitate labor migration to larger countries in the region, but without the automatic right of permanent residency (e.g. Samoans with New Zealand). It is worth noting here that residents of Funafuti atoll in Tuvalu have been described in the popular media and in the Al Gore film *An Inconvenient Truth* as already engaging in out-migration to New Zealand due to MSLR, but empirical research by Mortreux and Barnett (2009) found no evidence of such. Funafuti islanders do participate in labor migration to New Zealand under a formal agreement for that purpose but people participating in that program do not cite climate change as their rationale for doing so. That said, scholars have observed that circular labor migration such as this is an important component of household-level adaptive capacity to cope with climate risks in many Pacific island nations (Farbotko and Lazrus 2012).

Bilateral residency agreements and, to a lesser extent, labor migration agreements do offer some protection and hope of resettlement for residents of islands that may be lost to MSLR. Such arrangements are, however, subject to the good will of the more powerful partner. Moreover, right of residency is not the same as right of citizenship, and many countries differentiate residents from citizens when providing benefits and privileges. For countries that do not enjoy a guaranteed migration option, what alternatives might they have? One option already discussed would be the construction of sea defenses around the entire shoreline of an island state, such that the country would become a polder in the middle of the sea, indefinitely at risk of catastrophic inundation should the defenses ever be breached. The Maldives are pursuing a somewhat different and rather expensive alternative of building artificial islands to which residents would relocate if necessary (Sovacool 2012). This strategy, assuming it is viable, would generate unusual precedents under international law. For example, the laws of maritime territoriality do not apply to artificial islands (Gagain 2012). This means that the Maldives would not be legally entitled to claim an exclusive economic zone in the waters surrounding its artificial island, which would be essential to the economic well-being of the population. A naturally occurring island that is uninhabitable is also not eligible to have an exclusive economic zone under international law (Yamamoto and Esteban 2010), meaning that Maldivians living on their artificial islands would not maintain any legacy economic zone rights from their formerly inhabited islands. International agreements could, of course, be changed to account for such cases, which would be necessary if the artificial island option is to be sustainable in the long term.

Another alternative would be to find territory elsewhere to which citizens of disappeared islands might relocate and recreate their own state, or invite colonization by another country now in exchange for future citizenship and relocation assistance later. One analogous example is found in the run-up to the creation of the modern state of Israel. After decades of diplomacy, the Zionist movement was successful in getting the international community to allow the creation of the modern Israeli state in Palestine, but early leaders of the Zionist movement had actually toyed with the idea of obtaining an alternative location in East Africa (Gans 2008). Another example is the present-day state of Liberia, which was founded in the nineteenth century as an American colony to which freed slaves could move with financial assistance from an organization dedicated to that purpose (Burin 2012). A small island state at risk of MSLR might pursue a similar relocation strategy by a couple of options. One would be to actively pursue a formal dependency arrangement with another nation that is not threatened by MSLR, assuming such an agreement does not already exist. This would be a sort of reverse colonization process, whereby the weaker partner invites the more powerful one to administer it in exchange for the long-term security of the greater power's citizenship. This sort of idea was floated by the Turks and Caicos Islands in the 1970s, whose government sought to join the distant Canadian confederation, albeit for economic reasons and not environmental ones (Kavic 1975).

Another option for an island state with the financial means to do so could be to pursue the purchase of land in another nation for resettlement.[8] This would be an interesting variation of the global 'land grab' already taking place, whereby corporations and state-backed companies based in Asia have been steadily accumulating land in developing countries for conversion to export crop production (Cotula et al. 2011). It would not be sufficient simply to buy land for resettlement purposes; the island state in question would also need to negotiate terms of sovereignty, citizenship, and similar arrangements with the current government and seek recognition from the international community. While the aforementioned ideas might seem outlandish today, they are simply examples of the types of governance innovations that will become necessary in coming decades.

7.6.4 What an Enlightened International Community Might Do to Assist

If it has not already become abundantly clear, the international community is under no legal obligation to do anything to assist people who may be obliged to migrate in coming decades because of MSLR. African signatories to the Kampala Convention have committed to protect one another's IDPs, including those displaced for environmental reasons, but beyond that, population displacement because of MSLR remains a matter for individual states to deal with. Some legal scholars have argued that being displaced by any of the impacts of climate change amounts to a violation of basic human rights guaranteed under international law, thereby compelling action by the international community (e.g. Aminzadeh 2006, Knox 2009). While this may be so, human rights are violated egregiously on a daily basis in many countries while the international community stands idly by. If the international community is unwilling or unable to stop the Syrian government's use of incendiary devices in urban areas or

---

[8] There is no significant territory that does not already have at least a nominal sovereign government and to which displacees from an island state might freely move, apart from Antarctica, which is not particularly conducive to long-term human habitation and is in any event already subject to an international treaty regulating its occupancy.

the Sudanese government's indiscriminate attacks on civilians in the Blue Nile state,[9] it seems unlikely international policy makers will react swiftly to potential displacements due to MSLR out of concerns for how human rights are affected.

McAdam (2011) suggests that multinational, multilateral agreements to address climate change-related displacements should be avoided because there is so little likelihood the international community would carry out its obligations in a meaningful way. Just the same, let us assume that the international community does become genuinely concerned about MSLR and its impacts on populations living on coastal plains and low-lying islands, and is determined to do something right now. What are the options available for proactive action? The first and most obvious one is to quickly curtail greenhouse gas emissions, something that few countries seem interested in doing at the moment. The next option would be to provide adaptation assistance to people living in the most vulnerable areas, especially in less developed countries unable to fund their own adaptation programs adequately. Under the UN Framework Convention on Climate Change (UNFCCC), signatories are obliged to do just this. Although action has been slow in coming on creating the mechanisms and finding the financial resources to fund adaptation assistance, in 2010 developed country parties to the convention agreed to provide US$100 billion in funding for mitigation and adaptation in developing countries by the year 2020 through something called the Green Climate Fund (Smith et al. 2011). This is a much needed step in the right direction, but if estimates of MSLR are correct, $100 billion represents a small fraction of what will actually be needed over the long run. An ongoing commitment to extensive financial transfers from wealthier regions to less developed ones will be necessary to help densely populated low-lying areas in Africa, Asia, and the Pacific adapt; the size and duration of this commitment would likely dwarf anything previously experienced in modern history. And note, this would be in addition to the tremendous financial investments that developed countries may have to make to secure their own coastal populations.

Beyond general commitment and support for mitigation and adaptation, a proactive international community would want to begin planning strategies for protecting and assisting those who face displacement. A precursor step would be to reduce the size of the trapped population in the most highly exposed areas, and this would be best achieved by enhancing household-level adaptive capacity and improving freedom of mobility. As described earlier, state-organized population relocations have a very poor track record; it is therefore critical to keep to a minimum the number of people who might eventually need to rely on institutional relocation arrangements. One way this might be done would be through facilitating the ability of people living in exposed regions to participate in internal and international labor migration,

---

[9] Just two of many examples found on the Human Rights Watch webpage (www.hrw.org) as this chapter was being edited.

thereby expanding flows of remittances and building wider social networks along which knowledge and resources can flow. While this will not be a perfect solution for all people in all highly exposed areas, the research suggests such a strategy could help build adaptive capacity for many.

A final step would be to figure out how best to help those that do eventually need to relocate. Biermann and Boas (2012) and Gibb and Ford (2012) have suggested that the UNFCCC be amended, or a protocol added to it, to create a legal right of protection and assistance to those displaced by climate change impacts, including MSLR. The rationale for doing so is sensible, and may well be seen by international policy makers as preferable to amendments to the UN refugee convention. Biermann and Boas (2012) suggest the coordination of such a protocol could be performed by existing agencies like the UN Development Programme and the World Bank. They also highlight the need for a fund to assist the relocation of affected people, and have charted out a pathway to raising and administering the necessary resources. Whether the international community has the will to do so remains an open question; the authors suggest that wealthier nations' self-interest in global security and stability might encourage action – a subject that is a key focus of the next chapter.

7.7 Chapter Summary

Changes in sea levels relative to coastal settlements are driven by a combination of physical and human processes. Globally, sea levels are currently rising at an average of three millimeters per year, but the change at specific locations varies. It is conservatively estimated that sea levels may be twenty to sixty centimeters higher by the end of this century. The impacts will be felt on ecosystems, built infrastructure, and agriculture in low-lying coastal plains and deltas. Hundreds of millions of people worldwide live in areas exposed to the impacts of MSLR, with populations living on atoll islands especially exposed. Adaptation may include building expensive protective infrastructure, managed retreat, and migration out of areas at risk.

Future displacements because of MSLR will fall into two types: those where people become internally displaced within their own countries, and those where entire small island states might become practically uninhabitable, thereby rendering residents stateless. Existing examples of organized internal relocations of small populations from island environments show they are expensive, and that those relocated have not fared particularly well. There are no direct precedents of sovereign states disappearing for environmental reasons. A number of possible actions might be taken to assist those made stateless, most of which would seem unusual at present but may become necessary in coming decades. The international community is not legally obliged to do anything to assist either internal displacees or people made stateless by climate change. Despite popular use of the term, there is no such thing legally as an 'environmental refugee'. One path for action may lay in bilateral agreements or arrangements that allow freer labor migration, so that those exposed can build sufficient capital that their own household-level adaptive capacity is made more robust. Besides providing guidelines for reducing greenhouse gas emissions and providing adaptation assistance, the UNFCCC might also provide a vehicle for offering protection to those affected by MSLR if the international community is prepared to do so.

8

Emergent Issues in Climate and Migration Research

8.1 Introduction

The past two decades have brought a considerable surge in the amount of research done on issues related to climate and human migration. Even so, this is still an area of research very much in its infancy, and the overall volume of research and number of researchers working actively in this field are small in comparison with longer-established disciplines and subdisciplines in the natural and social sciences. This final chapter reviews some of the more important emergent themes in the field, including:

- How climate and migration may interact to create conditions of political instability and conflict
- The interplay of climate, global food systems, migration, and household food security
- The types of migration patterns and behavior that might be expected as a result of unexpected impacts or outcomes of climate change, which can be generally described as 'climate surprises'

This chapter then concludes this book by reviewing some of the key lessons from earlier chapters, and suggests a number of areas where future research is encouraged.

8.2 Climate Change, Migration, and State Security

Military and security organizations have shown growing interest in the relationship between climate change and migration in recent years, and in several countries have actively supported research in this field.[1] This creates an interesting opportunity for connecting climate and migration research with policy makers, for those who represent security interests typically sit at the inner circles of national and international governance, and security matters are first-order interest at cabinet tables and at the UN.

---

[1] Several paragraphs in this section appeared in similar form in the article O. Brown, R. McLeman (2009) A recurring anarchy? The emergence of climate change as a threat to international peace and security. *Conflict, Security and Development* 9: 289–305. My coauthor Oli Brown and the journal are thanked for allowing me to reproduce them here.

The way the climate-migration relationship is approached in security research may be somewhat unfamiliar to those studying migration in traditional social science disciplines, and some scholars have raised concerns about aspects of the 'securitization' of climate-migration research and the types of normative assumptions sometimes made (Brown, Hammill, and McLeman 2007). Nonetheless, this is an area where greater contributions from researchers would be well received, especially empirical studies. This section summarizes the origins of the security community's interests in climate and migration, its implications, and the opportunities for scholars to engage constructively with that community.

8.2.1 Origins of the Security Community's Interests in Climate and Migration

Researchers interested in the relationship between environmental change and state security were among the first to make concerted efforts to understand empirically the relationship between climate and migration. With the collapse of the Soviet Union in 1991, security scholars began to look beyond traditional Cold War issues like espionage and nuclear proliferation, and took greater interest in nontraditional security concerns, such as endemic poverty in developing nations, biological and disease outbreaks, water scarcity, and environmental degradation (Walt 1991). The link between environment and security caught the attention of Western policy makers with the publication of a widely read essay in *The Atlantic Monthly* by American journalist Robert Kaplan bearing the provocative title 'The Coming Anarchy' (1994). It is reported that this essay, which was based in large part on Kaplan's travels in West Africa and drew heavily on the writings of political scientist Thomas Homer-Dixon (1991), became required reading for senior advisors in the Clinton administration (Dabelko 1999). Kaplan's essay painted a bleak picture of Africa's future, predicting a descent into endemic conflict, disease, crime, resource scarcity, refugee migrations, and de facto rule by drug cartels and private armies. He further warned that this dynamic could spread throughout the less-developed regions of the world and would be exacerbated by climate change and mean sea level rise (MSLR).

The 1990s saw a steady stream of often sickening civil conflicts – many in Africa (e.g. Angola, Liberia, Mozambique, Rwanda, Sierra Leone, Somalia, and Zaire (Congo)), but also in other regions, such as Haiti, Iraq, and the former Yugoslavia – prompting policy makers to expand their international security focus from military aggression between states to concerns about how tensions within states could fuel regional instability and conflict. Independent academic research and studies funded by security organizations began looking into questions such as how fresh water shortages might be a potential trigger for violent conflict in water-scarce areas, how land degradation could become a source of conflict between agriculturalists and pastoralists, and similar types of resource-based conflicts (e.g. Homer-Dixon 1994a, Strizzi and Stranks 1996, Uvin 1996). Initially, anthropogenic climate change came fairly low on scholars' lists of potential environmental threats to security, ranking below agricultural land degradation, fresh water scarcity, deforestation, fisheries depletion, and stratospheric ozone depletion (e.g. Homer-Dixon 1994b). This is not surprising, for in the early 1990s, the physical science behind anthropogenic climate change science was still relatively new. The first assessment report of the Intergovernmental Panel on Climate Change (IPCC) had been released in 1990, but the general circulation models used to make projections of future climate were relatively crude, and knowledge of the role of oceans, airborne particulates, and other influences on atmospheric conditions was considerably poorer than it is today (though we still have a long way to go in improving our understanding of such things). The social science understanding of the impacts of climate change on human well-being was even less well developed, with Working Group II of the IPCC, which was charged with studying such questions, concluding, 'The results of the Working Group II studies highlight our lack of knowledge, particularly at the regional level and in areas most vulnerable to climate change' (Tegart, Sheldon, and Griffiths 1990: 4).

As scientific understanding of anthropogenic climate change improved over the following years, it steadily pushed its way to the top of the list of environmental threats to human security (Dabelko 2009). In 2007, the British delegation made climate change an agenda item for the UN Security Council, and in 2011 the Security Council acknowledged climate change was indeed a threat to global security (though it made no commitments to do anything substantive about it) (UN Security Council 2011). Meanwhile, studies commissioned for military and intelligence agencies warned that climate change would create conflicts and waves of environmental refugees in many regions, and these attracted attention in the popular media (Schwartz and Randall 2003, Center for Naval Analyses 2007, National Research Council 2011).[2] Popular books with provocative titles like *Climate Wars* (Dyer 2008) and *Global Warring* (Paskal 2010) created additional interest in the subject.

It is easy to understand why security and intelligence agencies, and the scholars who work to influence them, have maintained a relatively steady engagement with environmental migration research. Among their many duties, security agencies are charged with continually scanning the horizon, and occasionally trying to see over it, to identify emerging threats to national and international security. Further, people who work in the security field are encouraged to watch for potential connections between seemingly unconnected phenomena; to such eyes, the links between climate change, migration, and security are glaringly obvious. This makes for an interesting political dynamic, for the easy acceptance by the security intelligence community of the validity of climate science often runs very different from politicians' rhetoric and

---

[2] In interests of full disclosure, I have also written studies either directly or indirectly supported by security intelligence agencies (e.g. McLeman and Smit 2003, 2012). These are publicly available.

dialogue about climate change. This is especially so in the United States, where some of the most hawkish politicians publicly mock the validity of climate science even as the military and security agencies they champion so strongly actively plan strategies to deal with its impacts.[3]

8.2.2 Conceptualization of Climate and Migration in Security Research

The current trend in security circles is to treat climate change as a 'threat multiplier'; that is, an exogenous force with the potential to alter the severity of already-established threats to security (Brown et al. 2007, McLeman 2011b, UN Security Council 2011). Scholars have suggested at least five broad processes through which climate change could undermine peace and stability, be it locally, regionally, or globally, and migration figures prominently as a contributor to and/or outcome of each (Brown and McLeman 2009). First, volatile weather patterns, coupled with changes in rainfall and temperature, have the potential to adversely affect agricultural productivity and exacerbate food, water, and energy scarcities. Second, more frequent and intense natural disasters coupled with a greater burden of diseases such as malaria could stretch the coping capacity of developing countries. This could, in turn, tip poor countries into instability and plunge unstable states into upheaval or conflict. Third, natural disasters and a changing landscape could contribute to unregulated migration and displacement, forcing groups into competition for dwindling resources. Fourth, receding sea and land ice could enable access to previously inaccessible resources such as oil and gas supplies in the Arctic and to transit routes like the Northwest Passage, potentially triggering disputes over their ownership and control. Finally, soil salinization, rising sea levels, and severe droughts could make large areas uninhabitable, and in extreme cases jeopardize the very existence of small island states.

Within these five processes, the linkage with migration tends to be conceptualized in one of two related ways (McLeman 2011b). The first can be described as a scarcity-conflict scenario (Figure 8.1). This scenario assumes that the livelihoods and economic well-being of any given population will depend on a suite of resources particular to that population and setting. For an agricultural population, for example, these critical resources may be some combination of precipitation and soil fertility, while for an urban center they may be such things as stored surface water for municipal use and foodstuffs imported from the surrounding hinterland. Climate change holds the potential to upset livelihoods by triggering a decrease in resource quality, availability, or accessibility. A prolonged period of scarcity of critical resources may provoke competition among members of the affected population or push members into competition with other populations for those resources. If such a situation continues

---

[3] The most notorious of such politicians is Oklahoma senator James Inhofe, a senior member of the U.S. Senate's Armed Services Committee who, in addition to continuously advocating for ever greater military and security spending, also wrote a book expressing his views on climate change entitled *The Greatest Hoax*.

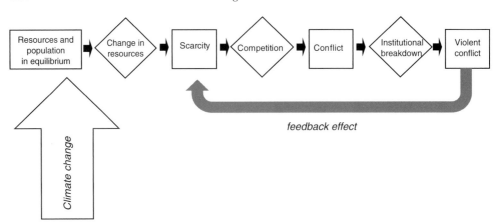

Figure 8.1. Scarcity-conflict scenario. Adapted from Brown and colleagues (2007); McLeman (2011b).

unabated, it may devolve into factionalized conflict, breakdown of public order and institutions, and, eventually, violence. Violence in turn reinforces conditions of scarcity and competition for resources, creating a feedback cycle. The Rwandan genocide and the Darfur conflict would seem to fit this model (Percival and Homer-Dixon 1996, Uvin 1996, UNEP 2007).

A variation of Figure 8.1 is an abundance-competition scenario (Figure 8.2), sometimes described as 'resource curse' conflict (Le Billon 2001, de Soysa 2002). This scenario emerges in places where a resource is geographically concentrated – like diamond mines or oil fields – enabling those who control it to extract economic rent from others who want access to it. In states where governments and institutions are weak or corrupt, the potential exists for degeneration into factionalization and violence when unresolved questions of competition and control emerge. Those living in the disputed resource area experience a rapid decline in living standards, may become victims of violence, and may be forced to choose between migration elsewhere or becoming participants in the violence. This situation currently exists, for example, in the Niger delta (Omotola 2009).

In this scenario, the impacts of climate change may work in one of two ways to stimulate new or greater incidence of conflict. The first is by increasing the value of the resources in question, either by further concentrating the geographical access to them or by elevating their market prices. This scenario could emerge, for example, in areas where water supplies are unevenly distributed, with past experience showing there is a risk of intergroup conflict within states over water supplies, though the risk of conflict between states over water is not as great (Wolf 1998, Gleditsch et al. 2006, Barnaby 2009). It is also possible to envisage climate change leading to an intensification and upscaling of local-level competition and conflicts over access to choice fishing locations, high-quality stands of timber, highly fertile soil deposits, and other strategic or common property resources. A second possibility is that climate change

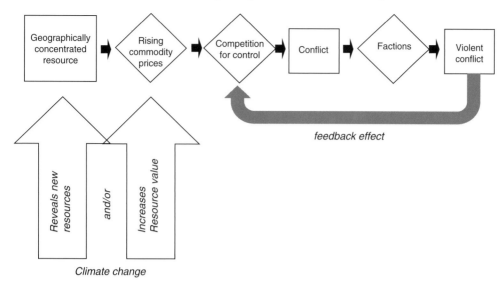

Figure 8.2. Abundance-competition scenario. Adapted from McLeman (2011b).

may reveal new, previously inaccessible resources over which there are no clearly established governance mechanisms or rights of control. Competition over shipping lanes and seabed resources in the increasingly ice-free Arctic is the best-known example (Young 2009), but others may emerge as the influence of climate change on ecosystem processes becomes more apparent. A less well-known example is that the melting of Siberian tundra is revealing fossil mammoth tusks that are making their way onto international markets for ivory (Kramer 2008). In this case, this new legal source of ivory could conceivably decrease prices for black market ivory, and thereby reduce the low-level violence and conflict that presently takes place between poachers, organized crime, and government authorities in Africa and Asia (Martin and Martin 2010).

It is important to recognize that these generalized scenarios are simply that – scenarios. While people can and do get into conflict with one another over natural resources, the types of resources that experience shows are most likely to be a source of violence or conflict – fossil fuels, minerals, and gems – are ones whose abundance and access are generally not influenced by climate.[4] In the case of resources whose abundance is influenced by climate – such as fresh water, grazing lands, fisheries – there are past examples of conflict during times and places of scarcity, but there are as many or more examples of cooperation and negotiation being the result. The Darfur conflict has been pointed to as an example of drought-induced scarcity triggering violent conflict (UNEP 2007), yet drought is an endemic risk across all of Sudano-Sahelian Africa, and has been for centuries. So why has such terrible violence been

[4] With the exception of deposits under retreating Arctic ice.

experienced in Darfur as compared with other parts of the region? The most likely explanation is that the government of Sudan allowed, and indeed encouraged, inter-group violence (Brown and McLeman 2009). In empirical studies done in north-ern Nigeria – an equally drought-prone region – Nyong, Fiki, and McLeman (2006) found that localized conflicts can occur between pastoralists and sedentary farmers during times of drought, but that local-level institutions have developed over genera-tions effective methods for resolving conflicts before they escalate. Similarly, in his studies of water scarcity, Wolf (1999, 2000) found that indigenous institutions typ-ically have built-in mechanisms for peaceful resolution of disputes during times of scarcity, and that even at the interstate level, disputes over shared resources are more often resolved through negotiation than through violence. Even those who were at the forefront in developing the environment and security literature were quick to high-light the importance of avoiding deterministic assumptions about outcomes, and to focus on the role stable institutions and governance structures play in reducing the risks of conflict (e.g. Homer-Dixon 1991, Lonergan and Kavanagh 1991, Dabelko and Dabelko 1995, Levy 1995).

8.2.3 Future Directions

It is important that social scientists, especially migration scholars, take it upon them-selves to play a greater role in research and public discussion of the security implica-tions of climate change, given the broad assumptions about migrants and refugees that are often made or implied. The scenarios suggested earlier are, from the perspec-tive of the migration scholar, largely atheoretical. They presume stimulus-response migration behavior on the part of people exposed to climatic risks when, as shown in previous chapters of this book, migration behavior is heterogeneous and context specific. Furthermore, it is the causes of refugeeism that need to be feared and not refugees themselves; yet, in the tone of security discussions about climate and migra-tion this distinction is not always apparent. For example, it is often presumed that refugees stimulate political instability in the places to which they flee. Sometimes this is true, as may be seen, for example, in how the unresolved situation of Palestinians helps drive regional tensions in the Middle East, or how the hundreds of thousands of impoverished Afghan refugees living in Pakistan provide a fertile recruiting ground for extremist organizations (Koser 2011). However, this need not always be the case. The potential for refugees to become a source of instability depends considerably on the extent to which they are allowed to settle and incorporate into the receiv-ing community. Confining refugees to camps and refugee-only settlements creates grim places that can become incubators for violence and extremism. The key, then, is to reduce the amount of time refugees must remain in such places. Another fre-quent assumption is that refugees become drivers of environmental degradation in the places to which they flee (see a useful review by Kibreab 1997). Again, this is true when refugees are confined to camps or specific areas of settlement, in which case they may indeed forage and scavenge every scrap of valuable resource until the landscape is denuded. But again, this situation is avoided when refugees are allowed to incorporate more freely into the receiving community, as shown, for example, in research done in the Senegal River valley (Black and Sessay 1997, 1998).

To summarize this section, environmentally based conflicts may emerge from conditions of abundance and of scarcity, and may stimulate migration outcomes that reinforce conditions of instability. Climate change will raise the risk of conflicts occurring in the future. However, it is important to recognize that the scenarios depicted earlier in this chapter represent *potential* progressions, not inevitable ones. Many possible intervention points exist along the pathways in each scenario, from reducing the impacts of climate change through mitigation of greenhouse gas emissions, to building and supporting robust governance structures and institutions, to enhancing local-level adaptability and conflict resolution mechanisms. Even in situations where distress migration does emerge, negative feedback effects on sending and receiving areas can be reduced through enabling the socioeconomic integration of migrants into receiving areas. Recognition of these systemic linkages between climate change, migration, and instability is important for developing appropriate policies to avoid the emergence of future conflict events, to enhance future prospects for international security, and to avoid worst-case scenario migration outcomes.

8.3 Climate Change, Food Security, and Migration

Research on climate change and food security draws upon an interesting range of disciplines, including climate scientists, agronomists, political scientists, and international development specialists, among many others. Pressures on global and regional food supplies are expected to grow in coming years as a result of population growth, urbanization, and consumer demand, with climate change likely to exacerbate the challenge. The role of migration in this context, as potentially an outcome or a moderator of food security crises, has only recently been considered in any systematic fashion, and only to a limited degree (McLeman 2013). Empirical research and policy contributions from migration scholars on questions related to climate and food security will be in greater demand in coming years, with the following section aimed at providing a starting point for those seeking to enter the fray.

8.3.1 Household Food Security

There is growing concern that anthropogenic climate change will have adverse impacts on global agricultural production, which will in turn affect food security among populations in lower-income countries (Gregory, Ingram, and Brklacich 2005; Schmidhuber and Tubiello 2007; Brown, Hintermann, and Higgins 2009; Douglas

2009). The term *food security* has had many definitions, which vary according to the scale of the system of interest. Originally, the term was used to determine whether, at a national level, countries had access to enough food to ensure all citizens could meet their basic dietary requirements, but the term has since been applied to more local scales and households as well (Pinstrup-Andersen 2009). Many factors may determine whether a household and all its members are food secure, factors that relate not only to the ability to produce or purchase sufficient food, but also to nonfood factors such as access to fresh water, sanitation, gender relations, and general health. Food insecurity at the household level may be temporary or seasonal, as seen in the Chapter 5 case study of Bangladesh, where rural households may go hungry during the annual *mangha*, or lean season, when food and agricultural wage labor are scarce. Food security may also be a chronic condition of undernourishment, with Barrett (2010) estimating the global undernourished population at nearly one billion.[5]

Three general factors contribute to household food security or lack thereof: the general availability of food, households' access to food, and their utilization of food (Barrett 2010). Availability of food at a global scale is rarely a challenge; numerous studies have shown that the world's food systems produce more than enough calories for every living human to have a robust diet, if only that food were evenly distributed and accessible to all (Gregory et al. 2005). In fact, Kummu and colleagues (2012) calculate that if the waste caused by inefficiencies in our food distribution systems were reduced, it would be possible to feed an additional 1 billion people with existing global agricultural production. Even in the face of rising human numbers and climate change, agricultural systems do in principle have the capacity to continue to produce sufficient food to keep pace with demand at the global scale (Godfray et al. 2010). There are, of course, discrepancies at any given moment in time with respect to the quantity, type, and price of food at local and regional levels, and climatic conditions can have a significant influence on these. Still, in terms of basic global food availability, the total number of food calories produced at a global level is more than sufficient to ensure that nobody should go hungry – yet they do.

Only a few generations ago, a large part of the global human population fed itself primarily on locally or self produced food. Food security at the household level was then very much a local supply problem. Household food security today – or lack thereof – is becoming less a supply problem than it is a distributional problem (Uvin 2009). Even in rural areas, it is becoming increasingly rare for households to subsist entirely on self-produced food, making the market price for food, the availability of wage labor, and the value of household wages relative to food prices key determinants of household food security. Using what has come to be known as *entitlement theory*, Nobel Prize winner Amartya Sen showed how hunger and food insecurity are

---

[5] The UN Food and Agriculture Organization (FAO) estimates the total number of people lacking food security at 800 million, although some scholars suspect the definitions and methods of calculation used by the FAO underestimate the true number (Pinstrup-Andersen 2009, Barrett 2010).

caused not by a lack of available food, but by the inability of poorer households to gain access to the food that is available (1981, 1999). Using case studies from South Asia, Sen (1977) demonstrated how people can easily go hungry even when food is plentiful on local markets – including people like fishermen who actually produce food for sale on local markets – when the local market price for food exceeds their financial means.

Food prices respond not simply to local supply and demand conditions, but are influenced by regional and international markets. For example, the price of corn tortillas in any given small town in Mexico[6] reflects not just local demand for tortillas and the amount of corn produced by Mexican producers, but also the amount of corn produced in the United States, agricultural policies in the United States that subsidize heavily American corn producers, currency exchange rates, growing demand for corn in China and other global markets, and many other factors well beyond the influence of Mexican farmers or tortilla buyers (Dyer and Taylor 2011). When the United States has a bumper crop of corn, it drives down the price of corn on Mexican markets – something that may be good for Mexican consumers but bad for Mexican producers. Conversely, when drought strikes the U.S. Corn Belt, as it did in 2012, global market prices for corn rise, which is bad for Mexican consumers but good for Mexican corn producers. Rural Mexican households do, of course, implement strategies to adapt to fluctuations in corn prices, but the point made here is that the global interconnectivity of food systems means that droughts, storms, and other climatic events that affect agricultural productivity in one region influence prices in another.

The volatility of prices for basic foodstuffs has been growing in recent years (recall Figure 6.1). This trend is worrisome because UN Food and Agricultural Organization statistics show that overall global production of common staple grains has increased by more than 25 per cent in the last decade or so.[7] Nonetheless, even slightly negative deviations from the general rate of increase spark price volatility, and as a result regional climatic events can have global consequences. For example, Russia suspended grain exports in 2010 in the wake of a severe drought. Around the same period, Australian grain production and exports also fell because of drought, with the combined effects causing a sharp rise in global grain prices (Wegren 2011). Although Russia and Australia are notable exporters of grain, their combined exports in a productive year do not amount to even one-third the volume of grain exported by Canada and the United States combined (McLeman 2013), highlighting the sensitivity of food prices to relatively small changes in total global output. A modest downturn in global food production due to a number of regional shortfalls stimulated sudden spikes in

---

[6] This example is chosen because corn is a basic staple grain consumed by most Mexican households, is a key crop grown by Mexican farmers, and is traded freely between Mexico, the United States, and Canada under the North American Free Trade Act. The United States is the world's largest producer of corn.

[7] For the most recent statistics on global food production, visit the UN FAO Cereal Supply and Demand Brief website at http://www.fao.org/worldfoodsituation/wfs-home/en/.

global food prices in 2007–8, which in turn led to riots in dozens of lower-income countries (O'Brien 2012). It is evident we have entered an era in which year over year increases in food productivity are necessary simply to maintain price stability; even producing the same amount of food as last year is insufficient. This dynamic would not be sustainable in the long run even in the absence of anthropogenic climate change. The situation is further exacerbated by commodity market speculators and the small but significant diversion of land and resources from food grains to biofuel production (Ghosh, Heintz, and Pollin 2012; Timlisina 2012).

8.3.2 The Role of Migration in the Climate Change/Household Food Security Dynamic

Migration is connected to the climate change/household food security dynamic in several ways. Two of these are in the context of voluntary labor migration, the first being the temporary migration of wage-seeking migrants in response to seasonal conditions or extreme events like droughts or floods, detailed in previous chapters. A second is through remittances of food or money that move through family or social networks between indefinite labor migrants and their home regions. These translocal or transregional networks help their members adapt proactively to food insecurity by maximizing their collective income and purchasing power. In Namibia, for example, migrants who settle in urban centers will often continue to receive food transfers from their rural relatives, with members of the family networks collaborating with one another to take advantage of food price discrepancies between locations when possible (Frayne 2005, Greiner 2011). Similar processes for maximizing food access occur within rural-urban networks in South Africa and Kenya (Smit 1998, Mberu et al. 2013) while in many parts of sub-Saharan Africa rural households invest cash remittances received from urban relatives to improve their food production capacity (Kruger 1998, Tiffen 2003). Remittances are not always invested in productive ways to enhance food security; studies from rural northern Ghana, for example, have shown remittances may be spent on eating in restaurants or purchasing low nutritional quality junk foods (Karamba, Quinones, and Winters 2011). There is also the chance that adaptive out-migration may leave insufficient labor in the source region to maintain food production.[8]

Nonetheless, studies from various countries suggest that long-run agricultural productivity, child nutrition, and rural household incomes tend to improve with the receipt of remittance income (de Brauw 2010; Azzarri and Zezza 2011; Carletto, Covarrubias, and Maluccio 2011). Remittances allow receiving households to spend less of their marginal income on basic needs like food, and to devote more resources

---

[8] Greiner (2011) reports how Namibian pastoralists who migrate to the city may end up hiring pastoralists from other areas to look after their livestock for them, creating new internal migration patterns.

to the quality of housing, to the education of younger household members, and to taking advantage of local entrepreneurial opportunities (Adams 2006; Lokshin, Bontch-Osmolovski, and Glinskaya 2010). This reduces their general vulnerability to food price fluctuations. Remittances can also help households cope with sudden-onset shocks to food security, with de Brauw (2011) observing that during the 2008 food price crisis in El Salvador, the physical development of children living in remittance-receiving households was less likely to be affected by dietary shortfalls.

Distress migration is a third way migration is linked to climate and food security, occurring in situations where food is simply unavailable or is so scarce as to be unaffordable. Extreme examples of famine and famine migrations were distressingly common in the second half of the twentieth century in parts of Africa and Asia where large rural populations practice rain-fed agriculture (Baro and Deubel 2006, Devereux 2009). Although climate-related short-term downturns in local or regional food production were often the proximate triggers, political and socioeconomic instability created the necessary conditions for food entitlement failures to degenerate into humanitarian disasters like the Bangladesh famine of the early 1970s and the Ethiopian famine of the 1980s (Quddus and Becker 2000, Block and Webb 2001). Hunger-related migration events are most often associated with movements of people between rural areas or from rural to urban areas, but it can also happen that people migrate out of cities during periods of urban food insecurity. This typically occurs only under conditions of exceptionally high urban unemployment that prompts people to go back to the land to become self-producers of food or to find work in agriculture. Researchers have observed recent examples in Zambia and Côte d'Ivoire (Potts 2005, Beauchemin 2011), while during the Great Depression this phenomenon occurred in various parts of North America (Boyd 2002, McLeman 2006).

8.3.3 Future Challenges

Climate change will put additional pressure on global food systems. It is reasonable to assume that some people in lower-income countries will adapt proactively through risk-reducing migration, and in some cases periodic food price shocks may stimulate reactive, distress-type migration. There is clearly an opportunity for more research, particularly empirical studies, on the migration decision making and behavior of households during periods of food price volatility. Two other phenomena have emerged in recent years that are likely to have additional implications for migration patterns in lower-income countries, and about which there is very little research. The first of these is the acquisition of lands in Africa and South and Southeast Asia by Middle Eastern and Asia-based investors for conversion to commercial export agriculture, generically referred to as 'land grabs'. These investors are a mix of private and state-backed corporations based in countries that are net food importers, whose motivations include the enhancement of their own national food security (Seo and

Rodriguez 2012). The nature of land grabs varies considerably from one example to the next in terms of their size, scale, purpose, legal arrangements, and number of people displaced as a result (Cotula et al. 2011). Land grabs appear to be rising in number, and there is considerable debate over the costs, benefits, winners, and losers (e.g. Chu 2011, Cotula et al. 2011, Deininger and Byerlee 2011, McMichael 2012).

At the time of this writing, no reliable empirical data is available on how many people these transactions have displaced, where they resettle, their welfare after they resettle, or the implications for local and regional labor movements. In many of the regions where land grabs occur, tenure rights are vague, informal, or customary, meaning that families that have occupied or used land for generations might find that their government has simply sold or leased it out from under them (Li 2011). There is also concern about the fate of female-headed households when land grabs occur in areas where tenure is typically vested in men (Chu 2011). Once land has been 'grabbed', the increased use of machinery and the types of crops produced mean less labor is required per unit area, thereby providing fewer local employment opportunities in agriculture than existed previously, and potentially triggering new food security problems for residents (Daniel 2011, Li 2011). Many African lands grabbed by outside interests are water scarce, which presents the additional risk of residents being pushed out over competition for water (Woodhouse 2012). There are examples of local-level and national-level resistance to land grabs, the best-known one in Madagascar, where the government had proposed to lease half the country's arable land to a Korean multinational (Daniel 2011). In most other cases, though, land grabs attract little attention outside the affected area. Any empirical research by migration scholars would be a welcome contribution to this subject.

A second area in dire need of research is the effects on migration of the diversion of agricultural land from food production to the production of feedstock for biofuels. Not all biofuels are made from food plants or require the conversion of productive agricultural lands, with willows, switchgrasses, crop-residues, slash from forestry (Figure 8.3),[9] and reprocessed cooking oils being just some of the many examples. However, in many parts of the world, land that has formerly produced food for people is being converted to growing biofuel feedstocks. Examples include Southeast Asia, where palm oil plantations are proliferating; sub-Saharan Africa, where jatropha acreages are expanding; and the United States, where up to one-third of corn production is used for biofuel production (Graham-Rowe 2011). In parts of Asia and Africa, this food-to-fuel land use conversion often occurs in concert with land grabs; in other regions, it is simply a case of market prices or government subsidies pushing farmers into making different crop choices. Assessments of the effects of biofuel production and climate change at broad scales have begun to appear in the scholarly

---

[9] *Slash* refers to smaller branches, unused smaller trees, and other forest materials that are typically not captured for use during conventional forestry. These can be chipped and used to fire steam boilers and home fireplaces.

Figure 8.3. Forestry slash, chipped and ready for use as biofuel, Addington Highlands, Ontario. The wood chips in the image were made from tree material left over after logs were removed from the sustainably managed forest in the background. The chips will be used to fire the boiler at the mill to which the logs were taken for processing into cardboard. Small-scale forestry is one of the few economic sectors that provide year-round gainful employment for households in this area of high out-migration of young people. Family-operated forestry companies have been struggling because of competition from foreign producers and slow economic growth in the United States. Biofuels, widely touted as a means of fighting global warming, are seen by residents of this region as an opportunity for sustaining the community economically in the future (see McLeman 2010b, Fast and McLeman 2012). Author's own photograph.

literature (e.g. Tirado et al. 2010), but the direct and indirect impacts of biofuel-driven land use change on the food security of households and local communities in lower-income regions have not yet been well studied. Research suggests that, if current trends continue, global food supplies will shrink slightly, with decreases in food availability being most pronounced in India and sub-Saharan Africa (Timlisina 2012). As already noted, the current global food system requires year-over-year increases in food availability to maintain price stability, so even a small diversion of food to fuel can be expected to have widespread repercussions for food security, state security, and migration patterns in lower-income regions. There is consequently an important opportunity here for research that looks at how migration patterns and behavior may already be responding and how they will respond in future.

To summarize this section, food security is for poorer households often less a question of food availability than it is accessibility and affordability. The interconnectedness of global food systems means that climate-related crop failure in one region can stimulate food price volatility in other regions. Migration is one of the ways households may adapt when their food security is threatened. Temporary labor migration can provide short-term relief. Translocal or transregional social networks between migrants and their places of origin provide opportunities for network members to share resources and take advantage of price discrepancies, with cash remittances potentially improving the food security, health, and well-being of receiving households. Land grabs run the risk of creating involuntary displacement in poorer rural areas in developing countries, while even small diversions of food production to biofuels raise the risk of food price shocks. Layered on top of all these are the risks presented by anthropogenic climate change. Again, there is here an opportunity for migration scholars to conduct considerably more empirical research.

8.4 Climate Surprise

8.4.1 What Is a 'Climate Surprise'?

A key premise of this book is that past human-climate interactions provide clues about how climate change may affect migration in the future. But – and this is an important 'but' – what if future climatic events and conditions do not conform to past patterns? Researchers cannot help but assume, somewhat hopefully, that the impacts of climate change will be experienced in a gradual, linear fashion that can be recognized, understood, planned for, and adapted to. For example, security analysts describe climate change as a 'threat multiplier'; climate researchers often say climate change 'exacerbates' other factors that create vulnerability. Scientist Michael Glantz[10] has warned we must also be concerned about 'climate surprise', and be aware that predictable, incremental, or observable changes in climate are less disruptive to human systems than unexpected ones (Streets and Glantz 2000). Not all 'surprises' are truly surprising or unforeseeable; humans are remarkably capable of willfully blinding themselves to environmental risks (McLeman and Smit 2006b). For example, people who live in floodplains should not be surprised when floods occur, yet often behave as though they are surprised and demand that governments come to their rescue. However, not all surprises are knowable or foreseeable, even with the best of current scientific knowledge. For example, Streets and Glantz (2000) note that chlorofluorocarbons (CFCs) were originally seen as a wonderful invention with all kinds of beneficial applications, and were in use for decades before scientists realized the harm they cause to the stratospheric ozone layer. This is an example of a

---

[10] Glantz was one of the early proponents of the 'research by analog' method for studying climate change impacts, an important inspiration for the present book.

'bad' surprise. There are also many examples from the past of 'good' surprises, such as Sir Alexander Fleming's accidental discovery of penicillin because he failed to maintain a tidy lab bench (Diggins 1999).

Anthropogenic climate change will hold its share of foreseeable and unforeseeable surprises, some good and some bad. The foreseeable ones like floods, droughts, storms, and rising sea levels – even if they surprise us with their frequency, severity, or by popping up in new places – will have potentially foreseeable impacts on migration, and these have already been reviewed in previous chapters. The final question to be considered in this book is, how will presently unknowable or unforeseeable climate surprises affect migration patterns in coming years? This question poses a challenge of logic, for if the 'surprising' climatic stimulus cannot be foreseen, how can its influences on migration be known until it happens? One way around the logic problem is to ignore whether the stimulus is of climatic origin or not, and identify past examples when populations or settlements experienced unforeseeable surprises that stimulated changes in migration patterns, and study these to see what happened and extract lessons.

8.4.2 Past Examples of 'Bad' Surprises Affecting Migration

What are some past examples of bad, unforeseeable surprises? For aboriginal peoples in the Americas and the Pacific, the arrival of Europeans between the sixteenth and eighteenth centuries would have certainly constituted an unforeseeable surprise, one that led to tremendous societal disruptions that included migration (Diamond 1997, 2005). Perhaps climate change will surprise modern societies the way modern societies surprised traditional ones in centuries past. Another past source of surprise has been changes in transportation technology. For example, the expansion of railways in the United States during the 1800s meant success or failure for frontier and rural settlements established in the pre-railroad era. If the railroad route passed through a town (and better yet, built a station and depot there) it survived, prospered, and grew (Handley 1974, Schwieterman 2004). If the railroad bypassed a settlement by even by a few miles, it ceased to grow, and withered. Towns and cities often lobbied like mad to avoid being passed by, but in many cases the decisions were out of their control. When railroads next switched from steam to diesel, many settlements that existed primarily to service the steam trains disappeared (Cottrell 1951). A similar transformation again swept through the United States in the mid-twentieth century when the interstate highway system was built and railways began abandoning unprofitable lines; although, by that point in time communities would already have been aware of the implications of being bypassed, and it would no longer have been a completely unforeseeable surprise.

A useful and relatively recent example of a 'bad' surprise is the case of the Aral Sea, one that has become famous (or infamous) for images of fishing boats stranded

Figure 8.4. Ships of the desert, Aral Sea. Photo by Staecker, public domain image.
http://upload.wikimedia.org/wikipedia/commons/2/21/AralShip.jpg.

in the deserts of Central Asia (Figure 8.4). Once an enormous inland lake, diversions
of its tributaries by Soviet planners in the 1960s led to a tremendous drop in water
levels and a retreat of the shoreline by up to 100 kilometers in some places (Zonn
1999, Micklin 2007). As the lake receded, people whose livelihoods depended on the
lake began leaving the region. The exposed lakebed sediments, which contained high
levels of agricultural chemicals, became airborne and created a respiratory health risk
for those who remained (Small, Van der Meer, and Upshaw 2001). The collapse of
the Soviet Union exacerbated unemployment and created political uncertainty in the
region around the lake. Out-migration spiked, with an estimated one hundred thousand people leaving in the years immediately surrounding the collapse, especially
young, skilled, ethnic Russians (Small et al. 2001, Crighton et al. 2003). Their departure left the region chronically short of health professionals at a time when environmental conditions created elevated health risks. This tale of an unexpected environmental disaster coinciding with a sudden political-economic change is worth keeping
in mind as a potential learning analog for 'bad' climate surprise (McLeman 2011a).

8.4.3 Past Examples of 'Good' Surprises Affecting Migration

By contrast, are there past examples of good surprises affecting migration patterns?
Examples to be looked for are cases where a location that once had few attributes
to invite settlement, relative to other locations, unexpectedly became attractive. The
rise of Chicago from lakeside hamlet to inland metropolis in just a few decades was

nothing short of remarkable, as Cronon (1991) carefully detailed. Henry Ford's revolutionary assembly plants, and those of manufacturers that copied him, attracted millions of rural migrants from the American South and Appalachia to the manufacturing centers of the Midwestern United States, in what has come to be known as the Great Migration (Tolnay et al. 2005). The technological innovation of air conditioning made the American Sun Belt more suitable for urbanization, with the warm-weather states of California,[11] Florida, Texas, North Carolina, and Georgia becoming main destinations of interstate migration (Meyer 2000, Gutmann and Field 2010).

Smaller, faster-moving examples of 'good' surprises that trigger migration are the gold rush towns and other resource-related 'boom towns' found on virtually every continent. An interesting one to consider is that of Fort McMurray, Alberta, the chief city of Canada's tar sands region. As the name suggests, tar sands are a thick, heterogeneous mixture of sand, clay, rock, and bituminous hydrocarbons with a consistency similar to road tar. Tens of thousands of square kilometers of land containing tar sands surround Fort McMurray, but before the 1960s they had little economic value. There was no efficient way of separating the bitumen from the sand, and high-quality, easily accessible crude oil found elsewhere was plentiful and cheap. Fort McMurray was back then a backwoods village that between 1956 and 1961 grew by a grand total of 76 people, from 1,110 to 1,186 (Statistics Canada 1971). Today, Fort McMurray and its surrounding area are home to over 115,000 people (Statistics Canada 2012). In the 1960s, technological innovations made it possible to extract a refinable oil product from tar sands, although it was still expensive. It took the 1973 OPEC crisis to raise world oil prices high enough that tar sand production became economically viable. These two 'good' surprises – technological innovation and an oil price shock – created a boom town that grew rapidly until oil prices fell in the late 1980s. When the slump in oil prices ended in the 1990s, Fort McMurray resumed its above-average population growth, as shown in Table 8.1. The city still shows some of the demographic characteristics of a boom town, the gender balance and average age reflective of a community that disproportionately attracts young men seeking employment. The Fort McMurray experience is one that may well be replicated in future boom towns that emerge as climate change presents new resource-related opportunities.

8.5 'Unknown Unknowns', Black Swans, and the Key Lessons of this Book

It seems fitting to begin wrapping up this book by summarizing the key lessons of previous chapters in the context of what former U.S. Secretary of Defense Donald Rumsfeld famously called *unknown unknowns* – surprise events that cannot possibly be anticipated because they are beyond our past experience. What if the Earth's

---

[11] With the caveat that northern California's San Francisco Bay area, which attracts a steady share of migrants, does not truly qualify as a 'warm weather' destination; more populous and continually growing southern California certainly does.

Table 8.1. *Comparison of selected population statistics for City of Fort McMurray, Province of Alberta, and Canada as a whole*

	Fort McMurray	Alberta	Canada
Population 2011	115,372	3,645,257	33,476,688
% population change, 2006–11	14.5	10.8	5.9
% population change, 2001–6	24.3	10.6	5.4
% population change, 1996–2001	17.8	10.3	4.0
% population change, 1991–6	–3.4	5.9	5.7
Median age, 2011	32.6	36.5	40.6
% population male, 2011	53	50.1	49
% population female, 2011	47	49.9	51

Source: Data from Statistics Canada (2012).

climate simply begins to behave in ways that it has not in the past? The future consequences of anthropogenic climate change will include unknown unknowns. Never before have humans experienced an atmosphere with this particular composition, and we modify it further by the day. It is a grand experiment, the early results of which will be manifest within our children's lifetimes, if not our own. Yet, even in the worst-case climate change scenarios that science fiction writers might dream up, most of the surface of the Earth presently suitable for human habitation will almost certainly remain habitable. Some of the choicest settlement locations, such as those situated in river valleys and in coastal deltas, as well as less choice locations where water resources are tenuous, could become uninhabitable, at least in terms of the present technologies we use for shelter, transportation, and economic activities. In 2009, a group of researchers gathered to consider the implications of a scenario where average global temperatures are by the end of the century four degrees Celsius above present temperatures – a scenario seen as possible but unlikely based on present science.[12] The researchers projected there would be tremendous disruptions to ecological and human systems and widespread human population displacements and migration. Gemenne (2011b) has suggested in such a world, the distinctions between forced and voluntary migration would become heavily blurred, and that one of the greatest threats to human well-being could be a lack of mobility. In other words, migration will grow in its importance for households and individuals as a means of adapting to climatic uncertainty. Similar concerns about immobility were echoed in the conclusions of the UK government's *Foresight* (2011) study on global environmental migration.

Future climate-related migration behavior and patterns will also contain their share of unknown unknowns. If we cannot be sure how future climate will behave, we

---

[12] The results of several studies emanating from the conference were published in 2011 in *Philosophical Transactions of the Royal Society London: Series A: Mathematical, Physical & Engineering Sciences* 369: 1934.

certainly cannot be sure how future climate-related migration will behave. Perhaps as a result, the lessons learned from past and present climate-related migration are not useful for understanding the future. This is a common difficulty when using inductive or analog-based reasoning: when attempting to forecast behavior that is rare or unusual, past evidence may be unreliable. Nassim Taleb calls this the problem of the *black swan*, a term he coined from a tale that suggests Europeans believed all swans were white until they first travelled to Australia and found black swans there, thereby changing everything they thought they knew about swans. In his book *The Black Swan: The Impact of the Highly Improbable* (2007) Taleb offers a prescription for success in a world where unknown unknowns are inevitable, which goes something like this: reduce potential exposure to negative black swans and create the potential to benefit from good black swans. Taleb's prescription is made in contemplation of future economic uncertainty, but his logic also applies here. It is not necessary to know exactly how future climate conditions will play out, so long as we (1) understand how human systems are sensitive to climatic changes; (2) take steps to reduce exposure to adverse climatic conditions and events that create distress migration (which is the least desirable form of migration); and (3) build adaptive capacity at local levels so that households have greater agency to choose the means of adaptation that best suit them, which may or may not include migration. The building of adaptive capacity also entails removing unnecessary institutional barriers to mobility and migration, and ensuring that those who are less mobile have improved access to the cultural, economic, and social capital necessary to adapt by other means.

This book has suggested a number of tools and insights that may help researchers and policy makers in figuring out how to meet future challenges. The MESA model provides a simple breakdown of the key functional components of migration under conditions of climatic variability and change. Figure 3.9 offers a process-based view of migration within an adaptive system, making it possible to better visualize how the process plays out and thereby identify potential intervention points. It also highlights how capital connects the macro, meso, and micro scales within that system, and helps shape their interactions. Of the many observations made about climate-related migration from examples from the recent past, several stand out as useful in anticipating migration patterns and behavior in an uncertain future:

Climate affects migration behavior directly and indirectly. Tropical cyclones, floods, and droughts provide the most obvious and visible examples of direct influences. There are many potential indirect and more subtle influences as well, such as climatic amenities that become desirable as people reach certain life stages, or events like heat waves that may exacerbate some individuals' respiratory conditions and cause them to consider moving closer to family or health facilities. The impact of climate on global food systems and food can be expected to have a growing influence on household adaptation and migration.

The theories and concepts scholars have traditionally used to study migration are also useful for understanding the relationship between climate and migration. They are particularly useful when combined with theories and concepts of vulnerability and adaptation as used in the climate impacts and adaptation research field. Migration in the context of climatic variability and change can as a result be seen as a function of the nature of the climatic exposure, the sensitivity of the human systems in place, and the range of adaptation options available to those exposed.

In most cases, climate-related migration is initiated at the household level. Adaptation options, migration options, and migrant agency are shaped and constrained by cultural, economic, political, and social factors that operate at multiple scales, often well beyond the direct control or influence of the individual, household, or local population. Flows of capital in its various forms, and household access to it, link local-level adaptation and migration decisions to larger-scale factors at work.

If people can adapt to climatic stresses in ways that do not entail indefinite migration, they typically will. Rates of long-distance, indefinite migration may go down during periods when climatic conditions are difficult, given its high up-front costs and uncertain return to the sending household. Households mobilize their economic, social, and cultural capital as efficiently as they can to respond to the threats posed to their livelihoods, and seek the least disruptive ways of adapting. Many types of capital, especially housing and land, are not portable, and are disincentives to adapting to climate through permanent migration. Loss or damage to housing has an important influence on migration patterns after extreme events because it creates a predisposition to relocation among those affected.

Where governments and institutions are stable, reliable, and capable of supporting adaptation at lower levels, distress migration in the face of extreme climate events or conditions is unlikely. Where institutions are weak, corrupt, or unreliable, households will adapt on their own, and this may well include migration. There is reason to believe that climate-related distress migration could act as a destabilizing political force in places with weak institutions, but outside intervention can offset this risk.

In many parts of the world, labor migration is a key means by which rural households adapt to reduce exposure to climatic risks, or to rebuild livelihoods and household assets in response to extreme climate events. Labor migration is most likely to follow established social networks to known destinations. Where the opportunity costs or monetary costs of migration are high, most migration will occur over modest distances to familiar places. Meso-level agents, such as migration facilitators, employer's agents, and smuggling organizations can play an important role where institutional barriers to migration exist.

Migration is a logical and legitimate means by which households adapt to climate-related challenges and opportunities. Immobility may create greater vulnerability to future climate change. As an adaptation strategy, migration is most effective and beneficial for sending area, receiving area, the migrants, and their social networks when it occurs under conditions of high agency. The most important thing that can be done to prepare for the climate-related black swans of the future is to create conditions that maximize household adaptive capacity and migrant agency.

8.6 Future Research Needs

The writing of this book began in 2011 and concluded in early 2013. Over this period the amount of scholarship devoted to climate and migration grew considerably. By the time the published book reaches its reader, aspects of it will already start to be out of date; such is the case when writing a 'state of the science' of a newly emerging field. Fortunately, excellent scholarly journals like *Population and Environment*, *Global Environmental Change*, and *Climatic Change*, among others, have shown a commitment to publishing new studies of climate and migration on a regular basis. For scholars who are new entrants to this field or are considering entering it, I offer these final, personal observations about questions that seem to be in particular need of greater research attention.

The most important need is empirical work, empirical work, and more empirical work. There is no shortage of papers, reports, and articles making normative observations about the links between environment and migration and offering policy prescriptions about what ought to be done about climate-change-induced migration. While these are appropriate topics for PhD qualifying exams, there is no urgent need for more publications of this type. What is lacking is empirical work, lots of it, that reflects a well-grounded understanding of both the natural and the social science relevant to climate and migration. Further, we need an expansion in the number of geographical regions studied. Excellent research continues to come out of Bangladesh, and Bangladeshi scholars, who are best placed to do it, are publishing more of it. A good body of research also exists on environment and migration in dryland Africa, though more work by African scholars (in addition to scholars who study Africa) needs to be published in mainstream journals. Journal editors are encouraged to find ways of getting work from scholars based in developing countries into peer-reviewed publications. In compiling this book I encountered relatively more English-language, peer-reviewed research about climate-related migration in Bangladesh, India, and dryland Africa than I did about such migration in South America, North America (apart from Katrina and the Great Plains Dust Bowl), Southeast Asia, and Europe. I would encourage more researchers to not only begin studying and writing about these regions, but also to start looking in their own communities and countries for opportunities to study climate and migration. I have learned much about the relationship between climate and migration from years of studying and observing a relatively anonymous set of small, rural communities in eastern Ontario, Canada that were a short drive from my Ottawa office.

Gender issues in the context of climate adaptation and migration are understudied. The experiences of women, children, and the elderly are difficult to find in the existing literature. I have flagged examples where I was able to find them. I have given great emphasis to the household as the adaptation and migration decision-making unit. Part of this is because the literature points to this as a logical thing to do, but part of it also reflects the fact that dynamics within the household as they relate to migration and adaptation behavior are not well studied. At recent conferences, I have seen promising signs of more research being done on these sorts of issues, and would encourage still more. By contrast, research on present-day climate-related migration of aboriginal peoples is also difficult to find, but I am seeing less of this presented at conferences. More voices are needed around the table.

There is also a need for researchers to focus attention on the more subtle linkages between climate and migration. Cases of people fleeing floods and droughts by the thousands are easy to identify and study, but as this book has pointed out, climate also influences migration behavior in less dramatic ways, and these also need to be studied systematically. I look forward to the day when scholarly articles on climate change and migration no longer feel a need to include a discussion of the environmental refugee scholarship or Myers (2002). The field is moving well beyond these. As part of this, coming years will hopefully see much more work on how climate affects labor migration and family-related migration which, after all, describe the vast majority of the world's migrants. There is also a need to look more carefully at how climate change, urbanization, and migration will interact with one another in coming decades, as humans continue to become an increasingly urban/suburban species.

As a companion to the study of the impacts of climate on migration, scholars are also encouraged to consider the impacts of migration on the capacity to adapt to climate and on food security. My own research in recent years has increasingly moved into this domain (e.g. McLeman 2010b, 2013, McLeman and Ford 2013) and, with the exception of a few bits and pieces of work done on specific issues such as the role of migration in UN National Plans of Action for Climate Change in less developed countries, much remains unstudied.

Finally, and this is directed specifically at the undergraduate or graduate student thinking about doing advanced research on climate and migration: do it! This is a field whose importance is growing by the year, and where every new study shows how little we actually know about the subject. New ideas, energy, and approaches are both welcome and desperately needed. Your contribution will be well received.

Annex

Estimates of Global Population Exposed to Tropical Cyclones

Table A1. *Global calculations (all figures in x000s)*

Country	Population year 2001	Population year 2010	Population change % since 2001	Notes on data dates
CARIBBEAN BASIN & CENTRAL AMERICA				All countries/all populations in region assumed to be exposed
Guadeloupe	432	404	−6.5	
Guatemala	11,678	14,362	23.0	
Haiti	8,720	10,085	15.7	
Honduras	6,530	8,046	23.2	
Jamaica	2,604	2,702	3.8	
Martinique	387	400	3.4	
Mexico	99,716	107,551	7.9	Data only until 2009
Montserrat	4.52	5	10.7	Data only until 2008
Netherlands Antilles	176	198	12.5	
Nicaragua	5,174	5,816	12.4	
Panama	3,004	3,504	16.7	
Puerto Rico	3,840	3,979	3.6	
Saint Kitts and Nevis – Saint-Kitts-et-Nevis	46	39	−15.4	Data only until 2005
Saint Lucia	158	168	6.4	Data only until 2007
Saint Vincent and the Grenadines	108	99	−8.3	Data only for 2002–8
Trinidad and Tobago	1,267	1,318	4.0	
Turks and Caicos Islands	20	40	102.9	

(continued)

Table A1 *(cont.)*

Country	Population year 2001	Population year 2010	Population change % since 2001	Notes on data dates
United States Virgin Islands	109	110	1.2	
Total	143,972	158,825	10.3	
SOUTH AMERICA				
Colombia	40,806	45,508	11.5	Colombia excluded from global totals as population statistics and hurricane risk not spatially compatible
Venezuela	24,766	28,834	16.4	
Total	65,572	74,342	13.4	
ASIA				
Bangladesh	131,000	146,600	11.9	Data only until 2009
Brunei Darussalam	333	406	22	Data only until 2009
Cambodia	12,922	14,303	10.7	
China – southern and eastern coast	536,220	576,170	7.5	See Table A2 for calculation, data source
China, Hong Kong SAR	6,714	7,068	5.3	
China, Macao SAR	434	545	25.5	
North Korea	23,149	23,612	2	Data only until 2004
India – eastern and southern coast	291,879	328,629	12.6	See Table A3 for calculation, data source
Indonesia	208,198	234,432	12.6	Data only until 2009
Japan	127,149	127,450	0.24	
Laos	5,377	6,310	17.3	
Malaysia	24,123	28,250	17.1	
Maldives	276	320	15.9	
Myanmar	51,138	58,377	14.2	Data only until 2008
Philippines	78,568	94,013	19.7	
Republic of Korea	47,357	48,875	3.2	
Singapore	4,138	5,077	22.7	
Sri Lanka	18,732	20,653	10.3	
Thailand	62,914	67,312	7	
Timor-Leste	1,115	1,115	0	No data except for 2009
Viet Nam	78,621	86,928	10.6	
TOTAL ASIA	1,710,358	1,876,443	9.7	

Country	Population year 2001	Population year 2010	Population change % since 2001	Notes on data dates
OCEANIA				
American Samoa	59	67	12.8	Data only until 2006
Australia – Queensland + Northern Territory	3788	4098	8.2	See Table A4 for calculation, data source
Cook Islands	18	23	26.5	
Fiji	810	882	8.9	y2009
French Polynesia	239	264	10.3	y2009
Guam	158	181	14.1	
Marshall Islands	55	54	-0.5	
Micronesia (Federated States of)	107	108	0.5	
Nauru	12	12	2.6	No data except 2001
New Caledonia	217	246	13.2	y2009
New Zealand	3,881	4,368	12.6	
Niue	2	1	−25.2	From 2002
Norfolk Island	3	2	−33.3	From 2002 to 2005
Northern Mariana Islands	72	48	−33	
Palau	20	21	7	Data only until 2008
Papua New Guinea	5,462	5,462	0	Only data from 2002
Samoa	178	184	3.4	Only data from 2002
Solomon Islands	426	542	27.3	
Tonga	101	103	2.3	Data only until 2007
Tuvalu	9	11	18.1	Data only until 2007
Vanuatu	216	221	2.3	Data from 2003–5
TOTAL OCEANIA	15,833	16,899	6.7	
AFRICA				
Madagascar	15,529	18,865	21.5	Data only until 2008
Mozambique	17,653	21,854	23.8	
Tanzania	36,308	41,900	15.4	Data only from 2003–9
Total	69,490	82,619	18.9	
USA – Carolinas to Texas	49,079	57,956	18.1	See Tables A5–6 for calculation, data source
GLOBAL TOTALS	1,988,733	2,192,742	10.3	

Source: Data from UN DESA (2010) except where otherwise noted.

Table A2. *Calculation of exposed population in China*
(all figures in x000s)

Province	year 2000	year 2009
Hainan	7,870	8,640
Guangdong	86,420	96,380
Guangxi	44,890	48560
Fujian	34,710	36,270
Zhejiang	46,770	51,800
Shanghai	16,740	19,210
Jiangsu	74,380	77,250
Shandong	90,790	94,700
Hebei	67,440	70,340
Lianing	42,380	43,190
Beijing	13,820	17,550
Tianjin	10,010	12,280
TOTAL	536,220	576,170

Note: Statistics represent population in China's coastal provinces.
Data source: China Statistics Press (2010).

Table A3. *Calculation of exposed population in India*
(all figures in x000s)

State	year 2001	year 2010
Tamil Nadu	62,405	72,139
Andhra Pradesh	76,210	84,666
Orissa	36,804	41,947
West Bengal	80,176	91,347
Tripura	3,199	3,671
Mizoram	888	1,091
Kerala	31,841	33,388
Andaman and Nicobar Islands	356	380
TOTALS	291,879	328,629

Note: Statistics represent population in India's coastal provinces.
Data source: Government of India (2011).

Table A4. *Calculation of exposed population in Australia*
(all figures in x000s)

State	year 2001	year 2006
Queensland	3,586	3,905
Northern Territory	202	193
TOTAL	3,788	4,098

Data source: Australian Bureau of Statistics (2013).

Table A5. *Calculation of exposed population in USA (all figures in x000s)*

State	year 2000	year 2010
Alabama	4,447	4,780
Florida	15,982	19,801
Georgia	8,186	9,688
Louisiana	4,469	4,533
Mississippi	2,845	2,967
North Carolina	8,049	9,535
South Carolina	4,012	4,625
Texas coastal counties	1,089	2,027
TOTAL	49,079	57,956

Data source: U.S. Census (2013).

Table A6. *Calculation of exposed population in Texas, USA coastal counties (all figures in x000s)*

County	year 2000	year 2010
Orange	85	82
Jefferson	252	252
Chambers	26	35
Galveston	250	291
Brazoria	242	313
Matagorda	38	37
Jackson	14	14
Victoria	84	87
Calhoun	20.6	21
Refugio	7	7
Aransas	22	23
San Patricio	67	65
Nueces	314	340
Kleberg	32	32
Kennedy	0.4	0.4
Willacy	20	22
Cameron	335	406
TOTAL	1,809	2,027.4

Data source: U.S. Census (2013).

References

Abel, N., Goddard, R., Harman, B., Leitch, A., Langridge, J., Ryan, A., & Heyenga, S., 2011. Sea level rise, coastal development and planned retreat: Analytical framework, governance principles and an Australian case study. *Environmental Science & Policy*, **14**(3), 279–88.

Adam, D., 2005. 50m environmental refugees by end of decade, UN warns. *Guardian Online*. Available at: http://www.guardian.co.uk/climatechange/story/0,12374,1589898,00.html.

Adams, R. H., 2006. International remittances and the household: Analysis and review of global evidence. *Journal of African Economies*, **15**(2), 396–425.

Adger, W. N., 1999. Social vulnerability to climate change and extremes in coastal Vietnam. *World Development*, **27**(2), 249–69.

Adger, W. N., 2003. Social capital, collective action, and adaptation to climate change. *Economic Geography*, **79**(4), 387–404.

Adger, W. N., 2006. Vulnerability. *Global Environmental Change*, **16**(3), 268–81.

Adger, W. N., Agrawala, S., Mirza, M. M. Q., Conde, C., O'Brien, K., Pulhin, J., Pulwarty, R., Smit, B., & Takahashi, K., 2007. Assessment of adaptation practices, options, constraints and capacity. In *Contribution of Working Group II to the Fourth Assessment Report of the Intergovernmental Panel on Climate Change, 2007* M. L. Parry, O. F. Canziani, J. P. Palutikof, P. J. van der Linden, & C. E. Hanson, eds. Cambridge: Cambridge University Press, 717–43.

Adger, W. N., Hughes, T. P., Folke, C., Carpenter, S. R., & Rockstrom, J., 2005. Social-ecological resilience to coastal disasters. *Science*, **309**, 1036–9.

Adger, W. N., Huq, S., Brown, K., Conway, D., & Hulme, M., 2003. Adaptation to climate change in the developing world. *Progress in Development Studies*, **3**(3), 179–95.

Adger, W. N., Kelly, P. M., Winkels, A., Huy, L. Q., & Locke, C., 2002. Migration, remittances, livelihood trajectories and social resilience. *Ambio*, **31**(4), 358–66.

Adhikari, P., Hong, Y., Douglas, K. R., Kirschbaum, D. B., Gourley, J., Adler, R., & Brakenridge, G. R., 2010. A digitized global flood inventory (1998–2008): Compilation and preliminary results. *Natural Hazards*, **55**(2), 405–22.

Adugna, A. & Thrift, N. J., 1989. The 1984 drought and settler migration in Ethiopia. In J. I. Clarke et al., eds. *Population and Disaster*. Oxford: Basil Blackwell, 114–27.

Ahamad, M. G., Khondker, R. K., Ahmed, Z. U., & Tanin, F., 2011. Seasonal unemployment and voluntary out-migration from northern Bangladesh. *Modern Economy*, **2**, 174–9.

Ahern, M., Kovats, R. S., Wilkinson, P., Few, R., & Matthies, F., 2005. Global health impacts of floods: Epidemiologic evidence. *Epidemiological Review*, **27**(1), 36–46.

Ahonen, E. Q., Benavides, F. G., & Benach, J., 2007. Immigrant populations, work and health – A systematic literature review. *Scandinavian Journal of Worker and Environmental Health*, **33**(2), 96–104.

Airriess, C. A., Li, W., Leong, K. J., Chen, A. C.-C., & Keith, V. M., 2007. Church-based social capital, networks and geographical scale: Katrina evacuation, relocation, and recovery in a New Orleans Vietnamese American community. *Geoforum*, **39**(3), 1333–46.

Ali, A., 2007. September 2004 flood event in southwestern Bangladesh: A study of its nature, causes, and human perception and adjustments to a new hazard. *Natural Hazards*, **40**(1), 89–111.

Aminzadeh, S. C., 2006. Moral imperative: The human rights implications of climate change. *Hastings International and Company Law Review*, **30**, 231–65.

Anderson, M. G., Holcombe, E., Esquivel, M., Toro, J., & Ghesquiere, F., 2010. The efficacy of a programme of landslide risk reduction in areas of unplanned housing in the eastern Caribbean. *Environmental Management*, **45**(4), 807–21.

Anderson-Berry, L. J., 2003. Community vulnerability to tropical cyclones: Cairns, 1996–2000. *Natural Hazards*, **30**(2), 209–32.

APHA, 1992. *Standard Methods for the Examination of Water and Wastewater*, Washington, DC: American Public Health Association.

Aragão, L., Malhi, Y., Roman-Cuesta, R. M., Saatchi, S., Anderson, L. O., & Shimabukuro, Y. E., 2007. Spatial patterns and fire response of recent Amazonian droughts. *Geophysical Research Letters*, **34**(L07701).

Arbour, L., 2008. The responsibility to protect as a duty of care in international law and practice. *Review of International Studies*, **34**(3), 445–58.

Archer, M. S., 2003. *Structure, Agency and the Internal Conversation*, Cambridge: Cambridge University Press.

Armah, F. A., Yawson, D. O., Yengoh, G. T., Odoi, J. O., & Afrifa, E. K. A., 2010. Impact of floods on livelihoods and vulnerability of natural resource dependent communities in northern Ghana. *Water*, **2**(2), 120–39.

Arnestam Gibbons, S. & Nicholls, R. J., 2006. Island abandonment and sea level rise: An historical analog from the Chesapeake Bay, USA. *Global Environmental Change*, **16**(1), 40–7.

Aronowitz, A. A., 2001. Smuggling and trafficking in human beings: The phenomenon, the markets that drive it and the organisations that promote it. *European Journal on Criminal Policy and Research*, **9**(2), 163–95.

Associated Press, 2007. Atlanta asks, 'Will we run out of water?' *NBC News.com* 19 October 2007. Available at: http://www.nbcnews.com/id/21382688/.

Autesserre, S., 2008. The trouble with Congo. *Foreign Affairs*, **87**, 94–110.

Azzarri, C. & Zezza, A., 2011. International migration and nutritional outcomes in Tajikistan. *Food Policy*, **36**(1), 54–70.

Bakewell, O., 2010. Some reflections on structure and agency in migration theory. *Journal of Ethnic and Migration Studies*, **36**(10), 1689–708.

Bakker, M. H. N., 2009. Transboundary river floods and institutional capacity. *Journal of the American Water Association*, **45**(3), 553–66.

Bales, K., 2004. *Disposable People: New slavery in the global economy* 2nd ed., Berkeley: University of California Press.

Ballu, V., Bouin, M.-N., Siméoni, P., Crawford, W. C., Calmant, S., Boréf, J.-M., Kanas, T., & Pelletier, B., 2011. Comparing the role of absolute sea-level rise and vertical tectonic motions in coastal flooding, Torres Islands (Vanuatu). *Proceedings of the National Academy of Sciences*, **108**(32), 13019–22.

Banerjee, L., 2010. Creative destruction: Analysing flood and flood control in Bangladesh. *Environmental Hazards*, **9**(1), 102–17.

Barber, R., 2009. The responsibility to protect the survivors of natural disaster: Cyclone Nargis, a case study. *Journal of Conflict and Security Law*, **14**(1), 3–34.

Barbier, B., Yacouba, H., Karambiri, H., Zoromé, M., & Somé, B., 2009. Human vulnerability to climate variability in the Sahel: Farmers' adaptation strategies in northern Burkina Faso. *Environmental Management*, **43**(5), 790–803.

Barbieri, A. F., Domingues, E., Queiroz, B. L., Ruiz, R. M., Rigotti, J. I., Carvalho, J. A. M., & Resende, M. F., 2010. Climate change and population migration in Brazil's northeast: Scenarios for 2025–2050. *Population and Environment*, **31**(5), 344–70.

Barden, T. E., 2004. Looking for humanistic stories: John Steinbeck as field ethnographer. *Steinbeck Review*, **1**(2), 63–77.

Bardsley, D. K. & Hugo, G. J., 2010. Migration and climate change: Examining thresholds of change to guide effective adaptation decision-making. *Population and Environment*, **32**(2–3), 238–62.

Barman, S. D., Majumder, S. C., Rahaman, M. Z., & Sarker, S., 2012. Foundations of migration from the disaster consequences coastal area of Bangladesh. *Developing Country Studies*, **2**(4), 22–9.

Barnaby, W., 2009. Do nations go to war over water? *Nature*, **458**, 282–3.

Barnes, W. J., 1989. A case history of vegetation changes on the Meridean Islands of west-central Wisconsin, USA. *Biological Conservation*, **49**(1), 1–16.

Baro, M. & Deubel, T. F., 2006. Persistent hunger: Perspectives on vulnerability, famine, and food security in sub-Saharan Africa. *Annual Review of Anthropology*, **35**, 521–38.

Barrett, C. B., 2010. Measuring food insecurity. *Science*, **327**(5967), 825–8.

Bassett, T. J. & Turner, M. D., 2007. Sudden shift or migratory drift? FulBe herd movements to the Sudano-Guinean region of West Africa. *Human Ecology*, **35**(1), 33–49.

Basu, R. & Samet, J. M., 2002. Relationship between elevated ambient temperature and mortality: A review of the epidemiologic evidence. *Epidemiology Review*, **24**, 190–202.

Bauder, H., 2003. 'Brain abuse', or the devaluation of immigrant labour in Canada. *Antipode*, **35**(4), 699–717.

Beauchemin, C., 2011. Rural-urban migration in West Africa: Towards a reversal? Migration trends and economic situation in Burkina Faso and Côte d'Ivoire. *Population, Space and Place*, **17**(1), 47–72.

Beine, M., Docquiera, F., & Rapoport, H., 2001. Brain drain and economic growth: Theory and evidence. *Journal of Development Economics*, **64**(1), 275–89.

Bellamy, A. J., 2005. Responsibility to protect or Trojan Horse? The crisis in Darfur and humanitarian intervention after Iraq. *Ethics & International Affairs*, **19**(2), 31–54.

Below, R., Grover-Kopec, E., & Dilley, M., 2007. Documenting drought-related disasters: A global reassessment. *The Journal of Environment & Development*, **16**(3), 328–44.

Beniston, M. & Stephenson, D. B., 2004. Extreme climatic events and their evolution under changing climatic conditions. *Global and Planetary Change*, **44**, 1–9.

Benson, L., Petersen, K., & Stein, J., 2007. Anasazi (Pre-Columbian Native-American) migrations during the middle-12th and late-13th centuries – Were they drought induced? *Climatic Change*, **83**(1–2), 187–213.

Berg, H., 2002. Rice monoculture and integrated rice-fish farming in the Mekong Delta, Vietnam – Economic and ecological considerations. *Ecological Economics*, **41**(1), 95–107.

Berkes, F. & Folke, C., 1994. Investing in cultural capital for sustainable use of natural capital. In A. Jansson et al., eds. *Investing in Natural Capital: The ecological economic approach to sustainability*. Washington, DC: Island Press, 128–49.

Berrang-Ford, L., Ford, J. D., & Peterson, J., 2011. Are we adapting to climate change? *Global Environmental Change*, **21**(1), 25–33.

Berz, G., 2000. Flood disasters: Lessons from the past – worries for the future. *Proceedings of the Institution of Civil Engineers: Water, maritime and energy*, **142**(1), 3–8.

Bhushan, L., Ladha, J. K., Gupta, R. K., Singh, S., Tirol-Padre, A., Saharawat, Y. S., Gathala, M., & Pathak, H., 2007. Saving of water and labor in a rice-wheat system with no-tillage and direct seeding technologies. *Agronomy*, **99**(5), 1288–96.

Biermann, F. & Boas, I., 2012. Climate change and human migration: Towards a global governance system to protect climate refugees. In J. Scheffran et al., eds. *Climate Change, Human Security and Violent Conflict*. Berlin, Heidelberg: Springer, 291–300.

Billings, S. A. & Phillips, N., 2011. Forest biogeochemistry and drought. *Forest Hydrology and Biogeochemistry*, **216**(5), 581–97.

Billson, J. M., 1990. Opportunity or tragedy: The impact of Canadian resettlement policy on Inuit families. *American Review of Canadian Studies*, **20**(2), 187–218.

Bin, O., Crawford, T. W., Kruse, J. B., & Landry, C. E., 2008. Viewscapes and flood hazard: Coastal housing market response to amenities and risk. *Land Economics*, **84**(3), 434–48.

Bin, O. & Polasky, S., 2004. Effects of flood hazards on property values: Evidence before and after Hurricane Floyd. *Land Economics*, **80**(4), 490–500.

Bing, L., Shao, Q., & Liu, J., 2012. Runoff characteristics in flood and dry seasons based on wavelet analysis in the source regions of the Yangtze and Yellow rivers. *Journal of Geographical Sciences*, **22**(2), 261–72.

Bingham, J., Hough, A., & Carter, C., 2010. Britain's cold weather: Deaths soar as winter takes its toll. *The Telegraph*. London, 16 January 2010. Available at: http://www.telegraph.co.uk/topics/weather/6997427/Britains-cold-weather-deaths-soar-as-winter-takes-its-toll.html.

Biswas, A. K., 1979. Water development in developing countries: Problems and prospects. *GeoJournal*, **3**(5), 445–65.

Bjarnadottir, S., Li, Y., & Stewart, M., 2011. Social vulnerability index for coastal communities at risk to hurricane hazard and a changing climate. *Natural Hazards*, **59**(2), 1055–75.

Black, R., Adger, W. N., Arnell, N. W., Dercon, S., Geddes, A., & Thomas, D., 2011. The effect of environmental change on human migration. *Global Environmental Change*, **21**(S1), S3–S11.

Black, R., Arnell, N. W., Adger, W. N., Thomas, D., & Geddes, A., 2012. Migration, immobility and displacement outcomes following extreme events. *Environmental Science and Policy*. DOI: org/10.1016/j.envsci.2012.09.001.

Black, R. & Sessay, M. F., 1997. Refugees, land cover and environmental change in the Senegal River Valley. *GeoJournal*, **41**(1), 55–67.

Black, R. & Sessay, M. F., 1998. Forced migration, natural resource use and environmental change: the case of the Senegal river valley. *International Journal of Population Geography*, **4**(1), 31–47.

Blaikie, P., 1985. *The Political Economy of Soil Erosion in Developing Countries*, London: Longman.

Blaikie, P. & Brookfield, H., 1987. *Land Degradation and Society*, London: Methuen.

Blaikie, P., Cannon, T., Davis, I., & Wisner, B., 1994. *At Risk: Natural hazards, people's vulnerability, and disasters*, New York: Routledge.

Blanchard-Boehm, R. D., Berry, K. A., & Showalter, P. S., 2001. Should flood insurance be mandatory? Insights in the wake of the 1997 New Year's Day flood in Reno-Sparks, Nevada. *Applied Geography*, **21**(3), 199–221.

Blanchflower, D. G. & Shadforth, C., 2009. Fear, unemployment and migration. *The Economic Journal*, **119**, F136–F182.

Block, S. & Webb, P., 2001. The dynamics of livelihood diversification in post-famine Ethiopia. *Food Policy*, **26**(4), 333–50.

Bloemraad, I., Korteweg, A., & Yurdakul, G., 2008. Citizenship and immigration: Multiculturalism, assimilation, and challenges to the nation-state. *Annual Review of Sociology*, **34**, 153–79.

Bloom, D. E. & Finlay, J. E., 2009. Demographic change and economic growth in Asia. *Asian Economic Policy Review*, **4**(1), 45–64.

Bocco, R., 2009. UNRWA and the Palestinian refugees: A history within history. *Refugee Survey Quarterly*, **28**(2–3), 229–52.

Bojanowski, A., 2011. Feared migration hasn't happened: UN embarrassed by forecast on climate refugees. *Spiegel Online*, 11 April 2011. Available at: http://www.spiegel.de/international/world/feared-migration-hasn-t-happened-un-embarrassed-by-forecast-on-climate-refugees-a-757713.html.

Bond, J. H., McKinley, R., & Banks, E. H., 1940. Testimony of J. H. Bond, Assistant Director; R. McKinley, Farm Placement Supervisor and E. H. Banks, Farm Placement Supervisor, Texas State Employment Service, Austin. In *Select Committee to Investigate the Interstate Migration of Destitute Citizens, Oklahoma City Hearings*. Washington, DC: U.S. House of Representatives, Sixty-seventh Congress, 1812–32.

Bongaarts, J. & Sinding, S., 2011. Population policy in transition in the developing world. *Science*, **333**(6042), 574–6.

Bonnard, C., 2011. Technical and human aspects of historic rockslide-dammed lakes and landslide dam breaches. In S. G. Evans, R. L. Hermanns, A. Strom, & G. Scarascia-Mugnozza, eds. *Natural and Artificial Rockslide Dams*. Berlin: Springer, 101–22.

Bonnifeld, P., 1979. *The Dust Bowl: Men, dirt and depression*, Albuquerque: University of New Mexico Press.

Borjas, G. J., 1989. Economic theory and international migration. *International Migration Review*, **23**(3), 457–85.

Borjas, G. J., 1994. The economics of migration. *Journal of Economic Literature*, **32**, 1667–717.

Bosello, F., Nicholls, R. J., Richards, J., Roson, R., & Tol, R. S. J., 2012. Economic impacts of climate change in Europe: Sea-level rise. *Climatic Change*, **112**(1), 63–81.

Bourdieu, P., 1984. *Distinction: A social critique of the judgement of taste*, Cambridge, MA: Harvard University Press.

Bourdieu, P., 1986. The forms of capital. In J. G. Richardson, ed. *Handbook of Theory and Research for the Sociology of Education*. New York: Greenwood Press, 241–58.

Bowers, D. E., Rasmussen, W. D., & Baker, G. L., 1984. *History of Agricultural Price-Support and Adjustment Programs, 1933–84*, Washington, DC: U.S. Department of Agriculture Economic Research Service, Agriculture Information Bulletin No. (AIB485). Available at: http://webarchives.cdlib.org/wayback.public/UERS_ag_1/20120306163040/http://www.ers.usda.gov/Publications/AIB485/.

Boyd, R. L., 2002. A 'migration of despair': Unemployment, the search for work, and migration to farms during the Great Depression. *Social Science Quarterly*, **83**(2), 554–67.

Bradley, D. E. & Longino, C. F., 2008. Geographic mobility and aging in place. In P. Uhlenberg, ed. *International Handbook of Population Aging*. Dordrecht: Springer, 319–40.

Bradshaw, C. J. A., Sodhi, N. S., Peh, K. S. H., & Brook, B. W., 2007. Global evidence that deforestation amplifies flood risk and severity in the developing world. *Global Change Biology*, **13**(11), 2379–95.

Brandimarte, L., Brath, A., Castellarin, A., & Di Baldassarre, G., 2009. Isla Hispaniola: A trans-boundary flood risk mitigation plan. *Physics and Chemistry of the Earth*, **34**(4–5), 209–18.

Brettell, C. B. & Hollifield, J. F., 2007. *Migration Theory: Talking across disciplines*, New York: Routledge.

Brodie, M., Weltzien, E., Altman, D., Blendon, R. J., & Benson, J. M., 2006. Experiences of Hurricane Katrina evacuees in Houston shelters: Implications for future planning. *American Journal of Public Health*, **96**(8), 1402–8.

Brondizio, E. S. & Moran, E. F., 2008. Human dimensions of climate change: The vulnerability of small farmers in the Amazon. *Philosophical Transactions of the Royal Society London: Biological sciences: Series B*, **363**(1498), 1803–9.

Broude, T., 2007. *The WTO/GATS Mode 4, International Labour Migration Regimes and Global Justice*, Jerusalem, International Law Forum of the Hebrew University. Available at: http://www.worldtradelaw.net/articles/broudemode4.pdf.

Brouwer, R., Akter, S., Brander, L., & Haque, E., 2007. Socioeconomic vulnerability and adaptation to environmental risk: A case study of climate change and flooding in Bangladesh. *Risk Analysis*, **27**(2), 313–26.

Brown, M. E., Hintermann, B., & Higgins, N., 2009. Markets, climate change, and food security in West Africa. *Environmental Science and Technology*, **43**(21), 8016–20.

Brown, O., 2008. The numbers game. *Forced Migration Review*, Issue **31**, 8–9.

Brown, O., Hammill, A., & McLeman, R., 2007. Climate change as the 'new' security threat: Implications for Africa. *International Affairs*, **83**(6), 1141–54.

Brown, O. & McLeman, R., 2009. A recurring anarchy?: The emergence of climate change as a threat to international peace and security. *Conflict, Security and Development*, **9**(3), 289–305.

Browne, C. V. & Braun, K. L., 2007. Globalization, women's migration, and the long-term-care workforce. *The Gerontologist*, **48**(1), 16–24.

Browne, M. J. & Hoyt, R. E., 2000. The demand for flood insurance: Empirical evidence. *Journal of Risk and Uncertainty*, **20**(3), 291–306.

Brunkard, J., Namulanda, G., & Ratard, R., 2008. Hurricane Katrina deaths, Louisiana, 2005. *Disaster Medicine and Public Health Preparedness*, **1**, 1–9.

Bucknam, R. C., Coe, J. A., Chavarría, M. M., Godt, J. W., Tarr, A. C., Bradley, L.-A., Rafferty, S., Hancock, D., Dart, R., & Johnson, M., 2001. *Landslides Triggered by Hurricane Mitch in Guatemala: Inventory and discussion*, Denver, U.S. Geological Survey. Available at: http://pdf.usaid.gov/pdf_docs/PNACP982.pdf.

Bugri, J. T., 2008. The dynamics of tenure security, agricultural production and environmental degradation in Africa: Evidence from stakeholders in north-east Ghana. *Land Use Policy*, **25**(2), 271–85.

Burby, R. J., 2001. Flood insurance and floodplain management: The US experience. *Global Environmental Change Part B: Environmental Hazards*, **3**(3–4), 111–22.

Burby, R. J., 2006. Hurricane Katrina and the paradoxes of government disaster policy: Bringing about wise governmental decisions for hazardous areas. *Annals of the American Academy of Political and Social Science*, **604**, 171–91.

Bures, R. M., 1997. Migration and the life course: Is there a retirement transition? *International Journal of Population Geography*, **3**(2), 109–19.

Burin, E., 2012. The Slave Trade Act of 1819: A new look at colonization and the politics of slavery. *American Nineteenth Century History*, **13**(1), 1–14.

Burke, E. J. & Brown, S. J., 2008. Evaluating uncertainties in the projection of future drought. *Journal of Hydrometeorology*, **9**(2), 292–9.

Burki, T., 2010. Aid slows to a trickle as Pakistan crisis enters a new phase. *The Lancet*, **376**(9746), 1041–2.

Burnette, D. J. & Stahle, D. W., 2013. Historical perspective on the Dust Bowl drought in the central United States. *Climatic Change*, **116**(3–4), 479–94.

Burton, C. & Cutter, S. L., 2008. Levee failures and social vulnerability in the Sacramento-San Joaquin Delta area, California. *Natural Hazards Review*, **9**(3), 136–50.

Burton, I., 1997. Vulnerability and adaptive response in the context of climate and climate change. *Climatic Change*, **36**(1–2), 185–96.

Burton, I., Kates, R. W., & White, G. F., 1978. *The environment as hazard*, New York: Guilford Press.

Byravan, S., Rajan, S. C., & Bangarajan, R., 2010. *Sea Level Rise: Impact on major infrastructure, ecosystems and land along the Tamil Nadu coast*, Madras: Centre for Development Finance, IFMR and Humanities and Social Sciences. Available at: http://ifmr-cdf.in/mod/file/pdfFiles/Report on Sea Level Rise and Impact on Coastal Infrastructure.pdf.

Cabrol, J.-C., 2011. War, drought, malnutrition, measles – A report from Somalia. *New England Journal of Medicine*, **365**, 1856–8.

Calder, I. R. & Aylward, B., 2006. Moving to an evidence-based approach to watershed and integrated flood management. *Water International*, **31**(1), 87–99.

Cannon, T., 2002. Gender and climate hazards in Bangladesh. *Gender and Development*, **10**(2), 45–50.

Cardoso, J. C., 2010. Immigration to Portugal. In Segal, U.A., Elliott, D., and Mayadas, N.S. eds. *Immigration Worldwide: Policies, practices and trends*. Oxford: Oxford University Press, 274–85.

CARE International, 2009. *In Search of Shelter: Mapping the effects of climate change on human migration and displacement*. Washington, DC. Available at: http://www.care.org/getinvolved/advocacy/pdfs/Migration_Report.pdf.

Carletto, C., Covarrubias, K., & Maluccio, J., 2011. Migration and child growth in rural Guatemala. *Food Policy*, **36**(1), 16–27.

Carr, D. L., 2008. Migration to the Maya Biosphere Reserve, Guatemala: Why place matters. *Human Organization*, **67**(1), 37–48.

Cassou, C., Terray, L., & Phillips, A. S., 2005. Tropical Atlantic influence on European heat waves. *Journal of Climate*, **18**, 2805–11.

Castles, S. & Miller, M. J., 2009. *The Age of Migration: International population movements in the modern world* 3rd ed., New York: The Guilford Press.

Cattiaux, J., Vautard, R., Cassou, C., Yiou, P., Masson-Delmotte, V., & Codron, F., 2010. Winter 2010 in Europe: A cold extreme in a warming climate. *Geophysical Research Letters*, **37**, L20704.

Caviedes, C. N., 2001. *El Nino in History: Storming through the ages*, Gainesville: University of Florida Press.

Cazenave, A. & Llovel, W., 2010. Contemporary sea level rise. *Marine Science*, **2**, 145–73.

Center for Naval Analyses, 2007. *National Security and the Threat of Climate Change*. Alexandria, VA. Available at: http://securityandclimate.cna.org/report/.

Cernea, M. M., 1997. The risks and reconstruction model for resettling displaced populations. *World Development*, **25**(10), 1569–87.

Cernea, M. M., 2000. Risks, safeguards and reconstruction: A model for population displacement and resettlement. *Economic and Political Weekly*, **35**(41), 3659–78.

Cernea, M. M., 2009. Resettlement – An enduring issue in development. *The Asia Pacific Journal of Anthropology*, **10**(4), 263–5.

Chagnon, S. A. & Chagnon, D., 2000. Long-term fluctuations in hail incidences in the United States. *Journal of Climate*, **13**(3), 658–64.

Chamlee-Wright, E. & Storr, V., 2009. There's no place like New Orleans: Sense of place and community recover in the Ninth Ward after hurricane Katrina. *Journal of Urban Affairs*, **31**(5), 615–34.

Chan, K. W. & Buckingham, W., 2008. Is China Abolishing the Hukou System? *The China Quarterly*, **195**, 582–606.

Chan, N. W. & Parker, D. J., 1996. Response to dynamic flood hazard factors in peninsular Malaysia. *The Geographical Journal*, **162**(3), 313–25.

Charmaz, K., 2004. Grounded theory. In S. N. Hesse-Biber & P. Leavy, eds. *Approaches to Qualitative Research: A reader on theory and practice*. New York: Oxford University Press, 496–521.

Chen, C.-C., McCarl, B., & Chang, C.-C., 2012. Climate change, sea level rise and rice: Global market implications. *Climatic Change*, **110**(3–4), 543–60.

Cheng, T. & Selden, M., 1994. The origins and social consequences of China's hukou system. *The China Quarterly*, **139**, 644–68.

Chimni, B. S., 2009. The birth of a 'discipline': From refugee to forced migration studies. *Journal of Refugee Studies*, **22**(1), 11–29.

Chinvanno, S., Souvannalath, S., Lersupavithnapa, B., Kersduk, V., & Thuan, N., 2008. Strategies for managing climate risks in the lower Mekong River basin: A place-based approach. In N. Leary, J. Adjuwon, V. Barros, I. Burton, J. Kulkarni, & R. Lasco, eds. *Climate Change and Adaptation*. London: Earthscan, 228–246.

Christian Aid, 2007. Human tide: The real migration crisis. London. Available at: http://www.christian-aid.org.uk/indepth/705caweekreport/index.htm.

Chu, J., 2011. Gender and 'land grabbing' in sub-Saharan Africa: Women's land rights and customary land tenure. *Development*, **54**(1), 35–9.

CIA, 2012. *World Fact Book 2012*, Washington, DC: Central Intelligence Agency.

Citizenship and Immigration Canada, 1996. *Immigration Statistics*, Ottawa. Available at: http://epe.lac-bac.gc.ca/100/202/301/immigration_statistics-ef/mp22–1_1996.pdf.

Citizenship and Immigration Canada, 2010. Canada – Permanent residents by source country. *Immigration Overview: Permanent and temporary residents*, Ottawa. Available at: http://www.cic.gc.ca/english/resources/statistics/facts2010/permanent/10.asp.

Citizenship and Immigration Canada, 2011. Facts and figures 2011. *Immigration Overview: Permanent and temporary residents*, Ottawa. Available at: http://www.cic.gc.ca/english/resources/statistics/facts2011/index.asp.

Clark, G. E., Moser, S. C., Ratick, S. J., Dow, K., Meyer, W. B., Emani, S., Jin, W., Kasperson, J. X., Kasperson, R. E., & Schwarz, H. E., 1998. Assessing the vulnerability of coastal communities to extreme storms: The case of Revere, MA., USA. *Mitigation and Adaptation Strategies for Global Change*, **3**(1), 59–82.

Clark, K. & McLeman, R., 2012. Maple sugar bush management and forest biodiversity conservation in eastern Ontario, Canada. *Small Scale Forestry*, **11**(2), 263–84.

Clarke, M., Rendell, H., Tastet, J.-P., Clavé, B., & Massé, L., 2002. Late-Holocene sand invasion and North Atlantic storminess along the Aquitaine coast, southwest France. *Holocene*, **12**(2), 231–8.

Coates, K. S., Healy, R., & Morrison, W. R., 2002. Tracking the snowbirds: Seasonal migration from Canada to the U.S.A. and Mexico. *American Review of Canadian Studies*, **32**(3), 433–51.

Codjoe, S. N. I. & Bilsborrow, R. E., 2011. Population and agriculture in the dry and derived savannah zones of Ghana. *Population and Environment*, **33**(1), 90–107.

Cohen, B., 2003. Urban growth in developing countries: A review of current trends and a caution regarding existing forecasts. *World Development*, **32**(1), 23–51.

Cohen, M. J. & Garrett, J. L., 2010. The food price crisis and urban food (in)security. *Environment and Urbanization*, **22**(2), 467–82.

Cohen, R., 1987. The 'new' international division of labour: A conceptual, historical and empirical critique. *Migration*, **1**(1), 22–40.

Cohen, R., 2004. The guiding principles on internal displacement: An innovation in international standard setting. *Global Governance*, **10**, 459–80.

Coleman, D., 2008. The demographic effects of international migration in Europe. *Oxford Review of Economic Policy*, **24**(3), 452–76.

Coleman, J. M., Huh, O. K., & Bruad, D., 2008. Wetland loss in world deltas. *Journal of Coastal Research*, **1**(S1), 1–14.

Coleman, J. S., 1988. Social capital in the creation of human capital. *American Journal of Sociology*, **94**(Supplement), S95–S120.

Coleman, W. J. & Hockley, H. A., 1940. Legal aspects of landlord-tenant relationships in Oklahoma. Stillwater: Oklahoma Agricultural Experiment Station.

Collins, T. W., 2010. Marginalization, facilitation, and the production of unequal risk: The 2006 Paso del Norte floods. *Antipode*, **42**(2), 258–88.

Comerio, M. C., 1997. Housing issues after disasters. *Journal of Contingencies and Crisis Management*, **5**(3), 166–78.

Comfort, L., Wisner, B., Cutter, S., Pulwarty, R., Hewitt, K., Oliver-Smith, A., Wiener, J., Fordham, M., Peacock, W., & Krimgold, F., 1999. Reframing disaster policy: The global evolution of vulnerable communities. *Global Environmental Change Part B: Environmental Hazards*, **1**(1), 39–44.

Comstock, R. D. & Mallonee, S., 2005. Comparing reactions to two severe tornadoes in one Oklahoma community. *Disasters*, **29**(3), 277–87.

Conelly, W. T., 1992. Agricultural intensification in a Philippine frontier community: Impact on labor efficiency and farm diversity. *Human Ecology*, **20**(2), 203–23.

Connell, J., 1990. The Carteret Islands: Precedents of the greenhouse effect. *Geography*, **75**(2), 152–4.

Connell, J., 2012. Population resettlement in the Pacific: Lessons from a hazardous history? *Australian Geographer*, **43**(2), 127–42.

Connell, J. & Conway, D., 2000. Migration and remittances in island microstates: A comparative perspective on the South Pacific and the Caribbean. *International Journal of Urban and Regional Research*, **24**(1), 52–78.

Connelly, R., Roberts, K., & Zheng, Z., 2011. The settlement of rural migrants in urban China – some of China's migrants are not 'floating' anymore. *Journal of Chinese Economic and Business Studies*, **9**(3), 283–300.

Conrad, C. P. & Husson, L., 2009. Influence of dynamic topography on sea level and its rate of change. *Lithosphere*, **2**, 110–20.

Cook, B. I., Miller, R. L., & Seager, R., 2009. Amplification of the North American 'Dust Bowl' drought through human-induced land degradation. *Proceedings of the National Academy of Sciences of the United States of America*, **106**(13), 4997–5001.

Cook, E. R., Anchukaitis, K. J., Buckley, B. M., D'Arrigo, R. D., Jacoby, G. C., & Wright, W. E., 2010. Asian monsoon failure and megadrought during the last millennium. *Science*, **328**(5977), 486–9.

Cook, E. R., Seager, R., Cane, M. A., & Stahle, D. W., 2007. North American drought: Reconstructions, causes and consequences. *Earth-Science Reviews*, **81**, 93–134.

Cooper, J. A. G. & McKenna, J., 2008. Social justice in coastal erosion management: The temporal and spatial dimensions. *Geoforum*, **39**(1), 294–306.

Cooper, J. A. G. & McKenna, J., 2009. Boom and bust: The influence of macroscale economics on the world's coasts. *Journal of Coastal Research*, **25**(3), 533–8.

Cottrell, W. F., 1951. Death by dieselization: A case study in the reaction to technological change. *American Sociological Review*, **16**(3), 358–65.

Cotula, L., Vermeulen, S., Mathieu, P., & Toulmin, C., 2011. Agricultural investment and international land deals: Evidence from a multi-country study in Africa. *Food Security*, **3**(1), 99–113.

Coutin, S., 2010. Confined within: National territories as zones of confinement. *Political Geography*, **29**, 200–8.

Craft, C. B., 2012. Tidal freshwater forest accretion does not keep pace with sea level rise. *Global Change Biology* **18**(12), 3615–3623.

CRED – Centre for Research on the Epidemiology of Disasters, 2013. EM-DAT International Disaster Database. Available at: http://www.emdat.be/.

Creese, G. & Wiebe, B., 2012. 'Survival employment': Gender and deskilling among African immigrants in Canada. *International Migration*, **50**(5), 56–76.

Crighton, E., Elliott, S. J., Meer, J. van der, Small, I., & Upshur, R., 2003. Impacts of an environmental disaster on psychosocial health and well-being in Karakalpakstan. *Social Science & Medicine*, **56**(3), 551–67.

Cronin, W. B., 2005. *The Disappearing Islands of the Chesapeake*, Baltimore, MD: Johns Hopkins University Press.

Cronon, W. 1991. *Nature's Metropolis: Chicago and the Great West*, New York: W. W. Norton.

Cross, P., Edwards, R. T., Hounsome, B., & Edwards-Jones, G., 2008. Comparative assessment of migrant farm worker health in conventional and organic horticultural systems in the United Kingdom. *Science of the Total Environment*, **391**(1), 55–65.

Cuba, L. & Hummon, D. M., 1993. Constructing a sense of home: Place affiliation and migration across the life cycle. *Sociological Forum*, **8**(4), 547–72.

Cui, X. F. & Graf, H. F., 2009. Recent land cover changes on the Tibetan Plateau: A review. *Climatic Change*, **94**(1–2), 47–61.

Cunfer, G., 2005. *On the Great Plains: Agriculture and environment*, College Station: Texas A&M University Press.

Cupples, J., 2007. Gender and Hurricane Mitch: Reconstructing subjectivities after disaster. *Disasters*, **31**(2), 155–75.

Currie, T. M., 2009. *The Ottawa Valley's Great Fire of 1870*, Ottawa: Creative Bound International.

Curtis, K. J. & Schneider, A., 2011. Understanding the demographic implications of climate change: Estimates of localized population predictions under future scenarios of sea-level rise. *Population and Environment*, **33**(1), 28–54.

Cutter, S., 2010. Social science perspectives on hazards and vulnerability science. In T. Beer, ed. *Geophysical Hazards*. Dordrecht: Springer, 17–30.

Cutter, S., Mitchell, J. T., & Scott, M. S., 2000. Revealing the vulnerability of people and places: A case study of Georgetown County, South Carolina. *Annals of the Association of American Geographers*, **90**(4), 713–37.

Dabelko, G. D., 1999. The environmental factor. *The Wilson Quarterly*, **23**(4), 14–19.

Dabelko, G. D., 2009. Planning for climate change: The security community's precautionary principle. *Climatic Change*, **96**(1–2), 13–21.

Dabelko, G. D. & Dabelko, D. D., 1995. Environmental security: Issues of conflict and redefinition. *Environmental Change and Security Project Report 1*, **1**, 3–13.

Daniel, S., 2011. Land grabbing and potential implications for world food security. *Sustainable Agricultural Development*, **1**, 25–42.

D'Aoust, S., 2012. *Immigration: An expedient complement to disaster response? An examination of Canada's post-earthquake immigration measures for Haiti and the influence of the Haitian diaspora in Canada*. MA thesis, International Development and Global Studies, University of Ottawa.

Darwin, C., 1859. *The Origin of Species*, Edison, NJ: Castle Books.

Das, S. & Vincent, J. R., 2009. Mangroves protected villages and reduced death toll during Indian super cyclone. *Proceedings of the National Academy of Science*, **106**(18), 7357–60.

Dasgupta, S., Laplante, B., Meisner, C., Wheeler, D., & Yan, J., 2009. The impact of sea level rise on developing countries: A comparative analysis. *Climatic Change*, **93**(4), 379–88.

Davies, J. & Hatfield, R., 2007. The economics of mobile pastoralism: A global summary. *Nomadic Peoples*, **11**(1), 91–116.

David, H. P., 1969. Involuntary international migration: Adaptation of refugees. *International Migration*, **7**, 67–105.

Davis, M., 2001. *Late Victorian Holocausts: El Nino famines and the making of the third world*, New York: Verso.

Dawe, D., Pandey, S., & Nelson, A., 2010. Emerging trends and spatial patterns of rice production. In S. Pandey, D. Byerlee, D. Dawe, A. Dobermann, S. Mohanty, S. Rozelle, & B. Hardy, eds. *Rice in the Global Economy: Strategic research and policy issues for food security*. Manila: International Rice Research Institute, 15–26.

De Brauw, A., 2010. Seasonal migration and agricultural production in Vietnam. *Journal of Development Studies*, **46**(1), 114–39.

De Brauw, A., 2011. Migration and child development during the food price crisis in El Salvador. *Food Policy*, **36**(1), 28–40.

De Haan, A., Brock, K., & Coulibaly, N., 2002. Migration, livelihoods and institutions: Contrasting patterns of migration in Mali. *The Journal of Development Studies*, **38**(5), 37–58.

De Haas, H., 2010. Migration and development: A theoretical perspective. *International Migration Review*, **44**(1), 227–64.

De Mendonca, M. J. C., Diaz, C. V., Nepstad, D., da Motta, R. S., Alencar, A., Gomes, J. C., & Ortiz, R. A., 2004. The economic cost of the use of fire in the Amazon. *Ecological Economics*, **49**, 89–105.

De Sherbinin, A., Castro, M., Gemenne, F., Cernea, M. M., Adamo, S., Fearnside, P. M., Krieger, G., Lahmani, S., Oliver-Smith, A., Pankhurst, A., Scudder, T., Singer, B., Tan, Y., Wannier, G., Boncour, P., Ehrhart, C., Hugo, G., Pandey, B., & Shi, G., 2011. Preparing for resettlement associated with climate change. *Science*, **334**(6055), 456–7.

De Silva, D. G., Kruse, J. B., & Wang, Y., 2008. Spatial dependencies in wind-related housing damage. *Natural Hazards*, **47**(3), 317–30.

De Soysa, I., 2002. Ecoviolence: Shrinking pie, or honey pot? *Global Environmental Politics*, **2**(4), 1–34.

Deccan H., 2012. *Mumbai Faces Serious Water Shortage*. Mumbai, 19 July 2012. Available at: http://www.deccanherald.com/content/265552/mumbai-faces-serious-water-shortage.html.

Debrah, C., 1989. *Address to the Conference on Implications of Climate Change for Africa*, Washington, DC: Howard University, 5 May 1989.

Deininger, K. W. & Byerlee, D., 2011. *Rising Global Interest in Farmland: Can it yield sustainable and equitable benefits?* Washington, DC: World Bank.

Del Ninno, C. & Dorosh, P., 2001. Averting a food crisis: Private imports and public targeted distribution in Bangladesh after the 1998 flood. *Agricultural Economics*, **25**(2–3), 337–46.

Dema, B., 2012. Sea level rise and the freely associated states: Addressing environmental migration under the compacts of free association. *Columbia Journal of Environmental Law*, **37**, 177–205.

Demerritt, D., Nobert, S., Cloke, H., & Pappenberger, F., 2010. Challenges in communicating and using ensembles in operational flood forecasting. *Meteorological Applications*, **17**(2), 209–22.

Denton, F., 2002. Climate change vulnerability, impacts and adaptation: Why does gender matter? *Gender and Development*, **10**(2), 10–20.

Deschenes, O. & Moretti, E., 2007. *Extreme Weather Events, Mortality and Migration*, Cambridge MA: National Bureau of Economic Research. Available at: http://www.econ.ucsb.edu/~olivier/w13227.pdf.

Deshingkar, P., Sharma, P., Kumar, S., Akter, S., & Farrington, J., 2008. Circular migration in Madhya Pradesh: Changing patterns and social protection needs. *European Journal of Development Research*, **20**(4), 612–28.

Deshingkar, P. & Start, D., 2003. *Seasonal Migration for Livelihoods in India: Coping, accumulation and exclusion*. London, Overseas Development Institute.

Devereux, S., 2009. Why does famine persist in Africa? *Food Security*, **1**(1), 25–35.

Dewing, R., 2006. *Regions in Transition: The northern Great Plains and the Pacific Northwest in the Great Depression*. Lanham, MD: University Press of America.

Di Baldassarre, G., Montanari, A., Lins, H., Koutsoyiannis, D., Brandimarte, L., & Blöschl, G., 2010. Flood fatalities in Africa: From diagnosis to mitigation. *Geophysical Research Letters*, **37**(22), L22402.

Diamond, J., 1997. *Guns, Germs, and Steel: The fates of human societies*. New York: W. W. Norton.

Diamond, J., 2005. *Collapse: How societies choose to fail or succeed*. New York: Viking.

Diaz, H. F., Trigo, R., Hughes, M. K., Mann, M. E., Xoplaki, E., & Barriopedro, D., 2011. Spatial and temporal characteristics of climate in medieval times revisited. *Bulletin of the American Meteorological Society*, **92**, 1487–500.

Diggins, F. W., 1999. The true history of the discovery of penicillin, with refutation of the misinformation in the literature. *British Journal of Biomedical Science*, **56**(2), 83–93.

Dixon, B., 2005. Groundwater vulnerability mapping: A GIS and fuzzy rule based integrated tool. *Applied Geography*, **25**(4), 327–47.

Dodds, R., 2012. Sustainable tourism: A hope or a necessity? The case of Tofino, British Columbia, Canada. *Journal of Sustainable Tourism*, **5**(5).

Dominion Bureau of Statistics, 1936. *Census of the Prairie Provinces, 1936, Volume 1: population and Agriculture*, Ottawa.

Donato, K. M., Trujillo-Pagan, N., Bankston, C. L., & Singer, A., 2007. Reconstructing New Orleans after Katrina: The emergence of an immigrant labor market. In D. L. Brunsma, D. Overfelt, & J. S. Picou, eds. *The Sociology of Katrina: Perspectives on a modern catastrophe*. Plymouth, UK: Rowman & Littlefield, 217–33.

Douglas, I., 2009. Climate change, flooding and food security in south Asia. *Food Security*, **1**(2), 127–36.

Douglas, I., Alam, K., Maghenda, M., Mcdonnell, Y., Mclean, L., & Campbell, J., 2008. Unjust waters: Climate change, flooding and the urban poor in Africa. *Environment and Urbanization*, **20**(1), 187–205.

Dowie, M., 2009. *Conservation Refugees: The hundred-year conflict between global conservation and native peoples*, Cambridge MA: MIT Press.

Drever, A., 2008. New Orleans: A re-emerging Latino destination city. *Journal of Cultural Geography*, **25**(3), 287–303.

Duan, Y. & Wilmsen, B., 2012. Addressing the resettlement challenges at the Three Gorges Project. *International Journal of Environmental Studies*, **69**(3), 461–74.

Duclos, P., Sanderson, L. M., & Lipsett, M., 1990. The 1987 forest fire disaster in California: Assessment of emergency room visits. *Archives of Environmental Health*, **45**(1), 53–8.

Dugmore, A. J., Keller, C., & McGovern, T. H., 2007. Norse Greenland settlement: Reflections on climate change, trade, and the contrasting fates of human settlements in the North Atlantic Islands. *Arctic Anthropology*, **44**(1), 12–36.

Duke, N. C., Meynecke, J.-O., Dittmann, S., Ellison, A. M., Anger, K., Berger, U., Cannicci, S., Diele, K., Ewel, K. C., Field, C. D., Koedam, N., Lee, S. Y., Marchand, C., Nordhaus, I., & Dahdouh-Guebas, F., 2007. A world without mangroves? *Science*, **317**(5834), 41–2.

Dun, O., 2011. Migration and displacement triggered by floods in the Mekong Delta. *International Migration*, **49**(1), e200–e223.

Duncan, O. D., 1935. Population trends in Oklahoma. Stillwater: Oklahoma Agricultural Experiment Station.

Duncan, O. D., 1940. The theory and consequences of mobility of farm population. Stillwater: Oklahoma Agricultural Experiment Station

Dux, L., 2008. The role of regional organizations in the protection of migrant workers' rights. In R. Blanpain, M. Tiraboschi, & P. A. Ortiz, eds. *Global Labour Market: From globalization to flexicurity*. Alphen aan der Rijn: Kluwer Law, 109–28.

Dyer, G. A., 2008. *Climate Wars*, Toronto: Random House.

Dyer, G. A. & Taylor, J. E., 2011. The corn price surge: Impacts on rural Mexico. *World Development*, **39**(10), 1878–87.

Eakin, H., 2005. Institutional change, climate risk, and rural vulnerability: Cases from central Mexico. *World Development*, **33**(11), 1923–38.

Easterling, W. E., Rosenberg, N. J., McKenney, M. S., & Jones, C. A., 1992. An introduction to the methodology, the region of study, and a historical analog of climate change. *Agricultural and Forest Meteorology*, **59**(1–2), 3–15.

Edwards, B., Gray, M., & Hunter, B., 2009. A sunburnt country: The economic and financial impact of drought on rural and regional families in Australia in an era of climate change. *Australian Journal of Labour Economics*, **12**(1), 109–31.

Egan, T., 2006. *The Worst Hard Time*, New York: Houghton Mifflin.

Egan, T., 2009. *The Big Burn*, New York: Houghton Mifflin.

El-Hinnawi, E., 1985. *Environmental Refugees*, Nairobi: United Nations Environmental Program.

Elliott, J. R. & Pais, J., 2006. Race, class, and Hurricane Katrina: Social differences in human responses to disaster. *Social Science Research*, **35**(2), 295–321.

Ellis, F., 2000. The determinants of rural livelihood diversification in developing countries. *Journal of Agricultural Economics*, **51**(2), 89–302.

Emanuel, K., 2005. Increasing destructiveness of tropical cyclones over the past 30 years. *Nature*, **436**, 686.

Emirbayer, M. & Mische, A., 1998. What is agency? *The American Journal of Sociology*, **103**(4), 962–1023.

Emrich, C. T. & Cutter, S. L., 2011. Social vulnerability to climate-sensitive hazards in the southern United States. *Weather, Climate and Society*, **3**, 193–208.

Engman, M., Onodera, O., & Pinali, E., 2007. *Export Processing Zones: Past and future role in trade and development. OECD Trade Policy Working Paper No. 53*, Paris. Available at: http://ideas.repec.org/p/oec/traaab/53-en.html.

Environment Canada, 2012. Canadian Climate Norms or Averages, 1971–2000. *National Climate Data and Information Archive*. Available at: http://www.climate.weatheroffice. gc.ca/climate_normals/index_e.html.

Erdlenbruch, K., Thoyer, S., Grelot, F., Kast, R., & Enjolras, G., 2009. Risk-sharing policies in the context of the French Flood Prevention Action Programmes. *Journal of Environmental Management*, **91**(2), 363–9.

Eriksen, S. & Lind, J., 2009. Adaptation as a political process: Adjusting to drought and conflict in Kenya's drylands. *Environmental Management*, **43**(5), 817–35.

Eriksen, S. & Silva, J. A., 2009. The vulnerability context of a savanna area in Mozambique: Household drought coping strategies and responses to economic change. *Environmental Science & Policy*, **12**(1), 33–52.

Ezra, M., 2001. Demographic responses to environmental stress in the drought- and famine-prone areas of northern Ethiopia. *International Journal of Population Geography*, **7**(4), 259–79.

Fagan, B., 2004. *The Long Summer: How climate changed civilization*. New York: Basic Books.

Fagan, B., 2008. *The Great Warming: Climate change and the rise and fall of civilizations*. New York: Bloomsbury Press.

Fagan, B., 2009. *Floods, Famines, and Emperors: El Nino and the fate of civilizations*. New York: Nation Books.

Faist, T., 1997. The crucial meso-level. In Thomas Hammer ed. *International Migration, Immobility and Development: Multidisciplinary perspectives*. Oxford: Berg, 187–218.

Faist, T., 1998. Transnational social spaces out of international migration: Evolution, significance and future prospects. *Archives Européennes de Sociologie* **39**(2), 213–47.

Fan, C. C. & Huang, Y., 1998. Waves of rural brides: Female marriage migration in China. *Annals of the Association of American Geographers*, **88**(2), 227–51.

Fang, X., Ye, Y., & Zeng, Z., 2007. Extreme climate events, migration for cultivation and policies: A case study in the early Qing Dynasty of China. *Science in China Series D: Earth Sciences*, **50**(3), 411–21.

Fankhauser, S., 2010. The costs of adaptation. *Wiley Interdisciplinary Reviews: Climate Change*, **1**(1), 23–30.

Farbotko, C. & Lazrus, H., 2012. The first climate refugees? Contesting global narratives of climate change in Tuvalu. *Global Environmental Change*, **22**(2), 382–90.

Farhana, K. M., Rahman, S. A., & Rahman, M., 2012. Factors of migration in urban Bangladesh: An empirical study of poor migrants in Rajshahi City. *Bangladesh e-Journal of Sociology*, **9**(1), 105–17.

Farley, R., Richards, T., & Wurdock, C., 1980. School desegregation and white flight: An investigation of competing models and their discrepant findings. *Sociology of Education*, **53**(3), 123–39.

Fast, S. & McLeman, R., 2012. Attitudes towards new renewable energy technologies in the Eastern Ontario Highlands. *Journal of Rural and Community Development*, **7**(3), 106–22.

Feng, S. F., Krueger, A. B., & Oppenheimer, M., 2010. Linkages among climate change, crop yields and Mexico-US cross-border migration. *Proceedings of the National Academy of Science*, **107**(32), 14257–62.

Feng, S. F., Oppenheimer, M., & Schlenker, W., 2012. *Climate Change, Crop Yields, and Internal Migration in the United States*, Cambridge MA: National Bureau of Economic Research Working Paper No. 17734. Available at: http://www.nber.org/papers/w17734.

Fernandez-Gimenez, M. E. & Le Febre, S., 2006. Mobility in pastoral systems: Dynamic flux or downward trend? *International Journal of Sustainable & World Ecology*, **13**(5), 341–62.

Few, R., 2003. Flooding, vulnerability and coping strategies: Local responses to a global threat. *Progress in Development Studies*, **3**(1), 43–58.

Few, R. & Matthies, F., 2006. *Flood Hazards and Health: Responding to present and future risks*, London: Earthscan.

Finch, C., Emrich, C. T., & Cutter, S. L., 2010. Disaster disparities and differential recovery in New Orleans. *Population and Environment*, **31**(4), 179–202.

Findley, S. E., 1994. Does drought increase migration? A study of migration from rural Mali during the 1983–1985 drought. *International Migration Review*, **28**(3), 539–53.

Fishback, P., Horrace, W., & Kantor, S., 2006. The impact of New Deal expenditures on mobility during the Great Depression. *Explorations in Economic History*, **43**(2), 179–222.

FitzGerald, D. M., Fenster, M. S., Argow, B. A., & Buynevich, I. V., 2008. Coastal impacts due to sea-level rise. *Annual Review of Earth and Planetary Sciences*, **36**, 601–47.

Fix, M. E. & Laglagaron, L., 2002. *Social Rights and Citizenship: An international comparison*, Washington, DC: The Urban Institute. Available at: http://www.urban.org/UploadedPDF/410545_SocialRights.pdf.

Flannigan, M., Stocks, B., Turetsky, M., & Wotton, M., 2009. Impacts of climate change on fire activity and fire management in the circumboreal forest. *Global Change Biology*, **15**(3), 549–60.

Fletcher, L. E., Pham, P., Stover, E., & Vinck, P., 2007. Latino workers and human rights in the aftermath of Hurricane Katrina. *Berkeley Journal of Employment and Labor Law*, **28**(1), 107–62.

Fonseca, I., 1996. *Bury Me Standing: The Gypsies and their journey*, New York: Vintage.

Ford, J. D., Keskitalo, E. C. H., Smith, T., Pearce, T., Berrang-Ford, L., & Duerden, F., 2010. Case study and analogue methodologies in climate change vulnerability research. *Wiley Interdisciplinary Reviews: Climate Change*, **1**(3), 374–92.

Ford, J. D., Pearce, T., Smit, B., Wandel, J., Allurut, M., Shappa, K., Ittusujurat, H., & Qrunnut, K., 2007. Reducing vulnerability to climate change in the Arctic: The case of Nunavut, Canada. *Arctic*, **60**, 150–66.

Ford, J. D., Pearce, T., Smit, B., Wandel, J., Shappa, K., Ittusarjuat, H., & Qrunnut, K., 2008. Climate change in the Arctic: Current and future vulnerability in two Inuit communities in Canada. *The Geographical Journal*, **174**, 45–62.

Foresight: Migration and Global Environmental Change, 2011. *Final Project Report*, London: Government Office for Science. Available at: http://www.bis.gov.uk/assets/bispartners/foresight/docs/migration/11–1116-migration-and-global-environmental-change.pdf.

Fourier, J., 1878. *The Analytical Theory of Heat*, Cambridge: Cambridge University Press.

Fratkin, E. & Roth, E. A., 1990. Drought and economic differentiation among Ariaal pastoralists of Kenya. *Human Ecology*, **18**(4), 385–402.

Frayne, B., 2005. Survival of the poorest: Migration and food security in Namibia. In L. J. A. Mougeot, ed. *Agropolis: The social, political, and environmental dimensions of urban agriculture*. London: IDRC/Earthscan, 31–50.

French, M. & Gardner, J., 2012. The health of informal settlements: Illness and the internal thermal conditions of informal housing. In S. Rassia & P. Pardalos, eds. *Sustainable Environmental Design in Architecture*. New York: Springer, 157–71.

Frey, W. H., Singer, A., & Park, D., 2007. *Resettling New Orleans: The first full picture from the census*, Washington, DC: Brookings Institution. Available at: http://www.brookings.edu/~/media/Files/rc/reports/2007/07katrinafreysinger/20070912_katrinafreysinger.pdf.

Friesen, G., 1984. *The Canadian Prairies: A History*. Toronto: University of Toronto Press.

Frihy, O. E. & El-Sayed, M. K., 2012. Vulnerability risk assessment and adaptation to climate change induced sea level rise along the Mediterranean coast of Egypt. *Mitigation and Adaptation Strategies for Global Change*. DOI 10.1007/s11027-012-9418-y

Fronstin, P. & Holtmann, A. G., 1994. The determinants of residential property damage caused by Hurricane Andrew. *Southern Economic Journal*, **61**(2), 387–97.

Fu, B., 1989. Soil erosion and its control in the loess plateau of China. *Soil Use and Management*, **5**(2), 76–82.

Funkhauser, E., 2009. The choice of migration destination: A longitudinal approach using pre-migration outcomes. *Review of Development Economics*, **13**(4), 626–40.

Fussell, E., 2007. Constructing New Orleans, constructing race: A population history of New Orleans. *The Journal of American History*, **94**(3), 846–55.

Fussell, E., 2009a. Hurricane chasers in New Orleans: Latino immigrants as a source of a rapid response labor force. *Hispanic Journal of Behavioral Sciences*, **31**(3), 375–94.

Fussell, E., 2009b. Post-Katrina New Orleans as a new migrant destination. *Organization and Environment*, **22**(4), 458–69.

Fussell, E. & Massey, D. S., 2004. The limits to cumulative causation: International migration from Mexican urban areas. *Demography*, **41**(1), 151–71.

Fussell, E., Sastry, N., & Van Landingham, M., 2010. Race, socioeconomic status, and return migration to New Orleans after Hurricane Katrina. *Population and Environment*, **31**(1–3), 20–42.

Gabriel, M., 2006. Youth migration and social advancement: How young people manage emerging differences between themselves and their hometown. *Journal of Youth Studies*, **9**(1), 33–46.

Gaetano, A. M. & Yeoh, B. S. A., 2010. Introduction to the special issue on women and migration in globalizing Asia: Gendered experiences, agency, and activism. *International Migration*, **48**(6), 1–12.

Gagain, M., 2012. Climate change, sea level rise, and artificial islands: Saving the Maldives' statehood and maritime claims through the constitution of the oceans. *Colorado Journal of International Environmental Law and Policy*, **23**, 77–120.

Galvin, K. A., 2009. Transitions: Pastoralists living with change. *Annual Review of Anthropology*, **38**, 185–98.

Gandy, M., 2008. Landscapes of disaster: Water, modernity, and urban fragmentation in Mumbai. *Environment and Planning A*, **40**(1), 108–30.

Gans, C., 2008. *A Just Zionism: On the morality of the Jewish state*. New York: Oxford University Press.

Garikipati, S., 2008. Agricultural wage work, seasonal migration and the widening gender gap: Evidence from a semi-arid region of Andhra Pradesh. *European Journal of Development Research*, **20**(4), 629–48.

Gastineau, G. & Soden, B. J., 2009. Model projected changes of extreme wind events in response to global warming. *Geophysical Research Letters*, **36**, L10810.

Geisen, T., 2010. New perspectives on youth and migration belonging, cultural repositioning and social mobility. In D. Cairns, ed. *Youth on the Move*. Dordrecht: Springer, 11–21.

Gelazis, N. M., 2004. The European Union and the statelessness problem in the Baltic states. *European Journal of Migration and Law*, **6**, 225–42.

Gemenne, F., 2011a. How they became the face of climate change: Research and policy interactions in the birth of the 'environmental migration' concept. In E. Piguet, A. Pecoud, & P. de Guchteneire, eds. *Migration, Environment and Climate Change*. Cambridge: Cambridge University Press, 225–59.

Gemenne, F., 2011b. Climate-induced population displacements in a 4°C+ world. *Philosophical Transactions of the Royal Society London: Series A: Mathematical, Physical & Engineering Sciences*, **369**(1934), 82–95.

Georges, E., 1992. Gender, class, and migration in the Dominican Republic: Women's experiences in a transnational community. *Annals of the New York Academy of Sciences*, **645**, 81–99.

Ghimire, Y. N., Shivakoti, G. P., & Perret, S. R., 2010. Household-level vulnerability to drought in hill agriculture of Nepal: Implications for adaptation planning. *International Journal of Sustainable & World Ecology*, **17**(3), 225–30.

Ghosh, J., Heintz, J. & Pollin, R., 2012. Speculation on commodities futures markets and destabilization of global food prices: Exploring the connections. *International Journal of Health Services*, **42**(3), 465–83.

Gibb, C. & Ford, J., 2012. Should the United Nations Framework Convention on Climate Change recognize climate migrants? *Environmental Research Letters*, **7**(4), 045601.

Gibson, C. & Argent, N., 2008. Getting on, getting up and getting out? Broadening perspectives on rural youth migration. *Geographical Perspectives*, **46**(2), 135–8.

Giczy, H., 2009. The bum blockade: Los Angeles and the Great Depression. *Voces Novae*, **1**(1), 97–122.

Gilbert, G. & McLeman, R., 2010. Household access to capital and its effects on drought adaptation and migration: A case study of rural Alberta in the 1930s. *Population and Environment*, **32**(1), 3–26.

Glantz, M. H., 1988. *Societal Responses to Regional Climatic Change: Forecasting by analogy*. Boulder, CO: Westview Press.

Glantz, M. H., 2001. *Currents of Change: Impacts of El Nino and La Nina on climate and society* 2nd ed., Cambridge: Cambridge University Press.

Glantz, M. H. & Ausubel, J. H., 1988. Impact assessment by analogy: Comparing the impacts of the Ogallala aquifer depletion and CO2-induced climate change. In M. H. Glantz, ed. *Societal Responses to Regional Climatic Change: Forecasting by analogy.* Boulder, CO: Westview Press, 113–42.

Glantz, M. & Jamieson, D., 2000. Societal response to Hurricane Mitch and intra- versus intergenerational equity issues: Whose norms should apply? *Risk Analysis*, **20**(6), 869–82.

Gleditsch, N. P., Furlong, K., Hegre, H., Lacina, B., & Owen, T., 2006. Conflicts over shared rivers: Resource scarcity or fuzzy boundaries? *Political Geography*, **25**(4), 361–82.

Godfray, H. C. J., Beddington, J. R., Crute, I. R., Haddad, L., Lawrence, D., Muir, J. F., Pretty, J., Thomas, S. M., & Toulmin, C., 2010. Food security: The challenge of feeding 9 billion people. *Science*, **327**(5967), 812–18.

Goffman, E., 2006. Environmental refugees: How many, how bad? *CSA Discovery Guides.* Available at: http://csaeditweb101v.csa.com/discoveryguides/refugee/review.pdf.

Gonzalez, N., 1961. Family organization in five types of migratory wage labor. *American Anthropologist*, **63**(6), 1264–80.

Goris, I., Harrington, J., & Köhn, S., 2009. Statelessness: What it is and why it matters. *Forced Migration Review*, **32**, 4–7.

Gorman, L. B., 2010. Latino migrant labor strife and solidarity in post-Katrina New Orleans, 2005–2007. *The Latin Americanist*, **54**(1), 1–33.

Gornitz, V., 1995. Sea-level rise: A review of recent past and near-future trends. *Earth Surface Processes and Landforms*, **20**(1), 7–20.

Gottschang, T. R., 1987. Economic change, disasters, and migration: The historical case of Manchuria. *Economic Development and Cultural Change*, **35**(3), 461–90.

Goudie, A. S., 2009. Dust storms: Recent developments. *Journal of Environmental Management*, **90**(1), 89–94.

Government of Alberta, 1993. Slave Lake – Sawridge Creek – Flood Hazard Study. *Environment and Sustainable Resource Development.* Available at: http://environment.alberta.ca/01697.html.

Government of Manitoba, 2012. Flood information. Available at: http://www.gov.mb.ca/flooding/index.html.

Government of Montserrat, 2012. Census 2011: Montserrat at a glance. Available at: http://www.gov.ms/wp-content/uploads/2011/02/Montserrat-At-A-Glance.pdf.

Grafton, R. Q. & Kompas, T., 2007. Pricing Sydney water. *Australian Journal of Agricultural and Resource Economics*, **51**(3), 227–41.

Graham-Rowe, D., 2011. Agriculture: Beyond food versus fuel. *Nature*, **474**, S6–S8.

Graumann, A., Houston, T., Lawrimore, J., Levinson, D., Lott, N., McCown, S., Stephens, S., & Wuertz, D., 2005. *Hurricane Katrina: A climatological perspective*, Asheville, NC, NOAA National Climatic Data Center. Available at: http://www.ncdc.noaa.gov/oa/reports/tech-report-200501z.pdf.

Gray, C. L. & Mueller, V., 2012a. Natural disasters and population mobility in Bangladesh. *Proceedings of the National Academy of Science*, **109**(16), 6000–5.

Gray, C. L. & Mueller, V., 2012b. Drought and population mobility in rural Ethiopia. *World Development*, **40**(1), 134–45.

Great Britain House of Commons International Development Committee, 2010. *The Humanitarian Response to the Pakistan Floods: Seventh report session 2010–12: Volume I*, London.

Great Plains Committee, 1936. *The Future of the Great Plains*, Washington, DC: United States Government Printing Office.

Green, R., Bates, L. K., & Smyth, A., 2007. Impediments to recovery in New Orleans' Upper and Lower Ninth Ward: One year after Hurricane Katrina. *Disasters*, **31**(4), 311–35.

Greenberg, M. R., Lahr, M., & Mantell, N., 2007. Understanding the economic costs and benefits of catastrophes and their aftermath: A review and suggestions for the U.S. *Federal Government*. **27**(1), 83–96.

Greenwood, M. J., 1997. International migration in developed countries. In M. R. Rosenzweig & O. Stark, eds. *Handbook of Population and Family Economics, Volume 1B*. 647–720.

Gregory, J. N., 1989. *American Exodus: The Dust Bowl migration and Okie culture in California*, New York: Oxford University Press.

Gregory, K. J., 2006. The human role in changing river channels. *Geomorphology*, **79**(3–4), 172–91.

Gregory, P. J., Ingram, J. S. I., & Brklacich, M., 2005. Climate change and food security. *Philosophical Transactions of the Royal Society London: Biological Sciences: Series B*, **360**(1463), 2139–48.

Greiner, C., 2011. Migration, translocal networks, and socio-economic stratification in Namibia. *Africa*, **81**(4), 606–27.

Grigg, D. B., 1977. E. G. Ravenstein and the 'laws of migration'. *Journal of Historical Geography*, **3**(1), 41–54.

Groen, J. & Polivka, A., 2010. Going home after Hurricane Katrina: Determinants of return migration and changes in affected areas. *Demography*, **47**(4), 821–44.

Grosfoguel, R. & Cordero-Guzman, H., 1998. International migration in a global context: Recent approaches to migration theory. *Diaspora*, **7**(3), 351–68.

Grove, J. M., 1988. *The Little Ice Age*. London: Routledge.

Grove, J. M., 2002. Climatic change in northern Europe over the last two thousand years and its possible influence on human activity. In G. Wefer, W. H. Berger, K.-E. Behre, & E. Jansen, eds. *Climate Development and History of the North Atlantic Realm, Hanse Conference on Climate History*. Berlin, Heidelberg: Springer, 313–26.

Grzegorzewski, A. S., Cialone, M. A., & Wamsley, T. V., 2011. Interaction of barrier islands and storms: Implications for flood risk reduction in Louisiana and Mississippi. *Journal of Coastal Research*, (Special Issue **59**), 156–64.

Gu, C., Hu, L., Zhang, X., Wang, X., & Guo, J., 2011. Climate change and urbanization in the Yangtze River Delta. *Habitat International*, **35**(4), 544–52.

Guikema, S., 2009. Infrastructure design issues in disaster-prone regions. *Science*, **323**(5919), 1302–3.

Guo, H., Hu, Q., Zhang, Q., & Feng, S., 2012. Effects of the Three Gorges Dam on Yangtze River flow and river interaction with Poyang Lake, China: 2003–2008. *Journal of Hydrology*, **416**, 19–27.

Gutmann, M. P., Deane, G. D., Lauster, N., & Peri, A., 2005. Two population-environment regimes in the Great Plains of the United States, 1930–1990. *Population and Environment*, **27**(2), 191–225.

Gutmann, M. P. & Field, V., 2010. Katrina in historical context: Environment and migration in the U.S. *Population and Environment*, **31**(1–3), 3–19.

Haberfeld, Y., Menaria, R. K., Sahoo, B. B., & Vyas, R. N., 1999. Seasonal migration of rural labor in India. *Population Research and Policy Review*, **18**(5), 471–87.

Hägerstrand, T., 1967. *Innovation Diffusion as a Spatial Process*, Chicago, IL: University of Chicago Press.

Hajat, S., Armstrong, B. G., Gouveia, N., & Wilkinson, P., 2005. Mortality displacement of heat-related deaths: A comparison of Delhi, São Paulo, and London. *Epidemiology*, **16**(5), 613–20.

Halli, S. S., Blanchard, J., Satihal, D. G., & Moses, S., 2007. Migration and HIV transmission in rural south India: An ethnographic study. *Culture, Health and Sexuality*, **9**(1), 85–94.

Hampshire, K., 2002. Fulani on the move: Seasonal economic migration in the Sahel as a social process. *The Journal of Development Studies*, **38**(5), 15–36.

Hampshire, K. & Randall, S., 1999. Seasonal labour migration strategies in the Sahel: Coping with poverty or optimising security? *International Journal of Population Geography*, **5**(5), 367–85.

Handley, L. R., 1974. Settlement across northern Arkansas as influenced by the Missouri & North Arkansas Railroad. *Arkansas Historical Quarterly*, **33**(4), 273–92.

Hannon, B., 1997. The use of analogy in biology and economics: From biology to economics and back. *Structural Change and Economic Dynamics* **8**(4), 471–88.

Hansen, E. & Donohoe, M., 2003. Health issues of migrant and seasonal farmworkers. *Journal of Health Care for the Poor and Underserved*, **14**(2), 153–64.

Hansen, H. K. & Niedomysl, T., 2009. Migration of the creative class: Evidence from Sweden. *Journal of Economic Geography*, **9**(2), 191–206.

Hansen, R., 2002. Globalization, embedded realism, and path dependence: The other immigrants to Europe. *Comparative Political Studies*, **35**(3), 259–83.

Hardy, J. T., 2003. *Climate Change: Causes, effects and solutions*, Chichester: Wiley.

Hare, D., 1999. 'Push' versus 'pull' factors in migration outflows and returns: Determinants of migration status and spell duration among China's rural population. *Journal of Development Studies*, **35**(3), 45–72.

Harpviken, K. B., 2009. *Social Networks and Migration in Wartime Afghanistan*. Palgrave: Houndmills.

Harrison, R. D., 2000. Repercussions of El Nino: Drought causes extinction and the breakdown of mutualism in Borneo. *Proceedings of the Royal Society B: Biological Sciences*, **267**, 911–15.

Hartmann, T., 2009. Clumsy floodplains and the law: Towards a responsive land policy for extreme floods. *Built Environment*, **35**(4), 531–44.

Hartmann, T., 2011. *Clumsy Floodplains: Responsive land policy for extreme floods*, Surrey, UK: Ashgate.

Haslam, G., 1977. What about the Okies? *American History Illustrated*, **12**(1), 28–39.

Haug, G. H., Günther, D., Peterson, L. C., Sigman, D. M., Hughen, K. A., & Aeschlimann, B., 2003. Climate and the collapse of Maya civilization. *Science*, **299**(5613), 1731–5.

Hays, S., 1994. Structure and agency and the sticky problem of culture. *Sociological Theory*, **12**, 57–72.

Hazell, P. B. R. & Hess, U., 2010. Drought insurance for agricultural development and food security in dryland areas. *Food Security*, **2**(4), 395–405.

Hazell, P. B. R., Poulton, C., Wiggins, S., & Dorward, A., 2010. The future of small farms: Trajectories and policy priorities. *World Development*, **38**(10), 1349–61.

He, X. & Jiao, J., 2000. The 1998 flood and soil erosion in the Yangtze river. *Water Policy*, **1**(6), 653–8.

Healy, T. & Soomere, T., 2008. Managed retreat – Is it really an option for mitigation of chronic erosion and storm surge flooding? In L. Wallendorf, L. Ewing, C. Jones, & B. Jaffe, eds. *Solutions to Coastal Disasters Congress 2008*. American Society of Civil Engineers.

Heberger, M., Cooley, H., Herrera, P., Gleick, P. H., & Moore, E., 2011. Potential impacts of increased coastal flooding in California due to sea-level rise. *Climatic Change*, **109**(1), S229–S249.

Heinonen, U., 2006. Environmental impact on migration in Cambodia: Water-related migration from the Tonle Sap Lake region. *International Journal of Water Resources Development*, **22**(3), 449–62.

Hellin, J., Haigh, M., & Marks, F., 1999. Rainfall characteristics of Hurricane Mitch. *Nature*, **399**, 316.

Henry, S., Boyle, P., & Lambin, E. F., 2003. Modelling inter-provincial migration in Burkina Faso, West Africa: The role of sociodemographic and environmental factors. *Applied Geography*, **23**, 115–36.

Henry, S., Piché, V., Ouédraogo, D., & Lambin, E. F., 2004. Descriptive analysis of the individual migratory pathways according to environmental typologies. *Population and Environment*, **25**(5), 397–422.

Hesketh, T., Lu, L., & Xing, Z. W., 2005. The effect of China's one-child family policy after 25 Years. *New England Journal of Medicine*, **353**, 1171–6.

Hewes, L., 1973. *The Suitcase Farming Frontier: A study in the historical geography of the central Great Plains*, Lincoln: University of Nebraska Press.

Hewitt, K., 1983. The idea of calamity in a technocratic age. In K. Hewitt ed. *Interpretations of Calamity from the Viewpoint Of Human Ecology*. Winchester MA: Unwin & Allen, 3–32.

Hillel, D., 1991. *Out of the Earth: Civilization and the life of the soil*. Los Angeles: University of California Press.

Hirabayashi, Y. & Kanae, S., 2009. First estimate of the future global population at risk of flooding. *Hydrological Research Letters*, **3**, 6–9.

Ho, J. C., 2010. An introduction to the debate on the Arizona immigration law. *Regent University Law Review*, **23**, 343.

Hodge, D. R. & Lietz, C. A., 2007. The international sexual trafficking of women and children: A review of the literature. *Affilia*, **22**(2), 163–74.

Hofer, T., 1998. Do land use changes in the Himalayas affect downstream flooding? Traditional understanding and new evidences. *Memoir of the Geological Society of India*, **19**, 119–41.

Hoffman, A., 1974. *Unwanted Mexican Americans in the Great Depression: Repatriation pressures, 1929–1939*, Tuscon: University of Arizona Press.

Hoffman, C. S., 1938. Drought and depression migration into Oregon, 1930 to 1936. *Monthly Labor Review*, **46**(1), 27–35.

Holt-Jensen, A., 1980. *Geography: Its history and concepts*. London: Harper & Row.

Holzschuh, A., 1939. A study of 6655 migrant households receiving emergency grants. San Francisco, CA: Farm Security Administration.

Homer-Dixon, T., 1991. On the threshold: Environmental changes as causes of acute conflict. *International Security*, **16**(2), 76–116.

Homer-Dixon, T., 1994a. Environmental scarcities and violent conflict: Evidence from cases. *International Security*, **19**(1), 5–40.

Homer-Dixon, T., 1994b. Environmental and demographic threats to Canadian security. *Canadian Foreign Policy Journal*, **2**(2), 7–40.

Homewood, K. & Lewis, J., 1987. Impact of drought on pastoral livestock in Baringo, Kenya 1983–85. *Journal of Applied Ecology*, **24**, 615–31.

Hondagneu-Sotelo, P. & Cranford, C., 2006. Gender and migration. In J. S. Chafetz, ed. *Handbook of the Sociology of Gender, Part II*. Dordrecht: Springer, 105–26.

Hong, C.-C., Lee, M.-Y., Hsu, H.-H., & Kuo, J.-L., 2010. Role of submonthly disturbance and 40–50–day ISO on the extreme rainfall event associated with Typhoon Morakot (2009) in southern Taiwan. *Geophysical Research Letters*, **61**.56.13.21.

Houze, R. A., Rasmussen, K. L., Medina, S., Brodzik, S. R., & Romatschke, U., 2011. Anomalous atmospheric events leading to the summer 2010 floods in Pakistan. *Bulletin of the American Meteorological Society*, (March 2011), 291–8.

Hsu, M. Y., 2000. *Dreaming of Gold, Dreaming of Home: Transnationalism and migration between the United States and South China, 1842–1943*, Palo Alto, CA: Stanford University Press.

Huang, C. C., Pang, J., Zha, X., Zhou, Y., Su, H., & Li, Y., 2010. Extraordinary floods of 4100–4000 a BP recorded at the Late Neolithic ruins in the Jinghe River Gorges, Middle Reach of the Yellow River, China. *Palaeogeography, Palaeoclimatology, Palaeoecology*, **289**(1–4), 1–9.

Huang, C. C. & Su, H., 2009. Climate change and Zhou relocations in early Chinese history. *Journal of Historical Geography*, **35**(2), 297–310.

Hugo, G., 1996. Environmental concerns and international migration. *International Migration Review*, **30**(1), 105–31.

Hugo, G., 2011. Future demographic change and its interactions with migration and climate change. *Global Environmental Change*, **21**(S1), S21–S33.

Hunt, L., 2008. Women asylum seekers and refugees: Opportunities, constraints and the role of agency. *Social Policy and Society*, **7**, 281–92.

Hunter, L. M., Murray, S., & Riosmena, F., 2011. *Climatic Variability and U.S. Migration from Rural Mexico*, Boulder: University of Colorado, Institute of Behavioral Science, Working Paper POP 2011–03. Available at: http://www.colorado.edu/ibs/pubs/pop/pop2011–0003.pdf.

Huntington, E., 1907. *The Pulse of Asia: A journey in Central Asia illustrating the geographic basis of history*, Boston, MA: Houghton Mifflin.

Huntington, E., 1924. *Civilization and Climate* 3rd ed., New Haven, CT: Yale University Press.

Huntington, H. P., Goodstein, E., & Euskirchen, E., 2012. Towards a tipping point in responding to change: Rising costs, fewer options for Arctic and global societies. *Ambio*, **41**(1), 66–74.

Huntley, I. D., 2012. The Thames in winter. *Weather*, **12**(12), 373–6.

Hurt, R. D., 1981. *The Dust Bowl: An agricultural and social history*, Chicago, IL: Nelson-Hall.

Hurt, R. D., 1986. Federal land reclamation in the Dust Bowl. *Great Plains Quarterly*, **6**(2), 94–106.

Hurt, R. D., 2011. *The Big Empty: The Great Plains in the twentieth century*, Tuscon: University of Arizona Press.

Hussain, I. & Hanjra, M. A., 2003. Does irrigation water matter for rural poverty alleviation? Evidence from South and South-East Asia. *Water Policy*, **5**(5–6), 429–42.

Huynen, M. M., Martens, P., Schram, D., Weijenberg, M. P., & Kunst, A. E., 2001. The impact of heat waves and cold spells on mortality rates in the Dutch population. *Environmental Health Perspectives*, **109**(5), 463–70.

Hyndman, J. & Mountz, A., 2008. Another brick in the wall? Neo-refoulement and the externalization of asylum in Australia and Europe. *Government and Opposition*, **43**, 249–69.

Hystad, P. & Keller, P., 2006. Disaster management: Kelowna tourism industry's preparedness, impact and response to a 2003 major forest fire. *Journal of Hospitality and Tourism Management*, **13**(1), 44–58.

IDMC, 2012a. *Global estimates 2011: People displaced by natural hazard-induced disasters*, Geneva, International Displacement Monitoring Centre. Available at: http://www.internal-displacement.org/8025708F004BE3B1/(httpInfoFiles)/1280B6A95F452E9BC1257A22002DAC12/$file/global-estimates-2011-natural-disasters-jun2012.pdf.

IDMC, 2012b. Internal displacement in Africa. Geneva: International Displacement Monitoring Centre. Available at: http://www.internal-displacement.org/africa

Iglesias, A., Garrote, L., Flores, F., & Moneo, M., 2007. Challenges to manage the risk of water scarcity and climate change in the Mediterranean. *Water Resources Management*, **21**, 775–88.

Ikeme, J., 2003. Climate change adaptational deficiencies in developing countries: The case of sub-Saharan Africa. *Mitigation and Adaptation Strategies for Global Change*, **8**(1), 29–52.

Inderberg, T. H. & Eikeland, P. O., 2009. Limits to adaptation: Analysing institutional constraints. In W. N. Adger, I. Lorenzoni, & K. L. O'Brien, eds. *Adapting to Climate Change: Thresholds, values, governance*. Cambridge: Cambridge University Press, 433–47.

International livestock Research Institute, 2011. Best ways to manage responses to recurring drought in Kenya's drylands. Available at: http://www.ilri.org/ilrinews/index.php/archives/6936.

IOM, 2010. *World Migration Report 2010*, Geneva: International Organization for Migration. Available at: http://publications.iom.int/bookstore/free/WMR_2010_ENGLISH.pdf.

IPCC, 2007. Summary for policymakers. In M. L. Parry, O. F. Canziani, J. P. Palutikof, P. J. van der Linden, & C. E. Hanson, eds., *Climate Change 2007: Synthesis Report. Contribution of Working Groups I, II and III to the Fourth Assessment Report of the Intergovernmental Panel on Climate Change*, Cambridge: Cambridge University Press, 7–22.

Iqbal, S., 2010. Flood and erosion induced population displacements: A socio-economic case study in the Gangetic Riverine Tract at Malda District, West Bengal, India. *Journal of Human Ecology*, **30**(3), 201–11.

IRIN, 2009. Syria: Drought response faces funding shortfall. Damascus, 24 November 2009. Available at: http://www.irinnews.org/Report/87165/SYRIA-Drought-response-faces-funding-shortfall.

IRIN, 2012. Time running out for solution to Yemen's water crisis. *The Guardian*, 27 August 2012. Available at: http://www.guardian.co.uk/global-development/2012/aug/27/solution-yemen-water-crisis.

Ishemo, A., 2009. Vulnerability of coastal urban settlements in Jamaica. *Management of Environmental Quality*, **20**(4), 451–9.

Isidoro, D. & Grattan, S. R., 2011. Predicting soil salinity in response to different irrigation practices, soil types and rainfall scenarios. *Irrigation Science*, **29**(3), 197–211.

Jacob, T., Wahr, J., Pfeffer, W. T., & Swenson, S., 2012. Recent contributions of glaciers and ice caps to sea level rise. *Nature*, **482**, 514–18.

Jacobson, J. L., 1988. *Environmental Refugees: A yardstick of habitability*. Washington, DC: Worldwatch Institute.

Jamieson, D., 1988. Grappling for a glimpse of the future. In M. H. Glantz, ed. *Societal Responses to Regional Climatic Change: Forecasting by analogy*. Boulder, CO: Westview Press, 73–94.

Jim, C. Y. & Yang, F. Y., 2006. Local responses to inundation and de-farming in the reservoir region of the Three Gorges Project (China). *Environmental Management*, **38**(4), 618–37.

Joffé, G., 2011. The Arab Spring in North Africa: Origins and prospects. *Journal of North African Studies*, **16**(4), 507–32.

Johnstone, S. & Mazo, J., 2011. Global warming and the Arab Spring. *Survival*, **53**(2), 11–17.

Jones, D. C., 1991. *Empire of Dust*. Edmonton: University of Alberta Press.

Jonkman, S. N., 2005. Global perspectives on loss of human Life caused by floods. *Natural Hazards*, **34**(2), 151–75.

Jonkman, S. N., Maaskant, B., Boyd, E., & Levitan, M. L., 2009. Loss of life caused by the flooding of New Orleans after Hurricane Katrina: Analysis of the relationship between flood characteristics and mortality. *Risk Analysis*, **29**(5), 676–98.

Jülich, S., 2011. Drought Triggered Temporary Migration in an East Indian Village. *International Migration*, **49**(S1), e189–e1999.

Kallis, G., 2008. Droughts. *Annual Review of Environment and Resources*, **33**, 85–118.

Kaplan, R. D., 1994. The coming anarchy. *The Atlantic Monthly*, February, **1**, 44–76.

Kaplan, T. & Hernandez, R., 2012. Cuomo, in aid appeal, cites broad reach of storm. *New York Times* **27** November. Available at: http://www.nytimes.com/2012/11/27/nyregion/governor-cuomo-says-hurricane-sandy-was-worse-than-katrina.html.

Karamba, W., Quinones, E., & Winters, P., 2011. Migration and food consumption patterns in Ghana. *Food Policy*, **36**(1), 41–53.

Karamera, D., Oguledo, V. I., & Davis, B., 2000. A gravity model analysis of international migration to North America. *Applied Economics*, **32**(13), 1745–55.

Karim, M. F. & Mimura, N., 2008. Impacts of climate change and sea-level rise on cyclonic storm surge floods in Bangladesh. *Global Environmental Change*, **18**(3), 490–500.

Karras, G. & Chiswick, C. U., 1999. Macroeconomic determinants of migration: The case of Germany 1964–1988. *International Migration*, **37**(4), 657–77.

Kartiki, K., 2011. Climate change and migration: A case study from rural Bangladesh. *Gender and Development*, **19**(1), 23–38.

Kasinsky, R. G., 1976. *Refugees from Militarism: Draft-age Americans in Canada.* New Brunswick NJ: Transaction Books.

Kates, R. W., Colten, C. E., Laska, S., & Leatherman, S. P., 2006. Reconstruction of New Orleans after Hurricane Katrina: A research perspective. *Proceedings of the National Academy of Science*, **103**(40), 14653–60.

Kavic, L., 1975. Canada and the commonwealth. *The Round Table: The Commonwealth Journal of International Affairs*, **65**(257), 37–49.

Keely, C. B., 2008. Replacement migration. In P. Uhlenberg, ed. *International Handbook of Population Aging.* Dordrecht: Springer, 395–406.

Keim, B. D., Muller, R. A., & Stone, G. W., 2007. Spatiotemporal patterns and return periods of tropical storm and hurricane strikes from Texas to Maine. *Journal of Climate*, **20**(4), 3498–509.

Kentayash, J. & Dracup, J. A., 2002. The quantification of drought: An evaluation of drought indices. *Bulletin of the American Meteorological Society*, **83**(8), 1167–80.

Khandker, S. R., Khalily, M. A. B., & Samad, H. A., 2012. Seasonal migration to mitigate income seasonality: Evidence from Bangladesh. *Journal of Development Studies.* DOI: 10.1080/00220388.2011.561325.

Khandker, S. R. & Koolwal, G. B., 2010. How infrastructure and financial institutions affect rural income and poverty: Evidence from Bangladesh. *Journal of Development Studies*, **46**(6), 1109–37.

Kibreab, G., 1997. Environmental causes and impact of refugee movements: A critique of the current debate. *Disasters*, **21**(1), 20–38.

Kikuchi, M. & Hayami, Y., 1983. New rice technology, intrarural migration, and institutional innovation in the Philippines. *Population and Development Review*, **9**(2), 247–57.

Kim, W.-B., 2010. Nostalgia, anxiety and hope: Migration and ethnic identity of Chosŏnjok in China. *Pacific Affairs*, **83**(1), 95–114.

King, R. & Skeldon, R., 2010. 'Mind the gap!' Integrating approaches to internal and international migration. *Journal of Ethnic and Migration Studies*, **36**(10), 1619–46.

Kirk, D., 1996. Demographic transition theory. *Population Studies*, **50**(3), 361–87.

Kirsch, T., Wadhwani, C., Sauer, L., Doocy, S., & Catlett, C., 2012. Impact of the 2010 Pakistan floods on rural and urban populations at six months. *PLoS Currents Disasters*, **4**(e4fdfb212d2432).

Kirwan, M. L., Guntenspergen, G. R., D'Alpaos, A., Morris, J. T., Mudd, S. M., & Temmerman, S., 2010. Limits on the adaptability of coastal marshes to rising sea level. *Geophysical Research Letters*, **37**(L23401).

Klein, H. S., 2010. *The Atlantic Slave Trade.* Cambridge: Cambridge University Press.

Klinenberg, E., 1999. Denaturalizing disaster: A social autopsy of the 1995 Chicago heat wave. *Theory and Society*, **28**(2), 239–95.

Knapp, K. R., Kruk, M. C., Levinson, D. H., Diamond, H. J., & Neumann, C. J., 2010. The International Best Track Archive for Climate Stewardship (IBTrACS): Unifying tropical cyclone best track data. *Bulletin of the American Meteorological Society*, **91**, 363–76.

Kniveton, D., Smith, C., & Wood, S., 2011. Agent-based model simulations of future changes in migration flows for Burkina Faso. *Global Environmental Change*, **21**(S1), S34–S40.

Knox, J. H., 2009. Human rights and climate change at the United Nations. *Harvard Environmental Law Review*, **33**, 477–98.

Knutson, T. R., McBride, J. L., Chan, J., Emanuel, K., Holland, G., Landsea, C., Held, I., Kossin, J., Srivastava, A. K., & Sugi, M., 2010. Tropical cyclones and climate change. *Nature Geoscience*, **3**, 157–63.

Kokelaar, B. P., 2002. Setting, chronology and consequences of the eruption of Soufriere Hills volcano, Montserrat (1995–1999). In T. H. Druitt & B. P. Kokelaar, eds. *Memoirs 2002*. London: The Geological Society, 1–43.

Kopp, R. E., Simons, F. J., Mitrovica, J. X., Maloof, A. C., & Oppenheimer, M., 2009. Probabilistic assessment of sea level during the last interglacial stage. *Nature*, **462**, 863–7.

Koser, K., 2011. The migration-displacement nexus and security in Afghanistan. In K. Koser & S. Martin, eds. *The Migration-Displacement Nexus: Patterns, processes, and policies*. New York: Berghahn Books, 131–44.

Koster, R. D., Dirmeyer, P. A., Guo, Z., Bonan, G., Chan, E., Cox, P., Gordon, C. T., Kowalczyk, E., Lawrence, D., Liu, P., Lu, C-H, Malyshev, S., McAvaney, B., Mitchell, K., Mocko, D., Oki, T., Oleson, K., Pitman, A., Sud, Y. C., Taylor, C. M., Verseghy, D., Vasic, R., Xue, Y., & Yamada, T., 2004. Regions of strong coupling between soil moisture and precipitation. *Science*, **305**(5687), 1138–40.

Kovats, R. S. & Kristie, L. E., 2006. Heatwaves and public health in Europe. *European Journal of Public Health*, **16**(6), 592–9.

Kramer, A. E., 2008. Trade in mammoth ivory, helped by global thaw, flourishes in Russia. *International Herald Tribune*, 25 March 2008. Available at: http://www.nytimes.com/2008/03/25/world/europe/25iht-mammoth.4.11415717.html?_r=1.

Krieg, A. S., 2006. Aboriginal incarceration: Health and social impacts. *Medical Journal of Australia*, **184**(10), 534–6.

Kruger, F., 1998. Taking advantage of rural assets as a coping strategy for the urban poor: The case of rural-urban interrelations in Botswana. *Environment and Urbanization*, **10**(1), 119–34.

Kugler, A. & Yuksel, M., 2008. *Effects of Low-Skilled Immigration on US Natives: Evidence from Hurricane Mitch*, Cambridge MA: National Bureau of Economic Research. Available at: http://www.nber.org/papers/w14293.pdf.

Kuks, S. M. M., 2009. Institutional evolution of the Dutch water board model. In S. Reinhard & H. Folmer, eds. *Water Policy in the Netherlands: Integrated management in a densely populated delta*. Washington, DC: Resources for the Future Press, 155–70.

Kumar, P., 2007. Providing the providers – remedying Africa's shortage of health care workers. *New England Journal of Medicine*, **356**, 2564–7.

Kummu, M., de Moel, H., Porkka, M., Siebert, S., Varis, O., & Ward, P. J., 2012. Lost food, wasted resources: Global food supply chain losses and their impacts on freshwater, cropland, and fertiliser use. *Science of the Total Environment*, **438**, 477–89.

Kummu, M. & Sarkkula, J., 2008. Impact of the Mekong River Flow alteration on the Tonle Sap Flood Pulse. *Ambio*, **37**(3), 185–92.

Kundzewicz, Z. W., Hirabayashi, Y., & Kanae, S., 2010. River floods in the changing climate – observations and projections. *Water Resources Management*, **24**(11), 2633–46.

Kunii, O., Nakamura, S., Abdur, R., & Wakai, S., 2002. The impact on health and risk factors of the diarrhoea epidemics in the 1998 Bangladesh floods. *Public Health*, **116**(2), 68–74.

Kurosaki, T., Khan, H., Shah, M. K., & Tahir, M., 2012. *Household-Level Recovery after Floods in a Developing Country: Further evidence from Khyber Pakhtunkhwa, Pakistan*, Tokyo, Hitotsubashi University, PRIMCED Discussion Paper Series, No. 27. Available at: http://www.ier.hit-u.ac.jp/primced/documents/No27-dp_up_Pdf_2012_000.pdf.

Kusch, L., 2012. Chief mum on ballooning evacuee stats. *Winnipeg Free Press*. 17 March 2012. Available at: http://www.winnipegfreepress.com/local/chief-mum-on-ballooning-evacuee-stats-143035185.html.

La Chapelle, P., 2007. *Proud to Be an Okie: Cultural politics, country music, and migration to Southern California*. Berkeley: University of California Press.

Laczko, F., 2005. Data and research on human trafficking. *International Migration*, **43**(1–2), 5–16.

Laczko, F. & Gramegna, M. A., 2003. Developing better indicators of human trafficking. *Brown Journal of World Affairs*, **10**, 185–98.

Laforge, J. & McLeman, R., In press. Social capital and drought-migrant integration in 1930s Saskatchewan. *The Canadian Geographer*.

Laird, K. R., Cumming, B. F., Wunsam, S., Rusak, J. A., Oglesby, R. J., Fritz, S. C., & Leavitt, P. R., 2003. Lake sediments record large-scale shifts in moisture regimes across the northern prairies of North America during the past two millennia. *Proceedings of the National Academy of Sciences*, **100**(5), 2483–8.

Lall, S. V. & Deichmann, U., 2011. Density and disasters: Economics of urban hazard risk. *World Bank Research Observer*. DOI: 10.1093/wbro/lkr006.

Lalonde, R. J. & Topel, R. H., 1997. Economic impact of international migration and the economic performance of migrants. In M. R. Rosenzweig & O. Stark, eds. *Handbook of Population and Family Economics, Volume 1* B. Amsterdam: Elsevier, 799–887.

Lamb, H. H., 1982. *Climate History and the Modern World*, London: Methuen.

Lambeck, K. & Chappell, J., 2001. Sea level change through the last glacial cycle. *Science*, **292**(5517), 679–86.

Landry, C. E., Bin, O., Hindsley, P., Whitehead, J. C., & Wilson, K., 2007. Going home: Evacuation-migration decisions of Hurricane Katrina survivors. *Southern Economic Journal*, **74**(2), 326–43.

Lange, D. & Taylor, P. S., 1939. *An American Exodus: A record of human erosion*. New York: Reynal & Hitchcock.

Laurance, W. F. & Williamson, G. B., 2001. Positive feedbacks among forest fragmentation, drought, and climate change in the Amazon. *Conservation Biology*, **15**(6), 1529–35.

Lawson, V., 2000. Questions of migration and belonging: Understandings of migration under neoliberalism in Ecuador. *International Journal of Population Geography*, **5**, 261–76.

Le Billon, P., 2001. The political ecology of war: Natural resources and armed conflicts. *Political Geography*, **20**(5), 561–84.

Lee, E., 1966. A theory of migration. *Demography*, **3**(1), 47–57.

Lee, H. F., Fok, L., & Zhang, D. D., 2008. Climatic change and Chinese population growth dynamics over the last millennium. *Climatic Change*, **88**, 131–56.

Legates, D. R., Mahmood, R., Levia, D. F., DeLiberty, T. L., Quiring, S. M., Houser, C., & Nelson, F. E., 2011. Soil moisture: A central and unifying theme in physical geography. *Progress in Physical Geography*, **35**, 65–86.

Lehmann, U., Dieleman, M., & Martineau, T., 2008. Staffing remote rural areas in middle- and low-income countries: A literature review of attraction and retention. *BMC Health Services Research*, **8**, 19.

Lein, H., 2000. Hazards and 'forced' migration in Bangladesh. *Norsk Geografisk Tidsskrift*, **54**(3), 122–7.

Lein, H., 2009. The poorest and most vulnerable? On hazards, livelihoods and labelling of riverine communities in Bangladesh. *Singapore Journal of Tropical Geography*, **30**(1), 98–113.

Lekson, S. H. & Cameron, C. M., 1995. The abandonment of Chaco Canyon, the Mesa Verde migrations, and the reorganization of the Pueblo world. *Journal of Anthropological Archaeology*, **14**(2), 184–202.

Levy, M. A., 1995. Is the environment a national security issue? *International Security*, **20**(2), 35–62.

Lewer, J. J. & Van den Berg, H., 2008. A gravity model of immigration. *Economic Letters*, **99**(1), 164–7.

Lewis, G. J., 1982. *Human migration: A geographical approach*. New York: St. Martin's Press.

Lewis, J., 1990. The vulnerability of small island states to sea level rise: The need for holistic strategies. *Disasters*, **14**(3), 241–9.

Lewis, M. E., 1989. National grasslands in the Dust Bowl. *Geographical Review*, **79**(2), 161–71.

Li, H., Waley, P., & Rees, P., 2001. Reservoir resettlement in China: Past experience and the Three Gorges Dam. *The Geographical Journal*, **67**(3), 195–212.

Li, J. & Zeng, Q., 2003. A new monsoon index and the geographical distribution of the global monsoons. *Advances in Atmospheric Sciences*, **20**(2), 299–302.

Li, T. M., 2011. Centering labor in the land grab debate. *Journal of Peasant Studies*, **38**(2), 281–98.

Liang, Z. & Ma, Z., 2004. China's floating population: New evidence from the 2000 census. *Population and Development Review*, **30**(3), 467–88.

Libecap, G. D., 1998. The Great Depression and the regulating state: Federal government regulations of agriculture: 1884–1970. In M. D. Bordo, C. Goldin, & E. N. White, eds. *The Defining Moment: The Great Depression and the American economy in the twentieth century*. Chicago, IL: University of Chicago Press, 181–224.

Lievins, J., 1999. Family-forming migration from Turkey and Morocco to Belgium: The demand for marriage partners from the countries of origin. *International Migration Review*, **33**(3), 717–44.

Lightfoot, D., 2009. *Survey of Infiltration Karez in Northern Iraq: History and Current Status of Underground Aqueducts*. UNESCO. Available at: http://www.iauiraq.org/ reports/UNESCO_Karez_survey_report_FINAL.pdf.

Lima, F. P. & Wethey, D. S., 2012. Three decades of high-resolution coastal sea surface temperatures reveal more than warming. *Nature Communications*, **3**, article 704.

Lindell, M. K., Kang, J. E., & Prater, C. S., 2011. The logistics of household hurricane evacuation. *Natural Hazards*, **58**(1), 1039–109.

Lindley, A., 2008. Crisis and displacement in Somalia. *Forced Migration Review*, **33**, 18–19.

Lindstrom, D. P., 1996. Economic opportunity in Mexico and return migration from the United States. *Demography*, **33**(3), 357–74.

Linnerooth-Bayer, J., Warner, K., Bals, C., Höppe, P., Burton, I., Loster, T., & Haas, A., 2009. Insurance, developing countries and climate change. *The Geneva Papers*, **34**, 381–400.

Lischer, S. K., 2008. Security and displacement in Iraq: Responding to the forced migration crisis. *International Security*, **33**(2), 95–119.

Liu, Z., 2005. Institution and inequality: The hukou system in China. *Journal of Comparative Economics*, **33**(1), 133–57.

Liverman, D. M., 1999. Vulnerability and adaptation to drought in Mexico. *Natural Resources Journal*, **39**, 99–115.

Lokshin, M., Bontch-Osmolovski, M., & Glinskaya, E., 2010. Work-related migration and poverty reduction in Nepal. *Review of Development Economics*, **14**(2), 323–32.

Lonergan, S. & Kavanagh, B., 1991. Climate change, water resources and security in the Middle East. *Global Environmental Change*, **1**(4), 272–90.

Luber, G. & McGeehin, M., 2008. Climate change and extreme heat events. *American Journal of Preventative Medicine*, **35**(5), 429–35.

Luginaah, I. N., Weis, T., Galaa, S., Nkrumah, M., Benzer-Kerr, R., & Bagah, D., 2009. Environment, migration and food security in the upper west region of Ghana. In I. N. Luginaah & E. K. Yanful., eds. *Environment and Health in Sub-Saharan Africa: Managing an Emerging Crisis*. Accra, 25–38.

Luo, C.-Z., 1987. Investigation and regionalization of historical floods in China. *Journal of Hydrology*, **96**(1–4), 41–51.

Lutz, H., ed., 2008. *Migration and domestic work: A European perspective on a global theme*. Burlington VT: Ashgate.

Le Sage, A. & Majid, N., 2002. The livelihoods gap: Responding to the economic dynamics of vulnerability in Somalia. *Disasters*, **26**(1), 10–27.

Makaske, B., De Vries, E., Tainter, J. A., & McIntosh, R. J., 2007. Aeolian and fluviolacustrine landforms and prehistoric human occupation on a tectonically influenced floodplain margin, the Méma, central Mali. *Geologie en Mijnbouw/ Netherlands Journal of Geosciences*, **86**(3), 241–56.

Manes, S., 1982. Pioneers and survivors: Oklahoma's landless farmers. In A. H. Morgan & H. W. Morgan, eds. *Oklahoma: New views of the forty-sixth state*. Norman: University of Oklahoma Press, 93–132.

Manly, M., 2007. The spirit of Geneva: Traditional and new actors in the field of statelessness. *Refugee Survey Quarterly*, **26**(4), 255–61.

Mann, M. E. & Kump, L. R., 2009. *Dire Predictions: Understanding global warming*, New York: DK Publishing.

Mann, M. E., Zhang, Z., Hughes, M. K., Bradley, R. S., Miller, S. K., Rutherford, S., & Ni, F., 2008. Proxy-based reconstructions of hemispheric and global surface temperature variations over the past two millennia. *Proceedings of the National Academy of Sciences*, **105**(36), 13252–7.

Marchildon, G. P., 2005. The great divide. In G. Marchildon, ed. *The Heavy Hand of History: Interpreting Saskatchewan's past*. Regina, SK: Great Plains Research Centre, 51–66.

Marchildon, G. P., Kulshreshtha, S., Wheaton, E., & Sauchyn, D., 2008. Drought and institutional adaptation in the Great Plains of Alberta and Saskatchewan, 1914–1939. *Natural Hazards*, **45**(3), 391–411.

Marengo, J., Nobre, C., Tomasella, J., Cardoso, M., & Oyama, M., 2008. Hydro-climatic and ecological behaviour of the drought of Amazonia in 2005. *Philosophical Transactions of the Royal Society London: Biological sciences: Series B*, **363**(1498), 1773–8.

Marger, M. N., 2001. Social and human capital in immigrant adaptation: The case of Canadian business immigrants. *The Journal of Socioeconomics*, **30**(2), 169–70.

Markowski, P. M. & Richardson, Y. P., 2009. Tornadogenesis: Our current understanding, forecasting considerations, and questions to guide future research. *Atmospheric Research*, **93**, 3–10.

Marshall, T. P., 2002. Tornado damage survey at Moore, Oklahoma. *Weather and Forecasting*, **17**(3), 582–98.

Martin, E. & Martin, C., 2010. Russia's mammoth ivory industry expands: What effect on elephants? *Pachyderm*, **47**, 26–35.

Martin, J. E., 1998. The structure and formation of a continental winter cyclone, Part II: Frontal forcing of an extreme snow event. *Monthly Weather Review*, **126**(2), 329–48.

Massey, D. S., 1990. The social and economic origins of immigration. *Annals of the American Academy of Political and Social Science*, **510**, 60–72.

Massey, D. S., Arango, J., Hugo, G., Kouaouci, A., Pellegrino, A., & Taylor, J. E., 1993. Theories of migration: A review and appraisal. *Population and Development Review*, **19**(3), 431–66.

Massey, D. S., Axinn, W. G., & Ghimire, D. J., 2010. Environmental change and out-migration: Evidence from Nepal. *Population and Environment*, **32**(2–3), 109–36.

Massey, D. S. & Capoferro, C., 2006. Sálvese Quien Pueda: Structural adjustment and emigration from Lima. *Annals of the American Academy of Political and Social Science*, **606**(1), 116–27.

Massey, D. S. & Espinosa, K. E., 1997. What's driving Mexico-US migration? A theoretical, empirical and policy analysis. *American Journal of Sociology*, **102**(4), 939–99.

Mavromaras, K., McGuinness, S., O'Leary, N., Sloane, P., & Fok, Y. K., 2010. The problem of overskilling in Australia and Britain. *The Manchester School*, **78**(3), 219–41.

Maxwell, D. & Fitzpatrick, M., 2012. The 2011 Somalia famine: Context, causes, and complications. *Global Food Security*, **1**(1), 5–12.

Mayda, A. M., 2009. International migration: A panel data analysis of the determinants of bilateral flows. *Journal of Population Economics*, **23**(4), 1249–74.

Mazzotti, S., Lambert, A., Van der Kooij, M., & Mainville, A., 2009. Impact of anthropogenic subsidence on relative sea-level rise in the Fraser River delta. *Geology*, **37**(9), 771–4.

Mberu, B. U., Ezeh, A. C., Chepngeno-Langat, G., Kimani, J., Oti, S., & Beguy, D., 2013. Family ties and urban-rural linkages among older migrants in Nairobi informal settlements. *Population, Space and Place*, **19**(3), 275–93.

McAdam, J., 2011. Swimming against the tide: Why a climate change displacement treaty is not the answer. *International Journal of Refugee Law*, **23**(1), 2–27.

McCormick, B. & Wahba, J., 2005. Why do the young and educated in LDCs concentrate in large cities? Evidence from migration data. *Economica*, **72**(285), 39–67.

McDean, H. C., 1978. The 'Okie' migration as a socio-economic necessity in Oklahoma. *Red River Valley Historical Review*, **3**(1), 77–92.

McDean, H. C., 1986. Dust Bowl historiography. *Great Plains Quarterly*, **6**(2), 117–26.

McDonald, B., Webber, M., & Duan, Y., 2008. Involuntary resettlement as an opportunity for development: The case of urban resettlers of the Three Gorges Project, China. *Journal of Refugee Studies*, **21**(1), 82–102.

McDonald, R. I., Green, P., Balk, D., Fekete, B. M., Revenga, C., Todd, M., & Montgomery, M., 2011. Urban growth, climate change, and freshwater availability. *Proceedings of the National Academy of Sciences*, **108**(15), 6312–17.

McGranahan, G., Balk, D., & Anderson, B., 2007. The rising tide: Assessing the risks of climate change and human settlements in low elevation coastal zones. *Environment and Urbanization*, **19**(1), 17–37.

McGregor, G., 1992. Climate change and Hong Kong: Possible implications and responses. *Hong Kong Meteorological Society Bulletin* **2**(1), 16–27.

McHugh, K. E., Hogan, T. D., & Happel, S. K., 1995. Multiple residence and cyclical migration: A life course perspective. *Professional Geographer*, **47**(3), 251–67.

McKenzie, S. & Menjivar, C., 2011. The meanings of migration, remittances and gifts: Views of Honduran women who stay. *Global Networks*, **11**(1), 63–81.

McLeman, R., 2006. Migration out of 1930s rural eastern Oklahoma: Insights for climate change research. *Great Plains Quarterly*, **26**(1), 27–40.

McLeman, R., 2007. Household access to capital and its influence on climate-related rural population change: Lessons from the Dust Bowl years. In E. Wall, B. Smit, & J. Wandel, eds. *Farming in a Changing Climate*. Vancouver: UBC Press, 200–16.

McLeman, R., 2008a. *Economic and Social Adaptation to Climate Change in Canadian Seasonal-economy Communities: Final Scientific Report for Natural Resources Canada*, Ottawa.

McLeman, R., 2008b. Climate change migration, refugee protection and adaptive capacity-building. *McGill International Journal of Sustainable Development Law and Policy*, **4**(1), 1–18.

McLeman, R., 2009. Climate change and adaptive human migration: Lessons from rural North America. In N. W. Adger, I. Lorenzoni, & K. O'Brien, eds. *Adapting to Climate Change*. Cambridge: Cambridge University Press, 296–310.

McLeman, R., 2010a. On the origins of environmental migration. *Fordham Environmental Law Review*, **20**(2), 403–25.

McLeman, R., 2010b. Impacts of population change on vulnerability and the capacity to adapt to climate change and variability: A typology based on lessons from a hard country. *Population and Environment*, **31**(5), 286–316.

McLeman, R., 2011a. Settlement abandonment in the context of global environmental change. *Global Environmental Change*, **21**(S1), S108–S120.

McLeman, R., 2011b. *Climate change, migration, and critical international security considerations*, Geneva, International Organization for Migration. Available at: http://publications.iom.int/bookstore/index.php?main_page=product_info&cPath=2_3&products_id=688.

McLeman, R., 2012. Developments in modelling of climate change-related migration. *Climatic Change*. DOI: 10.1007/s10584–012–0578–2.

McLeman, R. 2013. Labor Migration and Food Security in a Changing Climate. In C. Barrett (Ed.) *Food Security and Sociopolitical Stability*. (pp. 229-255). New York: Oxford University Press.

McLeman, R., Brklacich, M., Woodrow, M., Gallaugher, P., Vodden, K., & Sander-Regier, R., 2011. Opportunities and barriers for adaptation in Canadian rural and resource-based communities. In J. Ford & L. B. Ford, eds. *Climate Change Adaptation in Developed Nations*. Dordrecht: Springer, 449–60.

McLeman, R., Dupre, J., Ford, L. B., Ford, J., Gajewski, K., & Marchildon, G., 2013. What we learned from the Dust Bowl: Lessons in science, policy, and adaptation. *Population and Environment*. DOI10.1007/s11111-013-0190-z.

McLeman, R. & Ford, J. D., 2013. How demographic change and migration influence community-level adaptation to climate change: Examples from rural eastern Ontario and Nunavut, Canada. In T. Faist & J. Schade, eds. *Disentangling Migration and Climate Change: Towards an analysis of concepts, methodologies, and policies*. Berlin: Springer, 55–79.

McLeman, R., Herold, S., Reljic, Z., Sawada, M., & McKenney, D., 2010. GIS-based modeling of drought and historical population change on the Canadian prairies. *Journal of Historical Geography*, **36**(1), 43–56.

McLeman, R., Mayo, D., Strebeck, E., & Smit, B., 2008. Drought adaptation in rural eastern Oklahoma in the 1930s: Lessons for climate change adaptation research. *Mitigation and Adaptation Strategies for Global Change*, **13**(4), 379–400.

McLeman, R. & Ploeger, S. K., 2012. Soil and its influence on rural drought migration: Insights from Depression-era Southwestern Saskatchewan, Canada. *Population and Environment*, **33**(4), 304–32.

McLeman, R. & Smit, B., 2003. *Climate change, migration and security*. Ottawa: Canadian Security Intelligence Service. Available at: http://www.csis.gc.ca/eng/comment/com86_e.html.

McLeman, R. & Smit, B., 2006a. Migration as an adaptation to climate change. *Climatic Change*, **76**(1–2), 31–53.

McLeman, R. & Smit, B., 2006b. Vulnerability to climate change hazards and risks: Crop and flood insurance. *The Canadian Geographer*, **50**(2), 217–26.

McLeman, R. & Smit, B., 2012. Climate change and Canadian security. In C. Leuprecht, T. Hataley, & K. Nossal, eds. *Evolving Transnational Threats and Border Security: A new research agenda*. Kingston ON: Centre for International Defence and Policy, Martello Papers, 97–108. Available at: http://www.queensu.ca/cidp/index/Martello37E.pdf.

McMichael, P., 2009a. The world food crisis in historical perspective. *The National Review*, **61**(1). Available at: http://monthlyreview.org/2009/07/01/the-world-food-crisis-in-historical-perspective.

McMichael, P., 2009b. A food regime genealogy. *Journal of Peasant Studies*, **36**(1), 139–69.

McMichael, P., 2012. The land grab and corporate food regime restructuring. *Journal of Peasant Studies*. DOI: 10.1080/03066150.2012.661369.

McMillan, R. T., 1936. Some observations on Oklahoma's population movements since 1930. *Rural Sociology*, **1**(3), 332–43.

McMillan, R. T., 1943. *Migration and status of open-country families in Oklahoma*. Stillwater: Oklahoma Agricultural Experiment Station.

McWilliams, C., 1942. *Ill Fares the Land: Migrants and migratory labor in the United States*. Boston. MA: Little, Brown and Company.

Medina-Ramón, M. Zanobetti, A., Cavanagh, D. P., & Schwartz, J., 2006. Extreme temperatures and mortality: Assessing effect modification by personal characteristics and specific cause of death in a multi-city case-only analysis. *Environmental Health Perspectives*, **114**(9), 1331–6.

Meehl, G. A., Hu, A., Tebaldi, C., Arblaster, J. M., Washington, W. M., Teng, H., & Sanderson, B., 2012. Relative outcomes of climate change mitigation related to global temperature versus sea-level rise. *Nature Climate Change*, **2**, 576–80.

Meehl, G. A. Hu, A., Tebaldi, C., Arblaster, J. M., Washington, W. M., Teng, H., Sanderson, B. M., Ault, T., Strand, W. G., & White, J. B., 2012. Relative outcomes of climate change mitigation related to global temperature versus sea-level rise. *Nature Climate Change*, **2**, 576–80.

Meehl, G. A. & Tebaldi, C., 2004. More intense, more frequent, and longer lasting heat waves in the 21st century. *Science*, **305**(5686), 994–7.

Mehari, A., Schultz, B., & Depeweg, H., 2005. Where indigenous water management practices overcome failures of structures: The Wadi Laba spate irrigation system in Eritrea. *Irrigation and Drainage*, **54**(1), 1–14.

Mehari, A., Van Steenbergen, F., & Schultz, B., 2011. Modernization of spate irrigated agriculture: A new approach. *Irrigation and Drainage*, **60**(2), 163–73.

Meier, P., Bond, D., & Bond, J., 2007. Environmental influences on pastoral conflict in the Horn of Africa. *Political Geography*, **26**(6), 716–35.

Melton, G., Gall, M., Mitchell, J. T., & Cutter, S. L., 2009. Hurricane Katrina storm surge delineation: Implications for future storm surge forecasts and warnings. *Natural Hazards*, **54**(2), 519–36.

Memmott, P. & Long, S., 2005. Between places: Mobility in Aboriginal Australia. *Three60*, **4**, 25–9.

Mendelsohn, R., 2000. Efficient adaptation to climate change. *Climatic Change*, **45**(3), 583–600.

Mendelsohn, R., Basist, A., Kurukulasuriya, P., & Dinar, A., 2007. Climate and rural income. *Climatic Change*, **81**(1), 101–18.

Merli, M. G., 1998. Underreporting of births and infant deaths in rural China: Evidence from field research in one county of northern China. *The China Quarterly*, **155**, 637–55.

Mertz, O., Mbow, C., Reenberg, A., & Diouf, A., 2009. Farmers' perceptions of climate change and agricultural adaptation strategies in rural Sahel. *Environmental Management*, **43**(3), 804–16.

Metropolitan Water District of Southern California, 2012. *Annual Report 2012*, Los Angeles. Available at: http://www.mwdh2o.com/mwdh2o/pages/about/AR/AR12.html.

Meyer, W. B., 2000. *Americans and Their Weather*. New York: Oxford University Press.

Meze-Hausken, E., 2000. Migration caused by climate change: How vulnerable are people in dryland areas? *Mitigation and Adaptation Strategies for Global Change*, **5**(4), 379–406.

Michalowski, I., 2010. Immigration to France: The challenge of immigrant integration. In Segal, U.A. Elliott, D. Mayadas, N.S. eds. *Immigration Worldwide: Policies, Practices and Trends*. Oxford: Oxford University Press, 79–94.

Micklin, P., 2007. The Aral Sea disaster. *Annual Review of Earth and Planetary Sciences*, **35**, 47–72.

Millennium Ecosystem Assessment, 2005. *Ecosystems and Human Well-being: Synthesis*, Washington, DC: Island Press.

Milliman, J. D., Broadus, J. M., & Gable, F., 1989. Environmental and economic implications of rising sea level and subsiding deltas: The Nile and Bengal examples. *Ambio*, **18**(6), 340–5.

Milne, G. A., Gehrels, W. R., Hughes, C. W., & Tamisiea, M. E., 2009. Identifying the causes of sea-level change. *Nature Geoscience*, **2**, 471–8.

Milne, W. J., 1993. Macroeconomic influences on migration. *Regional Studies*, **27**(4), 365–73.

Mitchell, D., 1996. *The Lie of the Land: Migrant workers and the California landscape*. Minneapolis: University of Minnesota Press.

Mitchell, J. K., 2003. European river floods in a changing world. *Risk Analysis*, **23**(3), 567–74.

Mohan, G. & Mohan, J., 2002. Placing social capital. *Progress in Human Geography*, **26**(2), 191–210.

Moore, A. N. & Sanders, J. T., 1930. Credit problems of Oklahoma cotton farmers, with special reference to Garvin, Jackson, and Pittsburg counties. Stillwater: Oklahoma Agricultural Experiment Station

Morgan, K. M., 2007. Here comes the mail order bride: Three methods of regulation in the United States, the Philippines and Russia. *George Washington International Law Review*, **39**(2), 423–48.

Morin, J., Block, P., Rajagopalan, B., & Clark, M., 2008. Identification of large scale climate patterns affecting show variability in the eastern United States. *International Journal of Climatology*, **28**(3), 315–28.

Morris, S. S., Neidecker-Gonzales, O., Carletto, C., Munguia, M., Medina, J. M., & Wodon, Q., 2002. Hurricane Mitch and the livelihoods of the rural poor in Honduras. *World Development*, **30**(1), 49–60.

Morris, S. S. & Wodon, Q., 2003. The allocation of natural disaster relief funds: Hurricane Mitch in Honduras. *World Development*, **31**(7), 1279–89.

Morrow, B. H., 1999. Identifying and mapping community vulnerability. *Disasters*, **23**(1), 1–18.

Mortimore, M. J., 1989. *The Causes, Nature and Rate of Soil Degradation in the Northernmost States of Nigeria and an Assessment of the Role of Fertilizer in Counteracting the Process of Degradation*, Washington, DC: Environment Department Working Paper No. 17, World Bank.

Mortimore, M. J. & Adams, W. M., 2001. Farmer adaptation, change and 'crisis' in the Sahel. *Global Environmental Change*, **11**(1), 49–57.

Morton, J. F., 2007. The impact of climate change on smallholder and subsistence agriculture. *Proceedings of the National Academy of Sciences*, **104**(50), 19680–5.

Mortreux, C. & Barnett, J., 2009. Climate change, migration and adaptation in Funafuti, Tuvalu. *Global Environmental Change*, **19**(1), 105–12.

Mosse, D., Gupta, S., Mehta, M., Shah, V., & Rees, J., 2002. Brokered livelihoods: Debt, labour migration and development in tribal western India. *Journal of Development Studies*, **38**(5), 59–88.

Motsholapheko, M. R., Kgathi, D. L., & Vanderpost, C., 2011. Rural livelihoods and household adaptation to extreme flooding in the Okavango Delta, Botswana. *Physics and Chemistry of the Earth*, **36**(14–15), 984–95.

Munday, P. L., 2004. Habitat loss, resource specialization, and extinction on coral reefs. *Global Change Biology*, **10**(10), 1642–7.

Murphy, A. & Strobl, E., 2009. *The Impact of Hurricanes on Housing Prices: Evidence from US Coastal Cities*, Munich. Available at: http://mpra.ub.uni-muenchen.de/19360/3/MPRA_paper_19360.pdf.

Murrugarra, E. & Herrera, C., 2011. Migration choices, inequality of opportunities and poverty reduction in Nicaragua. In E. Murrugarra, J. Larrison, & M. Sasin, eds. *Migration and Poverty: Towards better opportunities for the poor.* Washington, DC: International Bank for Reconstruction and Development, 101–24.

Mushkat, R., 1987. The international legal status of Hong Kong under post-transitional rule. *Houston Journal of International Law*, **10**(1), 1–24.

Mustafa, D., 2002. Linking access and vulnerability: Perceptions of irrigation and flood management in Pakistan. *Professional Geographer*, **54**(1), 94–105.

Myers, N., 1993. Environmental refugees in a globally warmed world. *BioScience*, **43**(11), 752–61.

Myers, N., 2002. Environmental refugees: A growing phenomenon of the 21st century. *Philosophical Transactions of the Royal Society London: Biological sciences: Series B*, **357**(1420), 609–13.

Myers, S. M., 2000. The impact of religious involvement in migration. *Social Forces* **79**(2), 755–83.

Nagarajan, R., 2009. *Drought Assessment*. Dordrecht: Springer.

Nalbantis, I. & Tsakiris, G., 2009. Assessment of hydrological drought revisited. *Water Resources Management*, **23**, 881–97.

National Research Council, 2011. *National Security Implications of Climate Change for U.S. Naval Forces*, Washington, DC: National Academies of Science. Available at: http://image.guardian.co.uk/sys-files/Environment/documents/2011/03/10/PrepubAllClimateChange110218.pdf.

Nawrotzki, R. J., Riosmena, F., & Hunter, L. M., 2012. Do rainfall deficits predict U.S.-bound migration from rural Mexico? Evidence from the Mexican census. *Population Research and Policy Review*. DOI: 10.1007/s11113–012–9251–8.

Nee, V. & Sanders, J., 2001. Understanding the diversity of migrant incorporation: A forms-of-capital approach. *Ethnic and Racial Studies*, **24**(3), 386–411.

Neena, J. M., Suhas, E., & Goswami, B. N., 2011. Leading role of internal dynamics in the 2009 Indian summer monsoon drought. *Journal of Geophysical Research – Atmospheres*, **116**(D13103).

Nelson, D. R. & Finan, T. J., 2009. Praying for drought: Persistent vulnerability and the politics of patronage in Ceara, northeast Brazil. *American Anthropologist*, **111**(3), 302–16.

Neto, F. & Mullet, E., 1998. Decision-making as regards migration: Wage differential, job opportunity, and the network effect. *Acta Psychologica* **98**(1), 57–66.

Neumann, C. J., 1993. *Tropical cyclones of the North Atlantic Ocean, 1871–1977*, Washington, DC: National Oceanic and Atmospheric Administration.

Neumann, R. P., 2005. *Making Political Ecology* A. B. Murphy, ed., London: Hodder Arnold.

Neumayer, E., 2006. Unequal access to foreign spaces: How states use visa restrictions to regulate mobility in a globalized world. *Transactions of the Institute of British Geographers*, **31**(1), 72–84.

Ng, W.-S. & Mendelsohn, R., 2005. The impact of sea level rise on Singapore. *Environment and Development Economics*, **10**(2), 201–15.

Nguyen, H. N., 2007. *Flooding in Mekong River Delta, Viet Nam*, UNDP Human Development Report 2007/2008 Occasional Paper. Available at: http://78.136.31.142/fr/rapports/mondial/rdh2007–8/documents/Nguyen_HuuNinh.pdf.

Nicholls, R. J., 2004. Coastal flooding and wetland loss in the 21st century: Changes under the SRES climate and socio-economic scenarios. *Global Environmental Change*, **14**, 69–86.

Nicholls, R. J., 2011. Planning for the impacts of sea level rise. *Oceanography*, **24**(2), 144–57.

Nicholls, R. J. & Cazenave, A., 2010. Sea-level rise and its impact on coastal zones. *Science*, **328**(5985), 1517–20.

Nicholls, R. J., Marinova, N., Lowe, J. A., Brown, S., Vellinga, P., de Gusmão, D., Hinkel, J., & Tol, R. J., 2011. Sea-level rise and its possible impacts given a 'beyond 4°C world' in the twenty-first century. *Philosophical Transactions of the Royal Society A – Mathematical and Engineering Sciences*, **369**(1934), 161–81.

Nigg, J. M., Barnshaw, J., & Torres, M. R., 2006. Hurricane Katrina and the flooding of New Orleans: Emergent issues in sheltering and temporary housing. *Annals of the American Academy of Political and Social Science*, **604**(1), 113–28.

Niven, R. J. & Bardsley, D. K., 2012. Planned retreat as a management response to coastal risk: A case study from the Fleurieu Peninsula, South Australia. *Regional Environmental Change*.

Nkedianye, D., Leeuw, J. de, Ogutu, J. O., Said, M. Y., Saidimu, T. L., Kifugo, S. C., Kaelo, D. S., & Reid, R.S., 2011. Mobility and livestock mortality in communally used pastoral areas: The impact of the 2005–2006 drought on livestock mortality in Maasailand. *Pastoralism*, **1**(1), 1–17.

Nyong, A., Fiki, C., & McLeman, R., 2006. Drought-related conflicts, management and resolution in the West African Sahel: Considerations for climate change research. *Die Erde*, **137**(3), 223–48.

O'Brien, K. L., Leichenko, R., Kelkar, U., Venema, H., Aandahl, G., Tompkins, H., Javed, A., Bhadwal, S., Barg, S., Nygaard, L., & West, J., 2004. Mapping vulnerability to multiple stressors: climate change and globalization in India. *Global Environmental Change*, **14**, 303–13.

O'Brien, T., 2012. Food riots as representations of insecurity: Examining the relationship between contentious politics and human security. *Conflict, Security & Development*, **12**(1), 31–49.

Ohl, C. A., 2000. Flooding and human health. *BMJ*, **321**, 1167.

Omotola, J. S., 2009. 'Liberation movements' and rising violence in the Niger Delta: The new contentious site of oil and environmental politics. *Studies in Conflict & Terrorism*, **33**(1), 36–54.

Ong, A., 2006. *Neoliberalism as Exception: Mutations in citizenship and sovereignty*, Durham, NC: Duke University Press.

Opperman, J. J., Galloway, G. E., Fargione, J., Mount, J. F., Richter, B. D., & Secchi, S., 2009. Sustainable floodplains: Through large-scale reconnection to rivers. *Science*, **326**(5959), 1487–8.

Orlove, B., 2005. Human adaptation to climate change: A review of three historical cases and some general perspectives. *Environmental Science Policy*, **8**(6), 589–600.

Otsuka, K., Cordova, V. G., & David, C. C., 1990. Modern rice technology and regional wage differentials in the Philippines. *Agricultural Economics*, **4**(3–4), 297–314.

Oulahen, G. & Doberstein, B., 2012. Citizen participation in post-disaster flood hazard mitigation planning in Peterborough, Ontario, Canada. *Risk, Hazards & Crisis in Public Policy*, **3**(1), Article 4.

Owusu, V., Abdulai, A., & Abdul-Rahman, S., 2011. Non-farm work and food security among farm households in northern Ghana. *Food Policy*, **36**(2), 108–18.

Palloni, A., Massey, D. J., Ceballos, M., Espinosa, K., & Spittel, M., 2001. Social capital and international migration: A test using information on family networks. *American Journal of Sociology*, **106**(5), 1262–98.

Palmary, I., Burman, E., Chantler, K., & Kiguwa, P., 2010. *Gender and Migration: Feminist interventions*, London: Zed Books.

Pandey, S. & Bhandari, H., 2007. Drought: An overview. In S. Pandey, H. Bhandari, & B. Hardy, eds. *Economic Costs of Drought and Rice Farmers' Coping Mechanisms*. Manila: International Rice Research Institute, 11–30.

Pandolfi, J. M., Connolly, S. R., Marshall, D. J., & Cohen, A. L., 2011. Projecting coral reef futures under global warming and ocean acidification. *Science*, **333**(6041), 418–22.

Paris, T. R., Chi, T. T. N., Rola-Rubzen, M. F., & Luis, J. S., 2009. *Labour out migration on rice farming households and gender roles: Synthesis of findings in Thailand, the Philippines and Vietnam*, Rome: UN Food and Agricultural Organization. Available at: http://www.fao-ilo.org/fileadmin/user_upload/fao_ilo/pdf/Papers/16_march/Paris__Thelma_final_.pdf.

Paskal, C., 2010. *Global Warring: How environmental, economic and political crises will redraw the world map*. Toronto: Key Porter.

Passel, J., 2007. *Unauthorized migrants in the United States: Estimates, methods and characteristics. OECD Social, Employment and Migration Working Papers No. 57*, Paris. Available at: http://www.oecd.org/dataoecd/41/25/39264671.pdf.

Passel, J. & Cohn, D., 2011. *Unauthorized Immigrant Population: National and State Trends, 2010*, Washington, DC: Pew Hispanic Center. Available at: http://www.pewhispanic.org/files/reports/133.pdf.

Passel, J., Cohn, D., & Gonzalez-Barrera, A., 2012. *Net Migration from Mexico Falls to Zero – and Perhaps Less*, Washington, DC: Pew Hispanic Center. Available at: http://www.pewhispanic.org/files/2012/04/Mexican-migrants-report_final.pdf.

Pattanaik, D. R. & Rajeevan, M., 2010. Variability of extreme rainfall events over India during southwest monsoon season. *Meteorological Applications*, **17**, 88–104.

Paul, B. K., 1998. Coping with the 1996 tornado in Tangali, Bangladesh: An analysis of field data. *The Professional Geographer*, **50**(3), 287–301.

Paul, B. K., 2005. Evidence against disaster-induced migration: The 2004 tornado in north central Bangladesh. *Disasters*, **29**(4), 370–85.

Paul, B. K., 2009. Why relatively fewer people died? The case of Bangladesh's Cyclone Sidr. *Natural Hazards*, **50**(2), 289–304.

Paul, S. K. & Routray, J. K., 2010. Flood proneness and coping strategies: The experiences of two villages in Bangladesh. *Disasters*, **34**(2), 489–508.

Paxson, C. & Rouse, C. E., 2008. Returning to New Orleans after Hurricane Katrina. *American Economic Review*, **98**(2), 38–42.

Pedersen, J., 1995. Drought, migration and population growth in the Sahel: The case of the Malian Gorma: 1900–1991. *Population Studies*, **49**(1), 111–26.

Peet, R., 1985. The social origins of environmental determinism. *Annals of the Association of American Geographers*, **75**(3), 309–33.

Pelling, M., 1999. The political ecology of floodhazard in urban Guyana. *Geoforum*, **30**(3), 249–61.

Pelling, M. & High, C., 2005. Understanding adaptation: What can social capital offer assessments of adaptive capacity? *Global Environmental Change*, **15**(4), 308–19.

Penning-Rowsell, E. C., Sultana, P., & Thompson, P. M., 2013. The 'last resort'? Population movement in response to climate-related hazards in Bangladesh. *Environmental Science & Policy*, **27**(S1), S44–S59.

People's Daily Online, 2002. 1.8 Million people relocated to make way for floods. Beijing, 20 February 2002. Available at: http://english.people.com.cn/200202/20/eng20020220_90668.shtml.

Perch-Nielsen, S., Bättig, M., & Imboden, D., 2008. Exploring the link between climate change and migration. *Climatic Change*, **91**(3–4), 375–93.

Percival, V. & Homer-Dixon, T., 1996. Environmental scarcity and violent conflict: The case of Rwanda. *The Journal of Environment & Development*, **5**(3), 270–91.

Perreault, S., 2009. *The incarceration of Aboriginal people in adult correctional services*, Ottawa, Statistics Canada. Available at: http://www.statcan.gc.ca/pub/85–002-x/2009003/article/10903-eng.htm.

Persoons, E., Vanclooster, M., & Desmed, A., 2002. Flood hazard causes and flood protection recommendations for Belgian river basins. *Water International*, **27**(2), 202–7.

Peterka-Benton, D., 2011. Human smuggling in Austria: A comparative analysis of data on smuggled migrants from former Yugoslavia and the Russian Federation. *International Migration Review*, **45**(2), 215–42.

Peterson, G., 2009. Ecological limits to adaptation to climate change. In W. N. Adger, I. Lorenzoni, & K. L. O'Brien, eds. *Adapting to Climate Change: Thresholds, values, governance*. Cambridge: Cambridge University Press, 25–41.

Pettit, B. & Western, B., 2004. Mass imprisonment and the life course: Race and class inequality in U.S. incarceration. *American Sociological Review*, **69**(2), 151–69.

Pejic, J., 1998. Citizenship and statelessness in the former Yugoslavia: The legal framework. In S. O'Leary & T. Tiilikainen, eds. *Citizenship and Nationality Status in the New Europe*. London: Institute for Public Policy Research, 169–86.

Pielke, R. A., Gratz, J., Landsea, C. W., Collins, D., Saunders, M. A., & Musulin, R., 2008. Normalized hurricane damage in the United States: 1900–2005. *Natural Hazards Review*, **9**(1), 29–43.

Pielke, R. A., Rubiera, J., Landsea, C., Fernandez, M. L., & Klein, R., 2003. Hurricane vulnerability in Latin America and the Caribbean: Normalized damage and loss potentials. *Natural Hazards Review*, **4**, 101–15.

Pinstrup-Andersen, P., 2009. Food security: Definition and measurement. *Food Security*, **1**, 5–7.

Piore, M., 1979. *Birds of Passage: Migrant labor in industrial societies*. Cambridge: Cambridge University Press.

Pistrika, A. K. & Jonkman, S. N., 2009. Damage to residential buildings due to flooding of New Orleans after Hurricane Katrina. *Natural Hazards*, **54**(2), 413–34.

Pittock, J. & Xu, M., no date. *Controlling Yangtze River Floods: A New Approach*, Washington DC, World Resources Report. Available at: http://www.worldresourcesreport.org/files/wrr/wrr_case_study_controlling_yangtze_river_floods.pdf.

Plane, D. A., 1992. Age-composition change and the geographical dynamics of interregional migration in the US. *Annals of the Association of American Geographers*, **82**, 64–85.

Plane, D. A., 1993. Demographic influences on migration. *Regional Studies*, **27**(4), 375–83.

Plane, D. A., Henrie, C. J., & Perry, M. J., 2005. Migration up and down the urban hierarchy and across the life course. *Proceedings of the National Academy of Science*, **102**(43), 15313–18.

Plume, K., 2012. Iran buys U.S. wheat again, trade set to grow. *Reuters*, 15 March 2012. Available at: http://www.reuters.com/article/2012/03/15/us-usa-wheat-iran-idUSBRE82E15U20120315.

Plyer, A., 2011. *Homeownership, Household Makeup, and Latino and Vietnamese Population Growth in the New Orleans Metro*, New Orleans, Greater New Orleans Community

Data Center. Available at: https://gnocdc.s3.amazonaws.com/reports/GNOCDC_HomeownershipHouseholdMakeupAndLatinoAndVietnamesePopulationGrowth.pdf.

Poesen, J. W. A. & Hooke, J. M., 1997. Erosion, flooding and channel management in Mediterranean environments of southern Europe. *Progress in Physical Geography*, **21**(2), 157–99.

Porter, G., Hampshire, K., Abane, A., Tanle, A., Esia-Donkoh, K., Amoako-Sakyi, RO Agblorti, S., & Owusu, S., 2011. Mobility, education and livelihood trajectories for young people in rural Ghana: A gender perspective. *Childrens Geographies*, **9**(3–4), 395–410.

Portes, A., 2010. Migration and social change: Some conceptual reflections. *Journal of Ethnic and Migration Studies*, **36**(10), 1537–63.

Portes, A. & Landolt, P., 2000. Social capital: Promise and pitfalls of its role in development. *Journal of Latin American Studies*, **32**(2), 529–47.

Postel, S. L., 2000. Entering an era of water scarcity: The challenges ahead. *Ecological Applications*, **10**(4), 941–8.

Potts, D., 2005. Counter-urbanisation on the Zambian Copperbelt? Interpretations and Implications. *Urban Studies*, **42**(4), 583–609.

Powell, P. T., 1998. Traditional production, communal land tenure, and policies for environmental preservation in the South Pacific. *Ecological Economics*, **24**(1), 89–101.

Prabhakar, S. & Shaw, R., 2008. Climate change adaptation implications for drought risk mitigation: A perspective for India. *Climatic Change*, **88**(2), 113–30.

Prasad, N. P. & Rao, P. V., 1997. Adaptations of peasants in a stress environment. *Economic and Political Weekly*, **32**(5), 228–34.

Prevatt, D. O., Dupigny-Giroux, L.-A., & Masters, F. J., 2010. Engineering perspectives on reducing hurricane damage to housing in CARICOM Caribbean Islands. *Natural Hazards Review*, **11**(4), 140–51.

Prowse, T. D., Furgal, C., Bonsai, B. R., & Edwards, T. W. D., 2009. Climatic conditions in northern Canada: Past and future. *Ambio*, **38**, 257–65.

Pryce, G. & Chen, Y., 2011. Flood risk and the consequences for housing of a changing climate: An international perspective. *Risk Management*, **13**(4), 228–46.

Putnam, R., 2000. *Bowling Alone: The collapse and revival of American community*. New York: Simon and Schuster.

Quaye, W., 2008. Food security situation in northern Ghana, coping strategies and related constraints. *African Journal of Agricultural Research*, **3**(5), 334–42.

Quddus, M. & Becker, C., 2000. Speculative price bubbles in the rice market and the 1974 Bangladesh famine. *Journal of Economic Development*, **25**(2), 155–75.

Quiring, S. M. & Papakryiakou, T. N., 2003. An evaluation of agricultural drought indices for the Canadian prairies. *Agricultural and Forest Meteorology*, **118**(1–2), 49–62.

Quirk, J. F., 2006. The Anti-Slavery Project: Linking the historical and contemporary. *Human Rights Quarterly*, **28**(3), 565–98.

Rabby, T. G., Alam, Gazi Mahabubul Fredericks, L. J., Nair, S., Nurul Azam, M., & Al-Amin, A. Q., 2011. What offers solution to the poverty reduction of the Haor people in Bangladesh? Seasonal migration or a new inshore economic livelihood policy. *African Journal of Business Management*, **5**(23), 9979–91.

Rafique, A., 2003. Floods, poverty and seasonal migration. *Economic and Political Weekly*, **38**(10), 943–5.

Rahmstorf, S., Foster, G., & Cazenave, A., 2012. Comparing climate projections to observations up to 2011. *Environmental Research Letters*, **7**(4), 044035.

Rain, D., 1999. *Eaters of the Dry Season: Circular labor migration in the West African Sahel*, Boulder, CO: Westview Press.

Rajan, R. & Ramcharan, R., 2012. *The Anatomy of a Credit Crisis: The Boom and Bust in Farm Land Prices in the United States in the 1920s*, Cambridge, MA: National

Bureau of Economic Research Working Paper No. 18027. Available at: http://faculty.chicagobooth.edu/raghuram.rajan/research/papers/land_sales_5.pdf.

Rao, K. P. C., 2008. Changes in dry land agriculture in the semi-arid tropics of India, 1975–2004. *European Journal of Development Research*, **20**(4), 562–78.

Rashid, S. F., 2000. The urban poor in Dhaka City: Their struggles and coping strategies during the floods of 1998. *Disasters*, **24**(3), 240–53.

Rass, N., 2011. Livestock markets and drought in sub-Saharan Africa: Markets and livelihoods. In J. Gertel & R. Le Heron, eds. *Economic Spaces of Pastoral Production and Commodity Systems*. Surrey, UK: Ashgate, 249–64.

Ravenstein, E. G., 1889. The laws of migration (Second Paper). *Journal of the Royal Statistical Society*, **52**(2), 241–305.

Reilly, J. & Schimmelpfennig, D., 2000. Irreversibility, uncertainty and learning: Portraits of adaptation to long-term climate change. *Climatic Change*, **45**(1), 253–78.

Rendall, M. S., 2011. Breakup of New Orleans households after Hurricane Katrina. *Journal of Marriage and Family*, **73**(3), 654–68.

Resurreccion, B. P., 2009. Gender trends in migration and employment in Southeast Asia. In T. W. Devasahayam, ed. *Gender Trends in Southeast Asia: Women now, women in the future*. Singapore: ISEAS Publishing, 31–52.

Reuveny, R., 2008. Ecomigration and violent conflict: Case studies and public policy implications. *Human Ecology*, **36**(1), 1–13.

Riccio, B., 2001. From 'ethnic group' to 'transnational community'? Senegalese migrants' ambivalent experiences and multiple trajectories. *Journal of Ethnic and Migration Studies*, **27**(4), 583–99.

Riddle, L. A. & Buckley, C., 1998. Forced migration and destination choice: Armenian forced settlers and refugees in the Russian Federation. *International Migration*, **36**(2), 235–55.

Riebsame, W., 1986. The Dust Bowl historical image, psychological anchor, and ecological taboo. *Great Plains Quarterly*, **1**(1), 126–36.

Riney-Kehrberg, P., 1989. In God we trusted, in Kansas we busted … again. *Agricultural History*, **63**(2), 187–201.

Robbins, P., 1998. Nomadization in Rajasthan, India: Migration, institutions, and economy. *Human Ecology*, **26**(1), 87–112.

Robertson, G. W., 1974. Wheat yields for 50 years at Swift Current, Saskatchewan in relation to weather. *Canadian Journal of Plant Science*, **54**, 625–50.

Robinson, D. & Cruikshank, K., 2006. Hurricane Hazel: Disaster relief, politics, and society in Canada, 1954–55. *Journal of Canadian Studies*, **40**(1), 37–70.

Robinson, P. J., 2001. On the definition of a heat wave. *Journal of Applied Meteorology*, **40**(762–75).

Robinson, P. J., 2005. Ice and snow in paintings of Little Ice Age winters. *Weather*, **60**(2), 37–41.

Rogaly, B., Biswas, J., Coppard, D., Rafique, A., Rana, K., & Sengupta, A., 2001. Seasonal migration, social change and migrants' rights: Lessons from West Bengal. *Economic and Political Weekly*, **36**(49), 4547–59.

Rogaly, B., Coppard, D., Safique, A., Rana, K., Sengupta, A., & Biswas, J., 2002. Seasonal migration and welfare/illfare in eastern India: A social analysis. *Journal of Development Studies*, **38**(5), 89–114.

Rosegrant, S., 2007. *Wal-Mart's Response to Hurricane Katrina: Striving for a public-private partnership*, Cambridge, MA: Kennedy School of Government Case Program C16–07–1876.0, Case Studies in Public Policy and Management.

Rosenfeld, D. & Bell, T. L., 2011. Why do tornadoes and hailstorms rest on weekends? *Journal of Geographical Research*, **116**(D20211).

Rowell, E. J., 1936. Drought refugee and labor migration to California in 1936. *Monthly Labor Review*, **43**(6), 1355–63.

Ruane, A. C., Major, D. C., Yu, W. H., Mozaharul Alam, H., Sk. Ghulam Hussain, G., Khan, A. S., Hassan, A., Hossain, B., Goldberg, R., Horton, R. M., & Rosenzweig, C., 2013. Multi-factor impact analysis of agricultural production in Bangladesh with climate change. *Global Environmental Change*, **23**(1), 338–350.

Ruf, U. P., 1999. *Ending Slavery: Hierarchy, dependency and slavery in central Mauritania*, New Brunswick, NJ: Transaction Publishers.

Saleska, S. R., Didan, K., Huete, A. R., & Da Rocha, H. R., 2007. Amazon forests green-up during 2005 drought. *Science*, (**318**), 612.

Salt, J., 1997. Migration as a business: The case of trafficking. *International Migration*, **35**(4), 467–94.

Samers, M., 2010. *Migration*. London: Routledge.

Samra, J. S., 2004. *Review and analysis of drought monitoring, declaration and management in India*, Colombo, Sri Lanka: International Water Management Institute Working Paper No. 84.

Sanderson, D., 2000. Cities, disasters and livelihoods. *Environment and Urbanization*, **12**, 93–102.

Sassen, S., 2001. *The Global City (2nd)*, Princeton, NJ: Princeton University Press.

Sastry, N., 2009. Displaced New Orleans residents in the aftermath of Hurricane Katrina: Results from a pilot survey. *Organization and Environment*, **22**(4), 395–409.

Sauchyn, D. J., Stroich, J., & Beriault, A., 2003. A paleoclimatic context for the drought of 1999–2001 in the northern Great Plains of North America. *The Geographical Journal*, **169**(2), 158–67.

Scanlon, B. R., Faunt, C. C., Longuevergne, L., Reedy, R. C., Alley, W. M., McGuire, V. L., & McMahon, P. B., 2012. Groundwater depletion and sustainability of irrigation in the US High Plains and Central Valley. *Proceedings of the National Academy of Science*, **109**(24), 9320–5.

Schewe, J., Levermann, A., & Meinshausen, M., 2011. Climate change under a scenario near 1.5 C of global warming: monsoon intensification, ocean warming and steric sea level rise. *Earth System Dynamics*, **2**, 25–35.

Schindler, D. W. & Donahue, W. F., 2006. An impending water crisis in Canada's western prairie provinces. *Proceedings of the National Academy of Sciences*, **103**(19), 7210–16.

Schmalzbauer, L., 2004. Searching for wages and mothering from afar: The case of Honduran transnational families. *Journal of Marriage and Family*, **66**(5), 1317–31.

Schmidhuber, J. & Tubiello, F., 2007. Global food security under climate change. *Proceedings of the National Academy of Sciences*, **104**(50), 19703–8.

Schmidlin, T. W., Hammer, B. O., Ono, Y., & King, P. S., 2009. Tornado shelter-seeking behavior and tornado shelter options among mobile home residents in the United States. *Natural Hazards*, **48**(2), 191–201.

Schmidlin, T. W. & King, P. S., 1995. Risk factors for death in the 27 March 1994 Georgia and Alabama Tornadoes. *Disasters*, **19**(2), 170–7.

Schneider, S. K., 2005. Administrative breakdowns in the governmental response to Hurricane Katrina. *Public Administration Review*, **65**(5), 515–16.

Schneider, S., 2009. *Science as a Contact Sport: Inside the battle to save Earth's climate*. Washington, DC: National Geographic Society.

Schubert, S. D., Suarez, M. J., Pegion, P. J., Koster, R. D., & Bacmeister, J. T., 2004. On the cause of the 1930s Dust Bowl. *Science*, **303**(5665), 1855–9.

Schultz, B., 2001. Irrigation, drainage and flood protection in a rapidly changing world. *Irrigation and Drainage*, **50**(4), 261–77.

Schwabach, A., 2004. Ecocide and genocide in Iraq: International law, the Marsh Arabs, and environmental damage in non-international conflicts. *Colorado Journal of International Environmental Law and Policy*, **15**(1), 1–28.

Schwartz, B. S., Harris, J. B., Khan, A. I., Larocque, R. C., Sack, D. A., Malek, M. A., Faruque, A. S. G., Qadri, F., Calderwood, S. B., Luby, S. P., & Ryan, E. T., 2006. Diarrheal epidemics in Dhaka, Bangladesh, during three consecutive floods: 1988, 1998, and 2004. *American Journal of Tropical Medicine and Hygeine*, **74**(6), 1067–73.

Schwartz, P. & Randall, D., 2003. *An Abrupt Climate Change Scenario and Its Implications for United States National Security*. Emeryville, CA: Global Business Network.

Schwartz, R. M. & Schmidlin, T. W., 2002. Climatology of blizzards in the conterminous United States, 1959–2000. *Journal of Climate*, **15**, 1765–72.

Schwierz, C., Köllner-Heck, P., Mutter, E. Z., Bresch, D. N., Vidale, P.-L., Wild, M., & Schär, C., 2010. Modelling European winter wind storm losses in current and future climate. *Climatic Change*, **101**(3–4), 485–514.

Schwieterman, J. P., 2004. *When the Railroad Leaves Town: American Communities in the Age of Rail Line Abandonment*, Kirksville, MO: Truman State University Press.

Scudder, T., 2012. Resettlement outcomes of large dams. In C. Tortajada, D. Altinbilek, & A. K. Biswas, eds. *Impacts of Large Dams: A global assessment*. Berlin: Springer, 37–67.

Secretariat of the Pacific Community, 2011. *Pacific Islands' Population Tops 10 Million*, Noumea, New Caledonia. Available at: http://www.spc.int/sdp/index. php?option=com_content&view=article&id=74:pacific-islands-population-tops-10-million&catid=1&lang=en.

Segal, U. A., Mayadas, N. S., & Elliott, D., 2010. The immigration process. In U. A. Segal, D. Elliott, & N. S. Mayadas, eds. *Immigration Worldwide: Policies, Practices and Trends*. Oxford: Oxford University Press, 3–16.

Sellars, N. A., 2002. Treasonous tenant farmers and seditious sharecroppers: The 1917 Green Corn Rebellion Trials. *Oklahoma City University Law Review*, **27**, 1097–141.

Selman, P., 2011. Intercountry adoption after the Haiti earthquake Rescue or robbery? *Adoption & Fostering Journal*, **35**(4), 41–9.

Selth, A., 2008. Even paranoids have enemies: Cyclone Nargis and Myanmar's fears of invasion. *Contemporary Southeast Asia*, **30**(3), 379–402.

Selveraju, R., Subbiah, A. R., Baas, S., & Juergens, I., 2006. *Livelihood adaptation to climate variability and change in drought-prone areas of Bangladesh*, Rome. Available at: http://gcca.eu/usr/documents/Livelihood-Adaptation-and-Change-in-Bangladesh_201091418158.pdf.

Semple, E. C., 1911. *Influences of Geographic Environment on the Basis of Ratzel's System of Anthropo-geography*, New York: Henry Holt and Company.

Sen, A., 1977. Starvation and exchange entitlements: A general approach and its application to the great Bengal famine. *Cambridge Journal of Economics*, **1**(1), 33–59.

Sen, A., 1981. Ingredients of famine analysis: Availability and entitlements. *The Quarterly Journal of Economics*, **96**(3), 433–64.

Sen, A., 1999. *Development as Freedom*, Oxford: Oxford University Press.

Seo, K. & Rodriguez, N., 2012. Land grab, food security and climate change: A vicious circle in the Global South. In N. Chhetri, ed. *Human and Social Dimensions of Climate Change*. Open Access: InTech, 165–80.

Serageldin, I., & Grootaert, C. (2000). Defining social capital: An integrating view. In P. Dasgupta & I. Serageldin, eds, *Social Capital: A multifaceted perspective*. Washington, DC: The World Bank, 40–58.

Seto, K. C., 2011. Exploring the dynamics of migration to mega-delta cities in Asia and Africa: Contemporary drivers and future scenarios. *Global Environmental Change*, **21**(S1), S94–S107.

Shachar, A. & Hirschl, R., 2007. Citizenship as inherited property. *Political Theory*, **35**(3), 253–87.

Shah, S. A., 2012. Gender and building homes in disaster in Sindh, Pakistan. *Gender and Development*, **20**(2), 249–64.

Shahid, S. & Hazarika, M. K., 2010. Groundwater drought in the northwestern districts of Bangladesh. *Water Resources Management*, **24**, 1989–2006.

Shank, M., 1938. The 1937 flood in southern Illinois. *Journal of Geography*, **37**(2), 45–55.

Shankman, D., Davis, L., & De Leeuw, J., 2009. River management, landuse change, and future flood risk in China's Poyang Lake region. *International Journal of River Basin Management*, **7**(4), 423–31.

Shaw, A. G., 1977. *Convicts and the Colonies: A study of penal transportation from Great Britain and Ireland to Australia and other parts of the British empire*, Melbourne: Melbourne University Press.

Shaw, J. M., 2003. Climate change and deforestation: Implications for the Maya collapse. *Ancient Mesoamerica*, **14**, 157–67.

Shepherd, A., Ivins, E. R., Geruo, A., Barletta, V. R., Bentley, M. J., Bettadpur, S., Briggs, K. H., Bromwich, D., Forsberg, R., Galin, N., Horwath, M., Jacobs, S., Joughin, I., King, M., Lenaerts, J., Li, J., Ligtenberg, S., Luckman, A., Luthcke, S., McMillan, M., Meister, R., Milne, G., Mouginot, J., Muir, A., Nicolas, J., Paden, J., Payne, A., Pritchard, H., Rignot, E., Rott, H., Sandberg Sørensen, L., Scambos, T., Scheuchl, B., Schrama, E., Smith, B., Sundal, A., van Angelen, J., van de Berg, W., van den Broeke, M., Vaughan, D., Velicogna, I., Wahr, J., Whitehouse, P., Wingham, D., Yi, D., Young, D., & Zwally, H., 2012. A reconciled estimate of ice-sheet mass balance. *Science*, **338**(6111), 1183–9.

Shiblak, A., 2006. Stateless Palestinians. *Forced Migration Review*, **26**, 8–9.

Shin, S.-I., Sardeshmukh, P. D., & Yeh, S.-W., 2011. Sensitivity of the northeast Asian summer monsoon to tropical sea surface temperatures. *Geophysical Research Letters*, **38**, L22702.

Showers, K. B., 2002. Water scarcity and urban Africa: An overview of urban-rural water linkages. *World Development*, **30**(4), 621–48.

Siddiqui, T., 2003. Migration as a livelihood strategy of the poor: The Bangladesh case. In *Regional Conference on Migration, Development and Pro-Poor Policy Choices in Asia*. Dhaka, 22–24 June 2003. Available at: http://www.eldis.org/vfile/upload/1/document/0903/Dhaka_CP_5.pdf.

Silva, F. R., Molina, J. R., González-Cabán, A., & Machuca, M., 2012. Economic vulnerability of timber resources to forest fires. *Journal of Environmental Management*, **100**, 16–21.

Siminovic, S. P. & Carson, R. W., 2003. Flooding in the Red River Basin – Lessons from post flood activities. *Natural Hazards*, **28**(2–3), 345–65.

Simmons, A., Diaz-Brigquets, S., & Laquian, A. A., 1977. *Social Change and Internal Migration, A Review of Research Findings from Africa, Asia and Latin America*, International Development Research Centre.

Simmons, K. M. & Sutter, D., 2011. *Economic and Societal Impacts of Tornadoes*. Boston, MA: American Meteorological Society.

Silvey, R., 2004. Power, difference and mobility: Feminist advances in migration studies. *Progress in Human Geography*, **28**, 490–506.

Sjaastad, L. A., 1962. The costs and returns of human migration. *The Journal of Political Economy*, **70**(5), 80–93.

Skeldon, R., 2003. The Chinese Diaspora or the migration of Chinese peoples? In L. J. C. Ma & C. Cartier, eds. *The Chinese Diaspora: Space, place, mobility, and identity*. Oxford: Rowman & Littlefield, 51–68.

Skinner, J., 2000. The eruption of Chances Peak, Montserrat, and the narrative of containment of risk. In P. Caplan, ed. *Risk Revisited*. London: Pluto Press, 156–83.

Skinner, J., 2002. British constructions with constitutions: The formal and informal nature of 'island' relations on Montserrat and Gibraltar. *Social Identities*, **8**(2), 301–20.

Skogstad, G. D., 1987. *The Politics of Agricultural Policy-Making in Canada*. Toronto: University of Toronto Press.

Skopcol, T. & Finegold, K., 1982. State capacity and economic intervention in the early New Deal. *Political Science Quarterly*, **97**(2), 255–78.

Slovic, P., Kunreuther, H., & White, G. F., 2000. Decision processes, rationality and adjustment to natural hazards. In P. Slovic, ed. *The Perception of Risk*. London: Earthscan, 1–31.

Smakhtin, V. U. & Hughes, D. A., 2007. Automated estimation and analyses of meteorological drought characteristics from monthly rainfall data. *Environmental Modelling & Software*, **22**(6), 880–90.

Small, I., Van der Meer, J., & Upshaw, R. E. G., 2001. Acting on an Environmental Health Disaster: The case of the Aral Sea. *Environmental Health Perspectives*, **109**(6), 547–9.

Smika, D. E., 1970. Summer fallow for dryland winter wheat in the semiarid Great Plains. *Agronomy Journal*, **62**(1), 15–17.

Smit, B., Burton, I., Klein, R. J. T., & Wandel, J., 2000. An anatomy of adaptation to climate change and variability. *Climatic Change*, **45**(1), 223–51.

Smit, B. & Cai, Y., 1996. Climate change and agriculture in China. *Global Environmental Change*, **6**(3), 205–14.

Smit, B., McNabb, D. & Smithers, J., 1996. Agricultural adaptation to climatic variation. *Climatic Change*, **33**(1), 7–29.

Smit, B. & Skinner, M., 2002. Adaptation options in agriculture to climate change: a typology. *Mitigation and Adaptation Strategies for Global Change*, **7**(1), 85–114.

Smit, B. & Wandel, J., 2006. Adaptation, adaptive capacity and vulnerability. *Global Environmental Change*, **16**(3), 282–92.

Smit, W., 1998. The rural linkages of urban households in Durban, South Africa. *Environment and Urbanization*, **10**(1), 77–87.

Smith, J. B., Dickinson, T., Donahue, J. D. B., Burton, I., Haites, E., Klein, R. J. T., & Patwardhan, A., 2011. Development and climate change adaptation funding: Coordination and integration. *Climate Policy*, **11**(3), 987–1000.

Smith, K. & Ward, R., 1998. *Floods: Physical processes and human impacts*, Chichester: John Wiley & Sons.

Smith, V. H. & Glauber, J. W., 2012. Agricultural insurance in developed countries: Where have we been and where are we going? *Applied Economic Perspectives and Policy*, 34(3), 363–390.

Smoyer-Tomic, K. E., Claver, J. D., Soskolne, C. L., & Spady, D. W., 2004. Health consequences of drought on the Canadian prairies. *Ecohealth*, **1**(2), 144–54.

Snow, D. A., Vliegenthart, R., & Corrigall-Brown, C., 2007. Framing the French Riots: A comparative study of frame variation. *Social Forces*, **86**(2), 385–415.

Sobel, R. S. & Leeson, P. T., 2006. Government's response to Hurricane Katrina: A public choice analysis. *Public Choice*, **127**, 55–73.

Solomon, S., Qin, D., Manning, M., Chen, Z., Marquis, M., Averyt, K. B., Tignor, M., & Miller, H. L., 2007. *IPCC Fourth Assessment Report: Climate Change 2007: The Physical Science Basis*, Cambridge: Cambridge University Press.

Somerville, W. & Cooper, B., 2010. Immigration to the United Kingdom. In Segal, U.A. Elliott, D. and Mayadas, N.S. eds. *Immigration Worldwide: Policies, practices and trends*. Oxford: Oxford University Press, 124–37.

Southern, J. H., 1939. Farm tenancy in Oklahoma. Stillwater: Oklahoma Agricultural Experiment Station. Report no. B-239.

Sovacool, B. K., 2012. Perceptions of climate change risks and resilient island planning in the Maldives. *Mitigation and Adaptation Strategies for Global Change*, **17**(7), 731–52.

Stal, M., 2011. Flooding and relocation: The Zambezi River Valley in Mozambique. *International Migration*, **49**(1), e125–e145.

Stark, O., 1991. *The Migration of Labour*. Cambridge: Basil Blackwell.

Statistics Canada, 1971. *Census of Canada*, Ottawa.

Statistics Canada, 2012. *2011 Census*. Available at: http://www12.statcan.gc.ca/census-recensement/index-eng.cfm.

Stecker, T., 2012. Drought-tolerant corn efforts show positive early results. *Scientific American*, 27 July. Available at: http://www.scientificamerican.com/article.cfm?id=drought-tolerant-corn-trials-show-positive-early-results.

Steel, T., 1975. *The Life and Death of St. Kilda*. Glasgow: Fontana/Collins.

Steinberg, T., 2000. *Acts of God: The unnatural history of natural disaster in America*. New York: Oxford University Press.

Steinbock, D. J., 1998. Interpreting the refugee definition. *UCLA Law Review*, **45**, 733.

Stern, N., 2007. *The Economics of Climate Change: The Stern Review*, Cambridge: Cambridge University Press.

Sternberg, T., 2012. Chinese drought, bread and the Arab Spring. *Applied Geography*, **34**, 519–24.

Stewart, M. G., Rosowsky, D. V., & Huang, Z., 2003. Hurricane risks and economic viability of strengthened construction. *Natural Hazards Review*, **4**(1), 12–19.

Stewart, R. M. & Rashid, H., 2011. Community strategies to improve flood risk communication in the Red River Basin, Manitoba, Canada. *Disasters*, **35**(3), 554–76.

Stilwell, B., Diallo, K., Zurn, P., Vujicic, M., Adams, O., & Dal Poz, M., 2004. Migration of health-care workers from developing countries: Strategic approaches to its management. *Bulletin of the World Health Organization*, **82**(8).

Stone, B. & Rodgers, M. O., 2001. Urban form and thermal efficiency: How the design of cities influences the urban heat island effect. *Journal of the American Planning Association*, **67**(2), 186–98.

Streets, D. G. & Glantz, M. H., 2000. Exploring the concept of climate surprise. *Global Environmental Change*, **10**(2), 97–107.

Stringer, L. C., Dyer, J. C., Reed, M. S., Dougill, A. J., Twyman, C., & Mkwambisi, D., 2009. Adaptations to climate change, drought and desertification: Local insights to enhance policy in southern Africa. *Environmental Science & Policy*, **12**(7), 748–65.

Strizzi, N. & Stranks, R. T., 1996. The security implications for China of environmental degradation. *Canadian Security Intelligence Service Commentary*, **47**.

Stunden Bower, S., 2010. Natural and unnatural complexities: Flood control along Manitoba's Assiniboine River. *Journal of Historical Geography*, **36**(1), 57–67.

Sunil, T. S., Rojas, V., & Bradley, D. E., 2007. United States' international retirement migration: The reasons for retiring to the environs of Lake Chapala, Mexico. *Ageing and Society*, **27**, 489–510.

Sutter, D. & Simmons, K., 2010. Tornado fatalities and mobile homes in the United States. *Natural Hazards*, **53**(1), 125–37.

Sylvester, K. M. & Rupley, E. S. A., 2012. Revising the Dust Bowl: High above the Kansas grasslands. *Environmental History*, **17**, 603–33.

Syvitski, J. P. M., Kettner, A. J., Overeem, I., Hutton, E. W. H., Hannon, M. T., Brakenridge, G. R., Day, J., Vörösmarty, C., Saito, Y., Giosan, L., & Nicholls, R. J., 2009. Sinking deltas due to human activities. *Nature Geoscience*, **2**, 681–6.

Tacoli, C., 2009. Crisis or adaptation? Migration and climate change in a context of high mobility. *Environment and Urbanization*, **21**(2), 513–25.

Taleb, N., 2007. *The Black Swan: The impact of the highly improbable*. New York: Random House.

Tan, Y., Bryan, B. & Hugo, G., 2005. Development, land-use change and rural resettlement capacity: A case study of the Three Gorges Project, China. *Australian Geographer*, **36**(2), 201–20.

Tan, Y. & Hugo, G., 2011. Demographic impacts of the Three Gorges Dam. In S. Brunn, ed. *Engineering Earth*. Dordrecht: Springer Netherlands, 1583–98.

Tan, Y., Hugo, G., & Potter, L., 2003. Government-organized distant resettlement and the Three Gorges Project, China. *Asia Pacific Population Journal*, **18**(3), 5–26.

Tan, Y. & Qian, W. Y., 2004. Environmental migration and sustainable development in the upper reaches of the Yangtze River. *Population and Environment*, **25**(6), 613–36.

Tan, Y. & Yao, F., 2006. Three Gorges Project: Effects of resettlement on the environment in the reservoir area and countermeasures. *Population and Environment*, **27**(4), 351–71.

Tariq, M. A. U. R. & Van de Giesen, N., 2011. Floods and flood management in Pakistan. *Physics and Chemistry of the Earth*. DOI: org/10.1016/j.pce.2011.08.014.

Taylor, P. S., 1938. Migratory agricultural workers on the Pacific Coast. American Sociological Review, **3**(2), 225–32.

Taylor, P. S. & Rowell, E. J., 1938. Refugee labor migration to California, 1937. *Monthly Labor Review*, **47**, 240.

Tegart, W. J. M., Sheldon, G. W., & Griffiths, D. C., 1990. *Climate Change: The IPCC Impacts Assessment*, Canberra: Australian Government Publishing Service.

Terry, J. P., 2007. *Tropical cyclones: Climatology and impacts in the South Pacific*. Dordrecht: Springer.

Terry, J. P. & Falkland, A. C., 2010. Responses of atoll freshwater lenses to storm-surge overwash in the Northern Cook Islands. *Hydrogeology Journal*, **18**(3), 749–59.

Tesfai, M. & De Graaff, J., 2000. Participatory rural appraisal of spate irrigation systems in eastern Eritrea. *Agriculture and Human Values*, **17**(4), 359–70.

Texier, P., 2008. Floods in Jakarta: When the extreme reveals daily structural constraints and mismanagement. *Disaster Prevention and Management*, **17**(3), 358–72.

Thomas, D. S. G. & Twyman, C., 2004. Equity and justice in climate change adaptation amongst natural-resource-dependent societies. *Global Environmental Change Part A*, **15**(2), 115–24.

Thomas, D., Twyman, C., Osbahr, H., & Hewitson, B., 2007. Adaptation to climate change and variability: farmer responses to intra-seasonal precipitation trends in South Africa. *Climatic Change*, **83**(3), 301–22.

Thomas, J. C. & Torrone, E., 2008. Incarceration as forced migration: Effects on selected community health outcomes. *American Journal of Public Health*, **98**(S1), S181–S184.

Thurow, T. L. & Taylor, C. A., 1999. The role of drought in range management. *Journal of Range Management*, **52**(5), 413–19.

Tickell, C., 1989. *Environmental Refugees*, London: National Environment Research Council Annual Lecture, Royal Society, 5 June.

Tiffen, M., 2003. Transitions in sub-Saharan Africa: Agriculture, urbanization and income growth. *World Development*, **31**, 1343–66.

Tilt, B., Braun, Y., & He, D., 2009. Social impacts of large dam projects: A comparison of international case studies and implications for best practice. *Journal of Environmental Management*, **90**(S3), S249–S257.

Timlisina, G. R., 2012. Biofuels: The food versus fuel debate. *CAB Reviews*, **7**(36), 1–8.

Tirado, M. C., Cohen, M. J., Aberman, N., Meerman, J., & Thompson, B., 2010. Addressing the challenges of climate change and biofuel production for food and nutrition security. *Food Research International*, **43**(7), 1729–44.

Tissot, S., 2011. Excluding Muslim women: From hijab to niqab, from school to public space. *Public Culture*, **23**(1), 39–46.

Tobert, N., 1985. The effect of drought among the Zaghawa in northern Darfur. *Disasters*, **9**(3), 213–23.

Tockner, K. & Stanford, J. A., 2002. Riverine flood plains: Present state and future trends. *Environmental Conservation*, **29**(3), 308–30.

Todaro, M. P., 1969. A model of labor migration and urban unemployment in less developed countries. *American Economic Review*, **59**(1), 138–48.

Tolnay, S. E., White, K. J. C., Crowder, K. D., & Adelman, R. M., 2005. Distances traveled during the Great Migration: An analysis of racial differences among male migrants. *Social Science History*, **29**(4), 523–48.

Tong, Y., 2010. Place of education, gender disparity, and assimilation of immigrant scientists and engineers earnings. *Social Science Research*, **39**(4), 610–26.

Tory, K. J. & Frank, W. F., 2010. Tropical cyclone formation. In J. C. L. Chan & J. D. Kepert, eds. *Global Perspectives on Tropical Cyclones: From science to mitigation*. Singapore: World Scientific Publishing, 55–92.

Toth, S. A., 2006. *Beyond Papillon: the French overseas penal colonies, 1854–1952*, Lincoln: University of Nebraska Press.

Tschakert, P., Sagoe, R., Ofori-Darko, G., & Codjoe, S. N., 2010. Floods in the Sahel: An analysis of anomalies, memory, and anticipatory learning. *Climatic Change*, **103**(3–4), 471–502.

Tunas, D. & Peresthu, A., 2010. The self-help housing in Indonesia: The only option for the poor? *Habitat International*, **34**(3), 315–22.

Turner, M. D. & Williams, T. O., 2002. Livestock market dynamics and local vulnerabilities in the Sahel. *World Development*, **30**(4), 683–705.

UK Environment Agency, 2012. *Thames Barrier Project Pack*, London. Available at: http://www.environment-agency.gov.uk/static/documents/Leisure/Thames_Barrier_Project_pack_2012.pdf.

United Nations, 2009. *Trends in International Migrant Stock: The 2008 revision*, New York. Available at: http://www.un.org/esa/population/publications/migration/UN_MigStock_2008.pdf.

UN DAC, 2000. *1998 Floods in the People's Republic of China – Final Assessment Report*, Beijing, United Nations Disaster Assessment and Coordination Team. Available at: https://apps.who.int/eha/emergenc/china/intro.htm.

UN DESA, 2000. *Replacement Migration: Is it a solution to declining and ageing populations?* New York, UN Department of Economic And Social Affairs, Population Division. Available at: http://www.un.org/esa/population/publications/ReplMigED/migration.htm.

UN DESA, 2007. *World Population Prospects: The 2006 revision*. New York, UN Department of Economic and Social Affairs, Population Division. Available at: http://www.un.org/esa/population/publications/wpp2006/WPP2006_Highlights_rev.pdf.

UN DESA, 2011. *World Population Prospects: The 2010 revision: Highlights and advance tables*. New York, UN Department of Economic and Social Affairs, Population Division. Available at: http://esa.un.org/unpd/wpp/Documentation/pdf/WPP2010_Highlights.pdf.

UN ECLAC, 1999a. *Honduras: Assessment of the damage caused by Hurricane Mitch, 1998: Implications for economic and social development and for the environment*, Mexico City, United Nations Economic Commission for Latin America and the Caribbean. Available at: http://www.eclac.org/publicaciones/xml/6/15506/L367–1-EN.pdf.

UN ECLAC, 1999b. *Guatemala: Assessment of the damage caused by Hurricane Mitch, 1998: Implications for economic and social development and for the environment*, Mexico City, United Nations Economic Commission for Latin America and the Caribbean. Available at: http://www.eclac.org/publicaciones/xml/5/15505/L370–1-EN.pdf.

UNEP, 2007. *Sudan: Post-conflict environmental assessment*. UN Environment Programme. Available at: http://sudanreport.unep.ch/chapters/00_foreword_summary.pdf.

UN FAO, 2001. *Analysis of the Medium-term Effects of Hurricane Mitch on Food Security in Central America*. Rome, United Nations Food and Agriculture Organization.

Ungruhe, C., 2010. Symbols of success: Youth, peer pressure and the role of adulthood among juvenile male return migrants in Ghana. *Childhood*, **17**(2), 259–71.

UNHCR, 2011. *Statistical Handbook 2010*, Geneva. Available at: http://www.unhcr. org/4ef9cc9c9.html.

UNHCR, 2012. *Global Trends 2011: A year of crises*. Available at: http://www.unhcr. org/4fd6f87f9.html.

University of Virginia Geospatial and Statistical Data Center, 2012. *United States Historical Census Data Browser*. Available at: http://fisher.lib.virginia.edu/census.

Unruh, J., 2004. Migration induced legal pluralism in land tenure. In J. D. Unruh, M. S. Krol, & N. Kliot, eds. *Environmental Change and its Implications for Population Migration*. Dordrecht: Kluwer Academic, 101–18.

UN Security Council, Department of Public Information, News and Media Division, 2011. Security Council, in Statement, Says 'Contextual Information' on Possible Security Implications of Climate Change Important When Climate Impacts Drive Conflict. Media release. Available at: http://www.un.org/News/Press/docs/2011/sc10332.doc. htm.

UNU-EHS, 2005. As ranks of 'environmental refugees' swell worldwide, calls grow for better definition, recognition, support. Press release, Available at: http://www.ehs.unu. edu/index.php?cat=7&menu=44&page=12_October_-_UN_Disaster_Day.

Upadhyaya, H. K., Otsuka, K., & David, C. C., 1990. Differential adoption of modern rice technology and regional wage differential in Nepal. *Journal of Development Studies*, **26**(3), 450–68.

US Census Bureau, 2012. People and Households – Data by Subject. *People and Households*. Available at: http://www.census.gov/people/.

USDA, 2011. *Global Crop Production Review, 2010*, Washington DC. Available at: http:// www.usda.gov/oce/weather/pubs/Annual/CropProduction.pdf.

US Department of Labor, 2005. *Findings from the National Agricultural Workers Survey (NAWS) 2001–2002*, Washington, DC. Available at: http://www.doleta.gov/agworker/ report9/naws_rpt9.pdf.

US INS, 2002. *Statistical Yearbook of the Immigration and Naturalization Service, 1999*, Washington DC: US Government Printing Office. Available at: http://www.dhs.gov/ xlibrary/assets/statistics/yearbook/1999/FY99Yearbook.pdf.

Uvin, P., 1996. Tragedy in Rwanda: The political ecology of conflict. *Environment*, **38**(3), 6–15.

Uvin, P., 2009. The state of world hunger. *Nutrition Reviews*, **52**(5), 151–61.

Valdez, A., Cepeda, A., Negi, N. J., & Kaplan, C., 2010. Fumando La Piedra: Emerging patterns of crack use among Latino immigrant day laborers in New Orleans. *Journal of Immigrant and Minority Health*, **12**(5), 737–42.

Van der Bruggen, B., Borghgraef, K., & Vinckier, C., 2010. Causes of water supply problems in urbanised regions in developing countries. *Water Resources Management*, **24**, 1885–902.

Van der Geest, K., 2010. Local perception of migration from north-west Ghana. *Africa*, **804**(4), 595–619.

Vandentorren, S., Bretin, P., Zeghnoun, A., Mandereau-Bruno, L., Croisier, A., Cochet, C., Ribéron, J., Siberan, I., Declercq, B., & Ledrans, M., 2006. August 2003 heat wave in France: Risk factors for death of elderly people living at home. *European Journal of Public Health*, **16**(6), 583–91.

Vandersypen, K., Keita, A. C. T., Kaloga, K., Coulibaly, Y., Raes, D., & Jamin, J.-Y., 2006. Sustainability of farmers' organization of water management in the Office du Niger irrigation scheme in Mali. *Irrigation and Drainage*, **55**(1), 51–60.

Venot, J. P., Reddy, V. R., & Umapathy, D., 2010. Coping with drought in irrigated south India: Farmers' adjustments in Nagarjuna Sagar. *Agricultural Water Management*, **97**(10), 1434–42.

Vermeer, M. & Rahmstorf, S., 2009. Global sea level linked to global temperature. *Proceedings of the National Academy of Sciences*, **106**, 21527–32.

Viegas, D. X., 1998. Forest fire propagation. *Philosophical Transactions of the Royal Society A – Mathematical, Physical and Engineering Sciences*, **356**(1748), 2907–28.

Vigdor, J., 2008. The economic aftermath of Hurricane Katrina. *Journal of Economic Perspectives*, **22**(4), 135–54.

Villarejo, D., 1996. *93640 at Risk: Farmers, Workers and Townspeople in an Era of Water Uncertainty*, Davis CA, California Institute for Rural Studies. Available at: http://www.waterrights.ca.gov/IID/IIDHearingData/LocalPublish/CFBF2.pdf.

Vinck, P., Pham, P., Fletcher, L. E., & Stover, E., 2009. Inequalities and prospects: Ethnicity and legal status in the construction labor force after Hurricane Katrina. *Organization and Environment*, **22**(4), 470–8.

Vu, L., VanLandingham, M. J., Do, M., & Bankston, C. L., 2009. Evacuation and return of Vietnamese New Orleanians affected by Hurricane Katrina. *Organization and Environment*, **22**(4), 422–36.

Wadley, R., 2002. Coping with crisis – Smoke, drought, flood and currency: Iban households in West Kalimantan, Indonesia. *Culture & Agriculture*, **24**(1), 26–33.

Wahl, D. et al., 2007. Palaeolimnological evidence of late-Holocene settlement and abandonment in the Mirador Basin, Peten, *Guatemala*. **17**(6), 813–20.

Wahl, E. R. & Morrill, C., 2010. Toward understanding and predicting monsoon patterns. *Science*, **328**(5977), 437–8.

Wall, E., Ferrazzi, G., & Schryer, F., 1998. Getting the goods on social capital. *Rural Sociology*, **63**(2), 300–22.

Wallerstein, I., 1979. *The Capitalist World-Economy*. Cambridge: Cambridge University Press.

Walt, S. M., 1991. The renaissance of security studies. *International Studies Quarterly*, **35**(2), 211–39.

Wan, H., 2003. Policies and measures on flood mitigation in China since 1998. In *International Conference on Total Disaster Risk Management*, 2–4 December 2003. http://web.adrc.or.jp/publications/TDRM2003Dec/11_MR.%20HONGTAO%20WAN%20_FINAL_.pdf

Wang, B., Wu, R. & Li, T., 2003. Atmosphere-warm ocean interaction and its impacts on Asian-Australian monsoon variation. *Journal of Climate*, **16**, 1195–211.

Wang, F.-L., 2005. *Organizing through division and exclusion: China's Hukou system*, Palo Alto, CA: Stanford University Press.

Wang, H. & Chang, S. 2002. The commodification of international marriages: Cross-border marriage business in Taiwan and Viet Nam. *International Migration*, **40**, 93–116.

Wang, X. Cao, Z., Pender, G., & Tan, G., 2010. Modelling of urban flooding due to Yangtze River dike break. *Proceedings of the ICE – Water Management*, **164**(1), 3–14.

Wang, Y. P., Wang, Y. & Wu, J., 2009. Urbanization and informal development in China: Urban villages in Shenzhen. *International Journal of Urban and Regional Research*, **33**(4), 957–73.

Wang, Z., Song, K. & Hu, L., 2010. China's largest scale ecological migration in the Three-River headwater region. *Ambio*, **39**(5–6), 443–6.

Ward, R. C., 1978. *Floods: A geographical perspective*. London: MacMillan.

Warnes, A. M., 2008. International retirement migration. In P. Uhlenberg, ed. *International Handbook of Population Aging*. Dordrecht: Springer, 341–64.

Warraich, H., Zaidi, A., & Patel, K., 2011. Floods in Pakistan: A public health crisis. *Bulletin of the World Health Organization*, **389**(3).

Waters, J., 2006. Geographies of cultural capital: education, international migration and family strategies between Hong Kong and Canada. *Transactions of the Institute of British Geographers*, **31**(3), 179–92.

Watts, M., 1991. Entitlements or empowerment? Famine and starvation in Africa. *Review of African Political Economy*, **51**, 9–26.

Watts, M., 2000. Dependency theory. In R. J. Johnston, D. Gregory, G. Pratt, & M. Watts, eds. *The Dictionary of Human Geography* (4th ed.). Oxford: Blackwell, 164–5.

Watts, M. J. & Bohle, H. G., 1993. Hunger, famine and the space of vulnerability. *GeoJournal*, **30**(2), 117–25.

Watts, S. J., 1983. Marriage migration, a neglected form of long-term mobility: A case study from Ilorin, Nigeria. *International Migration Review*, **17**(4), 682–98.

Webb, A. P. & Kench, P. S., 2010. The dynamic response of reef islands to sea-level rise: Evidence from multi-decadal analysis of island change in the Central Pacific. *Global and Planetary Change*, **72**(3), 234–46.

Webb, J. D. C., Elsom, D. M., & Meaden, G. T., 2009. Severe hailstorms in Britain and Ireland, a climatological survey and hazard assessment. *Atmospheric Research*, **93**(1–3), 587–606.

Webb, W. P., 1931. *The Great Plains*. New York: Grosset & Dunlap.

Webster, P. J., Toma, V. E., & Kim, H.-M., 2011. Were the 2010 Pakistan floods predictable? *Geophysical Research Letters*, **38**(4), L04806.

Weeks, J. R., 2008. *Population: An introduction to concepts and issues*. Belmont, CA: Wadsworth.

Wegren, S. K., 2011. Food security and Russia's 2010 drought. *Eurasian Geography and Economics*, **52**(1), 140–56.

Wei, J., He, X., & Bao, Y., 2011. Anthropogenic impacts on suspended sediment load in the Upper Yangtze river. *Regional Environmental Change*, **11**(4), 857–68.

Weichselgartner, J., 2001. Disaster mitigation: The concept of vulnerability revisited. *Disaster Prevention and Management* **10**(2), 85–94.

Weil, J. H., 2009. Finding housing: Discrimination and exploitation of Latinos in the post-Katrina rental market. *Organization and Environment*, **22**(4), 491–502.

Weil, P., 2001. Access to citizenship: A comparison of twenty-five nationality laws. In T. A. Aleinikoff & D. B. Klusmeyer, eds. *Citizenship Today: Global perspectives and practices*. Washington, DC: Carnegie Endowment for Peace/Brookings Institution Press, 17–35.

Werner, A. D. & Simmons, C. T., 2009. Impact of sea-level rise on sea water intrusion in coastal aquifers. *Ground Water*, **47**(2), 197–204.

West, J., 2009. *Perceptions of ecological migration in Inner Mongolia, China: Summary of fieldwork and relevance for climate adaptation*, Oslo: Center for International Climate and Environmental Research. Available at: http://www.preventionweb.net/files/12537_7543.pdf.

Westerhoff, L. & Smit, B., 2009. The rains are disappointing us: Dynamic vulnerability and adaptation to multiple stressors in the Afram Plains, Ghana. *Mitigation and Adaptation Strategies for Global Change*, **14**(4), 317–37.

Westerling, A. L., Hidalgo, H. G., Cayan, D. R., & Swetnam, T. W., 2006. Warming and earlier spring increase western U.S. forest wildfire activity. *Science*, **313**(5789), 940–3.

Western, B. & Wildeman, C., 2009. The black family and mass incarceration. *The Annals of the American Academy of Political and Social Science*, **621**(1), 221–42.

Wheaton, E. E., 1992. Prairie dust storms – A neglected hazard. *Natural Hazards*, **5**, 53–63.

White, G., 1945. *Human adjustment to floods*. Chicago, IL: University of Chicago, Research Paper No. 29.

White, G. F., 1986. 'The future of the Great Plains' re-visited. *Great Plains Quarterly*, **6**(Spring), 84–93.

White, K. J. C., 2008. Sending or receiving stations? The dual influence of railroads in early 20th-century Great Plains settlement. *Population Research and Policy Review*, **27**(1), 89–115.

Whisenhunt, D. W., 1983. 'We've got the Hoover blues': Oklahoma transiency in the days of the Great Depression. In K. E. Hendrickson, ed. *Hard Times in Oklahoma: The Depression Years*. Oklahoma City: Oklahoma Historical Society, 101–14.

Wilmsen, B., Webber, M., & Duan, Y., 2011a. Development for whom? Rural to urban resettlement at the Three Gorges Dam, China. *Asian Studies Review*, **35**(1).

Wilmsen, B., Webber, M., & Duan, Y., 2011b. Involuntary rural resettlement: Resources, strategies, and outcomes at the Three Gorges Dam, China. *Journal of Environment and Development*, **20**(4), 355–80.

Winkels, A., 2012. Migration, social networks and risk: The case of rural-to-rural migration in Vietnam. *Journal of Vietnamese Studies*, **7**(4), 91–120.

Winklerprins, A. M. G. A., 1992. Seasonal floodplain-upland migration along the lower Amazon River. *Geographical Review*, **92**(3), 415–31.

Wishart, D. J., (Ed) 2007. *Encyclopedia of the Great Plains Indians*, Lincoln: University of Nebraska Press/Bison Books.

Wisner, B., Blaikie, P., Cannon, T., & Davis, I., 2004. *At Risk: Natural hazards, people's vulnerability and disasters*. London: Routledge.

Wolf, A. T., 1998. Conflict and cooperation along international waterways. *Water Policy*, **1**(2), 251–65.

Wolf, A. T., 1999. 'Water Wars' and Water Reality: Conflict and cooperation along international waterways. In S. C. Lonergan, ed. *Environmental Change, Adaptation, and Security*. Dordrecht: Kluwer Academic Publishers, 251–68.

Wolf, A. T., 2000. Indigenous approaches to water conflict negotiations and implications for international waters. *International Negotiation*, **5**(2), 357–73.

Woodhouse, P., 2012. New investment, old challenges. Land deals and the water constraint in African agriculture. *Journal of Peasant Studies*. DOI: 10.1080/03066150.2012.660481.

Woodroffe, C., McLean, R., Smithers, S., & Lawson, E., 1999. Atoll reef-island formation and response to sea-level change: West Island, Cocos (Keeling) Islands. *Marine Geology*, **160**(1–2), 85–104.

Woolcock, M., 1998. Social capital and economic development: Toward a theoretical synthesis and policy framework. *Theory and Society*, **27**(2), 151–208.

Wong, K.-K. & Zhao, X., 2001. Living with floods: Victims' perceptions in Beijiang, Guangdong, China. *Area*, **33**(2), 190–201.

World Bank, 2001. *Hurricane Mitch: The gender effects of coping and crises*, Washington, DC. Available at: http://www-wds.worldbank.org/external/default/WDSContentServer/WDSP/IB/2002/10/04/000094946_02092504034174/Rendered/PDF/multi0page.pdf.

World Commission on Dams, 2000. *Dams and Development: A new framework for decision making*, London: Earthscan.

Worster, D., 1979. *Dust Bowl: The southern plains in the 1930s*. New York: Oxford University Press.

Worster, D., 1986. The Dirty Thirties: A study in agricultural capitalism. *Great Plains Quarterly*, **6**(2), 107–16.

Wright, K. & Black, R., 2011. International migration and the downturn: Assessing the impacts of the global financial downturn on migration, poverty and human well-being. *Journal of International Development*, **23**(4), 555–64.

Wright, M. W., 2006. *Disposable Women and other Myths of Global Capitalism*, London: Routledge.

Xi, J. & Hwang, S.-S., 2011. Relocation stress, coping, and sense of control among resettlers resulting from China's Three Gorges Dam Project. *Social Indicators Research*, **104**(3), 507–22.

Xie, B., Zhang, Q., & Wang, Y., 2010. Observed characteristics of hail size in four regions in China during 1980–2005. *Journal of Climate*, **23**, 4973–82.

Xu, Y. P., Xu, J. T., Ding, J. J., Chen, Y., Yin, Y. X., & Zhang, X. Q., 2010. Impacts of urbanization on hydrology in the Yangtze River Delta, China. *Water Science and Technology*, **62**(6), 1221–9.

Yamamoto, L. & Esteban, M., 2010. Vanishing island states and sovereignty. *Ocean and Coastal Management*, **53**(1), 1–9.

Yang, H. & Zehnder, A., 2001. China's regional water scarcity and implications for grain supply and trade. *Environment and Planning A*, **33**, 79–95.

Ye, Y., Fang, X. & Khan, M. A. U., 2011. Migration and reclamation in Northeast China in response to climatic disasters in North China over the past 300 years. *Regional Environmental Change*, **12**(1), 193–206.

Ye, Q. & Glantz, M. H., 2005. The 1998 Yangtze Floods: The use of short-term forecasts in the context of seasonal water management. *Mitigation and Adaptation Strategies for Global Change*, **10**, 159–82.

Yin, H. & Li, C., 2001. Human impact on floods and flood disasters on the Yangtze River. *Geomorphology*, **41**(2), 105–9.

Yin, R. S., Xiang, Q., Xu, J. T., & Deng, X. Z., 2010. Modeling the driving forces of the land use and land cover changes along the upper Yangtze River of China. *Environmental Management*, **45**(3), 454–65.

Yohe, G. & Tol, R. S. J., 2002. Indicators for social and economic coping capacity – moving toward a working definition of adaptive capacity. *Global Environmental Change*, **12**(1), 25–40.

Young, O. R., 2009. Whither the Arctic? Conflict or cooperation in the circumpolar north. *Polar Record*, **45**, 73–82.

Yu, F., Chen, Z., Ren, X., & Yang, G., 2009. Analysis of historical floods on the Yangtze River, China: Characteristics and explanations. *Geomorphology*, **113**(3–4), 210–16.

Zaiotti, R., 2011. *Cultures of Border Control: Schengen and the evolution of European frontiers*, Chicago, IL: University of Chicago Press.

Zaum, D., 2011. Post-conflict statebuilding and forced migration. In A. Betts & G. Loescher, eds. *Refugees in International Relations*. Oxford: Oxford University Press, 285–304.

Zelinsky, W., 1971. The hypothesis of the mobility transition. *Geographical Review*, **61**(2), 219–49.

Zeng, N., Yoon, J.-H., Mariottie, A., & Swenson, S., 2008. Variability of basin-scale terrestrial water storage from a PER water budget method: The Amazon and the Mississippi. *Journal of Climate*, **21**(2), 248–65.

Zhang, D. D., Brecke, P., Lee, H. F., He, Y.-Q., & Zhang, J., 2007. Global climate change, war, and population decline in recent human history. *Proceedings of the National Academy of Sciences*, **104**(49), 19214–19.

Zhang, K. & Leatherman, S., 2011. Barrier island population along the U.S. Atlantic and Gulf coasts. *Journal of Coastal Research*, **27**(2), 356–63.

Zhu, Y., 2007. China's floating population and their settlement intention in the cities: Beyond the Hukou reform. *Habitat International*, **31**(1), 65–76.

Zisper, E. J., Cecil, D. J., Liu, C., Nesbitt, S. W., & Yorty, D. P., 2006. Where are the most intense thunderstorms on Earth? *Bulletin of American Meteorological Society*, **87**(8), 1057–71.

Zoleta-Nantes, D. B., 2002. Differential impacts of flood hazards among the street children, the urban poor and residents of wealthy neighborhoods in metro Manila, Philippines. *Mitigation and Adaptation Strategies for Global Change*, **7**(3), 239–66.

Zong, Y. & Chen, X., 2000. The 1998 flood on the Yangtze, China. *Natural Hazards*, **22**, 165–84.

Zonn, I. S., 1999. The impact of political ideology on creeping environmental changes in the Aral Sea basin. In M. H. Glantz, ed. *Creeping Environmental Problems and Sustainable Development in the Aral Sea Basin*. Cambridge: Cambridge University Press, 157–90.

Index